A Social and Cultural History of Late Antiquity examines the social and cultural landscape of the Late Antique Mediterranean. The text offers a picture of everyday life as it was lived in the spaces around and between two of the most memorable and towering figures of the time—Constantine and Muhammad. The author captures the period using a wide-lens, including Persian material from the mid third century through Umayyad material of the mid eighth century C.E. The book offers a rich picture of Late Antique life that is not just focused on Rome, Constantinople, or Christianity.

This important resource uses nuanced terms to talk about complex issues and fills a gap in the literature by surveying major themes such as power, gender, community, cities, politics, law, art and architecture, and literary culture. The book is richly illustrated and filled with maps, lists of rulers and key events. *A Social and Cultural History of Late Antiquity* is an essential guide that:

- Paints a rich picture of daily life in Late Antique that is not simply centered on Rome, Constantinople, or Christianity
- Balances a thematic approach with rigorous attention to chronology
- Stresses the need for appreciating both sources and methods in the study of Late Antique history
- Offers a sophisticated model for investigating daily life and the complexities of individual and group identity in the rapidly changing Mediterranean world
- Includes useful maps, city plans, timelines, and suggestions for further reading

A Social and Cultural History of Late Antiquity offers an examination of everyday life in the era when adherents of three of the major religions of today—Christianity, Judaism, and Islam—faced each other for the first time in the same environment.

Douglas Boin is Associate Professor in the Department of History at Saint Louis University in St. Louis, Missouri. He is the author of *Ostia in Late Antiquity* and *Coming Out Christian in the Roman World*.

Wiley Blackwell Social and Cultural Histories of the Ancient World

This series offers a fresh approach to the study of ancient history, seeking to illuminate the social and cultural history often obscured by political narratives. The books in the series will emphasize themes in social and cultural history, such as slavery, religion, gender, age, medicine, technology, and entertainment. Books in the series will be engaging, thought provoking accounts of the classical world, designed specifically for students and teachers in the classroom.

Published

A Social and Cultural History of Late Antiquity
Douglas Boin

Forthcoming

A Social and Cultural History of Archaic Greece
Adam Rabinowitz

A Social and Cultural History of Classical Greece
Elizabeth Kosmetatou

A Social and Cultural History of the Hellenistic World
Gillian Ramsey

A Social and Cultural History of Republican Rome
Eric M. Orlin

A Social and Cultural History of the Roman Empire
Jinyu Liu

A Social and Cultural History of Late Antiquity

Douglas Boin

WILEY Blackwell

This edition first published 2018
© 2018 John Wiley & Sons, Inc.

Registered Office(s)
John Wiley & Sons, Inc., 111 River Street, Hoboken, NJ 07030, USA

Editorial Office
101 Station Landing, Medford, MA 02155, USA

For details of our global editorial offices, customer services, and more information about Wiley products visit us at www.wiley.com.

Wiley also publishes its books in a variety of electronic formats and by print-on-demand. Some content that appears in standard print versions of this book may not be available in other formats.

Library of Congress Cataloging-in-Publication Data

Names: Boin, Douglas, author.
Title: A social and cultural history of late antiquity / by Douglas Boin.
Description: Hoboken, NJ : Wiley, 2018. | Series: Wiley Blackwell social and
    cultural histories of the ancient world | Includes bibliographical
    references and index.
Identifiers: LCCN 2017042187 (print) | LCCN 2017056942 (ebook) |
    ISBN 9781119076995 (pdf) | ISBN 9781119076988 (epub) |
    ISBN 9781119077008 (cloth) | ISBN 9781119076810 (pbk.)
Subjects: LCSH: Mediterranean Region–Civilization. | Mediterranean Region–History–
    To 476. | Mediterranean Region–History–476-1517. | Social change–Mediterranean
    Region–History–To 1500. | Romans–Mediterranean Region–History. |
    Romans–Mediterranean Region–Social life and customs. | Romans–Mediterranean
    Region–Social conditions.
Classification: LCC DE71 (ebook) | LCC DE71 .B59 2018 (print) | DDC 937/.06–dc23
LC record available at https://lccn.loc.gov/2017042187

Cover Design: Wiley
Cover Images: (Front cover) Juan Manuel Casillas Delgado / Alamy Stock Photo;
(Front cover background) © tomograf/iStockphoto; (Back cover) © OnstOn/iStockphoto

Set in 10.5/12.5pt Plantin by SPi Global, Pondicherry, India

Printed in Singapore by C.O.S. Printers Pte Ltd

10 9 8 7 6 5 4 3 2 1

Contents

Illustrations

Boxed Texts

Political Issues

Working With Sources

Preface: The Magic of History

History can be wondrous to watch, like beholding the act of an entrancing magician. With the right story, a compelling drama, and a dash of showmanship, people and periods long removed from us can dance almost inexplicably before our eyes. History, after all, is a performance of the past, though not everyone tells it the same way. That's why the discipline of history is still thriving. As specialists challenge each other with the discovery of new documents and overlooked clues force researchers to reassess the events that led to a war or an invasion, historians dust off material that can seem trite and familiar and dazzle audiences by turning it into something unexpected and new.

This book is a manual for teaching some of the basics of the craft of history. It's also an extended investigation into the secret behind what I like to think of as one of the world's most famous illusions: the "vanishing of Rome." Since that pivotal moment in the late fifth century CE – 476 CE – when the city of Rome was cut off from its own empire, many amateurs and professionals have puzzled and argued over the details of what happened. Centuries later, they still don't agree. Some say Rome's civilization disappeared, that the empire "fell" at just that precise moment in time. Others insist that Rome was already slowly being transformed – a few would even try to claim on a deep, spiritual level – with regions of the old empire moving to a new "Byzantine" state in the years before, during, and after 476 CE. Whatever explanation one prefers, in books that tell the story of the ancient Mediterranean, there routinely comes a point where something once great and majestic, the awesome world of Rome, vanishes. This book shows how that trick is done.

The people of the ancient Mediterranean knew something about magic and illusions. Consider this story of a visit to Athens, written in ancient Greek. It's dated to the end of the second century or the middle of the third century CE and alleges to be written by a farmer in Classical Greece. It's a skilled literary act, crafted by a smart author during a time when Romans governed Greece, Latin was the language of the state, and many people still had a fondness for Pericles' city.

In it, a farmer loads up his trusty donkey "with figs and fruit cakes" to join a dear friend in Athens. The two men are planning to go to the theater, and the thought of catching a show in the city, famous for its drama, excites the narrator:

> Most of the shows I don't recall, for I'm a poor hand at remembering and telling such things. But I can tell you that one thing I saw made me almost speechless with astonishment.
>
> A man came forward and, setting down a three-legged table, placed three little cups on it. Then under these cups he hid some little round white pebbles, such as we find on the banks of rapid streams. At one moment he would hide them one under each cup; and at another moment (I don't know how) he would show them all under a single cup. Then he would make them entirely disappear from under the cups and exhibit them between his lips. Then he would swallow them, and, drawing forward the spectators who stood near him, would take one pebble from a man's nose, another from a man's ear, and the third from a man's head! After picking them up, he would make them disappear from sight again. A very light-fingered gentleman…!
>
> I hope no creature like him ever gets on to my farm, though. No one would ever catch him. He would steal everything in the house and make off with all the goods. (Alciphron, *Letters* 2.17, LCL trans. by A. Benner and F. Fobes [1949], pp. 110–112)

Alciphron, the author of this Greek text, is not a household name. In fact, historians know next to nothing about him. But do you recognize the act he's describing? It's a classic of magic, performed by almost every magician from Harry Houdini to David Copperfield.

One of the most recent teams to perform the cups and balls, as it is known, was the iconoclastic duo Penn and Teller. In their signature style, they used clear plastic cups. Members of their guild were not amused. Can you guess why? They broke one of the first rules of their trade: People on the other side of the curtain are not supposed to know how the magic works. But does knowing the moves really make an act any less enjoyable? I don't think it does. Seeing an act for the first time, then taking it apart, dissecting the sleight of hand, is the first step in learning how to do it for yourself. The same is true for the practice of history. That's why I wrote this book.

While it is undeniably entertaining to sit back and watch someone else put on a show, history as a discipline will only continue to grow and thrive when people in the audience realize it's more than an act to cheer on, admire, and applaud. History is something people do, and that's why, in addition to appreciating good stagecraft, I believe everyone should know how to do a simple trick or two. What better illusion to practice with than the "vanishing" of Rome?

The challenge is that many people, at the outset, will already think they know what happened to Rome in Late Antiquity. It seems to be a trick so basic anyone would be able to retell it, or at least parts of it, if they were asked. Here's how one observer might describe it.

In the third century, the Roman Empire suffered a debilitating mix of political, military, economic, and spiritual crises that nearly tore its society apart. In the fourth century, its leaders managed to stabilize the state by embracing a new, spiritual faith, Christianity. By then, many Romans, itching for change, may even have been pushed in new pious directions by Constantine's conversion to Christianity. Soon, the emperor transferred the capital from Rome to Constantinople – a move that created the Byzantine Empire. A century later, when packs of frightening barbarians invaded western Europe, Rome finally crumbled. And although Byzantine emperors would belatedly strategize how to recapture parts of lost Europe and North Africa, their efforts would prove too late. The Roman Empire was gone.

This book takes its readers back stage to point out the strings, mirrors, and trapdoors that make this rather elegant historical illusion work. For even though the city of Rome did disappear from its own empire in 476 CE, at the time our book closes – in the eighth century CE – the Roman Empire itself will still, surprisingly, be standing. In order to understand how and why that happened, the pace with which history is performed has to be slowed down so that we can study each move, see every manipulation. That's what we'll do together in the next fourteen chapters.

A Note to Advanced Readers

This book is designed around case studies, questions, sources, and above all, problems of interpretation. But its structure largely unfolds in chronological order. This choice was deliberate. Some social and cultural histories become too muddled – overwhelming readers who have no prior familiarity with the subject matter – when they jump between times and places too casually. By trying to survey the entire history of a large topic in one small chapter – say, the history of cities, death, gender, or law – beginners are presented with a sweeping story that moves from one subject to the next without ever really being presented with a sequence of key events. This book takes a different approach.

Although structured around traditional social and cultural topics, like the household, law, and the family it starts at an earlier point in time and ends at a later one. Thus, the examples and case studies that appear in the earlier chapters are drawn from the third and fourth centuries CE whereas the material privileged in the latter chapters comes from the fifth, sixth, and seventh centuries CE. In this way, my hope is that readers who pick up this book gain a deep, nuanced appreciation for how to think about complex historical topics. By choosing *not* to frame my discussion of topics in usual, or expected, ways – there are no chapters here on "Church and State," "Byzantine Art and Architecture," or even the intriguing cultural phenomenon called "Religion" – what I hope to accomplish is that readers, from beginners to specialists, will realize that complex topics from the pre-modern world cannot and should not be shoehorned into artificial boxes.

One last note. Because this book lacks any formal conclusion, I would like to provide a commentary on one of the last lines of the book which a reader will encounter. It is the last of four questions in the final chapter, but it is the most important question that guided me as I was thinking about this subject matter. The question is this: "From a historical perspective, would you say that individuals and communities who hold monotheistic beliefs ('belief in one God') are fundamentally unable to live in a pluralistic society?" If there is one theme that unites the people and places of the proto-global world of Late Antiquity and if there is one topic which can inspire and motivate our own interest in their past lives, I can think of no better one than that which lies at the heart of this question. For the study of how people of different faiths and backgrounds choose to live in the complicated, complex, diverse world around them is not academic; it is an urgent one with relevance for today. If readers close this book with the recognition that pre-modern history still does have an urgency about it, then I will feel like I have done my job.

Late Antiquity is often imagined as a bridge, a welcome support that carries people from one side of a gap to another. In *A Social and Cultural History of Late Antiquity*, time does work that way – passing from the consular years of the old Roman Empire to the Christian hours of the Middle Ages – but place does not. For in crossing, we don't arrive in another land; we come upon a mysterious row of doors, behind which several stories are playing out simultaneously, in many places and many times. The trick of doing Late Antique history is knowing that the end will always pull us in multiple directions.

Acknowledgments

Two years out of graduate school, before I taught my first college seminar on "The World of St. Augustine," I suffered from that moment of crippling anxiety which young professors everywhere know first-hand. What books do I assign? There were good source collections for this period, like Michael Maas' outstanding *Readings in Late Antiquity* (London: Routledge, 2000, now in its second edition). Still, in 2010, I struggled to find an appropriate narrative. I wanted my students to have a book that was sufficiently up-to-date, archaeologically, linguistically, theoretically, and methodologically; one that described events of the time from both the ground-up and top-down; and last, and most important of all, one that challenged them to think about this transformative time beyond the vantage of someone standing inside the Christian church. When Wiley contacted me to contribute a volume on Late Antiquity to this new series, I was nervous to think I could contribute anything on such a topic. Four anonymous readers thought otherwise. The result is this book.

I cannot express enough my gratitude to the following colleagues with whom I have been lucky enough to be able to think and talk about Late Antiquity over the past few years. In no particular order, I would like to thank: Lorenzo DiTommaso, for the invitation to participate in a panel discussion about apocalyptic worldviews in Vienna, Austria; Maijastina Kahlos, for her invitation to discuss work in with her colleagues in Helsinki, Finland; Michele Salzman, Marianne Sághy, and Rita Lizzi Testa, for inviting me to discuss the fourth and fifth centuries with an outstanding group of Late Antique scholars in Rome, including Nicola Denzey Lewis, Neil McLynn, and Dennis Trout; Morwenna Ludlow and Richard Flower, for convening a similar group of like-minded researchers at the University of Exeter in the United Kingdom, including Barbara Borg, Robin Jensen, Aaron Johnson, Gillian Clark, Mark Humphries, and Carlos Machado; to Jörg Rüpke, Anna-Katharina Rieger, and Valentino Gasparini, for their organization of a panel on the archaeology of religion at La Sapienza, Rome; and their subsequent invitation to join an outstanding international community of scholars – funded by the European Research Council – investigating Lived Ancient Religion in Erfurt and Eisenach, Germany; to

Philip Rousseau, Scott Johnson, and Wendy Meyer, for our conversations in Washington, DC; to Maria Doerfler, Elizabeth Clark, Annabel Wharton, James Rives, and Erin Walsh in North Carolina, for including me in their joint Duke/UNC Late Antiquity colloquium; to Sarah Bond for her kind invitation to participate in the biennial Late Antique conference in Iowa; to Gregor Kalas, Tina Shepardson, and Jacob Latham, for asking me to share ideas with their Late Antiquity group in Knoxville; and to the Classics and Religious Studies departments at the University of Missouri, Columbia, for their invitation to speak on Christianity before and after Constantine.

Over all these coffees and adjournments, I have learned much more from this team of talented scholars than I could ever have hoped to contribute at one time. This book tries to repay all my debts, even to the reviewers of this manuscript. They, too, had a "thankless task"; and I'm appreciative of the time they took, on behalf of the press, to type up their constructive critiques. To those whose names I have inadvertently omitted, the error is most certainly mine, and it is one of oversight – not judgment.

Finally, there are the people closer to home I need to acknowledge: to the Dean of the College of Arts and Sciences at Saint Louis University, Chris Duncan; to the Provost, Nancy Brickhouse; and to the chairs of the History Department, Phil Gavitt and Charles Parker, I owe my debts for their intellectual encouragement and for the resources they provided for my work. In the History Department itself, Chris Pudlowski and Kelly Goersch were instrumental in helping me manage funding from a Mellon Faculty Grant which funded part of my travel. Among my colleagues in the Saint Louis University History Department, thank you to Luke Yarbrough, for help with the material on early Islam; Filippo Marsili, for his perspective on China and Central Asia; and to our library staff, especially Jamie Emery, without whose help I would not have been able to read and acquire so many necessary pieces of this puzzle; to my graduate research assistant, Robert Olsen, who, for nearly a year and a half, was stationed at the stacks, and helped immeasurably with the timeline; to his successor, Joel Cerimele, who carried the torch next. Special recognition is due to undergraduate Saint Louis University student Sophia Liu for kindly contacting museum officials in Urumqi on my behalf.

Last, to countless curious undergraduates at Saint Louis University who watched, semester after semester, as I stumbled through many of these tricks at the front of our classroom, please know that my family, especially Gardiner Rhoderick, thanks you for indulging me in this performance.

The inset plan of Rome used throughout the book was adapted by the author from the public domain work by A. Kuhn, *Roma: Ancient, Subterranean, and Modern Rome* (New York: Benziger Brothers, 1916), p. 70.

Annotated List of Abbreviations and a Note on Citations from Secondary Literature

Casual readers skip the abbreviations. They are conventional, didactic, and dull. The sooner a young historian learns them, however, the more quickly they will be able to start asking their own questions and designing their own projects to answer them. At the request of the series' editors, I have tried to keep abbreviations to a minimum, but these are some resources a beginner should know.

More experienced readers will probably notice the absence of footnotes or endnotes. These were not possible so as to fulfill the mission of the series: providing a book addressed to the curious, not the connoisseur. And yet, because this book would never have been possible without the scholarly endeavor of others, I have tried my best to show throughout the text who, how, and why the work of my peers has thrown new light on those hidden corners of Late Antiquity which were once dark and dusty. Other resources, from trusted books on specific subjects to provocative new takes on big historical questions, are listed at the end of every chapter. I hope that readers of every background will appreciate how accomplished and diverse these contributors are: male and female; gay and straight; scholars of many faiths or no faith. Perhaps the next generation will push these boundaries of scholarly diversity even more so that the discipline of Late Antiquity can remain a place proud of its camaraderie and collegiality. A more simple hope is that this book introduces readers to many of the scholars who have been working tirelessly – in libraries, museums, and at archaeological sites – to bring Late Antiquity back to life. It was an honor and a privilege to have had the chance to learn so immeasurably from their books and articles.

The following list of abbreviations is suggestive, not comprehensive.

AE   *L'Année épigraphique* [The Year of Inscriptions] Collects and categorizes new inscriptions related to the Roman world (Paris, 1888–present). It is available online through many research libraries. A useful database for searching Latin inscriptions is the Epigraphic Databank

Heidelberg, housed at the University of Heidelberg, Germany (uni-heidelberg.de).

ANF   *Ante-Nicene Fathers*, edited by A. Roberts, J. Donaldson, and A. Cleveland Coxe (Buffalo, NY: Christian Literature Publishing Co., 1886). Nine volumes of translated Greek and Latin texts that date before 325 CE. Available at newadvent.com, edited and revised by K. Knight. A good first step for students interested in reading these ancient sources.

CIL   *Corpus Inscriptionum Latinarum* [Collection of Latin Inscriptions]. Organized by region, then sub-organized chronologically and topically, these over-sized print publications are vital to know but not easy for a beginning student to use; all of the editorial descriptions, in addition to the texts, are written in Latin. A good companion resource is the Epigraphic Database, Heidelberg, available online.

CIMRM   *Corpus Inscriptionum et Monumentorum Religionis Mithriacae* [The Collection of Inscriptions and Monuments Related to the Study of Mithras], two volumes of material edited by M. J. Vermaseren (The Hague: Martinus Nijhoff, 1956–1960).

Duke Papyri   The study of papyri is a field that offers innumerable resources for historians, but papyrology can be an intimidating maze for beginning students and non-specialists to navigate. The *Checklist of Greek, Latin, Demotic and Coptic Papyri, Ostraca* [ceramic fragments with writing] *and Tablets*, at Duke University, is an important searchable guide.

EBW   *Egypt in the Byzantine World, 300–700*, edited by R. Bagnall (Cambridge: Cambridge University Press, 2007). An essential collection of essays covering a part of the Roman world which, due to language specialities, the amount of papyrological evidence, and the challenges of conducting archaeological field research, is not often integrated into studies of the later empire.

EI   *Encyclopaedia Iranica*, a comprehensive resource comprising fifteen volumes dedicated to the study of Iranian culture in the Middle East and Central and South Asia (London, 1982–present). Some entries are now available online, open access, at iranicaonline.org.

LAA   *Late Antique Archaeology*, an annual publication (Leiden: Brill, 2003–) available in print and online through many research libraries. Each volume is a curated collection of essays on topics with significant archaeological or material culture components. Each volume also features extensive lists of related books and resources.

LAGuide   *Late Antiquity: A Guide to the Postclassical World* (Cambridge, MA: Harvard University Press), edited by G. W. Bowersock, Peter

Brown, and Oleg Grabar. This book, divided into two parts, is a collection of essays followed by short encyclopedia entries on the Late Antique world. The mix of presentations gives readers an overview that is both broad and deep.

LCL
Loeb Classical Library, a collection of Greek and Latin sources in translation, published by Harvard University Press; available as a digital resource through many research libraries.

MGH
The Historical Records of "Germany" [Monumenta Germaniae Historica]. Although not limited to the history of Germany, this monumental collection (Berlin: Weidmann, 1892–) includes many documents relevant to Late Antiquity. It can be consulted and searched online at mgh.de.

NPNF
Nicene and Post-Nicene Fathers, First Series, edited by Philip Schaff (Buffalo, NY: Christian Literature Publishing Co., 1889). Translated texts from the period of Christian history post-325 CE, available at newadvent.com, edited and revised by K. Knight.

NRSV
New Revised Standard Version of the "Bible." One of the most scholarly translations of the Jewish and Christian Scriptures with Apocryphal and Deuterocanonical books. Academic, or scholarly, translations of the Jewish and Christian Scriptures are important because they include texts which some denominations do not consider sacred. The text of 2 Maccabees, for example, is not in the Hebrew Bible or the Protestant Christian one.

OEAGR
Oxford Encyclopedia of Ancient Greece and Rome, edited by M. Gagarin (New York: Oxford University Press, 2010). Available in print but also online in many research libraries, this encyclopedia gives more in-depth entries than the standard classical dictionaries and is useful for checking dates, reading biographies, and surveying historical topics.

OHLA
The Oxford Handbook of Late Antiquity, edited by Scott Johnson (New York: Oxford University Press, 2012). One of the most recent collections of essays on this field and one of the most geographically expansive, it contains thirty-nine individually authored chapters which can provide a good starting point for students interested in digging deeper.

Orbis
"Orbis: The Stanford Geospatial Network of the Roman World" is an online platform for calculating travel distances and costs in the Roman Empire, based on seasonal and financial factors.

PLRE
Prosopography of the Later Roman Empire: A.D. 395–527, three volumes [= Collected study of individuals and their family names from the later Roman period]. Edited by A. H. M. Jones, J. Martindale, J. Morris, E. Thompson, A. Cameron, and P. Grierson (Cambridge: Cambridge University Press, 1971–1992).

THH   Translated Texts for Historians series (Liverpool: Liverpool University Press). A useful and ever-expanding series of translated texts relevant to Late Antiquity. A good English translation of the late fifth-century or early sixth-century CE Greek historian Zosimus is here.

ZPE   *Zeitschrift für Papyrologie und Epigraphik* [Journal for the Study of Papyrus and Inscriptions]. This journal specializes in publishing the first editions of newly discovered papyrus texts and inscriptions. It is indexed in the online research database JSTOR.

Timeline

The historical people who are the actors in this book lived on three continents, over more than five hundred years, with shifting degrees of knowledge about each other, depending on the currents of their age. Some built extraordinary monuments that still stand or fashioned ideas that still resonate; the lives of others have been covered by dust. Although this timeline has been placed in the front matter to conform with the series, it is also intended, for readers, as a brief "roll of the credits" so that the names and dates of those who played a starring role here can quickly be identified.

*c.*165 BCE	A Jewish thinker, adopting the name of Daniel, articulates his view of world history structured as a sequence of four hostile empires
164 BCE	The Jewish community celebrates a victory over the Hellenistic kings and re-dedicates the Temple in Jerusalem (Hanukkah)
*c.*4 BCE–*c.*28 CE	Jesus is born and is executed by Roman government
*c.*50–60	Paul, a Hellenistic Jew who believes Jesus is the Messiah, travels and writes
70	A Roman army obliterates the Second Jewish Temple in Jerusalem
*c.*110	Ignatius of Antioch tries to convince followers of Jesus in Asia Minor that they should leave their Jewish rituals behind by acting "openly Christian"
212	Caracalla announces Roman citizenship for all free people throughout the empire
226	A family in Persia, the Sasanians, establishes a dynasty that will govern for nearly four centuries
249	Decius calls for everyone throughout the Roman Empire to participate in a sacrifice
239–272	Sapur I begins to grow the imperial profile of Sasanian Persia

260	The Roman Emperor Valerian is captured by a Sasanian army
267–274	Empress Zenobia claims power as Augusta in Roman Syria
294	Diocletian institutes a Rule of Four
303	Diocletian, despite having a Christian wife and daughter, institutes a legal policy targeting and punishing Rome's Christian community
309	A new Sapur, Sapur II, takes control of Persia; his reign will last seventy years
311	Emperor Galerius, a non-Christian, legalizes Christianity; after his death the same year, widespread legal uncertainty descends on the Christians of the Roman Empire
313	A meeting at Milan between Constantine and Licinius legalizes Christianity for a second time
324	Constantine removes Licinius from power
330	The city of Constantinople is dedicated
346	A local woman, Aurelia Ataris, is attacked and kidnapped in Roman Egypt; she files a petition with the authorities for justice
378	A Gothic army kills the Roman Emperor Valens on the battlefield at Adrianople, outside Constantinople
379	Theodosius begins his radically transformational rule of the Roman Empire
391–392	Christian extremists attack and destroy Alexandria's Temple of Serapis
392–394	A Roman civil war is fought with Christians on both sides
410	A Gothic leader, Alaric, attacks the city of Rome
415	Christian extremists murder Hypatia, a scholar and philosopher in Alexandria
408	Stilicho – of Vandal heritage but an official of Rome – is executed by the Roman government
417	Rutilius Namatianus begins his journey home
430	Augustine, the bishop of Hippo, in North Africa, dies; his theological fame begins to spread beyond North Africa
438	Emperor Theodosius II rejoices at the completion of a new Roman law code, named in his honor, the *Theodosian Law Code*
429–439	Vandals establish a government in post-Roman North Africa
476	The city of Rome disappears from its own empire
493	A man of Gothic heritage, Theoderic, a Christian "East Goth" (Ostrogoth), is appointed King of Rome
527	Justinian, looking over a withered Roman Empire, begins his rule
534–535	Justinian recaptures North Africa and then portions of Italy
537	Two clever architects, Anthemius of Tralles and Isidore of Miletus, celebrate the successful completion of Hagia Sophia in Constantinople
c.540	Plague ravages the pre-modern world; it reaches Constantinople

c.545–550	Cosmas, who sails to India, begins writing a text that will win him a lasting nickname, Indicopleustes
610	Heraclius is proclaimed ruler of the Roman Empire in Constantinople
614	Sasanian Persians attack Jerusalem; Heraclius vows to restore the true cross to Jerusalem
622	Rejected by local leaders, Muhammad and his followers, the "Believers," move from Mecca to Yathrib – an event to become known as the *hijra*; a "constitution" is drafted
632	Muhammad's death
636	An army of the "Believers" seizes Jerusalem from Roman control
641	An army of the "Believers" captures Egypt from the Roman Empire and establishes their own capital at Fustat (Cairo)
651	An army of the "Believers" overthrows the Sasanian Empire
c.690–691	For the first time since 70 CE, a building rises on the old Temple Mount in Jerusalem: the "Dome of the Rock," paid for by 'Abd al-Malik
c.723–743	A member of the Umayyad family, with an eye towards engaging his Greek-speaking neighbors, builds a hunting lodge at Qusayr 'Amra; the paintings are labeled in Greek and Arabic
1776	Edward Gibbon publishes his epic narration on *The Decline and Fall of the Roman Empire*
1980s	Archaeologists in Rome begin excavating the site that will become known as the Crypta Balbi Museum
1997	Fifty-eight tourists are murdered by religious extremists at Queen Hatshepsut's mortuary temple at Deir el-Bahari, Egypt
2001	Islamic extremists detonate the Buddhas at Bamiyan, Afghanistan
2015	Explosions at Palmyra. Temples crumble. The Syrian people suffer the humanitarian crisis of ongoing civil war

Map: The Late Antique World At-A-Glance

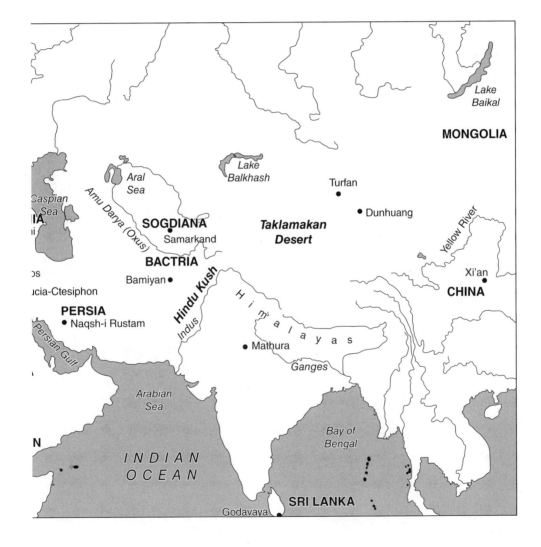

Part I
The "Vanishing" of Rome

1
Who and What Is Late Antiquity?

Rutilius Namatianus did not want to leave Rome; but as news of the attack trickled in, he managed his goodbyes and rushed down the Tiber to board the next ship. It cannot have been an easy decision, to give up his comfortable life in the imperial city to sail, at moment's notice, back to Gaul. But crisis had struck. The luxury of living away from home had come to a sudden halt. Friends and colleagues in Italy would have to understand. Many of them would probably have seen Rutilius' look of anxious confusion, for "eyes cannot, tearless, say goodbye." That, at least, is the way he describes his own departure in a Latin poem (Rutilius Namatianus, *On His Return to Gaul* 1.165, LCL translation by J. Duff and A. Duff [1935]).

The poetry of the line, like Rutilius' work as a whole, is arresting for many reasons, not the least of which are related to Rutilius' upbringing and career. A member of Rome's wealthy senatorial class, Rutilius had been raised by a hard-working father, a dedicated government official who had held the position of governor in central Italy and, perhaps more importantly, had fulfilled his duties without scandal. It was a solid reputation that would loom large over Rutilius' life for many decades. Stopping in Tuscany on his journey home, in 417 CE, Rutilius tells us how touched he was to learn that the citizens there fondly remembered his father's time in office. The residents of Pisa had paid to erect a statue of him in their Forum. "The honor done to my lost parent," Rutilius wrote, "made me weep" (*On His Return to Gaul* 1.575–580).

Rutilius' upbringing helped determine his career. An educated male, from a family who had already served the emperor, he can be counted among an elite group of people who, in the early fifth century CE, stood in the top 1 percent of Roman society. People like Rutilius moved easily through the halls of power. Three years earlier, in 414 CE, Rutilius himself had been Prefect of the City of Rome, *praefectus urbi*. Prior to that, he had already served at the pleasure of the emperor,

A Social and Cultural History of Late Antiquity, First Edition. Douglas Boin.
© 2018 John Wiley & Sons, Inc. Published 2018 by John Wiley & Sons, Inc.

acting as *magister officiorum*, "Master of the Imperial Offices." Like a modern politician's indispensable chief-of-staff, he oversaw the couriers, communications, interpreters, and audiences that kept the emperor's day in some semblance of order. Prefect of the City of Rome – a twelve-hundred-year-old city by Rutilius' day – was an extraordinary accomplishment. No surprise he was morose as he watched it disappear.

That's precisely why this chapter begins with him. Of all the writers who could have delivered the first lines of our story, of all the objects and monuments that could have been used to set the stage for what comes next in history, Rutilius Namatianus is indisputably not the most famous voice of his age. Yet I believe his minor, though heartfelt, reflections do merit top billing for an altogether different reason. I think the unhappiness that pervades his poem – the result of a highly educated, successful Latin speaker being forced to walk away from the ancient city he so deeply loved – is something that should resonate with many readers who pick up this book.

Planned as the last in a new series of volumes which explore the social and cultural world of the ancient Mediterranean, starting in Archaic Greece and finishing in Late Antiquity, this work is designed to take readers across the bridge that passes from classical antiquity to the Middle Ages. Now that the story has arrived in the fifth century CE, the time has come for us to bid goodbye to Rome, too. For students and scholars trained in classical history, who wouldn't be – like Rutilius Namatianus – just a tad nostalgic when they set foot nervously towards Late Antiquity? Many readers are leaving the world they love.

1.1   An Overview of the Book

History from the ground-up, all the way to the top

This book is built around people like Rutilius, second- or third-tier historical figures who are usually passed over in many traditional narratives of the time. That is not to say students won't learn about marquee names and dates, too: Constantine, the first Roman emperor to convert to Christianity, is here, as is the sixth-century Christian emperor of Constantinople, Justinian. Muhammad, the prophet who formed an important movement on the Arabian peninsula during the early seventh century, occupies these pages as well. But the emphasis throughout is not on the day-to-day record of wars, battles, and palace intrigue that largely predominates in our source material and gives us a narrative of what was happening at the top of society. This book focuses on reconstructing the period from the ground-up.

In many ways, it is a people's history of the time: a story of ambition and failure, of the daily grind around which people organized their hours and of their hopes and aspirations for change that sometimes materialized, sometimes did not. It is a picture not just of life in the Roman Empire's capital, Romulus' historic city, which Rutilius was fortunate to manage, or life in the empire's second capital, Constantinople – although it certainly will paint an impressionistic picture of both.

It takes readers, instead, on a tour: to the borderlands of the classical world to see what the people on the inside of the Mediterranean looked like to others who were looking in and then back again. In doing so, we have the opportunity to lay our eyes on a historical panorama that includes more than the isolated figures of emperors and kings.

In the fourteen chapters of this book, we will pause to inspect where the people of Late Antiquity lived and how they worshipped. We will explore the family bonds that sustained them and the economic structures that underpinned their daily life. We will encounter the fascinating literature they produced in a positively astounding number of languages, visit major monuments they built, and pick up the objects they left behind. This book is not a plodding survey of literature or archaeology, however. It is a social and cultural history – a story at its core about people, about the things and ideas that occupied their imaginations and shaped their world.

A reader could be forgiven for feeling enveloped, overwhelmed even, by such a broad, patchwork quilt of different cities, people, classes, and times. But there are recognizable faces here that are meant to comfort (and surprise, for those fortunate to meet them again for the first time). Augustine, the late fourth-century Christian author of the now world-famous spiritual autobiography called the *Confessions*, is but one of the familiar figures who hides in this landscape. Sometimes presumed to have dominated the period, Augustine will prove to be a much tougher person to hear than his later, saintly stature might imply, though. For the world we're about to put under our microscope hardly belonged to him. Even the map that we'll use to chart our journey will reveal itself to be more expansive and diverse than it sometimes appears in stories of Rome – with chapters featuring the history of South Asia, Central Asia, and the Arabian peninsula.

That is part of what makes Late Antiquity so exciting. It demands a deep, empathetic desire to inquire into the lives of ancient people who have outgrown the traditional labels, "Greek" and "Roman," with which the study of ancient Mediterranean history has traditionally been concerned. Their dramas played out on three continents – Europe, Africa, and Asia – and the richness of their experiences cannot be appreciated with the use of a simple, parochial lens like a focus on Christian theology or church history. In fact, a large number of its actors were not Christian at all: They were Jews shut out of their holiest site by an aggressive Christian take-over of Jerusalem; Muslims who wrestled with the complicated legacy of what had been revealed to Muhammad; and followers of the Buddha who worshipped in monastic communities over the din of Chinese and Persian traders passing outside their caves (*Exploring Culture* 1.1: Late Antiquity Lost; Figure 1.1). And among them was also a nameless, faceless, but no less important host of traders, laborers, wives, husbands, daughters, and sons who never declared any religious preference.

Their choices are the very things that make Late Antiquity so difficult to study. The question of why people at any time might choose to reveal meaningful things about themselves – in the imagery of a poem they composed or in the designs on a plate they commissioned or purchased in the market – is fundamentally connected with the power structures of the place and time around them. In short, although it's admirable and indeed necessary for us to dig deeper into history to study the borders,

Exploring Culture 1.1   *Late Antiquity Lost at the Start of the Twenty-First Century*

It can be difficult to think about the ancient past, let alone study it. Buildings, statues, even pieces of old cookware can breathe a little bit of life into people long gone. They bridge the distance and lend the past a more tangible presence. For archaeologists and historians, they also inform us about aspects of life not preserved in documents.

Stones and sherds are more than scientific artifacts, however. They are people's cultural heritage, and the loss of objects and monuments – whether through natural disaster like the sudden rumbling of an earthquake or through more nefarious means, described below – can strike like a gut-wrenching blow to communities who value the stories these precious pieces contain.

The start of the twenty-first century has witnessed some dramatic upheavals around the globe that have directly impacted how Late Antique scholars do their jobs. Regional conflicts, civil wars, international terrorism, and domestic disturbances have led, tragically, to the loss of many important examples of the historical and archaeological record. Two damaged sites, in particular, Bamiyan in Afghanistan and Palmyra in Syria, illustrate how truly expansive this period was and how interconnected its people were. Late Antiquity crossed many modern time zones.

Bamiyan lies in the center of Afghanistan. Located about 150 miles west of the Afghan capital, it is nestled in the tail of a mountainous ridge, the Hindu Kush, which snakes across northeastern Afghanistan before it merges with the Himalayas in Pakistan. Starting in the sixth century CE, two monumental statues of the Buddha were carved from the rock face. These towering Bamiyan statues were examples of Gandhara material culture. An ancient kingdom of the Indus River valley and Hindu Kush, with roots dating back to 1500 BCE, the people and culture of Gandhara began to see many Mediterranean customs and ideas come through the mountains in the wake of Alexander the Great's military excursions. Gandhara culture would flourish through the sixth century CE. A seventh-century Chinese traveler, Xuanzang, reports how impressive the rock-hewn Buddhas were.

In March 2001, however, the authorities in Afghanistan, the Taliban, deemed the Bamiyan statues "idolatrous" to their version of Islam and had them detonated. Today, after a U.S.-led invasion following the September 11, 2001, terror attacks, the people of Afghanistan are now picking up the pieces of their culture in more ways than one. There is a campaign to restore the Buddhas.

The all-too-familiar story of modern people suffering a cultural loss through violent destruction can be told about Palmyra (also known as Tadmur), Syria. Located at the opposite end of the Eurasian landmass from China, Palmyra was an important trading oasis in classical antiquity. During Roman rule, the city's temples, colonnades, and tombs reflected the cosmopolitan interests and personalities of its people.

In August 2015, in the middle of a heart-breaking civil war, the so-called Islamic State lined two important ancient temples and several tombs with explosives and blew them up. The largest of these buildings, the Temple of Bel, was situated inside a sanctuary that measured almost two American football fields on each side. The destruction of Palmyra's monuments was a heinous act of cultural cleansing intended to remove the pre-Islamic past from memories of war-torn Syria.

Figure 1.1 The Buddhist caves at Bamiyan, Afghanistan, where two colossal images of the Buddha once stood. Carved from the sandstone cliffs by a community of Buddhist monks – the smaller one in the middle of the sixth century CE, and the larger one (seen here) in the early seventh century CE – they were destroyed by the order of the Taliban government of Afghanistan in March 2001. The issue of how people of different faiths or no faith interacted with each other and with the diverse world around them is one of the key topics that we will explore in this book. It is a story that crosses three continents, five centuries, and involves Jews, Christians, Muslims, believers in the Olympian gods, Buddhists, Hindus, and people who had no religious preference at all. Originally 55 meters tall (c.180 feet). Copyright © DPA Picture Alliance Archive/Alamy Stock Photo.

beliefs, cities, families, economics, communities, literary culture, and material culture of the people who laid the foundation of this book, we cannot and must not leave conversations about politics, law, and power so casually behind. This book introduces readers to both, and it suggests that even bottom-up history must take account of people and events at the top of the social ladder.

Precisely for that reason, the intersection of power, politics, and society is a topic that haunts many episodes in this book. In the fourth century, we will consider whether Rome would remain true to its pluralistic past with the legalization of Christianity. In the fifth century, we will look at the social status which religious minorities, like Jews, had as citizens in a Christian empire. And in the sixth century, we will see how a contemporary empire, like that of the Persians, conceived of their own political mandate as divinely given, too. Finally, in the seventh and eighth centuries, we will search for evidence to show us how the first Muslims interacted with their neighbors – diplomatically or militarily? – and try to determine what effect their choices had on the lives of the people they unexpectedly came to govern. These are some of the avenues and questions we will wander down together in this book (*Key Debates* 1.1: Late Antiquity Found). In doing so, our guiding principle will be to eavesdrop on as many voices as possible, not just the testimony of the people who shouted loudest.

Key Debates 1.1 *Late Antiquity Found at the Start of the Twenty-First Century*

Was Jesus married? Did the Qur'ān exist prior to Muhammad? In the past decade, these two questions, which might scandalize some devout Christians or Muslims, have dominated the headlines. In each case, the news has been fueled by the discovery of new material culture.

In September 2012, American researchers at an international conference in Rome announced that they had translated a scrap of papyrus with a sensational phrase on it: "Jesus said to them, 'My wife….'" Written in eight lines of Coptic, a language used in Late Antique Egypt, the papyrus fragment had been assigned a sensational name by the researchers who were working on it. They called it a fragment of *The Gospel of Jesus' Wife*. The tiny artifact, which at c.1.5 × 3.0 inches is smaller than an iPhone, quickly lit a fuse in the academic community. A series of startling revelations followed.

Scientific tests used to determine the papyrus' date revealed that it had come from the seventh to ninth century CE. Consequently, the text offers no evidence at all about whether Jesus was *actually* married. It does, however, have a place in a long and important intellectual conversation, dating back to the late second century CE, in which Christian writers *speculated* about Jesus' marital status. The Late Antique Coptic fragment would fit within this vibrant tradition – if the text is authentic.

As soon as the fragment was unveiled, other researchers detected problems. The Coptic text was written in a dialect that had long died out in seventh- to ninth-century Egypt. In addition, the order of the words read less as fluent sentences and more as a series of patchwork phrases, cribbed from another source. One perceptive scholar identified a missing letter in the text's first line. It replicated the same error that appeared in the same words in an online edition of the much more widely known Coptic document, the *Gospel of Thomas*. Details of the fragment's exact collecting history, beyond a vague 1999 receipt and a few references to a mid-twentieth-century collector, were also never made public at the time. That point was particularly galling to the cultural heritage community, concerned with stopping the illicit trade of antiquities, which thrives on obscurity.

An announcement coming out of the United Kingdom, reported widely by outlets such as BBC and the *New York Times*, was similarly exciting. Charles Cadbury, a famous chocolate maker, had funded the acquisition of several ancient manuscripts in the 1920s. Purchased by a priest from Iraq, these artifacts were then brought to Birmingham in England.

In 2015, a graduate student made a stunning discovery. On two previously unidentified parchment folios, or individual leaves, she recognized the text of the Qur'ān. Muslims consider the Qur'ān to be the word of Allah revealed to Muhammad, starting in the 610s. No text of the Qur'ān has ever been dated to Muhammad's lifetime, however. He died in 632. The text is said to have been standardized by the Muslim community's third leader, Uthman, who ruled between 644 and 656 CE.

Scientific testing has now confirmed that the Birmingham parchments date between 568 and 645 CE. Though imprecise, the range of dates for the Birmingham folios distinguishes them as two of the world's oldest copies of the Qur'ān.

That's why, throughout this book, top-down history is interwoven with history from the ground-up. Famous names, momentous laws, and an emphasis on chronology: all these provide an essential ground line for registering the power dynamics within Late Antique society. When we pay attention to them, they can even help us see our sources in a higher relief – even "minor" poets like Rutilius Namatianus.

A top-down view of Rome in the fifth century CE

Let's consider an example of how to integrate top-down history with a more individualistic, local approach. Just what *was* happening in the Roman Empire at the time Rutilius set out for Gaul? Political changes before, during, and after the fifth century CE were certainly dramatic and, in many cases, socially disruptive. In 476 CE, the empire would shed the form it had assumed for roughly five centuries. Roman provinces across the landscape of Europe and North Africa, including the crucial territory of Italy, would be cut loose from imperial control, and many people would gradually adapt to life under new management: Christian kings, not Christian emperors.

To make matters more painful, at least for culturally conservative Romans, many of these new administrators were foreigners, and they had arrived in violent waves of migration. One group that rocked Rome into the fifth century CE were Vandals. A tribe from northern Europe, Vandals had crossed the Rhine River in the early fifth century CE. Later, they marched through modern Spain across to North Africa and, in 439 CE, eventually seized its cosmopolitan cultural capital, Carthage. The Rhine River wasn't the only site of border problems for the Roman Empire, though.

The Danube frontier was another. Since the mid-third century CE, other foreign tribes had been testing the vigilance of Roman armies stationed along the empire's northeastern frontier. These sporadic attacks began as third-century headaches for the Roman cities of eastern Europe and the Balkans. By the fourth century, they had turned into a full-blown, urgent political crisis. Athens was invaded in 267 CE. Areas of the historic city were torched. A century later, in 378 CE, the Emperor Valens would resolve to put an end to the confrontations. Backed by his powerful army and devoted soldiers, Valens met a band of Goths at Adrianople, outside modern Istanbul. The emperor may have been hoping for a swift victory. Instead, in a confrontation that left an open wound on the Roman state, Valens was killed in battle, his body never found. The emperor's death stung, an indictment of Rome's failed border policies. It was also a harbinger of more problems.

At the turn of the fifth century CE, two Gothic tribes, the Tervingi and the Greuthungi, living on the western shores of the Black Sea, were driven from their home by an unexpected invasion of Huns from Central Asia. Rome was ill prepared to handle the effect of foreigners driven from their home by other foreigners. This tense situation reached a breaking point in the first decade of the fifth century when a savvy Gothic leader, Alaric, began demanding a land settlement with Roman authorities. The government balked at ceding anything to Alaric's Goths.

In 410 CE, to prove the seriousness of his demands and to get the Senate's attention, Alaric attacked Rome. He and his army besieged the city to convince the
empire's stubborn bureaucrats that the Goths' concerns could no longer be ignored.
By holding the empire hostage, Goths won major territorial concessions, too. Around
413 CE, land was given to them in the province of Gaul, in the region of Aquitaine,
settling them far from the empire's capitals in Ravenna and Constantinople. Before
the end of the decade, the capital of the Gothic settlement in Aquitaine would be
based in the historical city of Roman *Tolosa*, modern Toulouse, France. From there,
Gothic settlers would continue to grow in power in Aquitaine and Spain and expand
militarily.

Rutilius Namatianus' family home was in Toulouse. In 417 CE, as word reached
Rome that the Goths had seized the city as their capital, the panic-stricken, one-time
Prefect of the City – fearing the worst for his hometown – rushed through his fare-
wells and arranged for passage on the next ship to Gaul. As historians, we don't have
to share Rutilius' sense of nostalgia to recognize how thankful we should be that we
have his poem. It allows us to experience a crucial transition in the story of the
Roman Empire through the eyes of a person who called two places home, Italy and
Gaul; but it also affords us a unique way of seeing the same period through several
of Rutilius' family and friends. Many of them were staking their hopes for the future
by looking in the opposite direction: east.

Rutilius' poetry, in effect, offers an excellent case study at the outset of our book
for observing how top-down narratives can inform our more minor sources, and vice
versa. Before starting, then, we should not push Rutilius off stage so quickly. We can
learn quite a bit more about how to do Late Antique history by listening to his
poem. This first chapter invites readers to join three figures, Rutilius' friends, all of
whom can help us put a human face on a pivotal age that is too often talked about
in generic terms.

1.2   Three Lives and the "Fall of Rome"

Rutilius' journey was delayed fifteen days on account of weather (*On His Return to
Gaul* 1.205). It must have been an agonizing two-week wait spent at the Roman
harbor. Although only one complete book, or chapter, survives, along with fragments of a second, Rutilius' poem *On His Return to Gaul* is our primary source for
his life, his family, and his career during the early fifth century CE. The precarious
circumstances under which he wrote peek through the lines of his text.

Throughout his poem (where the meter permitted it), Rutilius introduces friends
and relatives. The inclusion of their names and, in many cases, the details of their
professional or personal lives, helps us compile a profile of Rutilius' social network.
The following profiles will allow readers to personalize the dramatic decades of the
early fifth century. They will also help us begin to sketch, albeit impressionistically
at first, a more complex picture of how specific instances of change – like the migration of non-Roman citizens into the empire's borders and the violent conflict that
could accompany it or result from it – affected daily life in fifth-century Rome, Gaul,
and beyond.

Pictures of this period are sometimes painted in heavy black and white and for understandable reason. Greeks and Romans used these dark lines to stigmatize outsiders. They called foreign tribes "barbarians" (in the Greek, *barbaroi*; in Latin, *barbari*), "savages," whose perceived inability or even unwillingness to talk, act, or behave as Romans fundamentally disqualified them from being included in civic society. Since at least the republican age of Cicero in the late first century BCE and of Tacitus in the late first century CE, recourse to this kind of stereotyping, even dehumanizing language drove public conversation about who was worthy enough to be counted a real Roman (for example, see Cicero, *Against Verres* 2.4.112, evoking the image of inhumane "barbarian"; and Tacitus, *Annals* 14.39, characterizing the people of Britain as such). This book asks students to adopt a more empathetic approach to history.

Victorinus, vicarius *of Britain*

And yet we cannot underestimate the effect that this steady trickle of nativist ideology had on molding the minds of elite Romans over the course of five centuries. Rutilius attests its effects. From his poem, we learn that at least one Roman in Gaul was not willing to welcome this new wave of change brought by Gothic settlers. This man was Rutilius' friend Victorinus, a former *vicarius* of Britain and a native of Toulouse. "The capture of Tolosa," Rutilius tells us, "had forced Victorinus, a wanderer in the lands of Etruria, to settle there and dwell in a foreign home" (*On His Return to Gaul* 1.495–496). Victorinus' deliberate choice to relocate to Italy rather than continue to live in a city settled by Goths reveals much about his values and priorities.

The office of *vicarius*, "vicar," which Victorinus held prior to 414 CE, was a bureaucratic invention that had not existed in the earlier empire. At the end of the tumultuous political years of the third century CE, Emperor Diocletian (r. 284–305 CE) had instituted several constitutional changes that were designed to make governing such a vast empire more efficient. One of these had been the creation of twelve "dioceses," or super-provinces, which would become the second most senior structural unit of the Roman state (the prefectures, of which there were four, were super-dioceses). The long familiar units of empire, the provinces, meanwhile, were reduced in size – effectively allowing the provincial governor to manage a smaller, more self-contained area. In his role as *vicarius* of Britain, Victorinus would have coordinated reports from each of his provincial governors (there were five), and then channeled that information to the palace. Rutilius tells us that, for his service, Victorinus was awarded an honorary title, *comes*, "special advisor to the emperor."

In the early fifth-century CE western empire, however, none of this success apparently held any allure for Victorinus anymore. After a career that had taken him to the northwest territories, after a lifetime of calling the landscape of Roman Gaul his home, Victorinus opted for a pleasurable retirement in Tuscany, where, as "special advisor," he could be consulted if needed, rather than take a desk and an office with the emperor. By the time the Gothic settlers had won their concessions from the government, Victorinus must have thought that the world he loved was simply changing too fast for him to play an active role in it anymore. In this way, he moved out of his house in Gaul just as new, different people were moving in.

Was Victorinus' outlook commonplace, or unique? That's the question for the social and cultural historian. Rutilius' other friends certainly didn't share Victorinus' perspective. Notwithstanding the ongoing negotiations taking place with Alaric and the Goths, many Romans throughout the empire were striving to ensure that the government continued to function and that life as they knew it adapted to the times. One attack in 410 CE, however psychologically jarring, was not going to be the end of their world (*Political Issues* 1.1: "Are We Rome?" Apocalyptic Thinking, Then and Now). We can observe this alternate perspective if we look at the lives of two more of Rutilius' friends.

Political Issues 1.1   *"Are We Rome?" Apocalyptic Thinking, Then and Now*

Do you know the popular parlor game, "Are We Rome?" It's an amusing pastime in which people use the past to talk, in code, about current concerns. In this diversion, the "Fall of Rome" is assumed to be a historical event, usually dressed up with real dates: 410 CE, 476 CE, or 1453 CE. Yet Rome didn't "fall" in one year. Nor did it "fall" because of a series of mistakes. The "End of the Great Empire" is a powerful theological idea that has been around since antiquity. Scholars have identified it as one characteristic of an *apocalyptic worldview*.

Although many writings called "apocalypses" are known from antiquity, elements of an apocalyptic worldview transcend this specific genre. One biblical scholar, John Collins, has identified eight characteristic motifs of this worldview: There is (1) a frantic expectation that the world will end and a belief (2) that it will come as an utter catastrophe. This hope is based upon the conviction that (3) the world unfolds in neat, discrete time periods. In addition, writers may also characterize their present time (4) as a "cosmic struggle" in which heavenly actors, such as angels and demons, battle for the soul of humanity. The outcome of this battle is (5) salvation, often evoked through ecstatic visions of paradise. In the end, (6) a divine kingdom will arrive with the aid of (7) a royal, savior figure, who will come bringing (8) glory.

The roots of this worldview sink deep into time, perhaps dating back millennia to the Near East and Persia. One of the most famous – and influential – manifestations of it comes from the Hellenistic Jewish world: the Book of Daniel.

Most biblical scholars believe this Jewish text was written around 165 BCE. In the age of Alexander's successors, Hellenistic customs, ideas, and trade began arriving on the doorstep of Jerusalem in greater frequency. Their presence, including the practice of ruler cult, was sparking a heated debate among the Jewish people about how to balance cultural traditions and innovations, faith and politics. The Book of Daniel preserves a slice of this crucial historical moment.

In the text, Daniel is living in Babylon during the time of King Nebuchadnezzar. Nebuchadnezzar had destroyed the Temple in Jerusalem and taken the Jewish people as captives to Babylon in 586 BCE. While in prison, Daniel has a series of visions of "four great beasts [come] up out of the sea" (Daniel 7.2–8 [*NRSV*]). Puzzled by what they signify, he approaches an interpreter who tells him: "[They signify that] four kings shall arise out of the earth" (Daniel 7.16–17 [*NRSV*]). The author was using symbols to provide a coded message of hope for his readers. He was telling them that history had been "predicted" to unfold as a series of hostile empires. This divine plan had begun with Nebuchadnezzar's "Babylon." Daniel's readers would know that it had been followed by two of the most powerful empires of ancient history: the Median and Persian. The Hellenistic rulers were the last of these four maniacal "beasts."

The Book of Daniel suggests that their time, too, would soon reach its end and that the Hellenistic empire would "fall." This idea would have brought hope to people who saw the influx of Hellenistic ideals as incompatible with their Jewish faith. Both the Book of Daniel and the apocalyptic worldview which it encapsulates would be passed down to Late Antiquity. Many of these ideas still shape our own. They lie just beneath the surface of many "Are We Rome?" political laments.

Rufius Volusianus and Palladius were two other men whom Rutilius mentions in his poem. Their biographies suggest that not everyone in the early fifth century was necessarily demoralized or paralyzed by current events. These two men were not only staring head-on at the changing Roman world; they were eager to make the changing future their own.

Palladius, the law student from Gaul

Alaric's three-day siege of Rome, in 410, had clouded the mood of Rome's residents. Many wealthy Romans had fled, deciding to seek refuge from the aftermath of the precarious times by sailing to the comfort of their second homes in North Africa. Their stories, famously dramatized in a sermon on the Book of Daniel preached by Augustine that very year or the year following (Augustine, *Sermon* 397), create the impression of a city-wide exodus, a self-inflicted aftershock, that completed the decimation of the western capital. Yet during the first decades of the fifth century, not everyone was so eager to give up Rome.

Palladius – a young man from Gaul, perhaps in his twenties, maybe younger – had just arrived. And he had come with a purpose: to learn from the best teachers of the city. He "had been sent of late from the lands of the Gauls to learn the laws of the Roman courts" (*On His Return to Gaul* 1.208, 212–213). A close friend of Rutilius', Palladius was also the poet's relative, a boy who held "the fondest ties of my regard," Rutilius wrote. Their connection was deep and went back to two generations to Palladius' father, born in Poitiers in Gaul. An "eloquent youth," as Rutilius styles him, Palladius had potential. His family, however, was in a precarious state.

Palladius' father, Exuperantius, had been assigned the task of quelling Gothic disturbances in Gaul. "Even now his father, Exuperantius, trains the Armoric seaboard to love the recovery of peace; he is re-establishing the laws, bringing freedom back and suffers not the inhabitants to be their servants' slaves" (*On His Return to Gaul* 1.214–216). The duty was a thankless one. Roman Armorica occupied the peninsula of modern France which is roughly the region of Brittany, a territory that had, for geographic reasons, not been well integrated into the empire's road system. Routes to and from the coast, originating in the interior of Gaul, near Roman Limonum (Poitiers), took a circuitous path. Midsummer, the fastest journey to the center of Armorica from Exuperantius' home has been calculated to take almost twenty-one days; Romans fleeing to Carthage in the wake of Alaric's attack, by contrast, arrived at their destination in less than a week. Over the next two decades, the dedication that Palladius' father showed in fighting for Roman values would make him an easy target for the disreputable pool of usurpers and revolters hiding out the isolated Armorica.

In 424 CE, Palladius' father was murdered during an uprising in the south of France, as confirmed in a list of events, or "chronicle," compiled in Gaul in the midfifth century (*MGH, AA* volume 9, *The Gallic Chronicle of 452* CE, entry at year 424–425 CE). Sadly, we do not know what effect his father's death had on Palladius. The student who had come to Italy to learn law, the boy who had bid goodbye to his father while he was policing Gaul, vanishes from the historical record after his appearance in Rutilius' poem. Whatever dreams the young Palladius had for making a name for himself in the wake of Alaric's attack may have been lost in Rome.

Rufius Volusianus, the prodigy who went to Constantinople

Anonymity was not a choice for our third and final individual: Rufius Antonius Agrypnius Volusianus. Rufius Volusianus was a child of an indisputable privilege; his father's family traced its lineage through Rome's historic *Decii* and *Caeonii* lines. His great-grandfather had been a senator. His status among the membership of the empire's elite was unimpeachable. His mother's name is unknown. He was also a loyal friend who thought nothing about accompanying Rufinus on his trip to the harbor.

"And now while others wend their way back to Rome, Rufius, living glory of his father Albinus, clings close to me on my way" (*On His Return to Gaul* 1.165–166). One imagines two young men running frantically to catch a ferry down the Tiber or a chariot down the Ostia Way. All the while, Rutilius must have appreciated the ridiculousness of the scene. His friend had forever bragged of having acquired his nickname – Volusianus – "from the ancient pedigree of [the name] Volusus," one of the local Italian tribes that had risen to power during the first years of the Roman Republic, back during the sixth century BCE. An impressive connection, if it were true. When people pressed him to substantiate it, Rutilius says, Volusianus would hem and haw, boldly brandishing stories about the authority of "Rutilian kings on the witness of Virgil" (*On His Return to Gaul* 1.170). Whether anyone ever mocked such outrageous claims of lineage is never documented; Virgil's Rutilian kings, their stories dramatized in the *Aeneid*, were fictional characters.

Rufius Volusianus may have seen himself in Virgil's poetry, but poetry could not contain someone who presented himself as larger than life. It was Rufius' impressive "power of eloquence" that, Rutilius says, had skyrocketed his friend's career (*On His Return to Gaul* 1.171). One of his earliest jobs was in the imperial house, acting as *quaestor sacri palatini*, or "Chief Legal Officer in the Sacred Palace." The number of positions in the administration had grown since Diocletian's time, just as the number of provinces had, at the end of the third century and beginning of the fourth century CE. Diocletian's successors, among them chiefly Constantine, had continued to create new positions to assist in the day-to-day running of the empire. The "Communications Officer in the Sacred Palace" was one of these new roles.

Historians would be at a loss to decode the roles in this puzzling bureaucracy were it not for the fact we fortunately possess a document that helps us crack it. Written around 400 CE and preserved in several early medieval manuscripts, it is titled the *List of Offices* (in Latin, the *Notitia Dignitatum*). It charts many government positions in both the western and eastern branches of the empire and, in some cases, explicitly states the duties associated with these roles. Unquestionably dry to read, lacking any plot or character, the *List of Offices* is, nevertheless, a valuable reference for understanding Rufius Volusianus' political world. It tells us that Rufius Volusianus would have been responsible for "the formulation of laws [and] the formulation of petitions." It also mentions that he would have been fortunate to have a staff ("subordinate clerical assistants from the various bureaus" [*List of Offices*, translation by W. Fairley, 1901]).

With this government job came a high salary and the potential for advancement to an even higher salary, with more access and prestige. And less than two years after Alaric's attack, Volusianus seems to have been on a path towards acquiring just that. By then, his ambition – with hints of political ruthlessness – had clearly imprinted itself on Rutilius. "In youth he was the fitting spokesman of the emperor [*quaestor sacri palatini*]. Still earlier [probably before 412 CE], a mere stripling, he had governed as pro-consul the Carthaginian peoples and among the Tyrian folk [the Punic people of North Africa] inspired dread (in Latin, *terror*) and love (*amor*) alike" (*On His Return to Gaul* 1.171–174). It was these qualities, his ability to be a feared paper-pusher with a delicate touch, that led Rutilius to speculate freely about his friend's future: "His zealous energy gave promise of highest office. If it is permitted to trust desert, a consul he will be" (*On His Return to Gaul* 1.175–176).

Rufius Volusianus never became consul, one of the honorary chief executives of the state, a position often held ceremoniously by many emperors during their own reign. He did, however, earn another one of the elite titles of the empire: *vir illustris*, "Illustrious Man." Like the top-tier "Platinum Status" for today's frequent fliers, this Latin rank had been created in the fourth century CE to help distinguish levels of wealth and success among the already wealthy and successful. *Vir clarissimus*, "Distinguished Man," and *vir spectabilis*, "Admirable Man," functioned in similar, but less elevated, ways. Public texts inscribed in Greek and Latin throughout the Mediterranean usually include a proud reference, on the part of the dedicator, to one of these three levels of elite status.

Rufius Volusianus, the platinum-level office holder, would capitalize on it. By 418 CE, he would become the Prefect of the City of Rome. A decade later, in 428–429 CE, he would be given even more responsibility: the control of an entire praetorian prefecture. There were four of these state units: the prefectures of Gaul, Italy–North Africa, the Balkans, and the eastern Mediterranean, according to the *List of Offices*. Each had been drawn onto the map of the Roman state by Emperor Constantine (r. 313–337 CE) and functioned as the super-provinces of the fourth-century empire, just as Diocletian dioceses once had. The result of Constantine's tweak to Diocletian's design was a three-tiered level of Roman government – prefecture, diocese, province – that would survive into the seventh century CE.

The boy who had raced to the harbor with Rutilius would eventually command one of these four territories, "Italy–Africa," and he would end his career as a confidant of the Roman emperor. When, in 437 CE, the ruler in the west, Valentinian III (r. 425–455 CE), announced his plan to marry the daughter of the emperor of the east, Volusianus' connections must have opened doors. He was invited to the eastern capital to be a part of the ceremony. This imperial wedding must have been one of the grandest state functions in Constantinople's young history. We know these things not from anything Rufius Volusianus wrote down but because his niece was living in the east, and she was eager to see her uncle.

It is one of history's great ironies that the story of her life – not his – would soon be circulating as a book. Motivated by an ascetic urge, Melania (383–439 CE) had convinced her husband they should sell their homes, in North Africa and elsewhere, and move to Jerusalem. There, they would endow monastic communities for Christian men and women in the city where Jesus had been executed. By the late fifth century, a *Life of Melania*, written in ancient Greek, would be providing inspiration for pious Christian ascetics and pilgrims throughout the empire. A Latin edition would shortly follow. Uncle Volusianus, who traced his lineage to Rutilian kings, political striver and platinum-status aristocrat, would be reduced to a bit player in the *Life* of his ascetic Christian niece (*Working With Sources* 1.1: Writing History vs. Writing Church History).

A withdrawn, monastic world was certainly not the one Rufius Volusianus saw when he looked around. After a century and a half in which emperors had redrawn the administrative boundaries of the state, the two most important politicians of the Roman world now stood united, in marriage, over a political territory that stretched from western Europe to Asia Minor and from North Africa to the eastern Mediterranean. If a sad plume of smoke had been rising over Rome, in 410 CE, as Rutilius Namatianus sailed away, by the mid-fifth century its cloud had dissipated. And Rufius Volusianus was there to capitalize on what happened next, wherever it happened.

Thirty years later, in 476 CE – just as Melania's life story was put down on parchment or papyrus – a new group of Christian foreigners would negotiate the fiercest settlement yet with the rulers of the empire. They called for the western emperor's resignation and demanded sole political control over the western capital. By the time they had worked their magic, the city of Rome had been erased from the map of a now-diminished Roman Empire. How had that happened? What did it mean? And what were the effects of the "vanishing" of Rome on the people of antiquity? Did Rome really disappear from history in 476 CE, or might it be an illusion?

Working With Sources 1.1

Writing History vs. Writing Church History

When the author of the Book of Daniel, in c.165 BCE, "predicted" the rise of the Hellenistic empire, Rome was a distant star. The maturing Republic on the Tiber was also at that time a potential ally in the Jewish struggle against the Hellenistic kings. In 164, that hoped-for allegiance became a reality. Jewish communities asked the Roman Senate to intervene on their behalf in their struggles with the Hellenistic kings (2 Maccabees 11.34–38).

By year's end, one Jewish family, the Maccabees, had seized the Jewish Temple and ousted the Seleucid dynasty from the Jewish homeland. That same year, in the Jewish month of Chislev, 164 BCE, they purified and rededicated the Temple, establishing a new line of high priests. The Maccabean victory is commemorated today during Hanukkah. In this way, the prophet Daniel's "fourth beast" was finally, triumphantly, erased from time.

By Late Antiquity, however, that's not what many Christians had been taught to believe. Rather than accept the fact that the visions of Daniel had now been "fulfilled," many Christians resorted to highly creative interpretations to convince others that the "fourth beast" was still alive. Daniel, they claimed, had really been talking about "Rome." This fanciful interpretation provided the starting point for many Christian writers who wanted to reassure their listeners that God had been guiding history to its present age. Some were writing at times of genuine crisis.

After Goths attacked Rome in 410 CE – something no foreign army had accomplished in almost eight hundred years – the writer Orosius tried to justify the attack. In a treatise he titled *Against the Non-Christians*, he explained the calamity as part of God's plan. Adopting Daniel's worldview, Orosius presents history as the story of four kingdoms: "In the beginning there was the Babylonian, then the Macedonian [Hellenistic] kingdom, later the African [Carthaginian], and finally," he wrote, there was "the Roman Empire" (*Against the Non-Christians* 2.1). By reworking the scheme to allow room for "Rome," Orosius was suggesting that the Christian empire had not only been predicted by Daniel; it would last until the end of time, a moment which – despite the Gothic attack – had not yet come. Hearing that the end times were postponed must have buoyed the spirits of many Christian communities in Orosius' time. It also must have given them a sense that the story of the world was being written by providence.

At its core, Orosius' history is rooted in an apocalyptic worldview. From a historian's perspective, however, his way of reading Daniel is too theological to be an objective starting point for narrating the events of the past. Still, many Christians could not be convinced to read the text any other way.

Porphyry, who lived in the late third and early fourth centuries CE, was a particularly righteous fact-checker. Daniel did not foretell the future, Porphyry tried to explain to Christians. He was talking about the Hellenistic world. In fact, he was describing the time of Antiochus IV Epiphanes (Prologue to Jerome's *Commentary on the Book of Daniel*, translated by G. Archer, 1958). Given the later success of Orosius' text – *Against the Non-Christians* was immensely popular during the Middle Ages – it is clear that many Christians did not care to be so rigorously fact-checked.

Summary

In many history books, the tumultuous events of the fifth century CE are presented as the "Fall of Rome." In this chapter, we used the poetry of one fifth-century writer, Rutilius Namatianus, to give some human faces to a time period that is often written about in cataclysmic, world-ending terms. Rutilius' poetry introduced us to the different fortunes of his friends and, above all, to their own ideals and aspirations during an age that is traditionally characterized as one of decline, decay, and ruin. A careful reading of this fifth-century poem also revealed many details about the changing administration and constitutional structures of the Roman state.

By introducing readers to a select group of people from the fifth-century Roman world, this exercise raises questions about which individuals or groups might be left out of our sources. (Readers who wish to learn more about the historical data we have for all these men, outside the lines of Rutilius' poetry, should consult the "Study of the People of the Late Roman Empire" [*PLRE*], volume 1.)

Study Questions

1. Who is Rutilius Namatianus? When did he live? What did he do for a living?
2. What were some of the key political and military events that shaped the fifth-century CE Roman Empire?
3. How does Rutilius' poetry help historians investigate this same time period?
4. How have others characterized life in the fifth century CE? Do you agree with the way this time is traditionally presented as the "Fall of Rome"?

Suggested Readings

Peter Heather, *Empires and Barbarians: The Fall of Rome and the Birth of Europe* (Oxford: Oxford University Press, 2009).

Johannes Lipps, Carlos Machado, and Philipp von Rummel (eds.), *The Sack of Rome in 410 AD: The Event, Its Context and Its Impact* (Wiesbaden: Reichert Verlag, 2013).

Martha Malamud, *Rutilius Namatianus' Going Home: De Reditu Suo* (New York: Routledge, 2016).

Danuta Shanzer and Ralph W. Mathisen (eds.), *Romans, Barbarians, and the Transformation of the Roman World: Cultural Interaction and the Creation of Identity in Late Antiquity* (Burlington: Ashgate, 2011).

2

When Does Late Antiquity Begin? When Does it End?

The law student, the manager of a diocese, a legacy child with the gift of speaking and arguing, and a Prefect of the City of Rome – urgently rushing westward to check on imperial developments involving foreigners, the same foreigners who had attacked their western capital – each of these figures gives us a different vantage for reconstructing what happened in 410 CE and afterwards.

Is it too much to claim that all of Late Antiquity can be seen in and around the lines of Rutilius' poem? Of course it is. Rutilius has given access to a micro-history, a more personal reconstruction of his age, a drama enacted on a smaller, quieter stage than the stadium venues of prefectures, dioceses, and provinces – and battlefields – of his day. We should be wary, however, of what he never shows us. Without a doubt, the events that led to his journey home had immediate effects on countless thousands in Rome, North Africa, and Gaul. They also posed new questions for people throughout the empire, including for those high-powered politicos formulating new strategies of diplomacy inside Rome's parallel palace in Constantinople. The questions these elite officials faced were related to nothing less than territorial stability of the Roman state – the very idea of Rome – yet even amid these grand, idealistic strategy sessions, the people around the table were driven by other concerns: individual aspirations, ambitions, and their beliefs about what Rome as a civic society should or should no longer be in the fifth century CE. There is much in and around Rutilius' poem to help us put a human face on this crucial transition point.

There is much that is not here, too. Parts of the Roman Empire are never mentioned: Egypt, Asia Minor, or the borders beyond, for example. An entire gender of the Late Antique population is missing; and the people who do appear, meanwhile, are recruited from the writer's own network of friends. Finally, scenes of daily life are given with Latin subtitles without any acknowledgment that the languages used by the empire's nearly 60 million people were astoundingly diverse. In short, in

A Social and Cultural History of Late Antiquity, First Edition. Douglas Boin.
© 2018 John Wiley & Sons, Inc. Published 2018 by John Wiley & Sons, Inc.

order to appreciate Rutilius Namatianus' poem as a historical document, we have to read it closely. But we also have to learn how to integrate it with other sources so that we are constantly re-evaluating the claims we make about the past. To make claims about an entire century from one poem is not really to write history at all, not even a micro-history; it's more akin to literary analysis.

The goal of a social-historical approach is different. It is to integrate as many voices as possible back into a larger story about the past while respecting the local, individual backgrounds of the sources. It demands detailed criticism and analysis – of texts and material culture – but it also requires thoughtful synthesis and a constant, careful attention to a bigger picture. Historians who specialize in the early modern and modern world have advocated this method forcefully: "[M]icro-history that fails to reconnect to larger narratives, and to state frankly what it hopes to overturn and what to uphold, may court antiquarianism," write historians David Armitage and Jo Guldi in their provocatively titled book, *The History Manifesto* (Cambridge: Cambridge University Press, 2014, p. 121). Historians of the pre-modern world, which includes the ancient Mediterranean, share these ideals.

But what exactly *is* the "larger narrative" of Late Antiquity? When does it begin? When does it end? And how do the people and events of the fifth century CE, such as those described in the last chapter, fit into this bigger story?

2.1   The Third through Fifth Centuries CE: A Narrated Timeline

A solid understanding of chronology is an essential starting point for researchers ready to experiment with new lines of investigation. For students new to the period, however, a lack of familiarity with big names and dates can make doing Late Antique history a frustrating enterprise. Who are the important figures? What questions should we learn to ask of them? Above all, how will we be able to tune into the important conversations that might be worth a second analysis?

The first step in doing a social and cultural history of Late Antiquity, then, is learning exactly what kinds of issues are at stake, why these issues matter, and to whom. Without any engagement with this larger picture, our own attempt at doing history will risk "courting antiquarianism."

The third-century crisis

By 250 CE, the Roman Empire, from palace to army camp, apartment house to town house, lay beaten and battered. Public memorials in many Roman towns – the kinds of Greek and Latin inscriptions that might tell us about the health of civic life – start to disappear; archaeologists have had a hard time finding them. The implication of this silence seems dire. Cities and civic society must have been in tatters. Buildings that had stood for centuries were no longer being repaired; town councils could not function in ways to meet their residents' needs. For Romans, two hundred years of relative political stability and economic growth had finally come to an end, and with it, the vision of the house of the first emperor, Augustus. "Crisis" would define the third century CE.

For the people who lived through it, it was an empire unraveling in real time and a period in which nostalgia likely ran high. From 27 BCE to 14 CE, Augustus had repaired the fractured Republic and set Rome on a series of strong, new foundations that ensured its successes in the coming decades. From the Julio-Claudian rulers to the end of the second century CE, Rome developed a sophisticated administration of its provincial territories, invested in Mediterranean trade, local enterprise, architectural achievement, and literary culture. By the time roots of imperial power began to shoot up in other provinces – in 193 CE, the patriarch Septimius Severus from Roman Libya would inaugurate a new ruling family, the Severan dynasty – Rome's formula for political, military, and cultural dominance seemed unassailable.

Rather than continuing on this course, the death of the last Severan emperor, Alexander Severus (d. 235), inaugurated the opposite: an age of angst. Over the next fifty years, twenty-five men would try to claim the mantle "emperor." The empire itself would be precariously split in three as enterprising yet radical local leaders – in Gaul and in Roman Syria – tried to secede. Between 260 and 268, General Postumius would lead a break-away confederacy in Gaul and Roman Spain. In 268, he would be assassinated by troops eager to acquire yet more territory; this breakaway Gallic confederacy would last for almost another decade, until 273.

At the very same time, political events in the eastern Mediterranean were following an eerily similar pattern. In 268, tribes from the northern reaches of the Black Sea, the Heruli, found their way to Athens and burned the city. Further east still, between 267 and 274, Zenobia of Palmyra, an oasis city in the trading routes of Roman Syria, would take advantage of the imperial chaos to establish herself as head of state. Calling herself "Augusta" (in Greek "Sebastē," a word meaning "Roman empress"), she and her family would rule the territories of Roman Egypt and Syria until 275 CE (Figure 2.1). Some contemporary historians often call her "Queen" to belittle her Roman identity. But a century after the house of Septimius Severus had come to power in Rome, the fabric of the empire was literally being unstitched by people who had grown up inside it – and by forces tearing at it from the outside.

No family throughout the third century would hold power as long as the memorable figures of the Julio-Claudian dynasty or the Severans, and the speed with which leaders were being removed from their position – on the battlefield in tragic circumstances or in their sleep in devious ones – cast a wide pall on Rome's future. In 251, Emperor Decius did not return from battle with Goths. In 260, Emperor Valerian was captured by a Persian army. The rise of this strong-willed, culturally sophisticated empire on the Roman world's eastern border would exacerbate problems at home, as well. Founded in 224 CE, the empowered Persian state, organized under the leadership of the Sasanian family, would remain a threat to Roman officials for the next three hundred years.

Figure 2.1 A coin from the third century CE with a portrait of the Empress Zenobia (271–275 CE). Zenobia is shown here wearing an imperial diadem, or crown. The text surrounding her portrait identifies her as "Sebastē," the Greek word for "Augusta," that is, Roman empress. The personification on the back is of one of the most essential Roman imperial ideals; she is the goddess Harmony ("Homonoia" in ancient Greek; "Concordia" in Latin) and is holding a cornucopia, suggesting prosperity. This coin, made from a copper alloy, was part of a series issued from Alexandria. © The Trustees of the British Museum (British Museum inventory number 1860,0327.273).

Naturally, as a result of so much turmoil, social, cultural, and spiritual malaise seeped into the once resilient marrow of the Roman people (this, at least, is how the story is usually told). The economy was thrown into crisis, and inflation began to cause once quaint and stable prices across the Mediterranean to skyrocket. Amid the panicked confusion, new, exotic "eastern" beliefs – or so we are led to believe – snaked their way inside the minds of Romans. As a result of this tsunami of spiritual proportions, against the backdrop of war, economic crisis, and political turmoil, Christians allegedly gained the cultural high-ground in Rome (*Exploring Culture* 2.1: Christianity before "The Bible").

Even the outbreak of a devastating disease, a plague that struck North Africa between 249 and 270 CE, conspired to spread the Christian faith in pagan Rome because Romans had no innate ability, no resilient traditions of their own, to cope emotionally with a sequence of such catastrophic events. Numbers of Jesus' followers swelled, and the emperors rushed to restore order to the third century. Soon, they would start to pursue more discriminatory policies against Jesus' followers.

Emperor Aurelian stopped the territorial hemorrhaging. During a short but transformative five-year reign, between 270 and 275 CE, he repaired the torn empire, even humiliating "Queen" Zenobia by marching her through the streets of Rome as a prisoner of war. Rome, too, was the canvas for his most daring venture. Residents watched as a towering brick wall gave a new shape to the city on the Tiber. It included, for the very first time in Rome's history, residents who lived on the city's second largest hill, the Janiculum – on the west side of the Tiber – and it encompassed

Exploring Culture 2.1 *Christianity before "The Bible"*

Reading "The Bible" offers tantalizing glimpses of the life of the earliest church. "Every scripture inspired by God," says the author of 2 Timothy, "is also useful for teaching, for reproof, for correction, and for training in righteousness" (2 Timothy 3.16 [*NRSV*]). The author of 2 Peter claims that "the ignorant and unstable" twist scriptures "to their own destruction" (2 Peter 3.16 [*NRSV*]).

Neither writer was talking about the Christian "Bible" however. Both 2 Timothy and 2 Peter were written at the end of the first century CE, at a time when the Christian "Bible" did not exist. These references are to Jewish Scriptures, which many Christians and Jews consulted in the Greek version of the Jewish Bible known as the Septuagint. To understand the historical process by which these later letters were sorted, edited, and assembled into a specifically Christian holy book means looking beyond Jesus, Paul, and the gospel writers.

"The Bible" acquired its name from the city of Byblos. Located in modern Lebanon, Byblos was a Phoenician port, millennia-old even by the time of Homer. Because of its trade connections with Egypt, it became known for the import of papyrus, an important early writing material. Greeks called a papyrus roll "byblos" (βύβλος), or "biblos" (βίβλος). Biblia is the plural Greek noun which means "books." "The Bible," then, is a library – not a single book. How this anthology came to be considered one "book" is an important question.

Many people might suppose that, by Constantine's day, a standard "Bible" was known to every Christian. That's only partly true. The divine authority of many commonly revered written documents did help many Christians structure their life and liturgy and were often used to chastise others. For long stretches of Roman history, however, Christians argued passionately about which foundational documents actually mattered. Many conversations about the Christian canon led to arguments over writings that were deemed heretical or have now been lost. Christianity's relationship to its Jewish roots – a winding, sometimes tortured relationship – would also influence the creation of "The Bible."

The first attempt at a Christian canon, or list of agreed-upon scriptures, would not be proposed until c.140 CE. According to Marcion, Jewish Scriptures were irrelevant to Christians, and so he excluded them. By the 170s CE Irenaeus of Lyon countered these claims, making reference for the first time to an "Old Testament" and a "New Testament." Many Christians still maintain this highly inflammatory terminology, separating Jewish and Christian Scripture into "old" and "new," as if the living traditions of Jews had been replaced by Christianity's arrival. For historians, the use of these terms is not recommended practice.

Even Irenaeus' suggested list was open to challenge. Almost one hundred and fifty years later, debates about what constituted Christian Scripture were still ongoing. Eusebius reports that, when it came to the apocalyptic Book of Revelation, some considered it canonical. Others "rejected the book altogether, criticizing it chapter by chapter, and pronouncing it without sense or argument" (Eusebius, *Church History* 7.25, trans. by A. McGiffert in the *NPNF* series [1890]). In 394 CE a church council at Carthage took up the issue – and gave their blessing to the book. By that time, John Chrysostom of Constantinople seems to have been the first to refer to all these writings as "ta biblia," that is, as "The Bible." Today, it is impossible to be historically precise when using this term.

neighborhoods, like the Campus Martius, which for centuries had not properly been integrated into the city. Rome was changing. It was growing. Its cityscape and its people were witnesses to that evolution.

Constitutional stability followed, led by the brilliant administrative mind of Emperor Diocletian (r. 284–305 CE). Power-sharing was the new managerial principle of the day. In 294 CE, two Augustuses (*Augusti*, in the Latin plural) were assigned two halves of the empire and two junior partners, Caesars (*Caesares*), were posted to train under them. In effect, a Rule of Four now oversaw a Mediterranean state that had, since the time of Augustus, been guarded by a single man. Shockingly, none of these constitutional innovations were written down. As with the series of negotiations that had brought Augustus to power, the Senate and the People of Rome operated by consensus, not by formal document. There never was nor would there ever be in its thousand-year history a piece of writing that functioned as the "Roman Constitution." Power, personality, prestige, compromise, respect for tradition, and a recognition that innovation was sometimes necessary to save the state: this was the language of the Roman government. It was a system written in shared ideas and values, not set in stone.

The fact that Diocletian, a military child from the Adriatic coast, was able to marshal consensus during a period of political rupture is a testament to his charisma. Rome's third-century storm had been weathered.

All that remained, as Diocletian walked away from power in 305, was for the shell-shocked Roman people to come into their city centers to survey the damage of a century of war, to pick up the pieces of their towns, and begin the process of repairing the civic fabric of their lives. The unresolved issue – what no one had ever provided guidance on – was what things to keep and what to throw away.

The fourth-century crisis

As the Rule of Four moved into imperial palaces now strategically being erected throughout the Mediterranean and as Diocletian himself moved out – the first Roman ruler in nearly a century to voluntarily set aside his constitutional power – Rome would come to face a fourth-century crisis. This crisis was social, not a military one, but that doesn't mean it can't or shouldn't be characterized in the same terms as the events of the last century. At its heart was a debate about who was allowed to be included in the body of the Roman state. This battle, too, would threaten to tear Rome apart from the inside-out.

In 303 CE, before leaving power, Diocletian had inaugurated a vicious anti-Christian program directed at purging the empire of a community who had gained significant visibility during the last century. The "Great Persecution" would target Christian property and worship spaces, earmarking them for government confiscation. Churches were burned without any legal ramification, and Christians themselves, under penalty of law, were required to turn over both their sacred books and their community funds (*Key Debates* 2.1: Are There Forgeries in Christian Scripture?). By the time a new emperor, someone sympathetic to Christian Romans, could

Key Debates 2.1 *Are There Forgeries in Christian Scripture?*

Around 256 CE, Cyprian, a Christian bishop in North Africa, decided to meddle in church affairs in Spain. Cyprian wrote a letter attacking a Spanish bishop who had been seen participating at a Roman sacrificial banquet. Cyprian insisted that the bishop, Martial, be removed from church office.

Martial's "deceitful" decision to participate in the banquet "cannot profit him anything," Cyprian wrote, "since he who also is involved in great crimes should not hold the office of bishop since the apostle also warns and says, 'A bishop must be blameless as the steward of God'" (Cyprian, *Letter* 67.5, translation slightly adapted from R. Wallis in the *ANF* series [1886]). To support his argument against Martial, Cyprian has quoted the words of "the apostle," Paul, a central figure of the first-century church, as preserved in the text known as the Letter to Titus (1.7). Cyprian's appeal to "history" was an attempt to show the Spanish bishop that he was straying far from the traditions of the earliest church. Martial was acting against teachings of Paul, or so Cyprian wanted his readers to believe.

There's one problem. Paul didn't write the Letter to Titus. In fact, of the fourteen writings in Christian Scripture attributed to "Paul," only half of them – seven – are securely thought to be authentic. These are: Romans, 1 and 2 Corinthians, 1 Thessalonians, Philippians, Galatians, and Philemon. The Pauline authorship of the remaining books is either strongly doubted or widely agreed upon to be "pseudepigraphic," that is, falsely written.

The debated documents are Ephesians, Colossians, and 2 Thessalonians. The doubtful ones are 1 and 2 Timothy, as well as Titus, which Cyprian has quoted as if it had Paul's stamp of authority. Beyond these now canonical texts, there are still other forged texts from Late Antiquity which are associated with Paul's name and memory. These include a highly fanciful meeting between Paul and the first-century CE Roman philosopher Seneca.

Which is an authentic text and which is a forgery is much more than an innocent, antiquarian exercise played by biblical scholars. Who used what texts and when – and what authority later writers, like Cyprian, presumed such false documents to have – is an important subtext to many Late Antique Christian arguments. Getting these facts right has important implications for how history is told.

Consider this short overview of the office of "bishop," the title Cyprian held and the one which he tried to deny to Martial in Spain. "It is striking that the word *episkopos* [meaning "overseer" in Greek] and its cognates appear only rarely in the New Testament," one Late Antique historian has observed. "It ... appears in the letters of the apostle Paul for a total of seven times.... In the most significant passage ... Paul advised his close associate Timothy on how to regulate the internal structure of the Christian communities (1 Timothy 3:1–7)" (in C. Rapp, *Holy Bishops in Late Antiquity* [Berkeley: University of California Press, 2005], p. 25). On first look, that's certainly what the "New Testament" texts appear to suggest. According to this interpretation, the office of bishop is ancient, dating back to the very first documents of church history.

Other scholars, more attuned to the issues surrounding the authentic, debated, and pseudepigraphic letters in Pauline studies, might write the history of the office of "bishop" in a different way. Since Titus was written at the end of the first century CE, a generation after Paul, it testifies to a growing need for organization in the young church – a social feature of the Jesus community that was absent from Paul's own day.

address the terrible damage, the compromises that had given birth to the Rule of Four, including an acknowledgment of each individual's proper turf, were no longer respected.

In 312 CE, Diocletian's system entered cardiac arrest. That year, the junior emperor Constantine – stationed at York, England, with his troops – would march on Rome to acquire the capital for his own portfolio, breaking the political consensus that had been so important to Rome's recovery. By the year's end, the ruler of Rome, Emperor Maxentius, would be dead. Constantine had drawn him and his army out of the city to the northernmost bridge over the Tiber River, the Milvian Bridge. The climactic battle between two leaders was one that likely shocked those who heard about it or watched it from the river banks. Two generals, fighting a civil war to control the capital, must have seemed to many like a horrible, frustrating flashback to an age that was supposed to have come to an end.

Constantine's calculus, however disrespectful it had been of Diocletian's settlement, did provoke a change in policy in other regards. The emperor, according to some, had converted to Christianity before his victory – a momentous personal experience that would haunt political conversations for centuries to come. Its effects were immediate.

In 313, as Augustus of the west, Constantine and his now co-ruler, Licinius in the east, would meet in Milan to address the status of Roman Christians. Christians, the two emperors acknowledged, were no longer to be discriminated against by Roman law. They were to be given full rights to worship as members of the Roman state, and nothing in their legal status would stigmatize them anymore as second-class citizens. The "Edict of Milan," as the emperors' decision is known, gave Jesus' followers an explicit legal protection that had never before been granted to any other worship community in Rome, not even Jews, who had been worshipping openly throughout the empire for centuries.

This decision about the empire's Christian community marked a monumental reversal – a true social triumph – for Jesus' followers. It also re-ignited a poisonous debate, one that had been kindling within the Christian community for three centuries, about whether being "Christian" allowed one to participate in all the facets of Roman social life or whether it required believers to oppose Roman customs and values, without any compromise. Christians were not in agreement on this point (*Political Issues* 2.1: What Role Did Martyrdom Play in the Rise of Christianity?). In the aftermath of Constantine and Licinius' major policy announcement, their disputes with each other would begin to flare up again. By the century's end, it would also ensnare non-Christian politicians, as well. On the outside, these arguments, by turns intense and occasionally sophomoric, must have looked – only to the most naive – as proof of a clash of cultures.

At stake in these battles (and the prize awaiting those who fought hardest in them) was possession of the palace. Since the Rule of Four, this residency was more a traveling road-show than any one prestige building. The Palatine Palace in Rome had not disappeared. A majestic architectural residence, of marble-clad hallways, luxurious rooms, and over-life-size emperors whose names were synonymous with the glory of Rome – Trajan, Hadrian, Antoninus Pius – the Palatine would continue to host rulers when they lived in the city through at least the sixth century CE.

Political Issues 2.1 *What Role Did Martyrdom Play in the Early Church?*

Tertullian (160–220 CE) enjoyed defending Christianity almost as much as he did instigating his opponents. In *The Apology*, he savages Roman culture – the mainstream culture of the early third century CE – and couples his criticisms with unwavering claims of Christian superiority.

"You accuse us of refusing to worship the gods and to spend money on sacrificing for the emperors," he wrote. "We cease to worship your gods, from the moment we learn that they are no gods!" (*Apology* 10, trans. by A. Souter [1917]). Tertullian's public denial of the gods would have struck quite a shrill, even treasonous tone in the public square, but he was likely talking to a much smaller audience. As with other examples of "apologetic," or defense, literature, the *Apology* was probably designed to be read by those already within the Christian community.

The extent to which Christians antagonized their non-Christian family, neighbors, and Roman public officials is a thorny question. It is also related to the issue of martyrdom and the growth of the church. Tertullian claimed that "the blood of the martyrs was like the seed" that grew the early church (*Apology* 50), a germination process that had taken root as early as Nero (*Apology* 21). A century later, Eusebius would use the same framework to tell his version of the *History of the Church*. "[P]ublicly announcing himself as the first among God's chief enemies, Nero [r. 54–69 CE] was led on to the slaughter of the apostles," Eusebius wrote (2.25, trans. by A. McGiffert in the *NPNF* series [1890]).

Scholars are extremely interested in the sources for these early "martyrdoms." Many Greek and Latin texts which purport to tell of these brutal executions date centuries after the "martyrs'" deaths. The *Martyrdom of Polycarp*, about the bishop of Smyrna who died in the mid-second century CE, is filled with so many allusions to Jesus' passion and the Maccabean resistance that some scholars question its historical reliability.

The presence of literary borrowings, even outright invention, does not deny that "martyrs" could and did become powerful cultural symbols. For many of Jesus' followers, "martyr" stories confirmed that being Christian meant always acting in a counter-cultural way.

Perhaps to support those claims – which not every Christian in Rome agreed with – Eusebius was adamant about verifying the history behind the martyr legends. For example, although there is not a single piece of reliable evidence to confirm whether Peter or Paul were actually killed in Nero's Rome, Eusebius claimed otherwise. "[T]heir names are preserved in the cemeteries of that place even to the present day" (*Church History* 2.25). According to a source allegedly seen by Eusebius, a man named "Gaius" who lived *c.*217 CE had spoken about these burial sites, "these places where the sacred corpses of the aforesaid apostles are laid [saying]: 'But I can show [you] the trophies of the apostles. For if you will go to the Vatican [Hill] or to the Ostian Road, you will find the trophies of those who laid the foundations of this church" (*Church History* 2.25).

What do historians make of this testimony? Given that so many links in the chain of evidence are broken, it is difficult to know what is real and what is fiction. This conundrum has led some historians to ask different kinds of research questions, focusing instead on the ideology of martyrdom as it was articulated by living Christian writers or on the construction of gender codes as presented in the martyr stories.

But the military mayhem that had devolved upon the empire in the third century had given Diocletian and many of his advisors the idea that the emperor and his staff should be more mobile.

Trier in Germany, Antioch in the eastern Mediterranean, Nicomedia in the vicinity of the Black Sea: the location of the imperial court in the early fourth century reflected a keen desire that, however big the empire, it would help the administration to have a power base nearby. Constantine would add yet another capital city to that list, the year he treated Romans to the gift of an empire ruled again by one man, not four.

In 324 CE, Constantine removed Licinius from power and dismantled the last vestiges of Diocletian's system. For the first time in a generation, the Roman Empire was governed by one Augustus, evoking the glory of a bygone age. That year, Constantine also set in motion plans to build a capital city in Licinius' old territory, at the ancient Greek city of Byzantium, now to be named after Constantine. Six years later, in 330 CE, Constantinople's streets would be filled with joyous citizens for its inauguration. By decade's end, in 337, the Christian emperor who had done so much to fight for the Christian community of the wider Roman world would be dead.

Like all conscientious dynasties, Constantine's sons would make sure power did not leave the family at the emperor's last breath. From 337–363, a member of the Constantinian household would govern Rome from its multiple capitals. All were raised Christian, even the last, Emperor Julian (361–363 CE). And contrary to the way scholars characterize their mission, none of them knew anything about the "Byzantine Empire." Not one fourth-century ruler of Constantinople ever believed their capital was anything but a branch of Rome's power in the wider Mediterranean.

But an unmistakable center of authority it was. By the late fourth century CE, certain Christian politicians and advisors had taken a gamble and convinced the occupants of the palace that their version of Christianity should be announced as the only legitimate state religion. In 380, Emperor Theodosius (r. 375–395 CE), raised in Spain, ruling from Constantinople, signed off on that decree. In the coming decades, the people of the Roman world would watch as a chilling legal curtain fell on practices and beliefs that had, for millennia, sustained countless families, their households, and their civic life.

To Christians who saw their beliefs as fundamentally incompatible with other people's traditions and customs, the imperial palace had been won and with it, the right to shape the laws that came out of it. Even if many Christians disagreed, even if Christians themselves were a demographic minority in the Roman Empire, none of that mattered. Rome was not nor had it ever been a democracy. For that reason alone, there is no need for us to try to reverse-engineer the rise of Christianity to explain the alleged growth of Christianity. However many Christians there were in the empire at this time is a fascinating question. But in trying to explain why the empire became a Christian state, it may also be a red herring. Emperors set the laws. Everyone else lived by them. A more interesting historical question may be how it came about that Christians in Rome thought it perfectly proper to use the power of the law to enact their strict, zealous vision for society.

The fifth-century crisis

Between Spain and the Sea of Marmara, outside the Black Sea, Emperor Theodosius had seen a lot of the Roman world for himself. He had also inherited an empire that was more openly, viciously partisan than that governed by any of his predecessors. Whatever may have motivated him to make the choices that he did – wading into the politics of church councils or waging war on other Romans, Christian and non-Christian alike, who opposed his policies – the effects of his rule are undeniably revolutionary. Nicene Christianity, based on a platform drafted by bishops in 325 CE, would forever remain the Roman Empire's official religion. That was the substance of Theodosius' decree in 380, and it would never be replaced or repealed. (The language of Nicaea insisted that God and Jesus were equally divine and that they had both existed from the beginning of time; Jesus may have been born later, the bishops acknowledged, but he had always existed.)

Not every Christian throughout the empire was eager to sign off on this document. Consequently, Christian wrangling over the party platform, combined with still other, more pressing geopolitical concerns, would fall to the house of Theodosius to address. The events of Rutilius Namatianus' day – a spike in border infractions, a need for urgent diplomatic meetings, and negotiated land settlements – were the pressing issues seen by Theodosius' sons. The two of them, Arcadius (r. 395–408) and Honorius (r. 395–423 CE), succeeded in staying true to their father's imperial vision. In simplest terms, Rome was now a Christian state. And although their decision to share authority over the Mediterranean may seem, to us, to belie the unity of the empire they governed, Rome in the fifth century CE was no longer experiencing an existential crisis. It was now facing a territorial one.

Emperor Honorius, who was 11 years old when he was appointed to power, lived this reality every day. His palace guardian, Stilicho, was the face of the fifth-century world. Son of a Roman mother but of a Vandal father, Stilicho had served in the Roman army and married into Theodosius' family. For the child emperor Honorius, as for his advisors who held more traditional, stereotypical views of foreigners like "the Vandals," there could be no more immediate sign that the idea of Rome was changing. Stilicho himself had won a consulship in 400 and 405 CE. He had also won fame by aggressively policing Rome's borders. By 408, however, those same rising fortunes would seal Stilicho's fate among the conservative members of the senate. Suspected of betraying Rome, he was assassinated.

One political execution, motivated by jealousy and fear, however, could not stop Rome's borders from receding. Nor could it correct the inability or, worse, the unwillingness of its most talented politicians and diplomats to create a sustainable policy for the border. In 410 CE, authorities made the decision to withdraw the army from Britain, effectively abandoning the island – its farthest northwest possession – to local control. That year, in Italy, we have already seen how the government grappled with Alaric, the Gothic leader who forced Rome's hand by holding the city of Rome hostage. Alaric himself was also a Christian.

The awkwardness of foreign tribes "daring" to assert their own political voices would not be resolved on the watch of Arcadius or Honorius. Much would come to the desk of Theodosius II, grandson of the dynasty's founder, to resolve. Seven years old at the time of his elevation, Emperor Theodosius II may not have grasped the depth of Rome's problems right away. But he would govern for nearly four decades (r. 408–450 CE), the longest ruler in all of Rome's storied history. Before his death, he would also see the beginnings of the complicated, stunning dismantling of the Roman state.

Between 429 and 439 CE, Vandals conquered North Africa. Still other tribes were lurking beyond the frontiers. The Huns, a people of the steppes of the northern shores of the Black Sea, found their voice in a leader named Attila. By 451, Attila had led his band of Huns across northern Europe. They attacked Gaul that year – a shocking strike to the northern territories to be matched, four years later, from the south. Sailing from their base in Carthage, Vandals raided the coast of Italy in 455, even reaching Rome.

Theodosius II himself did not live long enough to see or hear about the attack in 455 CE, but his daughter and son-in-law experienced it first-hand. It was Theodosius II's daughter who was the bride at the joyful wedding in Constantinople attended by Rufius Volusianus, with which we ended the last chapter. Her husband, Emperor Valentinian III of Rome, would be murdered later that year.

Within two decades, command over the Italian peninsula was given to one of Attila's own loyal companions. His name was Odoacer, and he was installed as king in 476 CE. Parts of the old Roman world, particularly in the northwest territory, were cut loose from the imperial map at this time. Lands in northern Gaul united under the leadership of a Frankish king, Clovis (r. 481–511 CE). In Italy itself, Odoacer's rule proved unstable. A wealthy Goth named Theoderic, educated in Constantinople, took it from him. His victory was a defining moment for the Gothic communities of western Europe, which included Spain, southern Gaul, and now Italy. Theoderic's "Eastern Goths" (Ostrogoths), so named to distinguish themselves from the "Western Goths" (Visigoths), would govern Rome into the sixth century. The branches of the Roman Empire, at the turn of 500 CE, had been pruned (*Working With Sources* 2.1: The Lost Syriac Chronicle of Theophilus of Edessa).

Working With Sources 2.1
The "Lost" Syriac Chronicle of Theophilus of Edessa

Brutal tales of war dominate the story of the sixth-century CE Roman Empire, thanks to the authors who chronicled them. Trying to hear the events of the next century, however, can be more difficult. There are few Greek and Latin writers who wrote about the seventh century although it's not because history grew dull. An Islamic army would soon defeat the Sasanian state; they would take Egypt, Jerusalem, and Syria from Rome, a catastrophic territorial loss.

There is one unique, contemporary witness to this key moment in history. He was an astrologer who did not write in a classical language: Theophilus of Edessa (Urfa, in modern Turkey). Theophilus composed a *Chronicle* of the seventh and eighth centuries in his local language, Syriac. A dialect of Aramaic, the language spoken in first-century Judaea by Jesus and many Jews, Syriac was still used extensively in Late Antiquity by people in Roman Syria, in and around Jerusalem, and in the cities of the Roman–Sasanian frontier like Edessa, where Theophilus grew up.

Edessa was not just located near the ever-fluctuating eastern borders of the Roman and Persian Empires. It also lay within reach of,the often disputed territory of the Armenian Kingdom. For this reason, Theophilus likely spoke multiple languages from an early age; he is especially known for having translated several Greek works into Syriac: the epic poetry of Homer, the medical texts of Galen, and the philosophy of Aristotle. None of these texts survive, and neither does his valuable *Chronicle* – at least, not exactly. So how is it that this multilingual astrologer from Edessa has become such an essential source for the seventh century CE?

Many later writers, working in Syriac, Greek, and Arabic, referred to Theophilus' work. Some, like Michael the Syrian (d. 1199 CE), acknowledge they borrowed material directly from him. Others, like the Greek writer Theophanes (d. 818), never make their citations explicit. But based on uncanny similarities that emerge when comparing these authors side-by-side, scholars can reconstruct the contents of Theophilus' text.

Here is an example of how that works. These two writers are describing what happened when the Sasanian Persians captured Jerusalem in 614 CE:

"The Persians took the Jordan, Palestine, and the Holy City by force of arms and killed many people therein through the agency of the Jews. Some say it was 90,000. For the Jews bought the Christians [as slaves], each man according to his means, and killed them" (from the Greek text written by Theophanes, trans. by Hoyland [2011]).

"In year six of [Emperor] Heraclius, Shahrbaraz attacked Jerusalem, subdued it, and killed 90,000 persons. The Jews, because of their hatred for them, were buying Christians from the Persians for a low price and killing them" (from the Syriac text written by Michael the Syrian, trans. by Hoyland [2011]).

Neither of these writers was familiar with the other's work, which suggests they consulted a common, third source independently. That author is now thought to be Theophilus of Edessa.

Theophilus' *Chronicle* is a tantalizing source because it gives us a non-Muslim view of Islam's rise and spread. In fact, Theophilus was one of the first Christian writers to incorporate early Arabic traditions about Muhammad into his history of early Islam. The fact that Theophilus had access to these Arabic texts and could read them is remarkable. It suggests that "a lot more historical material was circulating between the Muslim and Christian communities [of the seventh and eighth centuries CE] than is usually assumed" (Robert Hoyland, *Theophilus of Edessa's Chronicle and the Circulation of Historical Knowledge in Late Antiquity and Early Islam* [Liverpool: Liverpool University Press, 2011], p. 29).

2.2   A Warning about Periodization

Dividing time into discrete periods is something historians do, but it's also character-istic of people who think theologically. As we learned in the last chapter, many people in antiquity believed that they were living in a time of corrupt morals and decadent behavior and that their world was in urgent need of spiritual renewal. They placed their hopes in the notion that the present age would eventually come to an end and that a new chapter in the divine plan for humanity would begin – perhaps soon, in their lifetime. Whether they were Jew or Christian or neither, the people who looked at their world through these powerful lenses magnified (some would say, distorted) the social problems around them and turned them into signs with a cosmic significance.

Therein lies an important but often unaddressed problem in the study of ancient history, particularly Late Antique history. Because many people in the ancient world were eager to divide time into separate periods for theological reasons, our own, dispassionate attempt to work with the sources they left behind – to subject them to laboratory analysis and to write up the findings from our experiment – is always at risk of producing history with a theological glow. Even the apparent casualness with which historians wave their wand and change Constantine's Roman Empire or Justinian's Roman Empire into an entirely different state ("The Byzantine Empire") has much to tell us about the agendas that lie behind periodization. We need to look more closely at what's going on behind these tricks of the trade.

The attack in 410 CE and the removal of Rome from its own empire, in 476 CE, were two events that led Christians of the time to reflect more intently about God's plan for their world. From Jerome to Orosius, Christians of the fifth century and later, in Latin and in Greek, drew upon their own hopes and fears to try to make sense of these changing circumstances, which many framed in apocalyptic terms as if it were an event trumpeting the arrival of the end of the world.

For later historians, particularly those of the eighteenth century like Edward Gibbon, it became hard to separate these doleful, biblically inspired lamentations about the "Fall of Rome" from more dispassionate descriptions of the fifth century. Gibbon's own epic contribution to this conversation was titled *The Decline and Fall of the Roman Empire* and the first volume in his magnum opus, published in 1776, set off an explosion of interest into causes of Rome's "fall." By the late twentieth century, two hundred and ten reasons had been deduced to explain what had alleg-edly happened that caused Rome's empire to crumble. These explanations range from the apparently plausible to the wildly improbable: from lead poisoning to gay people ("homosexuality") to inflation. The most frightening are still trudged out during modern political debates, particularly in America and western Europe.

In the 1960s, one scholar hit upon an ingenious way to short-circuit this unhelp-ful obsession with Rome's decline. His name was Peter Brown. Beginning with a new biography of Augustine and proceeding to write, over the course of sixty years, about the vibrant social milieu of the fourth through sixth centuries CE, Brown built a field of inquiry around a more optimistic idea, even a spiritually comforting one. This was an age of transitions and of transformations, of exciting religious dialogue and a vibrant interchange of ideas, not collapse and decay. Brown's was a vision of the period we now call "Late Antiquity." And for three generations, that vision has worked like a masterful check-mate in the ongoing chess match against Gibbon and his acolytes, many of whom, for example, still equate the rise of Christianity with Rome's decline. In this, Brown's new approach worked at its best, drawing attention to fascinating, although usually ecclesiastical, stories of innovation that earlier historians were eager to dismiss.

Brown's move has also, whether it was originally intended to or not, obscured one of the more troubling features of the age: the sheer number of fanatics living in the fourth, fifth, and sixth centuries who believed that the Roman world really was coming to an end. Many of these Christians thought they were living in the eye of the "end times," that the events of their day should be seen as if they were the manifestation of God's final plan for Jesus' Second Coming. These people and their strange faith-based beliefs can be rather embarrassing to twenty-first-century students. The ideas themselves are particularly quixotic to skeptical researchers who think that history's door should be forceably shut on such nonsense. But the people who held these beliefs cannot be written out of history simply because they might make us feel uncomfortable.

The reasons why Christians might burn a Jewish synagogue or the beliefs that may have motivated a Christian emperor to start a war over Jerusalem – even the root of the Christian conviction that the world of old "Rome" had fallen because a new, "more Christian" Rome had stepped in to replace it – all of these extraordinary ideas shaped the history of the Mediterranean world before and after 476 CE. We will see when, how, and ask why throughout this book.

And so, even as "Late Antiquity" and the "Byzantine Empire" bring many recognizable benefits to the study of history today, helping us gerrymander the ancient Mediterranean into discrete, more manageable disciplines, we should not let either concept deflect our gaze from some of the key problems that accompany them. The reason why an individual might want to draw boundaries around a particular historical age – erect a barrier between "Old Rome" and "New Rome," as many Christians would do; or between the "Age of Revelation" and the "Age of Ignorance" (*Jahiliyyah*), as many Muslims would do to characterize the period before Muhammad's revelation – is precisely what we're trying to capture with our historical instruments. It is the historian's job to describe and analyze these individuals and their behavior, not fall victim to their misdirection.

Summary

In this chapter, we met several political figures and learned about key events which shaped Mediterranean history between the third and fifth centuries CE. A broad outline of important names and dates should now be apparent. By combining Rutilius' more personal perspective from the previous chapter with an appreciation for this larger historical context, we can now begin to look at Late Antiquity more systematically. The next chapter, the last in this introduction, discusses important interpretive tools that will be useful for our study.

Study Questions

1. Identify the following people. State when they lived and why they are important: Zenobia of Palmyra, Diocletian, Constantine, Theodosius, and Theoderic.
2. Explain why every century between the third century and the fifth century CE can be characterized as a time of "crisis."
3. How has Edward Gibbon influenced the study of the later Roman Empire?
4. Consider the reasons why a historian might be skeptical of periodization.

Suggested Readings

Peter Brown, *The Rise of Western Christendom: Triumph and Diversity, A.D. 200–1000*, second edition (Oxford: Blackwell, 2003).

Averil Cameron, *The Mediterranean World in Late Antiquity: AD 395–700*, second edition (London: Routledge, 2012).

Judith Herrin, *Byzantium: The Surprising Life of a Medieval Empire* (Princeton: Princeton University Press, 2009).

Chris Wickham, *The Inheritance of Rome: Illuminating the Dark Ages, 400–1000* (New York: Penguin, 2009).

3

How Do We Do Late Antique History?

Rutilius needed someone to blame. Forced from his comfortable life in Rome – taken away from "the noise of the circus games" and the "blaze of cheers" from the theater; even cut off from the city's welcoming mood, where "the very daylight which Rome makes for herself seems purer than all else" (*On His Return to Gaul* 1.200–203, LCL trans. by Duff and Duff [1935]) – he blamed Stilicho. Guardian of the child emperor Honorius, born of a mixed ("non-Roman") marriage, Stilicho was a convenient scapegoat. Many elite and non-elite Romans, not just Rutilius, had lived through the attack on their city in 410 CE and were keen to identify who let this catastrophe happen and how. They pointed to the compromised "foreigner."

Never mind that Stilicho's foreign lineage was Vandal and that Rome's attackers had been of a different tribe entirely: Goths. To Rutilius and others who thought like him, all "barbarians" were the same. This man was a "traitor" to Rome whose back-channel bargaining with Goths during the first decade of the fifth century had opened the door for "skin-clad menials" to ravage the capital (*On His Return to Gaul* 2.49–51).

In a way, Rutilius was doing what historians do. He was scouring his world for clues and causes to explain why things had turned out this way, not that way. In their research, historians, too, try to reassemble the web of explanations that might have motivated individuals, communities, and even states in the past to behave as they did. Rutilius, who blamed Stilicho's ethnic identity and his questionable allegiances, found the causes for the attack on Rome in this one wisp of a web. Historians have traditionally been uncomfortable with these kinds of single-issue explanations. The structure of a web is usually more complex.

Therein lies a challenge for the Late Antique historian. Now that we've put a few names and faces on one of the most central turning points in our period and now that we've taken a more bird's-eye view of the crises that led to 410 CE, we should

A Social and Cultural History of Late Antiquity, First Edition. Douglas Boin.
© 2018 John Wiley & Sons, Inc. Published 2018 by John Wiley & Sons, Inc.

pause to reflect on our methods. How exactly do we start to do the history of this time? Where does the evidence come from: for the battles, for the biographies, for the political debates?

3.1 Evaluating Sources, Asking Questions

Comparing and contrasting

The answers to these questions cannot be relegated to the teacher's edition of a textbook, kept away from the eyes of students who don't really need to know them. Every source that exists from antiquity, even a Latin poem like the one Rutilius wrote, needs to be interrogated for what it provides to our story before it can be deemed historically useful. Sources, put simply, do not just provide the "facts" of history. Sources beget questions that challenge the very outline of history. For that reason, this book is structured around discussions of specific pieces of evidence and how to interpret them.

Comparison will be a crucial tool in this journey because it helps historians build a set of checks-and-balances for sources that would otherwise lack any real value if they weren't compared or contrasted to something else. After all, there is no way to fact-check a single writer or an isolated text unless it is brought into dialogue with another.

Rutilius' opinion of Stilicho offers a good reminder of the need for tracking down and lining up the right sources. Were Rutilius' bigoted views of the Vandal-Roman leader unique or were they widespread, and what might the answer tell us about Roman society on the eve of so much political crisis? There is no way to begin compiling this information from the poem; it's simply not there. We have to interview other sources.

In this case, the contemporary writer Claudian provides additional, helpful information. Claudian lived in the late fourth century and early fifth century CE. Educated at Alexandria in Egypt, he wrote fluently in two languages, Greek and Latin. His works in Greek no longer survive. His Latin writings are a fascinating set of archives because of when and why Claudian produced them. Invited to go to Emperor Honorius' court in the western empire, with its capital moving between the northern Italian cities of Milan and Ravenna, Claudian wrote poetry praising the fortunes of the imperial family and lauding the achievements of other officials. He worked as a public relations guru who played up his clients' accomplishments to drew more attention to them. Specialists call him a panegyrist.

Among the many panegyric poems he wrote for Emperor Honorius, Claudian composed one three-book work extolling the virtuous character of Stilicho. Written in 400 CE, to commemorate Stilicho's successful term as consul of Rome, it features personifications of Spain, Gaul, Africa, and Italy who sing his military praises. It also is filled with Claudian's optimistic take on the wide public support that Stilicho enjoyed as a Roman politician. "In Stilicho's case alone, class rivalry has not raised its head: the knights welcome him with joy, the senate with enthusiasm, while the people's prayers rival the goodwill of the nobles" (Claudian, *On the Consulship of Stilicho* 3.49–50, LCL trans. by M. Platnauer [1922]). The successes of previous military leaders had led to faction and partisanship. Not so in Stilicho's case, Claudian argued. The soldier-turned-consul had brought Rome together when it needed it the most. The fact that he happened to have a complicated family story, born of a Vandal father and Roman mother, never merited any suspicion.

Claudian's poetry is important because it allows us to appreciate Stilicho's successes whereas Rutilius, writing a decade later, wanted us to remember him as an unmitigated disaster. Both texts are important for piecing together the lost transcript of what people were talking about in the first decades of the fifth century CE. The search for answers to explain what had led to Alaric's attack involved a debate about the legacy of a half-Vandal, half-Roman who had been given guardianship of the child emperor. This debate would have profound personal consequences for Stilicho. By 408 CE, he was dead on the road between Rome and Ravenna – assassinated by members of the emperor's staff.

Incorporating textual and material culture

How had public opinion turned against such a talented politician so quickly? It's an interesting question, and another piece of evidence suggests how and why it may have happened. This evidence comes not from a published, polished piece of Latin or Greek literature, although it is written in an ancient language. It is a marble statue base that had been set up in one of the most prominent outdoor spaces in Rome, the Forum. The statue base had been put there, in the early fifth century CE, by Stilicho himself to honor the Roman troops who had fought with him against invading armies on the borderlands.

By the time Rutilius Namatianus saw it as Prefect of the City, Stilicho had been murdered and his name had been violently scratched out of the marble. The message to anyone who walked past it was meant to be crystal clear. Stilicho died as an enemy of the state he had fought so bravely to protect his entire career. The stone's erasure is perhaps the most vivid illustration of what a partisan hack-job could look like in fifth-century Rome. The statue base, missing Stilicho's name, still survives (Figure 3.1); it has been catalogued in the Collection of Latin Inscriptions from Rome (*CIL* volume 6.31987).

This archaeological object is an example of what historians call, more broadly, material culture. Material culture comprises many things that might look on first glance like simple works of art – mosaics, architecture, wall paintings, jewelry, or kitchenware. For historians, however, much of this material has a story to tell about the people who paid for it, used it, stole it, or destroyed it. In this approach, the aesthetic value of the objects is but one part of what makes them historically significant.

Figure 3.1 This Latin inscription praises the Roman Emperor Honorius and is currently on display in the Roman Forum. It was erected in view of the Senate House in the early fifth century CE. Interestingly, the text also originally honored a talented Roman general, Stilicho (d. 408 CE), for his help in repelling a Gothic attack from Italy. Born to a Vandal father, with a Roman mother, Stilicho had married into the imperial family and in the process had become a trusted advisor of Honorius. After his death, some people questioned his loyalty to Rome. Later, they erased Stilicho's name from the monument. The inscription is printed in the Collection of Latin Inscriptions (*CIL* 6.31987). Photo credit: Gregor Kalas, with permission.

Material culture and textual culture can also overlap. The face of a coin might reveal an important "legend," or set of promotional words; a marble block might be unearthed which has a public announcement chiseled on one side. In these cases, there is little use in trying to classify these objects as either textual or material evidence; they're both. A broader, more important point to keep in mind is that text and material culture mutually inform each other as historical sources. Both sets of evidence are indispensable archives. Together, they fill out the stories of people like Rutilius, Claudian, Stilicho, and the boy emperor Honorius.

A piece of material culture like Stilicho's statue base, with its rubbed-out lines, also teaches another powerful lesson. History is not just a list of names and dates to be studied and memorized; history is a continuing conversation about which names and dates should be considered important. History, in short, is an argument – supported with evidence – about who or what deserves to be remembered and why. Stilicho's detractors knew this aspect of history well. That's why they tried to erase him from it.

3.2 The Past in the Past

Doing Late Antique history should start to be a little less mystifying now. It involves finding texts and pieces of material culture, describing what they say, identifying who wrote them or made them, and why. It means considering when they were written so that we can analyze, compare, and contrast them while respecting the circumstances that led to their creation. And it involves putting them together, synthesizing them, so that we can step back and re-evaluate what the big picture looks like.

If applying this formula were all there was to doing history, however, the end result would hardly be satisfying. We would be writing about programmed robots, not real, three-dimensional people. For people are not just filled with current ideas. People carry memories, too. Sometimes, things that they're taught as children or learn as adolescents even go on to mold the way they see the world – for years, decades, sometimes their entire lives.

One Late Antique example of this phenomenon comes from the world of the pharaohs. At the Egyptian city of Deir el-Bahari, across the Nile from the regal Luxor, a powerful queen once built a large funerary monument for herself (Figure 3.2). Queen Hatshepsut constructed her memorial there during the Eighteenth Dynasty of Egypt, a period which we would date to the early fifteenth century BCE. Designed as a series of terraces, each raised above the desert valley and faced with a majestic row of columns, Queen Hatshepsut's grand tomb complex is one of Egypt's most iconic sites and a testament to ambitions of this powerful female ruler. It also continues to draw visitors who seek to behold the Egypt of the ancient pharaohs.

It would be easy to compartmentalize a monument like Queen Hatshepsut's funerary monument in historical studies by relegating it to art history classes on the pre-Christian world. Queen Hatshepsut lived and died fifteen hundred years before Jesus was born; why should someone so old steal the spotlight from much later figures? A closer look at the site of Deir el-Bahari, however – and a better appreciation for how the past was a living presence for people of the Late Antique ancient Mediterranean world – tells a more complex story. For there, on the upper terrace of Hatshepsut's sanctuary complex, a Christian monastery was established in Late Antiquity. This monastery was dedicated to a man named St. Phoibammon. Textual records dating from the sixth century CE make abundant reference to St. Phoibammon's monastery although nothing of the monastic community building remains today. Astonishingly, its traces were largely destroyed not by later, religious militants but by "modern" excavators, who tore the archaeological site to pieces without any proper record keeping. (To learn more about this story, consult the contribution by F. Dunand in *EBW* [2007].)

Figure 3.2 The funerary and temple complex of Queen Hatshepsut at Deir el-Bahari in Upper Egypt. Hatshepsut was one of the rulers of the Eighteenth Dynasty of Egypt (d. 1458 BCE). More broadly, she holds the distinction of being among a unique group of ancient female rulers, like Nefertiti and Cleopatra, who shaped the long history of ancient Egypt. That story would continue at Deir el-Bahari two thousand years after the queen's burial. In the sixth century CE, according to textual records from the time, a Christian monastery had been built somewhere in the vicinity of Hatshepsut's tomb. Why Christians chose to use this ancient complex as the site of their monastic community is not entirely clear, but the site's remarkable preservation today makes clear they did not destroy it. The funerary complex remains a popular destination for tourists intrigued by the pharaohs and queens of "Ancient Egypt." Copyright © Ian Dagnall/Alamy Stock Photo.

As this example shows, Queen Hatshepsut's sanctuary held many Christians in Roman Egypt under its cultural spell. Other Christians would pay to be mummified to maintain their connections to Egyptian mores, continuing a cultural tradition that Queen Hatshepsut herself would have valued and appreciated. For these reasons, Late Antique history is more than a collection of sources arranged in chronological order. Childhood joys, long-standing cultural customs, even traumatic events can seep into people's lives in different ways at different times. All of these episodes affect how a person responds to their surroundings and influence the decisions they make. There would always be those who naturally tried to escape the more haunting realities. But in Egypt and elsewhere, a swirl of memories would worm its way into the minds of poets, home decorators, even the people who paid for fancy tombs. That's why researchers have to find a way to describe how the people in the past carried the past with them, too. Memories shaped their present lives.

Our poet Rutilius Namatianus was also someone for whom, even in the early fifth century CE, the memory of the past was still regrettably a feature of the present. In this case, Rutilius didn't like Jews. "Would that Judaea had never been subdued by Pompey's wars and Titus' military power," the poet writes after meeting a Jewish merchant on his way home. Rutilius was unrelenting in his vitriol, calling him "a creature that quarrels with sound human food." The poem continues:

> He charges in our bill for damaging his bushes and hitting the seaweed, and bawls about his enormous loss in water we had sipped. We pay the abuse due to the filthy race that infamously practices circumcision: a root of silliness they are. Chill Sabbaths are after their own heart, yet their heart is chillier than their creed. Each seventh day is condemned to ignoble sloth, as if it were an effeminate picture of a god fatigued. The other wild ravings from their lying bazaar methinks not even a child in his sleep could believe. (*On His Return to Gaul* 1.384–394, LCL trans. slightly modified)

These appaling sentiments are usually left out of historical commentaries or only embarrassingly alluded to. One can understand why. Amid all Rutilius' lyricism about fifth-century Rome and his father's accomplishments, amid all his reflections on the successes of his friends and of the failures of men like Stilicho, Rutilius' opinions about Jews seem like an irrelevant theological aside, something best kept away from more serious history students of the period. And yet, Rutilius' anger was scathing and his rhetoric about Jewish people, disease-driven: "The infection of this plague, though excised, still creeps abroad the more: and it is their own conquerors that a conquered race [now] keeps down" (*On His Return to Gaul* 1.397–398). Late Antique historians should not dismiss these lines as literary imagination.

Rutilius' bigotry rips the band-aid off the idea that Late Antiquity represents a cleaned, sterilized time, fundamentally different from more difficult periods of early Christian history. Rutilius' view of Jews, in particular, shows us that many people in Late Antiquity lived with a deep wound that was still fresh. This wound was suffered when Judea, the territory around Jerusalem, was first captured by the Roman general, Pompey, in 63 BCE. It was exacerbated by the events of 70 CE, when another Roman general destroyed the Jewish Temple in Jerusalem itself. It would be easy, if not perhaps justifiable, to crop these difficult events out of Late Antiquity because they do not fall within the period's chronological limits. Rutilius' poetry, however – and other disturbing events, like the destruction of synagogues and the drafting of legislation which targeted the rights of Jewish people living in the Christian Roman Empire – provides an important counterweight. Earlier historical periods cannot necessarily be omitted from our story because they don't fit within the boundaries we've decided to draw around our sources.

In the end, the history of Late Antiquity, as much as it can be narrated sequentially year after year, is one in which complicated memories snagged the straightforward unspooling of time (*Exploring Culture* 3.1: Studying Memory, or the Past within the Past). The Christians who tried to heal this open wound and the Christians who let it fester and rot – until it would become a debilitating infection on their history – cannot be omitted from the narrative.

Exploring Culture 3.1   *Studying Memory, or the Past within the Past*

In antiquity, fiery attacks like the Persian sack of Athens, in 480 BCE, or Rome's destruction of the Jewish Temple, in 70 CE, seared the land and smoldered in the memory of people who witnessed them. Conflict scars a country. Even political fights can bruise it.

Yet people who live through such acute moments of change are not exactly scrubbed clean of their memories when they wake up from them. In the days, months, and sometimes years that follow, the past stays with them. In this way, history doesn't just move forward, a series of names and dates cascading endlessly in time. Time itself can be torn, or snagged on past events. Scholars who try to study this phenomenon are searching for the traces of social or cultural memories.

Memory was an important concept in classical antiquity. One Roman writer conceived of it like a vast mental mansion, where objects or emotions could be retrieved by walking through the rooms. In the slowly changing Roman Empire of Late Antiquity, memory could awaken in many individuals and communities a sense of nostalgia or inspire a new course of action for the future. "There are present within me," Augustine of Hippo wrote in his *Confessions*, "heaven, earth, sea, and whatever I could think on therein – besides what I have forgotten. There also I meet with myself and recall myself and when, where, and what I have done and under what feelings. There is everything which I remember [in the "vast court" of memory], either on my own experience or on another's credit" (*Confessions* 10.8, trans. adapted from Pusey [1907]). In Augustine's retelling, the sum of his past experiences profoundly shaped the person whom he became. Or so he wanted us to believe.

The process of remembering and its opposite, forgetting, can work in different ways for different people. Historians need to be carefully attuned to these traces of the "past in the past."

The life of the Greek philosopher Proclus (412–485 CE), who taught in Athens in the fifth century CE, testifies to competing value systems – and memories – aswirl in major metropolises. Athens itself offered many opportunities for Christians and non-Christians to reflect on the cultural importance of the past.

According to the philosopher's biography, the aspect of Athenian life which Proclus appreciated most was owning a home next to several historic landmarks. "This indeed was one of Proclus' good fortunes: that he lived in the house that suited him best … It was in the vicinity of the Temple of Asklepios [the healing god] which the tragedian Sophocles had immortalized. It was also next to the Temple of Dionysus near the theater and was in sight of the Acropolis, too [the hill dedicated to Athena]" (Marinus, *Life of Proclus* 29–30, trans. adapted from Guthrie [1925]). Even with the increasing legislation against non-Christian worship that had taken place during the Theodosian period, Proclus prided himself on his proximity to these majestic venues, haunted by larger-than-life figures, like the ghost of the talented literary star Sophocles.

For Proclus the memories of this culturally sophisticated age were so strong, in fact, that, when a group of Christian citizens tried to remove the cult statue of Athena from the Parthenon, he took the statue into his house (Marinus, *Life of Proclus* 30). Proclus' "house of memories" would have looked quite a bit different from Augustine's.

3.3 Acquiring Cultural Competence: The Study of Religion in History

The fact that Rutilius himself never once, in his entire poem, clearly or unequivocally states his religious identity makes it all the more important to understand what was happening in Late Antique society and culture. Rutilius himself was an equal opportunity religious critic. Passing an island of Christian ascetics – followers of Jesus who had retreated to an isolated world where they could deepen their faith and their connection to each other – he characterizes their choices as the "silly fanaticism (*rabies*, in Latin) of a distorted brain" (*On His Return to Gaul* 1.445, LCL trans.). Because of Rutilius' low, apparently equal disregard for Jews and Christian monks, some scholars describe Rutilius as a "pagan," that is, a non-Christian.

There is no need for us to be so gullible or naive. Nothing prohibits a Christian, either then or now, from looking upon many of the beliefs and practices of their Christian peers and seeing the "silly fanaticism of a distorted brain." In fact, there were many Christians in Late Antiquity who thought the same thing about their own Christian peers.

Lactantius and Augustine were two men who spoke out about the degrees of Christian madness around them. Lactantius wrote at the end of the third century CE and start of the fourth century; Augustine at the end of the fourth century and into the first three decades of the fifth century. Both were Christians, and both were aghast at some of the eyebrow-raising beliefs held by their peers. Some in Lactantius' community were prophesying that Antichrist would soon arrive in the guise of the beast, Emperor Nero, and that with Nero's arrival, the world would come to an end. Lactantius called these Christians *deliri*, or "crazies," for assuming they could foresee the future and for speculating wildly about the return of a dead emperor (*On the Death of the Persecutors* 2.8).

Augustine, writing nearly a century later, observed a similarly inexplicable phenomenon among Christians who were trying to make sense of difficult scripture passages. At issue was the interpretation of a difficult passage in his Bible. In the text known as "Paul's Second Letter to the Thessalonians," the writer hints that "the secret power of lawlessness is already at work [in society]; but the one who now holds it back will continue to do so till he is taken out of the way" (2 Thess 2.7 [*NRSV*]). This text was written in the late first century CE, and Augustine confesses that he is "completely at a loss" as to what the writer of the passage was saying.

Augustine also states that many Christians of his own day were absolutely certain that they knew the secret meaning behind it:

> Some suggest that [it means] Nero himself will rise again and will become Antichrist; others think that [Nero] was not slain, but was rather withdrawn so that he might be thought to have been slain and that he is still living in concealment in the vigor of the age that he had reached at the time when he was supposed to have died until in his own time he shall be revealed and restored to his kingdom. But I am amazed at the great audacity of those who hold these opinions. (Augustine, *City of God* 20.19, LCL trans. by W. Greene [1960])

According to Augustine, then, some Christians of his day believed that Nero would return from the dead and play the role of "Antichrist." When he did, his reappearance would inspire the Second Coming of the Messiah, Jesus.

The nature of these convictions will likely astonish scientifically attuned ears. The important point here is to note that they were equally baffling to Christian men of the fourth and fifth century. Both Christian writers, Augustine and Lactantius, were disturbed by those people who, just like them, identified as "Christians" yet held these kinds of groundless beliefs. Lactantius' disdain for these "crazies" and Augustine's amazement that some Christians had the "great audacity" to read and interpret the Bible in this fantastical way provide us a useful warning. For historians who write about religion, it is extremely difficult to draw a complete picture of someone's religious identity by making inferences from the poems they write, the goods they leave behind in their tombs, or even from the politicians they may support.

In the end, a writer like Rutilius Namatianus may not tell us anything about his own religious identity, but his blanket hatred for the Jewish people and his disdain for the "silly fanaticism" of monks do not make him a "pagan" by default. They certainly don't disqualify him from being a Christian. The study of Late Antiquity requires a careful attention to social and cultural forces that shaped individual and community beliefs and behavior (*Key Debates* 3.1: Can We Ever Really Know What Happened?). Most important of all, there is no reason for historians to expect that all members of a religious group acted the same way at all times or even according to gross stereotypes.

Key Debates 3.1   *Can We Ever Really Know What Happened?*

Is history a science? In the field of modern history, it can sometimes seem that way. Data collection – from U.S. census figures to polling numbers to inflationary spending – shapes the questions historians ask about the past. In the field of ancient history, by contrast, archives filled with raw numbers rarely exist. Will ancient historians ever know what happened to the same degree of specifity?

The parallel lives of two nineteenth-century German men illustrate the nature of this challenge and its lasting impact on contemporary ideas about doing history.

Leopold van Ranke (1795–1886) grew up in a world shaped by Enlightenment values of rationalism, empirical inquiry, and hard fact. Later, he excelled as a scholar of classical and European history. He was committed to using contemporary evidence, not secondary materials; and he advocated (though not always faithfully practiced) the importance of giving proper citations. Van Ranke believed his scientific methods would help scholars recover the past in a fresh way. "History has had assigned to it the office of judging the past and of instructing the present for the benefit of the future ages," he commented in the preface to his *History of the Latin and Teutonic Nations from 1494 to 1514* (1824). "To such high offices, the present work does not presume: it seeks only to show *what actually happened*," translated by R. Wines in *The Secret of World History* (New York: Fordham University Press, 1981), p. 58.

This short German phrase, *wie es eigentlich gewesen*, "as it actually happened," would nag, puzzle, and hound generations of historians, curious students, and dedicated amateurs.

Heinrich Schliemann (1812–1890) belongs in the latter category. Schliemann, a sly businessman, was deeply interested in what really happened. Using his wealth to hunt for gold, he set off to search for the legendary city of Troy. Schliemann's "excavations" in modern Greece and Turkey succeeded in uncovering many spectacular artifacts, like gold jewelry and funerary masks, which still dazzle museum-goers. Almost all these objects have little or nothing to do with the time of Homer.

Today, many scholars would prefer to cover the tracks of men like van Ranke and Schliemann, as well as their quest to discover history "as it really was." Statues, paintings, and *objets d'art* are no longer used, like Schliemann once advocated, to dress up the "real" history deduced from textual sources; archaeological methods have become more precise, and material culture is now seen as an important source of primary evidence. Other researchers have turned a critical eye to the rhetorical nature of ancient texts. When discussing the lives of women, foreigners, or political opponents, these "primary sources" may not be as innocent as van Ranke once trusted they were. History as it actually happened seems a fool's errand.

So where does that leave ancient historians? Is the study of the past merely the study of rhetoric, or can it still be something more comprehensive – a narrative?

One prominent twentieth-century scholar has suggested a middle road between these extremes. *"Wie es eigentlich gewesen* [means] the right portrayal of relations" (M. Finley, *Ancient History: Evidence and Models*, 1985, p. 52). As the amount of Late Antique evidence expands to include new texts and new archaeological discoveries, the "right portrayal of relations" among these disparate pieces might be the best historians can aim for.

A cultural competency talking about religion in people's lives is one of the first techniques an aspiring Late Antique historian has to master before advancing in the field. A key component of this competency is being able to recognize that the values which can bring people together – and the disputes that drive them into different factions and constituencies – can frequently cross the theological aisle. Just because someone identifies with the label "Christian" doesn't mean they believe or act the same way as their neighbors, their family, or even their bishop.

3.4 Linking, not Disconnecting, Different Periods of Early Christianity

In the case we just examined, many Christians living in the fourth and fifth centuries CE were passionately fixated on the notion that the Roman Empire would very soon come to an end. To them, signs of Rome's fall would be clear: "Antichrist," the cosmic opponent of the Messiah, would arrive as a harbinger of the approaching battle. Then, Jesus' Second Coming would follow. How had these odd seeds taken root in the landscape of later Rome? Where had they blown in from, and when? To answer these questions requires that we build a sturdy bridge between the time of Jesus and his first followers and the later world of "Late Antiquity Christianity."

The need to link events in the first century CE to the fourth century CE will seem basic to many history students. That's what historians are trained to do. They laboriously construct a framework for their analysis by looking carefully at everything that happened before. What could be more foundational to the study of Late Antiquity, then, than to follow the footsteps of people from Jesus' time into the later landscape of Lactantius and Augustine? Ruefully, very few historical narratives interrogate the rise of Christianity from the first century to the fourth century without relying explicitly or implicitly upon assumptions about the superiority of the Christian faith.

The following examples illustrate why the Second Temple period of Jewish history and early Christian history cannot be so easily cut off from the world of Late Antiquity.

Paul and the context of the late Second Temple period

Paul is the Jewish writer who left behind, in ancient Greek, the earliest written accounts of the Jesus movement. In 2014, one historian of Late Antiquity called him "a Jewish convert to Christianity," but this characterization is regretfully inaccurate. Paul was a Jewish man who believed that the risen Jesus (the "Christ," a Greek adjective which means "the Anointed One," or the "Messiah") provided a path to salvation without the need for him to abandon his own Jewish upbringing. Perhaps for this reason, Paul never referred to the early Jesus movement as a separate religion – which we call "Christianity" – nor did he ever preach about the moral requirements of being a "Christian" or even self-identify with that label.

We know these things because seven of Paul's writings have been preserved in Christian Scripture, and neither the word "Christianity" nor the term "Christian" appears in any of them. All of these authentic texts date to the 50s CE, making them earlier even than the Gospels. In not one does Paul ever claim to be "a Jewish convert to Christianity." Even in sentences which might imply, in English, that Paul has parted ways from his Jewish roots, the reality is more complex.

At the one place where Paul mentions his "earlier life in Judaism" (Galatians 1.13), he uses the Greek word *Ioudaïsmos*. Often erroneously translated as "Judaism," this word did not refer to the "religion of the Jewish people," as we might use that English word now. Invented in the second century BCE by the anonymous author of the text known as Second Maccabees, *Ioudaïsmos* was a curious, contested word. It had been coined during a Jewish revolt against the Hellenistic rulers of Jerusalem, a military battle which led to the creation of the festival of Hanukkah in 164 BCE. This victory also gave a Jewish family, the Hasmoneans, direct control over the priesthood of the Second Temple in Jerusalem. The Maccabean revolt is one of the most important, transformational events of the late Second Temple period.

According to the writer of Second Maccabees, the word *Ioudaïsmos* was being waved like a political banner during this polarizing age. On the one hand, it united Jews who were fighting with the Maccabees against the incursion of Hellenistic influences on Jerusalem. On the other hand, given that many of their Jewish friends and family were quite comfortable adapting to Hellenistic customs and social practices, this word would have divided Jews as much as it united them. *Ioudaïsmos* advocated only one specific way of being Jewish. (The ultimate irony is that the text of Second Maccabees, which laments the spread of Hellenistic influences, was written in Hellenistic Greek.)

Paul is the first person we know of in all of Greek literature to use the word *Ioudaïsmos* after the Second Maccabees, and for that reason, we can be certain he was drawing upon the meaning of the word as it was used in the late Second Temple context. And so, when he claims to have left behind his "earlier life in *Ioudaïsmos*," he was not stating that he had radically parted ways from his Jewish upbringing. He was making an alternate claim about "being Jewish." For him, it was one that now depended upon a belief that Jesus had been the Messiah. Many of Jesus' first followers, raised in the Jewish tradition, would make the same faith leap.

Paul's legacy, forged texts, and the rise of Christianity

This conversation continued after Paul's death, often in his name and obviously without his knowledge. According to a majority of biblical scholars, the text Augustine was looking at, "Paul's Second Letter to the Thessalonians," was not written by Paul. It had been composed after Paul's death (d. *c.*62–64 CE) by someone pretending to be him. For that reason, scholars categorize it as a "pseudepigraphic" text. This technical term is derived from the Greek words meaning "to write" [*graphein*] "falsely" [*pseudos*].

The idea that there might be forgeries in Christian Scripture shocks students who have been taught to believe that the "Bible" is the literal word of God and that it would not contain such falsehoods and deceits. But Second Thessalonians is not the only pseudepigraphic text in the Bible. The First and Second Letters to Timothy, as well as the Letter to Titus, are the three other pseudepigraphic texts of Christian Scripture. Like the Second Letter to the Thessalonians, all were written and circulated after Paul's death. The circumstances that led a now-anonymous writer to draft a sequel to Paul's "First Letter to the Thessalonians" are fascinating. In his own letter, Paul had used language which alluded to a coming end time (1 Thess 5.1–3).

Because the world did not end in Paul's lifetime, however, many who had remembered hearing Paul preach may have started to doubt his authority in the years after he died. For if Paul had been mistaken about the timetable for the Second Coming of the Messiah, what else might he have gotten wrong, they would have wondered? The writer of "Second Thessalonians" invented a creative way to airbrush these concerns. Drafting a letter that mimicked Paul's style, the now-anonymous author expanded, elaborated on, and corrected Paul's teachings about "The End." By including predictions that even Augustine found impossible to understand ("[T]he one who now holds [the mystery of lawlessness] back will continue to do so till he is taken out of the way"), the writer who forged this document reinforced the core of Paul's authority while casually updating Paul's teachings. "Second Thessalonians" reassured the wider community that Paul had not been wrong about the Second Coming after all.

Like many other Christians in the Roman Empire, Augustine of Hippo didn't actually care whether Paul had authored Second Thessalonians. Nor did many other

Christian writers ever take care to distinguish Paul's genuine letters from the ones forged in his name. They simply included these texts in their Bible and began relying upon them as authoritative documents. Bishop Cyprian of Carthage, who lived in the middle of the third century CE, shows us the power these texts could have. Cyprian wanted to convince follow bishops to stop attending civic events in their Roman cities, so he appealed to the authority of Scripture: "[T]he Apostle [Paul] warns [you] and says, 'A bishop (*episkopos*, written in Greek) must be blameless being the steward of God'" (Cyprian, *Letter* 67.5, trans. adapted from R. Donna). The text which Cyprian quotes is not the "Apostle," however. It is the pseudepigraphic "Letter of Titus" (Titus 1.7), written after Paul's death.

These later texts were undeniably instrumental in giving shape to early Christianity as an institution. Many of them articulated an organizational structure – of deacons, priests, and bishops – that helped the Jesus movement gain momentum as a group. But historians of Late Antiquity cannot treat these early texts so carelessly. One scholar has proposed the following reconstruction about the history of church leadership: "Paul advised his close associate Timothy on how to regulate the internal structure of the Christian communities," and then, "Paul repeated several of these injunctions in his Letter to Titus" (1 Timothy 3.1–7 [*NRSV*]). Unfortunately, neither text, First Timothy or the Letter to Titus, was written by Paul. In fact, none of Paul's authentic letters sheds any light on the status of "bishops" in the early church because the office did not exist in the middle of the first century CE. In history, facts are still important.

That's why, whether one is exploring the role of martyrs in promoting or damaging the profile of the early church, or investigating how a hierarchy of church offices developed over time, historians of Late Antiquity can't simply bypass the bridge connecting early Christian history to later Christian history. Late Antique Christians did not live in a self-enclosed world, cut off from the roots of the Jesus movement. Jesus' followers in the third, fourth, fifth, and sixth centuries CE were inventing a future for themselves by actively engaging with the memory of who they were, where their movement had come from, and where Christianity was going (*Political Issues* 3.1: Emperor Galerius' Edict of Toleration, 311 CE).

Political Issues 3.1 *Emperor Galerius' Edict of Toleration, 311 CE*

In 303, many Christians in the Roman Empire were suddenly nervous. Eusebius, bishop of Caesarea Maritima and writer of a contemporary church history, explains why.

It was in the nineteenth year of the reign of Diocletian, in the month Dystrus [a way of recording time used in Macedonia, roughly February], called 'March' by the Romans, when the feast of the Savior's passion was near at hand, that royal edicts were published everywhere, commanding that the churches be leveled to the ground and the scriptures be destroyed by fire, and ordering that those who held places of honor be degraded, and that the household servants, if they persisted in the profession of Christianity, be deprived of freedom. (Eusebius, *Church History* 8.2, trans. by A. McGiffert in the *NPNF* series [1890])

For only the second time in Rome's history, Jesus' followers were being targeted with legal discrimination. The first period of Roman conservative ire had come two generations earlier. In 257–258 CE, two years before being killed in a battle with the Sasanians, the short-lived Emperor Valerian had compelled wealthier Christians to forfeit their property. Valerian also singled out institutional leaders – deacons, priests, and bishops – for arrest. That, at least, is the account given in the one source, a third-century Christian text known as the *Proconsular Acts of St. Cyprian*.

A half century later, Roman authorities remained convinced that "Christians," as these people called themselves, were enemies of the state. Within a few months of Diocletian's hostile campaign against them, "other decrees were issued," Eusebius reports, which ordered "that all the rulers of the churches in every place be first thrown into prison and afterwards by every artifice be compelled to sacrifice" (Eusebius, *Church History* 8.2). For individuals and families who suffered through these two, intense periods of state-sanctioned prejudice – the only two documentable periods of "persecution" on record in the first four hundred years of Christian history – the emotional, even physical toll must have been high.

The politician traditionally seen as ending this age of intolerance is the emperor and general Constantine. In 312 CE, after seeing a vision in the sky, he instructed soldiers to emblazon their shields with the *chi-rho*, the two-letter Greek monogram corresponding to the word for the "Messiah" ("Christ"). One year later, he and his co-ruler Licinius gave Christians the legal protection they had been seeking.

Constantine's beliefs and the reasons behind his toleration decree have been endlessly debated ever since. Amid the fixation on Constantine's Christianity, though, another edict, published by an equally fascinating figure, remains relatively overlooked.

In 311 CE, Emperor Galerius made a similar decree. After Galerius' death, it was quickly repealed, but its import cannot be dismissed. Galerius' act of toleration shows that at least one high-powered official, a non-Christian, was ready to accept Christians as part of society.

Constantine's conversion makes for a more compelling drama, naturally. So, too, does Galerius' death. One Christian writer claimed Galerius was devoured by worms, the same malady that had stricken Antiochus IV Epiphanes in 2 Maccabees (Lactantius, *On the Death of the Persecutors* 33). Scholars can debate the veracity of Galerius' death, but Christianity's acceptance was not necessarily dependent on having a Christian in the imperial palace.

The bridge from the Christianity of today to the Christianity of the ancient Roman world zig-zags quite a bit; it is not a straight crossing. But the world of the Second Temple period, of Jesus and of Paul provides an essential context for understanding the concerns of Christians, Jews, and others in the third through eighth centuries CE. The time has now come to shine our spotlight on them.

3.5 Pre-Modern vs. Early Modern History: A Note on Sources

Where will we look for our evidence? A historian of the medieval or modern period has access to caches of documents. These can include town archives, state archives, journalists' interviews, newspaper accounts, and legal documents. These historians also use material culture – Thomas Jefferson's writing desk, family photographs, posters advertising the sale of humans into slavery in the Caribbean – to broaden the body of evidence on which they draw. The result is a mash-up of voices, recorded from different sources, that allow us to see history from multiple perspectives.

For pre-modern history, such as that of the Mediterranean world in Late Antiquity, the challenges of our evidence are similar but different. Although there are no state archives to visit, there are certainly texts: sermons, law codes, records of church councils, letters, even treatises on various subjects like architecture and war. There is very little data, however, which directly pertains to the kinds of questions a historian of the modern period might want to ask: no data-heavy economic reports, no government white papers on trade or inflation, no public policy memos on health issues or plague. The ancient historian's task is made more difficult by the fact that many features of the pre-modern landscape do not map easily onto the terrain of the modern world (*Working With Sources* 3.1: Was There an Ancient Word for Our Idea of "Religion"?).

Working With Sources 3.1
Was There an Ancient Word for Our Idea of "Religion"?

The Edict of Galerius and the Edict of Constantine and Licinius pose challenges for historians. One of the foremost issues is how to translate the technical ancient terms. The Latin word *religio* (plural *religiones*), a concept rendered in Greek by the word *threskeia*, is a particularly vexing case. Adding an -n to the Latin word makes it look like a familiar English one. But is that what it meant to Greek and Latin speakers?

In recent years, this question has captivated scholars of religion. One researcher has observed that most studies on ancient "religion" treat the topic with "a surprising, and amusing similarity [to] the way people talk about defining hard-core pornography," that is, "I know it when I see it" (B. Nongbri, *Before Religion* [New Haven: Yale University Press, 2013], p. 15). Some find this call for more precise definitions too pedantic, but the issues are not trivial. The categories scholars use to classify their subjects can say much more about their own interests than they do about how the people of the past saw themselves.

Consider the word *religio* in the two edicts granting Christians freedom of worship. Galerius' edict is known from a Latin text. Constantine and Licinius' is preserved in both a Greek and a Latin version.

Galerius uses *religio* exactly once. The emperor claimed he had been motivated to act because Christians were refusing to demonstrate "the care and proper worship (*cultus et religio*) owed to the gods" (Lactantius, *On the Death of the Persecutors* 34.4). Here, the translation, "proper worship," makes the most sense because it is consistent with four hundred years of Latin usage.

To Romans, *religio* was a word that referred to the socially acceptable way that people of all classes and backgrounds showed their respect and reverence for the gods. Anyone who dared to harness the power of the gods for their own gain – by putting a hex on their neighbor, for example, or by praying for the ruin of a former lover – practiced a different kind of worship, one that was socially *unacceptable*. When Romans talked about these devious ne'er-do-wells, they denigrated them as engaging in *superstitio*, or "delusion."

Today's observer might describe both of these behaviors as forms of religion. But to Romans, only those rituals that benefited the state could properly be termed a *religio*. It's an important distinction, and one that the emperors Constantine and Licinius understood, as well.

In the so-called Edict of Milan, the two men explained the rationale behind their decree. They wanted "to give to Christians and to everyone else a free ability to follow the form of worship (*religio*) which each person wished" (Lactantius, *Death of the Persecutors* 48.2; Eusebius, in his Greek version, uses *thrēskeia*, *Church History* 10.5.2). By rendering this legal language in a more precise, culturally sensitive and specific way, it becomes clear that Christians were not being granted "religious liberty" in the modern sense of the term – as if they were now released from the basic rules of decent, civic engagement.

Christians were now expected to worship in a socially acceptable way that benefited the state, just like everyone else. Neither edict established Christianity as the state religion.

What we have, in short, is a massive puzzle – of tens of thousands of seemingly random pieces, strewn across the borders of the sixty-two modern nations where the Roman Empire once existed – with no cardboard box cover to show us what our final picture should look like. How is it possible to take these pieces and assemble a historical landscape? In the following chapters, you will begin to learn how, as Late Antiquity, magically, begins to appear.

Summary

The task of a historian is challenging. By comparing and contrasting sources, drawn from textual and material culture, historians not only try to determine what happened in the past; they also try to explain change over time. To do so, sources are evaluated in their specific context, giving proper attention to time and place. As we learned from the example of Stilicho's statue base in Rome, however, or from Rutilius Namatianus' opinions about Jews, historians also need to investigate how memories of other times and places can shape or even warp an individual's thoughts, actions, and motives. When studying the nature of people's religious beliefs or how they might affect political behavior, historians also need to exercise care, so as not to suggest that all members of a faith group are programmed to act in an identical fashion. The fact that both Lactantius and Augustine tried to push back against irrational tendencies within their own communities – as evidenced by those who were interpreting current events as if they heralded the coming of the Antichrist – demonstrates that Christians did not always share the same understanding of their scriptures, either in the early fourth century or the early fifth century CE.

Finally, we looked at the long, complicated process by which Christianity sprouted from its Jewish roots. This topic, which includes having a greater understanding of the Jewish figure Paul, cannot be left unaddressed by Late Antique historians because it affects how we read texts that were written in his name. The emergence of the church office of bishop, for example, is a development in Christian leadership that dates to the early second century CE, not the period of Paul.

Study Questions

1. Who was Stilicho and what did Claudian, the public relations poet, think of him? How did other people view Stilicho?
2. In your own words, retell the story of Jesus' followers in the first century CE. What about the group had changed by the fourth century CE? What had stayed the same?
3. In this chapter we saw that history is an argument, based on evidence, about who should be remembered and why. Can you think of another example that illustrates this idea?
4. Explain some of the challenges ancient historians face in finding historical evidence.

Suggested Readings

Bart Ehrman, *Forgery and Counterforgery: The Use of Literary Deceit in Early Christian Polemics* (New York: Oxford University Press, 2012).

Karl Galinsky (ed.), *Memory in Ancient Rome and Early Christianity* (New York: Oxford University Press, 2016).

Candida Moss, *The Myth of Persecution: How Early Christians Invented a Story of Martyrdom* (New York: HarperOne, 2013).

L. Michael White, *From Jesus to Christianity* (San Francisco: HarperCollins, 2001).

Part II
Late Antiquity Appears

4
Power

How did people understand their place in the Late Antique world? How did political boundaries define their allegiances, and how did their identities change when those boundaries were redrawn? How is it even possible for us to stand outside some groups, looking out, while adopting the perspective of other groups, looking in? The questions are difficult to answer in any period. They are especially hard to tackle when the two groups we have our eyes trained on didn't give much thought to engaging each other in neutral terms. Is it fair, for example, to stigmatize an entire population of Late Antique men and women as "uncultured," "uncivilized," or "barbaric" simply because they had the misfortune of being on the wrong side of our written sources?

The third century CE is an excellent starting point for this discussion, for it witnessed the rise of Sasanian Persia, which would parry with the Roman state both militarily and politically over the next three hundred years. Although the relationship between these two empires can be told as one of hostilities and conflict, as we saw in Chapter 2, this chapter digs beneath that rough exterior to find signs of more constructive communication. Both Roman and Sasanian monuments, rituals, artifacts, and texts reveal the nature of this quieter conversation unfolding in the background of so much political bluster. This chapter begins, then, not at the bottom of history but with the shifting power dynamics that affected the Mediterranean and broader world at the top.

4.1 Third-Century Politics

For Rome in the third century CE, an empire that had dominated ancient Mediterranean life for more than three hundred years, the balance of power was about to change. Their new geopolitical neighbor was assembling that empire out of

A Social and Cultural History of Late Antiquity, First Edition. Douglas Boin.

the pieces of old Parthia. It was an empire that would encompass modern Iran and, to its west, Iraq (the so-called Fertile Crescent between the Tigris and Euphrates Rivers), as well as land to the north and west: portions of modern Armenia and territory in the southern regions of the Caucasus Mountains, between the Black Sea and Caspian Sea. Founded in 226 CE when a member of the Sasanian family deposed the previous ruling dynasty, the Arsacids, the Sasanian Empire would remain a crucial power player in Late Antique history through the reign of its last king, 651 CE. Its capital was located at Ctesiphon, a suburb of modern Baghdad.

Romans had a long strategic interest in this region. They captured it once but ultimately decided not to control it. In the early second century CE, Emperor Trajan (r. 98–117) envisioned creating an official Roman province here, "Mesopotamia." That political territory was carved from the land belonging to the Parthians, whom Trajan's army had defeated. But the project never went forward. For much of the second and early third centuries, the Parthians continued to govern the land that lay just beyond the Tigris and Euphrates Rivers. Their presence there also kept several smaller, political entities in check. Territories in Armenia, Osrhoene (a kingdom to the northwest of Mesopotamia), and Hatra (a kingdom located south of Mosul, Iraq) were governed by local officials who allied with Parthia or Rome when, or if, they thought it convenient.

By the 160s CE – the time when the great philosopher-emperor and Roman general Marcus Aurelius governed Rome – the territory along the Euphrates had been incorporated into the Roman state. Lands beyond the Tigris River now lay just within reach. The geopolitical situation would change again in the early third century, during the reign of the young Alexander Severus. When Alexander seized Osrhoene, it may have been the spark that set in motion the overthrow of the old ruling order within Parthia.

In 224, the Arsacid family was expelled from the capital in a coup led by the Sasanian leader Ardashir. Ardashir would be the first king of this new empire, soon to be called – for the first time in history – the land of "Iran." Who were these people just beyond Rome's borders?

4.2   Mithras and a Roman Fascination with the Mysteries of Persia

For centuries, Western historians have operated with an insidious case of "Orientalism." The people and cultures of the east have been branded different, exotic, and unique. The "East," as it provocatively came to be imagined, was the source of magic and mystery. Even in antiquity, Romans fell prey to these stereotypical ideas.

The Roman god Mithras, wildly popular during the second, third, and fourth centuries CE, was once thought by researchers to have come from Persian, or "Eastern," origins. In art and sculpture, Romans always dressed Mithras in loose-flowing clothes and fitted him with a floppy hat, the hackneyed image of an non-Roman "Easterner" (Figure 4.1). Initiates into the private communities of Mithras worshippers were

Figure 4.1 A bronze plaque showing the Roman god Mithras slaying a bull. Depicted in wall paintings and sculptural reliefs, the scene was one of the most popular among Mithraic communities in the Late Antique Mediterranean. Mithras himself was worshipped across a wide geographic span, from the northern frontier cities of the Roman Empire, along the Rhine and Danube valleys, to the city of Rome itself and the territory of Roman Syria. This plaque, whose findspot is unfortunately not known, dates to the late second or early third century CE. It is currently in the Metropolitan Museum of Art, New York. Gift of Mr. and Mrs. Klaus G. Perls, 1997 (accession number: 1997.145.3). Dimensions: 14 × 11 5/8 × 1 3/4 in. (35.6 × 29.5 × 4.4 cm). Open-access Met collection.

given a series of titles, which may have been awarded based on an individual's level of financial contribution to the group. (The worship of Mithras itself was never granted the status of a publicly funded state cult.) Among these seven "grades," one title was, appropriately, "the Persian." Its symbol was a floppy, "Persian" hat and it is seen widely in the artwork of many community centers where Mithras' worshippers met, called Mithraea (the Latin singular is Mithraeum). We will look more closely at an example of a Mithraeum, as well as consider the titles and artwork associated with the other "grades" of initiation, when we investigate what it meant to join such a group in later chapters.

This evidence points us in a rather peculiar direction. By the third century CE, it would appear that many Romans were worshipping a Zoroastrian god even as their government was waging a war against the leaders of the Sasanian Empire. But can the evidence stand the weight of this interpretation? Recently, scholars have suggested not. In fact, the story of how Romans began to worship Mithras is much more complex – and quite eye-opening. It began not with a specific act of cultural borrowing but with a more general Roman fascination for all things "Eastern."

In Zoroastrian worship, the god "Mitra" was a a solar deity. His name, spelled "Mitra," appears on inscriptions as early as the fifth century BCE. By the time of Alexander the Great and his successors, knowledge about this Persian sun god "Mitra" had spread to the world of the Hellenistic kings. There, one Hellenistic ruler – King Antiochus (r. c.69–c.31 BCE), ruler of the kingdom of Commagene, located in far eastern Asia Minor – took the Persian cult and transformed it in a way that carefully and cleverly advanced his own political agenda. The Hellenistic king erected statues dedicated to the god "Mithras" which depicted a panoply of stars and at least one symbol of a constellation, the Lion, which were meant to celebrate the king's birthday. By mixing a Hellenistic fascination with astrology with the symbols of a Persian solar deity, King Antiochus – a descendent of both Hellenistic and Persian families – created a space where cooperation and shared tradition were uniquely built into the fabric of his kingdom.

Romans eventually conquered and replaced the Hellenistic kingdoms, but to many people of the Roman Empire, the worship of Mithras would always feature this important astrological component, inherited from the Hellenistic world. In short, just like the name of the god itself ("Mithras," not "Mitra"), many aspects of Mithras worship did not come from Persia. That is why, as we have now seen, very little evidence exists to substantiate the claim that a Persian god was directly imported into Rome. The Roman god "Mithras," rather, emerged organically as the creative result of many individuals – living at the borderlands of the Roman Empire – who wanted to capitalize on the appeal of a "foreign"-sounding god to create a stronger community for themselves at home, even going so far as to dress up their private meetings with these aesthetically Persian veneers. None of these traits say anything about the origins of "Mithras," but they do tell us quite a bit about the Romans. In the case of Mithras, they were allured by the "magic" and "mystery" of Persia.

So it will be, in Roman writers, for the people of Sasanian Persia themselves. Although Romans discuss aspects of the Sasanian Empire and how it came to power, ultimately, few writers were ever really interested in telling the history of its people from their own perspective. Romans used "Persian" culture to tell comforting tales about themselves. So where *do* we find evidence to understand the Sasanian Empire from the inside?

4.3   The Material Culture of Sasanian Persia

One answer is to look to archaeological evidence. King Ardashir (r. 224–239) and his transformational successor, King Sapur I (r. c.242–270), left behind a stunning record of monumental building that allows us to glimpse how the Sasanian rulers wanted people to view them. These pieces of material culture also allow us to explore how the Sasanian kings saw their own mandate to rule.

Some of the most important archaeological evidence comes from the cities of Behistun, Bishapur, and Naqsh-i Rustam, all in modern Iran. All had been important places of political ritual for the leaders of the Achaemenid dynasty, the family of kings who had governed the last great Persian Empire in the fifth century BCE. The Achaemenid family had included such notable figures as Darius I, whose dramatic rise to power was narrated on a trilingual inscription on the face of a mountain at Behistun. The classical Greek historian Herodotus, who recounts the events that led Darius to attack Greece, knew this inscription and used it to draw his own biography of the Persian king. Behistun was a place rich with history and memory. It is no surprise the Sasanians wanted to build near there, too.

At Naqsh-i Rustam, we see the Sasanian family articulating their political ideologies and cultural values. We should visit it and look at these remains more closely. The city itself is 12 kilometers, less than 8 miles, from the old Achaemenid capital at Persepolis, a city whose fields of tall columns still mark the place where King Darius and his son, Xerxes, ruled their empire. It was Xerxes himself who had famously battled Athens and Sparta for Persia's stake in the Mediterranean until they were repelled and driven back to Asia Minor. Just as they had at Behistun, rather than relegate the powerful memory of this earlier age to oblivion, by letting these cities and monuments fall into further disrepair or by actively demolishing them, the first Sasanian rulers returned to these historic sites and referenced them by building around them.

At Naqsh-i Rustam, several stunning reliefs have been cut into the cliff face that provide important historical information about Sasanian rulers. These sculptural reliefs depict Ardashir's rise to power, the event which marked the establishment of the new Persian dynasty. In one scene, Ardashir receives his crown from the God of Light, Ahura Mazda (also known as Ohrmazd), the most important divinity to Zoroastrian worshippers (Figure 4.2). In another, Ardashir is shown trampling his enemies. The first person to be conquered is his rival, Ardawan IV, also known as Artabanus, the last of the Arsacid rulers.

King Ardashir's victories are not limited to the human realm. The triumphant king is also shown celebrating a victory in the cosmic realm. In yet another relief, the artists have depicted King Ardashir vanquishing the Zoroastrian God of Evil, Ahriman. As a sign of thanks for his divinely inspired victory over his foes, King Ardashir is then shown touching his index finger to his mouth, a gesture of reverence. Behind him is an anonymous attendant who carries a fan or royal canopy.

What can we learn about the Sasanian king and his relationship to the divine forces of the Zoroastrian world from these monuments at Naqsh-i Rustam? For one, we can see how the king presented himself on an equal plane with the gods. Battling the God of Evil, as if face-to-face with his spiritual enemy, Ardashir had crafted a subtle message that Persia's new successes were a product of divine support. Ardashir's diadem, in particular, awarded to him by Ahura Mazda, marks him as the divinely backed victor over the forces of evil. This ideology, intertwining the ruler's successes with the Zoroastrian forces of Light (Good) and Darkness (Evil), would be promoted by all subsequent Sasanian kings. At the city of Bishapur, for example, Ardashir's successor, Sapur I, would be shown in almost exactly the same fashion. Ahura Mazda gives King Sapur I his diadem, the symbol

Figure 4.2   Carved into the cliff face at Naqsh-i Rustam, in modern Iran, is an image of the first Sasanian king, Ardashir of Persia (r. 224–242 CE). Ardashir, the founder of the Sasanid dynasty, is shown here on horseback, at left. He is meeting the Zoroastrian God of Light, Ahura Mazda, at right, who is depicted as his equal. By offering the new ruler a crown, Ahura Mazda invests the head of the Sasanian family with a symbol of divine authority. Zoroastrian values, beliefs, and worship were foundational to the Sasanian Empire. Third century CE. Photo credit: Saman Tehrani, with permission.

of his ruling power. Here, too, as in Naqsh-i Rustam, the Sasanian king is seen defeating his adversaries and triumphing over spiritual forces.

One of the more thought-provoking aspects of Sapur I's monument at Bishapur is the man over whom the Persian king is claiming victory. The general depicted in the relief is the Roman emperor Gordian III (r. 238–244), an inexperienced ruler who led the Romans against the Sasanians in 244. In a traumatic loss for the Roman people, Gordian III never returned from battle.

4.4   Rome and Sasanian Persia in Conflict

The death of the Roman emperor, against the rising Sasanian power, was not something many Roman historians dwelled upon in their texts. In fact, if chance had preserved for us only our Latin and Greek texts, we would have a rather distorted view of what happened on the battlefield in 244 CE, when Gordian III died. Here is the report of the one Latin writer who describes the Roman march to war against Persia and the disastrous outcome of Gordian's battle:

> There was a severe earthquake in Gordian III's reign, so severe that whole cities with all their inhabitants disappeared into the opening in the ground. Vast sacrifices were offered throughout the entire city and the entire world because of this. And Cordus [a historian] says that the Sibylline Books were consulted and everything that seemed ordered in them was done, whereupon the worldwide evil was stayed.
>
> But after this earthquake, in the consulship of Praetextatus and Atticus, Gordian III opened the twin gates of Janus, which was a sign that war had been declared, and set out against the Persians with so much gold as easily to conquer them with either his regulars or his auxiliaries. He marched into Moesia....
>
> From there, he stormed through Syria to Antioch, which was then in Persian hands. There he fought and won repeated battles and drove out Shapur, the Persian King. After this Gordian recovered Artaxanses, Antioch, Carrhae, and Nisibis, all of which had been included in the Persian empire. Indeed, the Persian king had become so fearful of Emperor Gordian that ... he evacuated cities and restored them unharmed to their citizens, nor did he injure their possessions in any way. (*Writers of the Imperial History* [*Scriptores Historiae Augustae*], "Lives of the Three Gordians," LCL trans. by D. Magie [1924], 26.1–27.1)

The text, which is anonymous, comes from a collection of biographies of third-century emperors known to later tradition as the *Writers of the Imperial History* (*Scriptores Historiae Augustae* in Latin, often abbreviated to *SHA*). The text continues by narrating Gordian III's triumphs in Rome. There, like previous emperors, Gordian reported to the Senate and boasted of his victories, which he had achieved with the help of his father-in-law. The Senate itself decreed a victory parade, an important political ritual in Rome known as a triumphal procession. The writer of the *Imperial History* tells us that Gordian III's parade was truly remarkable for featuring four elephants to show "that Gordian might have a Persian triumph in as much as he had succeeded in conquering the Persians." If we were to end our reading here, Gordian III would enter the history books as a hero!

At this point, the biographer reports the upsetting news. While on a subsequent campaign, the head of the Roman emperor's bodyguard, the praetorian prefect – a man named Philip who hailed from Roman Syria – conspired to arrange the emperor's death. Philip spread rumors and slander among the soldiers, implying that Gordian III was too young to capably manage the empire. Soon, the praetorian prefect had convinced a group of soldiers to grant him and Gordian equal rank. A short while later, Philip arranged for the young emperor to be "carried out of sight, shouting in protest, where he was despoiled and slain." As the writer of the *Imperial History* characterizes it, "At first [Philip's] orders were delayed, but afterwards, it was done as Philip had bidden. And in this unholy and illegal manner, Philip became emperor" (*SHA*, "Lives of the Three Gordians," 29.4, 30.8–9).

Philip's cover-up of the assassination was diabolically deceitful:

> And now, that Philip might not seem to have obtained the imperial office by bloody means, he sent a letter to Rome saying that Gordian III had died of disease and that he, Philip, had been chosen emperor by all the soldiers. The Senate was naturally deceived

in these matters about which it knew nothing, and so it gave Philip the imperial title, *Augustus*, and then voted to place Gordian III among the gods, bestowing on him the divine epithet *Divus*. (SHA, "Lives of the Three Gordians," 31.2–3)

Is it fair to take this anonymous text at face value? The larger collection to which it belongs is a set of biographies of the rulers from the turbulent years of the third century CE. In it, the third-century political and military world is beset by political killings, military defeats, and rapid turnover in the palace (*Key Debates* 4.1: Was There a "Third-Century Crisis" in Roman History?). There are lots of reasons to be skeptical of the collection as a historical document, not the least of which is that the *Imperial History* was composed a hundred years after the events it describes – when Rome's fortunes had rebounded and writers could begin to look back with some distance, mixing nostalgia for better times with hope about their present day.

Key Debates 4.1   *Was There a Third-Century Crisis in Roman History?*

When Emperor Alexander Severus died in 235 CE, it was the end of a dynasty. For many historians, it was the ruin of Rome. For four decades, from 193–235 CE, a member of the Severan family had governed the empire. Their patriarch had been Septimius Severus, and he and his successors had presided over an age of stable leadership matched with a commitment to urban investment.

Born in Lepcis Magna, Libya, to a Phoenician family and proclaimed emperor by an army outside Vienna, Septimius had been the first Roman ruler to hail from North Africa. He would sponsor public building across the empire, outfitting his hometown with extravagant new baths, colonnades, basilicas, and temples. In 212 CE, one of the Severans, Caracalla, extended citizenship to every free-born man and woman of the Roman Mediterranean. A welcome feel of innovation and transformation blew through the empire. It lasted until Alexander's death.

Generations of students have come to learn about the subsequent period as the "third-century crisis." It is distinguished by a tragic series of assassinations, bold military coups, a plague that decimated North Africa, unchecked inflation, a loss of religious values, even widespread urban decay, or so the traditional telling goes. But what is the evidence for this catastrophic model of third-century daily life, and can it still hold up to scrutiny?

A closer look at one set of sources, the biographies of the third-century rulers, exposes the difficulties of doing third-century history.

Textual sources are sparse. Two Greek writers, Cassius Dio and Herodian, end their narrative, frustratingly, in the first decades of the third century, the very time when single-minded generals and senators began vying with each other for power. Latin historians are non-existent, a disheartening loss. During this period of historical silence, twenty-five emperors would rule Rome in the course of a fifty-year period. Almost all of what survives about their careers – and in one case about a famous empress, Zenobia of Palmyra – comes from a later source. Known in Latin as the *Scriptores Historiae Augustae*, or *Writers of the Augustan [Imperial] History*, this anonymous collection of biographies was composed in the mid- to late fourth century, almost a century or more after the events it purports to describe.

It is riddled with errors. The most jaw-dropping fiction of the *Writers* (or *SHA*, as it is commonly abbreviated) is that Emperor Gordian III was killed by a Roman military plot – not, as attested on the inscription at the Ka'ba-i Zardusht, by the Sasanian king. Today, most scholars believe that the story of Gordian's assassination was invented to cover up the scandalous, indeed, shocking memory of the emperor's death at the hands of a foreign enemy. Not without reason, the third century does seem, on first glance, as calamitous as once thought.

But did this crisis of governance trickle down to the lives of the empire's citizens, and if so, to what extent did they feel the uncertainty in their daily life? These questions demand a closer look at the archaeology of cities, including the study of inscriptions, papyrus documents, and coins. Just like the imperial biographies, this material evidence presents its own challenges of interpretation, but with plenty of room for debate, the study of third-century society is an exciting area of research.

There is a good reason to doubt whether Philip had ever really plotted to kill Gordian III, however. It comes from an inscription which was carved onto a monument at Naqsh-i Rustam. After his many military victories, Sapur I, following the model of Darius, erected a trilingual victory inscription there. It was chiseled onto three sides of a rectangular tower, known as the Ka'ba-i Zardusht, or the Ka'ba (or "Cube") of Zoroaster (*Exploring Culture* 4.1: The People of "Iran"; Figure 4.3). It is an important third-century document drafted by a Sasanian ruler and is a solid reminder that researchers need to work cautiously, especially when they depend on only one source to write their histories. For contrary to the way the Roman writer reports on Gordian III's death, the Persian text makes no mention of the emperor dying at the hand of a treacherous praetorian guard. The text at Naqsh-i Rustam says Gordian III died in battle. It says King Sapur I killed him.

Weighing the accounts, making a decision

What is a historian to do given that the Sasanian text so baldly contradicts the Roman one? How do we judge and weigh the validity of these sources? Who is right? In the end, does it really matter?

One school of thought would argue that Sapur I's testimony is closer to the events he purports to describe and, hence, the more reliable testimony. Second, the writer of the *Imperial History*, looking back on the turbulent years of the third century, would have had a good reason to cover up the circumstances of Gordian's death; Persia and Rome were locked in a fierce rivalry during this time, and it would not have helped the current Roman emperors' diplomatic maneuvers with the Sasanian kings to popularize a story of Roman defeat. Lastly, there is the scandalous element

Exploring Culture 4.1   *The People of "Iran"*

The Ka'ba-i Zardusht is an important monument in Iran. It stands in the valley of Naqsh-i Rustam in the Fars province outside the old Persian capital of Persepolis. The Arabic word *ka'ba* means "cube," and the Ka'ba-i Zardusht means the "Cube of Zoroaster," a moniker which suggests that the structure relates to the chief deity of the Zoroastrian religion.

Unfortunately, this name was bestowed on the monument at a much later time. The structure is a royal shrine which once housed a sacred fire for the Persian King Darius I. It was built in the sixth century BCE.

Like other royal monuments erected by Darius and his family, such as the captivating trilingual autobiography inscribed on the rock face at Mt. Bihistun for all to read, the so-called Ka'ba-i Zardusht was intended to glorify Darius' family, the Achaemenids, who had ruled during this important period of Persian history. Darius himself would become famous for having expanded the Persian Empire. Breaking out of its regional borders, Achaemenid Persia would eventually expand beyond the Zagros Mountains of modern Iran, beyond Mesopotamia, to the Aegean Sea and Sea of Marmara. After attacking the Aegean city-states, Darius would inaugurate almost a decade of war famously chronicled by the "father of history," Herodotus.

Persia's advances into the Mediterranean were thwarted; and after the last of the Achaemenid family rulers died, Persia's empire crumbled, taken over by the Parthians. Thereafter, Persia was the quieter sibling in Mediterranean affairs – until the third century CE. In 224 CE the Persian family known as the Sasanids changed the balance of power once again, asserting their own political interests in the Roman regions of Syria and Mesopotamia.

One of the most influential leaders of the new Sasanian dynasty was Sapur I (r. c.242–270 CE). And, in order both to establish the legitimacy of his rule and to proclaim the great ambitions of the Sasanian family, he made an important addition to Darius' old monument, the Ka'ba-i Zardusht.

Sapur told his workmen to add an inscription of his own in the three languages of the Sasanian government: Parthian, Middle Persian, and Greek. Although the languages were different from the ones used by Darius, this powerful evocation of the past, almost nine hundred years after the Achaemenid family had vanished, must have inspired many Persians who suddenly felt that they were witnessing the rebirth of their once glorious empire. In many ways, they were. But there were also significant differences.

In the inscription on the ka'ba at Naqsh-i Rustam, Sapur I describes himself as "King of the kings of Iran and non-Iran" (trans. by B. Dignas and E. Winter, *Rome and Persia in Late Antiquity* [Cambridge: Cambridge University Press, 2007], p. 56). It is the first time in history that the word "Iran" had been chiseled into existence. Sapur I and the Sasanian dynasty, which would rule until the seventh century CE, were responsible for giving a name to a political territory and a culture that still thrives today.

Figure 4.3 The Sasanids were not the only ones who used the landscape at Naqsh-i Rustam to promote their family's authority and power. The relief sculpture of Ardashir, for example, is carved out of the same cliff where the mighty Persian kings Darius and Xerxes (fifth century BCE) were buried. Darius and Xerxes belonged to the Achaemenid family, the great Persian dynasty founded by King Cyrus in the sixth century BCE. His successors would rule for three hundred years and expand Persian territory westward to Egypt and Asia Minor and eastward to the Indus River in modern Pakistan. They were eventually overthrown by Alexander in the third century BCE. Six hundred years later, the Sasanids returned to the burial sites of these long-gone cultural heroes to express their own hopes for a new empire. An inscription on the Ka'ba, a shrine for Zoroaster at Naqsh-i Rustam, refers to the new Sasanian leaders as the kings of the people of "Iran." It is one the earliest documented references to the name of the modern country. Copyright © Leonid Andronov/Alamy Stock Photo.

of the Roman emperor himself dying at the hands of a foreigner. Because Romans were stubbornly proud of their military prowess and looked down on "barbarian" tribes, it is likely that the writer of the *Imperial History* changed the events that led to Gordian's demise by blaming an upstart, conniving Roman soldier, Philip – in effect, framing the emperor's murder as the result of an internal army squabble, not as the disastrous result of a foreign policy decision gone horribly wrong (*Political Issues* 4.1: Stigmas, Stereotypes, and the Uglier Side of Imperialism).

A second, alternative interpretation is also possible. Because Sapur's inscription was intended to augment his own power and stature in Sasanian society, it may have deliberately manipulated the events of the battlefield to present the Sasanian king, not the Roman emperor, in the more flattering light. Whichever side of the story one chooses to believe, a broader vantage provides a clearer picture. The rise of Sasanian

Political Issues 4.1 *Stigmas, Stereotypes, and the Uglier Side of Imperialism*

According to the biographer Plutarch, Romulus had founded Rome as an asylum, a place where people of all repute – from debtors to murderers to refugees – would be embraced. Romans of later periods were not always eager to offer this warm welcome to others. Ethnic and cultural stereotyping was, unfortunately, rampant and long lasting in the Roman world.

In 175 CE, Emperor Marcus Aurelius faced a grave internal threat. A Roman general based in the eastern Mediterranean, Avidius Cassius, had decided to challenge the emperor's rule. Avidius' father, who had served under a previous administration, had been born in Cyrrhus, in Roman Syria – a city located about 40 miles from Aleppo. Avidius himself, who would try to claim the throne, was born in Egypt while his dad was stationed there.

When Marcus Aurelius rallied his troops to quash the rebellion, he laid bare the uglier side of Roman society. "Fellow-soldiers," he said, "you ought to be of good cheer. For surely Cilicians [a province on the southern coast of Turkey], Syrians, Jews, and Egyptians have never proved superior to you and never will, even if they should muster as many tens of thousands more than you as they now muster fewer" (Cassius Dio, *Roman History* 72.25, LCL trans. by Cary and Foster [1914]). The sharp rhetoric would have stung, if Avidius had heard it. Before his failed attempt to become emperor, Avidius had already served as a senator and consul. He was no less Roman than Marcus Aurelius. This kind of ethnic stereotyping had a disturbing history in Rome and Greece. The first-century CE poet Juvenal rued the spread of "foreign" customs. In his poetry, he lamented that "the Syrian Orontes," a river near Antioch, had "polluted the Tiber" (Juvenal, *Satires* 3).

Three centuries later, at the end of the fourth century CE, the same tired tunes were still being played. Those who did so spared no victim. According to the *Writers of the Imperial History*, Emperor Severus Alexander himself "felt shame at being called a Syrian" (*Severus Alexander* 28, LCL trans. by D. Magie [1924]). Whether the report is true or not, the claim suggests that social stigma was commonly used in public debates. Shame knew no boundary, either.

When problems developed in the fourth century with Germanic and Gothic tribes on the northern frontier, stereotyping became an easy way for emperors and their speech writers to promote the idea that Romans were a superior breed to foreign tribes.

In 370 CE, the Roman statesman Themistius, who served as city prefect of Constantinople and later as tutor to the imperial house (d. 388 CE), praised the Emperor Valens for brokering a Gothic truce. This act of diplomacy, Themistius argued in ancient Greek, highlighted Valens' skill at bringing "civilization" to the disorganized tribal folk beyond Rome's borders.

"There is in each one of us a barbarian tribe, extremely overbearing and intractable," Themistius told the emperor and Senate in Constantinople during his oration. "I mean the temper and the insatiate desires, which stand opposed to the rational elements, as the Scythians and Germans do to the Romans" (*Oration* 10, section 199, trans. by D. Moncur in the series *TTH*, vol. 11 [1991], p. 35). Themistius argued that, by using diplomacy to establish peace, Valens had wisely relied upon Roman values. Reason and intellect had triumphed over wild, erratic foreigners.

Themistius' speech was but the latest chapter in an ongoing story of Romans who wanted to claim cultural superiority over their neighbors.

Persia was a trying time for third-century Romans. Perhaps for that reason and for others, no continuous narrative of imperial politics exists for the middle of the third century CE. The monuments at Bishapur and Naqsh-i Rustam offer vital perspective on the history of Sasanian–Roman relations during this tense time, seen from the outside and from the top-down.

Admittedly, the picture that emerges from this perspective may look like one of constant clash and conflict. But, as we recall from our study of the origins of Mithras, not everything about Persia was necessarily seen as suspicious to Roman audiences. In the Sasanian Empire, too, many smaller artifacts attest to a level of dialogue that should cause us to question whether this was really a time of irrational, open hostility between two groups of people – or whether the conflict was limited to the officials in the palaces of the emperor of Rome and king of Iran (*Working With Sources* 4.1: A Cameo Glorifying the Sasanian King; Figure 4.4).

Working With Sources 4.1
A Cameo Glorifying the Sasanian King

In 288 CE, Emperor Diocletian would sign a peace treaty with King Bahram II of Persia to bring stability to the two empires, a truce that would last into the fourth century. It would be natural to assume that the one hundred years prior to this truce were a time of endless conflict.

Material evidence, however, suggests a level of peaceful, if not tense, dialogue that may have counter-balanced the open hostility of the battlefield. One piece of surprising evidence comes in the form of a delicately carved piece of jewelry, a cameo.

Cameos are carved from a single gemstone which has colored bands of minerals on the interior. A deep black onyx cameo, for example, might have layers of white embedded within it, visible only as a thin line on the stone surface. The craftsman's job – a careful one – is to shave the stone down to the surface of the contrasting color, and then to sculpt an image against the dark background.

Romans had perfected this technique as early as the first century BCE. Famous classical cameos include the Gemma Augustea, or Augustan gem, which depicts the Emperor Augustus as Jupiter, king of the gods of Mt. Olympus. Augustus is shown with bare feet, like a god, and he receives a crown from the goddess Victory for his triumph over foreign nations.

Cameos stayed an important Roman luxury item into the third century CE. One good example is in the Bibliothèque Nationale, Paris. On it, two adversaries, Emperor Valerian, on the left, and the contemporary King of Persia, Sapur I, on the right, go to battle. Valerian wears a billowing cloak, a *paludamentum* in Latin. This draped garment was one of the most noticeable expressions of a military commander in third-century Rome. Sapur is decked out with the regal symbols of the Sasanian kingdom. The globes at each of his shoulders, for example, signify the king's divine authority. Sapur's helmet is in the shape of the royal Sasanian crown.

As the iconography, or imagery of the scene, makes clear, the Paris cameo commemorates a known event: Sapur's capture of Valerian in 260. Equestrian duels between the two leaders figure prominently in Sasanian art. The way the artist has depicted this particular event is especially telling. In Sasanian artwork, like rock-cut reliefs and other sculpted monuments, the act of grabbing an opponent by the wrist symbolizes victory.

Who was the recipient of this expensive jewel, glorifying the capture and defeat of the Roman emperor? Who wore it, when, and in what settings? These questions cannot be answered, but one surprising side of cultural history is hidden in the nature of the artwork itself. Cameos are rare in Sasanian culture. Very likely, this one was executed by a craftsman familiar with the long, storied *Roman* tradition of cameo production. Yet few Romans would have dared pin this scene on their own togas or stole.

The cameo is a reminder that behind battle lines were many more subtler encounters.

Figure 4.4 This piece of jewelry is a cameo, carved from sardonyx, a shiny black gemstone with bands of brownish red. On its face it depicts a battle between the Sasanian King Sapur I (r. c.242–270 ce) and the Roman Emperor Valerian. Cameo craftsmanship was a highly valued trade. Starting with a stone that contains a thin band of contrasting color (a stripe of white, as seen here), the artist would begin to shave away its exterior. When the two colors of the stone were dramatically exposed, a scene would be carved on its surface. This cameo, originally from Iran, is now in the collection of the Bibliothèque Nationale, Paris, France. Measurements: height 6.8 cm, width 10.3 cm (3.5 in. × 4.0 in.). Photo credit: Erich Lessing/Art Resource.

To consider this matter in a slightly different way, we might try asking a slightly broader question: What did it mean to be or to identify as a Roman in the third-century world? Was there one answer? Or were there many? If the latter, how did Romans grapple with so much diversity in a political system that was supposed to be unified and cohesive?

4.5 The Roman World of the Third Century CE

Empire-wide citizenship is decreed

Looking back at the years before Sasanian Persia's rise, we can quickly see that the Roman people and their leaders were already grappling with widespread social change at home. In 212 CE, Emperor Caracalla had announced that all free-born residents of Rome's territorial holdings – from the seasonally clammy isle of Britain to the perpetually dry sands and welcome oases of Egypt – would be granted Roman citizenship.

It was a momentous legal victory. For generations, many in the Roman world worked as second-class residents of its empire. Although they may have held jobs that serviced the Roman army or provided food and goods to Roman politicians, families, and businessmen in their local towns, the Senate and People of Rome – the constitutional advisory bodies to the emperors – had never guaranteed any of these residents the same access to protections and rights that a real "Roman" had. Those protections were known as the *ius Italicum*, a Latin legal term roughly meaning "Italian rights," and the *ius Latinum*, or "Latin rights."

The idea of these rights had a long backstory. "Latin rights" had first become a pressing issue during the turbulent years of Rome's growth as a republic. As cities throughout Italy began to demand access to the same kinds of laws and protections that citizens of Rome took for granted, they petitioned the Senate and People of Rome to share in the benefits of citizenship. By the early first century BCE, the cities of Italy would go to war to win these rights from Rome. Three hundred years later, by the time of Emperor Caracalla (r. 211–217 CE), "Italian rights" were bestowed on cities that had been founded with the approval of the Senate or the emperor, or awarded as a gift as a sign of the emperor's graciousness. They could also be passed down generationally. These rights were a highly prized social ticket for residents of a Mediterranean city. They allowed one to live and work in Lepcis Magna (Roman Libya) or in Aquincum (Roman Vienna) and feel that he belonged to the same class of people in Italy, the heart of the empire, or in its capital, the city of Rome. They also guaranteed one's access to the codified protections of the Roman legal system.

By chance, the text of Caracalla's announcement survives. A copy of it was written on a small piece of papyrus that was later thrown into an ancient trash dump in Roman Egypt, where it was later fished out. Today, this scrap is known as *P. Giss*. 40 because it belongs to the papyrus collection ("P.") at the University of Giessen ("Giss.") in Hesse, Germany. Although torn and tattered, which makes piecing the lines of text back together again a frustrating exercise, *Giessen Papyrus* no. 40 (*P. Giss.* 40) offers a ghostly record of Caracalla's voice:

> I grant ... to all [free persons of the Roman] world the citizenship of the Romans ... For it seems fair [that the masses not only] should bear all the burdens [of empire] but participate in the victory as well. [This my own] edict is to reveal the majesty of the Roman people. [For this majesty happens] to be superior to that of the other [nations]. (*P. Giss.* 40, trans. by F. M. Heichelheim, "The Text of the 'Constitutio Antoniniana' and the Three Other Decrees of the Emperor Caracalla Contained in Papyrus Gissensis 40," *Journal of Egyptian Archaeology* [1941], p. 12)

This piece of papyrus is also important because it preserves a story that speaks to Caracalla's motivations. In the opening lines of the decree, Caracalla alludes to a recent assassination attempt. The emperor makes clear that his citizenship decree was a way of giving thanks to Rome's divinities for saving him. Caracalla would not be the last third-century emperor to appeal to the gods as part of a policy initiative for uniting the Roman Empire. The role that the Roman gods played as a kind of civic glue, keeping the diverse people of the Roman world together, is one that we will look again in the next chapter.

As for reaction to the news, only one writer – a man who wrote comfortably in ancient Greek – provides us any immediate comment on Caracalla's decree. Cassius Dio (d. 235 CE) was a senator, a consul, and a provincial manager, and he was also not entirely convinced by the sincerity of the emperor's piety. "This was the reason why [Caracalla] made all the people in his empire Roman citizens," Cassius Dio says in his *Roman History*. "Nominally he was honoring them, but his real purpose was to increase his revenues by this means, inasmuch as aliens [non-citizens] did not have to pay most of these taxes" (*Roman History* 78.9, LCL trans. by E. Cary [1927]).

Was the senator pulling back the curtain on the policy deliberations which had led to Caracalla's announcement? Or was his cynicism a personal gripe, the result of his own cultivated contempt for Caracalla's decision to knock down Rome's borders and admit a whole host of "new Romans" to the empire? It would be helpful if we had more sources. As it stands, one has to start to wonder from what corners of Rome the notion of a third-century "crisis" may have originated. For the new citizens of Rome, Caracalla's decree marked the start of a new day, a new way of being Roman.

Rome's birthday is celebrated, a *saeculum* is renewed

To think that third-century Rome was a festive place – a place where cultural traditions continued, social customs were passed on, and the composition of the empire grew larger – cuts against the standard view of crisis. But there is every reason to look behind the curtains of gloom and doom, hanging in the palace, and see what was happening outside. The streets of Rome, even its most resplendent entertainment venues, were about to be filled with a celebration.

The faces of this new, changing Rome were everywhere, starting with Emperor Philip. In 248 CE, the soldier who would later be remembered for having murdered Gordian III would preside over the thousand-year birthday of Rome. The city which had been founded by Romulus at the mythical moment of April 21, 753 BCE – the asylum city, the open city of debtors and creditors and murderers and magistrates (Plutarch, *Life of Romulus* 9.3) – was now run by a man, Philip, who had been raised in Roman Syria. Tradition, which is to say, the awkward customs of other history writers, would prefer that we label him as "Philip the Arab"; generations of history students have reduced Philip's biography to this one ethnic attribute. But we should do better for the leader of 60 million people. Philip was Roman; he just happened to come from a corner of the Mediterranean most traditionalists in Italy couldn't bring themselves to admit was part of their same world.

Like Caracalla, however, Philip, too, would depend upon the gods to unite the Roman people. And the thousandth-year birthday party was a fitting time to give thanks for the empire's resilience. Bronze coins that were circulated during Philip's reign (r. 244–249 CE) show one of the most iconic symbols of Rome's empire, the she-wolf who had taken care to nurse the young Romulus and Remus after their birth. On the legends of these coins, a Latin text announced to everyone who picked them up that a new *saeculum*, or "divine age," had been inaugurated.

The new *saeculum* would have given all residents of the empire enthusiastic reason for celebrating the gods, paying thanks to Rome's long-standing divine protection. Students approaching ancient history for the first time, however, may have some difficulty grasping the cultural significance of this word. Because it looks deceptively like the English word "secular," it can lead aspiring historians to imagine that daily life in ancient Rome was similarly divided into the neat and tidy boxes which we use to organize our lives today: "religious" and "secular."

Unfortunately, the Latin word *saeculum* did not carry that connotation. Romans had no word for distinguishing, or isolating, the "religious" elements of their daily life from the "secular" state. Both these concepts are borrowed from more recent periods of history, specifically the intellectual exploration of the Enlightenment, when thinkers and politicians began to devise conceptual frameworks for quarantining clergy from managing the government. By creating the idea of a "secular" space, one that was divorced from the influences of "religion," Enlightenment thinkers engineered one of the most important social and cultural developments of the eighteenth century. Neither of these categories applies to Rome, to Late Antiquity, or to any period of pre-modern history, however. And to write about the people who lived during this time as if they understood our modern terms is not recommended.

When Emperor Philip inaugurated the new *saeculum* for Rome, he was writing the next chapter in a divine story that stretched all the way back to the Etruscans – for whom the history of the world had been divided into discrete segments of time, or *saecula* (the Latin plural of *saeculum*). Only Etruscan priests knew the exact length of time that each *saecula* lasted, but the passing of one and the coming of the next marked a momentous occasion which had to be celebrated. Romans, who from the time of the earliest Republic had invited Etruscan priests into their governmental system, had continued this practice. It served to remind all Romans that the gods were truly looking out for the health of the Roman people and their empire. Caracalla, Philip, and still other third-century emperors would all strike this optimistic note in their public policies, as we will see very clearly in our next chapter, which explores the role of worship in the Roman Empire.

New walls and city borders are constructed

As the Roman people took account of the Sasanian Empire on their eastern border, as they wrestled with the presence of "new Roman citizens" in their own streets and city centers, Rome and its emperors began to work to repair the snags and tears at

Figure 4.5 In the late third century CE, the Roman Emperor Aurelian constructed a new brick-and-mortar wall for the city of Rome. The capital had long since outgrown its earlier defenses, constructed out of volcanic rock seven hundred years earlier during the city's Republican period. Aurelian's new wall would begin to redefine life in Rome and play a lasting role, in many urban forms, throughout the Middle Ages. This view of Rome faces to the west from the ramparts of the ancient gate now called the Porta San Sebastiano, leading to the church of St. Sebastian. With this new spectacular fortification, the neighborhoods in the distance, on the west bank of the Tiber, were included in Rome's walls for the first time in the third century CE. Photo credit: Author's photograph, 2012.

the edges of society. Break-away provinces were reincorporated. By the 280s CE, the Rule of Four would move into palaces throughout the empire. Throughout this time, the city of Rome matured.

By 275 CE, the capital would be encircled by a towering new wall, both a practical defensive posture and a powerful statement about the city's grandeur. (For material culture works in both these ways. It occupies a physical place in the landscape but it also shapes the world people live in.) In this way, the walls of Emperor Aurelian (r. 270–275 CE) would come to define the urban appearance of Rome for the next seventeen centuries (Figure 4.5). Designed to keep out raiders, at the same time they embraced parts of Rome – like the right bank of the Tiber and the tallest hill of Rome, the Janiculum – which had never been incorporated into the city. At the conclusion of the third century, then, even Rome's city boundaries were changing, just as the boundaries of the empire were in flux around it. Aurelian's walls are not a monument that can be easily made to disappear from history, either. Their durability and their lasting physical authority help explain why Rome would always carry the memories – even in the city's darkest hours – of its once glorious empire.

If there was one hard-and-fast way to define what it meant to live within these borders, however, neither Emperors Caracalla, Philip, nor Aurelian had been able to articulate it. The best that some Roman writers seemed capable of mustering – if we consider the subtext to Cassius Dio's discussion of the citizenship decree or, later, the fabricated tales told about Gordian's death – was the highly debatable idea that being a real Roman simply meant not being or acting like "them," whoever it is "they" actually were.

Summary

In the third century CE, another empire was formed at the eastern border of Rome's. This Sasanian state would remain an important conversation partner for the Roman government and Roman people until it was conquered in 651 CE. Here, at sites in modern Iran like Naqsh-i Rustam, Sasanian kings drew upon a wealth of Persian history, combining it with a divinely inspired understanding of their status as rulers, to evoke their strong vision for the Sasanian Empire. Kings like Sapur I used these sites to advertise their military victories over Rome's emperors.

The Roman people themselves had long been fascinated by Persian culture and told themselves stories that the popular god Mithras, whom many Roman communities worshipped, had come from Persia. We also saw, however, that many of the traits and characteristics which Romans believed were "exotic" and "Persian" had been filtered through Hellenistic and Roman customs, transforming Mithras into something that tells us very little about the Persian people. Still, traces of dialogue between the two empires and their people can indeed be detected in the third century CE by looking at material evidence, which speaks to a level of artistry and craftsmanship that was crossing the newly erected political borders.

Lastly, we saw that, inside the borders of Rome during this same time, a simmering conversation about what it meant to be a Roman had led many emperors – Caracalla, Philip, and Aurelian – to take a more active role in promoting social and cultural unity among the people of the Roman provinces and the residents of the city of Rome itself.

Study Questions

1. Who was Ardashir? What did he do, and why are his actions historically significant?
2. Did the Roman and Persian people always live in conflict? How do you know?
3. Evaluate the evidence for the death of the Roman Emperor Gordian III, using both Persian and Roman sources. How do you make sense of the conflicting reports?
4. What do the policies and programs of Emperors Caracalla, Philip, and Aurelian tell you about Roman society in the third century CE?

Suggested Readings

Matthew Canepa, *The Two Eyes of the Earth: Art and Ritual of Kingship between Rome and Sasanian Iran* (Berkeley: University of California Press, 2010).

Hendrik Dey, *The Aurelian Wall and the Refashioning of Imperial Rome, AD 271–855* (New York: Cambridge University Press, 2011).

Beate Dignas and Engelbert Winter, *Rome and Persia in Late Antiquity: Neighbors and Rivals* (New York: Cambridge University Press, 2007).

Jaś Elsner, *Imperial Rome and Christian Triumph: The Art of the Roman Empire AD 100–450* (Oxford: Oxford University Press, 1998).

5
Worship

Less than a year after Emperor Philip had staged grand celebrations for Rome's thousandth birthday – to which he had treated the people of the capital to parades of elk, lions, leopards, hippopotami, giraffes, and hordes of gladiatorial games, according to *Writers of the Imperial History* (*Life of the Three Gordians* 33.1) – Rome's first Syrian-born ruler died. The year was 249 CE. Whether he was assassinated by his own soldiers or was killed in a civil war being fought against the Senate's new favorite choice for emperor, Decius, is unclear. But in the aftermath of the loss, the Roman government, its military, and the new citizens of the Roman Empire remained fractured politically and socially. Looking for ways to heal the divisions, Emperor Decius (r. 249–251 CE) used a bold solution to try to address the problems. He called for a universal act of sacrifice to be performed in cities throughout the Roman world.

To modern commentators, Emperor Decius will look like yet another tired example of a manipulative politician who, in the long history of government officials, used "religion" to advance his own ideological agendas. This analysis makes a mockery of Roman history and has to be avoided by researchers writing about Rome. Here's why.

As we saw in our previous discussion of ancient Greek and Latin sources in Chapter 3, neither Decius nor any other politician, in his day or after, had the intellectual tools to think of the idea of "religion" as a sphere of private, individual behavior. The proper worship of the gods, what Romans referred to as the practice of their *religio*, was an integral, necessary part of the good management of the state. Priests and priestesses who oversaw these public rituals held positions that were the equivalent of government offices. To put it in simpler terms, then, "the proper worship of the gods" functioned like a branch of the Roman constitutional system. *Religio* provided support to the empire's very fabric and foundations. As an idea, then, it went to the very heart of what it meant for a man or a woman to call themselves a Roman.

A Social and Cultural History of Late Antiquity, First Edition. Douglas Boin.
© 2018 John Wiley & Sons, Inc. Published 2018 by John Wiley & Sons, Inc.

This ongoing political conversation about what it meant to be a Roman had profound effects on Rome over its long history. To start, individuals and groups who happened to find their rituals and beliefs outside the mainstream faced an uphill battle for greater social integration. However important their own sets of worship practices might be to them – indeed, however legitimate their "religious beliefs" may be in our eyes – the people associated with these outside groups were looked down upon. They were stigmatized for practicing an unhealthy, detrimental form of worship. To conservative Romans, their rituals and beliefs were called in Latin a *superstitio*.

People who were mocked for practicing a *superstitio* were not seen as successfully integrated into the life of the empire. To some second-century CE Romans, for example, Jews counted among the empire's most harmful practitioners of *superstitiones*. On the eve of Rome's cataclysmic war with the Jewish people in Judaea, which was waged between 66 and 74 CE, the historian Tacitus tried to explain what made Jews so fundamentally different: "Prodigies had indeed occurred [announcing the signs of a coming war in Jersualem], but to avert them either by victims or by vows [as a Roman politician might] is held unlawful by a people which, though prone to *superstitio*, is opposed to all propitiatory rites" (Tacitus, *Histories* 5.13, LCL trans. by C. Moore [1931]). Tacitus and his contemporaries would characterize Jesus' worshippers with the same derogatory word (Tacitus, *Annals* 15.44; Pliny the Younger, *Letters* 10.96).

Throughout the empire the hostile headwinds faced by these groups were strong and at times destructive, but that does not give historians license to write about this tense social dynamic as if it were the same as widespread, legally backed persecution. Even facing the challenges that they did, many Jews and Jewish communities lived openly throughout the Mediterranean alongside their Roman neighbors, friends, and co-workers, as we will see later. Jews themselves did not need to win a special legal status to achieve this level of interaction and integration. Their small successes, notwithstanding the profoundly devastating wars fought against Rome, suggest that precisely what kind of worship counted as *religio* was a topic Romans themselves would contest and debate – at home, in the forum, or at a local town council. Despite harsh policies being imposed from the top-down, in Roman culture there was always the potential for a bottom-up conversation to shape Roman society.

5.1   The Civic Sacrifice Policy of 250 CE

In 250 CE, Decius would attempt to legislate and legally enforce what was culturally "proper" or socially "acceptable." He did so by calling for an empire-wide moment of civic sacrifice. Facing the realities of Roman citizens living on three continents, it makes sense that one of Decius' first goals for his administration would be to find a way to unite the people of his disparate empire and to do so with an act that could strengthen the bonds of its community. It's also natural that he and his advisors chose to make sacrifice the central component of their plan.

Public sacrifices to the Roman gods had long been a feature of Mediterranean cities, even before the people who lived in them had won Roman citizenship. At the most important festivals, there were even public banquets where the leading figures of town, Romans and locals alike, were present among the people. Participation at a sacrifice, meeting one's neighbors, seeing and being seen, had long been a way to bridge economic and social divides that existed in Roman towns.

Unfortunately, however noble Decius' policy may have seemed in theory, the plan to implement it was not the most bureaucratically efficient. At every performance of sacrifice – whether an animal was being slaughtered or incense and wine were being offered to thank the gods and the divine emperors for protecting the state – Decius ordered that signed receipts be given out so that Rome's citizens could prove they had attended. The number of officials involved in these transactions must have been staggering. Thanks to the arid climate of Egypt, many of these receipts from Decius' civic sacrifice policy have survived.

The following receipt is dated June 27, 250 CE. It was written on parchment in ancient Greek and was pulled from the garbage at Oxyrhynchus, Egypt, by scholars hunting for scraps of ancient texts. "To the commissioners of sacrifices at Oxyrhynchus from Aurelius Gaius son of Ammonius and Taeus," it begins.

> Always has it been my habit to sacrifice and pour libations and worship the gods in accordance with the orders of divine decree, and now I have in your presence sacrificed and made libations and tasted the offerings together with Taos my wife, Ammonius and Ammonianus my sons, and ... my daughter, acting through me. I request you to certify my statement. [Dated] Year 1 of the Emperor Caesar Gaius Messius Quintus Trajanus Decius Pius Felix Augustus, Epeiph 3 [an Egyptian month]. I, Aurelius Gaion, have delivered [this petition]. I, Aurelius Sarapion, also called Chaeremon, wrote on his behalf, as he is illiterate. (*Oxyrhynchus Papyri* number 12.1464 [*P. Oxy.* 12.1464], trans. by AnneMarie Luijendijk, *Greetings in the Lord: Early Christians and the Oxyrhynchus Papyri* [Cambridge, MA: Harvard University Press, 2008], pp. 163–164)

The specificity of the information written is astounding and is seen on other receipts dated to *c.*250 CE. The logistics of this imperial record-keeping must have been mind-bogglingly complicated, especially if copies were required to be filed in the local records' hall. What people were expected to do with their receipts once they received them is also unclear. Did Romans need to carry them around, the equivalent of an ancient identity card? Or could they be kept safely at home – stored in a kitchen cupboard, for example, or under the bed – to be retrieved only in the event that a local official needed to confirm that a resident had participated? Historians don't know.

Implementation of the policy

What we can say more confidently is this. The available historical evidence makes overwhelmingly clear that individuals and groups whose worship practices might have been deemed potentially questionable – like Mithras' followers or Jews – never contested, opposed, protested, or objected to the terms of Decius' civic sacrifice policy.

This silence is significant, and historians must engage with it. For the actions of the worshippers of Mithras or the empire's many Jewish communities speak quite loudly to the delicate social status of many minority groups throughout the Mediterranean. Neither group was an official Roman *religio*, yet both found ways to coexist in Roman cities alongside friends and neighbors who did not identify with either of these communities.

The challenges faced by groups like these were steep. For its entire history, the cult of Mithras was not explicitly recognized, funded, or even socially sanctioned by the Roman state – not at the time of Decius' decree in the mid-third century nor even in the last years of the fourth century CE. Consequently, individuals and groups who worshipped Mithras may have born a mark of shame among friends and family. Their willing participation in Decius' civic sacrifice decree was likely part of a strategy to ensure the successful integration of their cult.

In the same way, there is no evidence that Jews or any Jewish communities throughout the Mediterranean caused a political revolt because of Decius' decree. Nor is there evidence that Jews ever sought to be exempted from participating in it because they felt it infringed on their liberty as a faith community (*Exploring Culture* 5.1: A Rich Legacy of Human Figures in Jewish Art; Figure 5.1). These points cannot be written out of the third century. Tellingly, they suggest that one did not need to be a member of a polytheist faith to support the Roman emperor's political policies.

The absence of any public dispute among followers of Mithras and the Jewish community suggests that both polytheist and monotheist minority individuals and groups were able to find intellectual and social reasons to justify their civic participation in the sacrifice. We will look at these groups more closely in this and the next chapter.

This perspective gives the more famous story of the third century a sharper context. For what most people know is that some Roman Christians would forever lament Decius' call to civic sacrifice as a period of "persecution." This retelling of history cannot be supported by any evidence. Although it may be convenient, even comforting, for the Christian faith community to remember their complicated early history in dualistic terms, this "church view" of the larger Roman story is inside-out. It also provides subtle misdirection for an inconvenient truth: Many of Jesus' followers actually took part in Decius' civic sacrifice because they did not see any problem reconciling it as part of their Roman and Christian identity (Cyprian, *Letter* 67; Cyprian, *On the So-Called "Lapsed"*).

The historian's delicate task: writing about the policy

Decius' sacrifice decree needs to be described in neutral terms in order for the emperor's goals and political vision to make historical sense. That's not what usually happens. By seeing it and narrating it from the perspective of the most intransigent Christian writers – those who brooked no act of Christian compromise with Roman culture – historians become complicit in telling the story of the empire's 60 million people from the vantage of its most extreme voices.

Exploring Culture 5.1   *A Rich Legacy of Human Figures in Jewish Art*

As Moses led the Israelites out of Egypt, Yahweh gave them a set of laws. These included the "Ten Commandments," related in the Book of Exodus, an account likely written down in the sixth to fifth centuries BCE. The "Ten Commandments" are not the only laws in Jewish Scripture – one rabbi, writing in the third century CE, counted 613 commandments – but one Mosaic law has loomed large over many artists' shoulders.

The second commandment reads as follows: "You shall not make for yourself an idol, whether in the form of anything that is in heaven above, or that is on the earth beneath, or that is in the water under the earth. You shall not bow down to them or worship them; for I the Lord [Yahweh] your God am a jealous God, punishing children for the iniquity of parents, to the third and the fourth generation of those who reject me, but showing steadfast love to the thousandth generation of those who love me and keep my commandments" (Exodus 20.4–6 [*NRSV*]).

Generations of historians have cited this one passage to claim Jews never developed a figural artistic tradition because scripture forbade it. Archaeological evidence from many Roman cities proves otherwise.

In northern Israel, just south of the Sea of Galilee at the Roman city of Beth Alpha, one synagogue preserves a mosaic floor with human and animal figures. The mosaic shows Abraham preparing to sacrifice his son Isaac. Elsewhere on the floor, a zodiac calendar was created, depicting astrological (animal and figural) signs with Hebrew labels. In the center, it even included a personification of the sun god riding a four-horse chariot. Assembled from thousands of tiny pieces of colored stone, *tesserae*, the mosaic at Beth Alpha was laid in the fifth or sixth century CE.

Perhaps the most significant discovery has come from Syria. At the Roman city of Dura Europos, on the west bank of the Euphrates River, archaeologists working in the 1930s uncovered a room of painted walls showing scenes from the Hebrew Bible. This building, a synagogue, was later destroyed – deliberately – in 256 CE by Dura's residents as they fortified their town during a war with Persia, but their loss preserved one of the most important examples of Jewish artwork.

From floor to ceiling, the synagogue was covered with three rows, or registers, of scenes. They show royal episodes, such as Samuel anointing King David; iconic moments from the life of Moses, such as his discovery by the Egyptian pharaoh's family in a basket on the Nile; as well as stories from other books, like 1 Kings, in which the prophet Elijah demonstrates Yahweh's power in front of priests of Ba'al, a local Syrian god. All are preserved today, in reconstructed form, in the National Museum in Damascus.

Exciting discoveries like those at Beth Alpha and Dura Europos also continue to be announced. In 2015, excavators in Huqoq, Israel, revealed that they had uncovered a synagogue mosaic floor with depictions of humans and an elephant. The interpretation of the puzzling group is ongoing, but while scholars pore over its meanings, the assumption of an earlier day – that Jews did not make figural art because it broke one of their laws – can be safely left behind.

Figure 5.1 In this fresco from the synagogue at Dura Europos, Syria, the pharaoh's daughter finds the infant Moses in the Nile River – a story preserved in the Hebrew Bible. The synagogue at Dura Europos was constructed, c.239 CE, by renovating a private home. When the transformation was complete, the synagogue's hall of assembly was painted with scenes like this one. The paintings prove definitively that Jewish individuals and communities in antiquity did not interpret the second commandment of the Hebrew Bible as a prohibition against making figural art. This nuanced observation is an important point with relevance for understanding the history of early Christianity, as well. Although Hebrew Scripture instructs Jews not to worship idols, it did not prevent them from drawing, painting, or sculpting pictures of their sacred stories. Photo credit: Art Resource.

The bishop of Caesarea in Roman Palestine, Eusebius, born just after Decius' reign (c.260–c.339), is one of those influential voices who has distorted the picture. As a church official, he has disproportionately shaped Christians' understanding of Roman imperial history. In his monumental *History of the Church* he writes:

> After a reign of seven years, [Emperor] Philip was succeeded by Decius. On account of his hatred of Philip, he commenced a persecution of the churches, in which Fabianus suffered martyrdom at Rome, and Cornelius succeeded him in the episcopate. (Eusebius, *History of the Church* 5.39, trans. by A. McGiffert in the *NPNF* series [1890])

Contrary to what Eusebius and other modern church historians who follow his lead assert, however, Decius' decree was not directed against Christians; nor was it designed to "persecute" them. As Eusebius makes clear from testimony quoted later in his *History of the Church*, the struggles of some Christian communities, in fact, *pre-dated* Decius' decree. Such was the case in Alexandria ("The persecution among us [in Alexandria] did not begin with the royal decree [of Decius]," reported Bishop Dionysius of Alexander, "but preceded it an entire year," Eusebius, *History of the Church* 41.1). Oddly, some Christians were claiming "persecution" before any Roman law was ever announced compelling people to sacrifice.

This complicated evidence suggests that simple stories of "pagans" and "Christians" clashing because of Decius' civic sacrifice decree will not suffice to explain the challenges faced by both Rome's leaders and its people (*Key Debates* 5.1: When Did Christianity Split from Judaism?). The third-century Roman world was a melting point of different ethnicities and minority groups; and rulers like Caracalla, Decius, and others were engaged in an earnest, perhaps even urgent desire to keep the empire socially coherent. All of Rome's politicians and their new citizens were working out the dynamics of what it meant to be a Roman, even the empire's Christians and Jews.

The following survey of the different types of worship available to people in Roman cities will illustrate the richness of its traditions and the high level of diversity among them. The person who can open this wider Mediterranean world to us is a Latin writer, Minucius Felix, and the city whose streets can provide a compelling look at it is Rome's old harbor town, Ostia.

Key Debates 5.1   *When Did Christianity Split from Judaism?*

Jesus was a Jewish teacher born in the last years of King Herod's reign, around 4 BCE. Herod had been a client king of Rome. Three decades later, around 28 CE, Jesus would be executed by Roman authorities. Those thirty years may not seem like much, but they led to the birth of a far different Roman world. After one of Herod's sons proved inept at governing, a Roman official was ordered to control the region, in 6 CE. This event officially created the Roman province of Judaea. With it, a procurator was installed in Jerusalem. Taxes were collected. The Roman army moved in.

Because of these changes, the first century CE was a tumultuous time in Jerusalem. According to Josephus (c.37–100), at least fifteen rebels tried to foment a Jewish revolt against Roman rule. Their motivations often differed. Some opposed Roman taxes (Josephus, *Jewish Antiquities* 18.3–10, 23–25). Others, like Jesus son of Ananias, preached a message of apocalyptic doom (Josephus, *Jewish War* 6.301–309). The hopes of all the leaders were systematically snuffed out by Roman authorities. Jesus' preaching about an imminent end time likely led to his crucifixion by Roman authorities, too.

In later telling, however, many of Jesus' most vocal followers – called by tradition "Matthew," "Mark," "Luke," and "John" – would insist that rival Jewish voices had arranged to kill the "Messiah" ("Christ"). These texts, authored after the Temple's destruction, would play a key role in derailing Jewish–Christian relations. In particular, they gave rise to an ugly belief that, because "the Jews" had killed the "Messiah," their unconscionable act demanded retribution. Centuries of anti-Semitism would be born from this messy world of first-century Jewish politicking.

But when did Judaism and Christianity split from each other? There is no evidence that Jesus, Paul, or any of the early disciples articulated their mission as one of founding a new religion, "Christianity." And all the canonical Gospels show signs of working within a Jewish worldview. Only around 80–90 CE, in the letter 1 Peter, does the first evidence emerge that Jesus' followers had begun, willingly, to call themselves "Christian," or "follower of the Messiah." Prior to this time, the word had been tossed about by many Romans as a derogatory term for Jesus' followers.

At the start of the second century CE, unresolved identity debates among Jesus' followers about their own Jewish roots and traditions – the group included a number of Gentile converts by now – grew more intense. Ignatius, a bishop in Antioch (d. 110 CE), testifies to that phenomenon.

"Having become disciples of Christ," Ignatius wrote to a community in Magnesia, Asia Minor, "let us learn to live by openly embracing the name 'Christian' (in Greek, *Christianismos*); for whoever is called by any other name than this does not belong to God.... [I]t is utterly absurd to proclaim Jesus Christ and to continue to act 'openly Jewish' (in Greek, *Ioudaïsmos*)" (*Letter to the Magnesians* 10.1–3, trans. by the author). Ignatius is the first person we know to juxtapose the words *Ioudaïsmos* and *Christianismos*, often translated as "Judaism" and "Christianity." His letter has even led some scholars to deduce that Christianity and Judaism had parted ways by this time.

The substance of Ignatius' letter makes clear, however, that the writer was concerned with group members who were still meeting on the Jewish Sabbath and practicing circumcision. The "parting of the ways" between the two groups is now dated much later than the second century CE.

5.2 How Did Romans Worship Their Gods? Text and Material Culture, *c.* Third Century CE

In Minucius Felix's *Octavius*, three dear friends are enjoying a pleasurable stroll at the shore amid the streets of Ostia. During the course of the dialogue, Octavius, a committed Christian, debates his non-Christian friend, Caecilius, about the legitimacy of Christianity while a third friend, although admittedly on Octavius' side, plays the role of referee. How can historians use this one, theologically biased Latin text to illuminate the history of Roman society in the third-century empire?

Let's start by exploring the author, the text, and the setting together and then connect all three to additional evidence. We do not know the precise details of Minucius Felix's birth and death. Those details are lost, but we are fortunate to have the document he wrote. It is the kind of philosophical performance piece that had made Plato, teller of the tales of Socrates, so famous. The text can be dated to the early third century based on the fact that mid-third-century Christian writers later borrowed and cited it.

Unfortunately, it is impossible to specify the extent to which a text like the *Octavius* was addressed to Christian insiders or intended for a wider audience. Like all apologetic texts written in the ancient world, that is, documents penned to "defend the faith," these kinds of stories usually shore up the faith of people who have already made their choice to join the group. They only rarely do the hard work of recruiting others to join. The *Octavius* itself consistently casts Christianity as if it were a culturally superior way of worshipping God. As the passionate, even borderline fanatical Christian Octavius Ianuarius taunts his non-Christian interlocutor:

> "[Y]ou say this superstitious worship of yours (*superstitio*) gave you your world-empire, increased and established it, for your strength lay not so much in valor as in your proper sense of worship and your devotion to the gods, the family, and the state [*pietas*]. You say the noble and majestic fabric of Roman justice drew its auspices from the cradle of infant empire! Yet were your ancestors not in origin a collection of criminals? Did they not grow by the iron terror of their own savagery? ... All that the Romans hold, occupy and possess is the spoil of outrage; your temples are all of loot, drawn from the ruin of cities, the plunder of gods and the slaughter of priests." (Minucius Felix, *Octavius* 25.1–5, 5, slightly modified from the LCL trans. by T. Glover and G. Rendhall [1931])

The brazen way in which the Christian speaker Octavius mocks established, conservative Roman values – embodied in the Latin concepts of *religio* and *pietas* – suggests this "apologetic" text may not have been intended as a recruitment pamphlet at all. By turning Roman culture on its head, Octavius presents Christianity as if it were incompatible with Rome's customs, values, and traditions. If the text really had been meant for outsiders, its strategy to grow the Christian church cannot have won the author many fans. In fact, it may have done the opposite: radicalize Christians who already identified with the group (*Political Issues* 5.1: Are All Christian References to Jews "Rhetorical"?).

As a text that sheds light on how one Christian author conceived of his own faith, then, Minucius Felix's *Octavius* is only marginally interesting. Among the most historically significant elements of the dialogue, however, is its setting: Rome's harbor town. The wider landscape of Ostia is a good starting point for understanding the third-century Mediterranean because its streets were packed with hordes of busy people who worked in long-distance trade and shuffled their goods and ideas between the port and the capital. The city itself was considered to be Rome's first colony, thought to have been founded by one of Rome's kings, Ancus Marcius, in the sixth century BCE. Archaeology has shown that the city was actually developed more recently: in the third century BCE. That did not prevent the people of Ostia from believing that their city was older than it really was.

By the time of Minucius Felix, Ostia's residents lived among streets and neighborhoods that were nearly six centuries old. For us, the archaeological history of Ostia is also important because the city was filled with Roman temples, as any colony would be. And what makes the city so fascinating to study is that – unlike Pompeii, which was destroyed dramatically in the cataclysmic eruption of Mt. Vesuvius in 79 CE – neither Ostia's residents nor their customs were wiped out

Political Issues 5.1   *Are All Christian References to Jews "Rhetorical"?*

One of the most uncomfortable aspects in the history of Christianity is the religion's rocky relationship to Jewish faith, scripture, customs, and traditions. Late Antique historians have to confront this difficult subject, too. John Chrysostom (c.354–407 CE) is one of several Christians whose writings take us into the dark caverns of this important topic.

John Chrysostom began his public career as a deacon in Antioch and soon distinguished himself as a priest and bishop in the same city. By 398, he had accepted a post to the privileged position of bishop of the eastern imperial capital at Constantinople.

From a Christian perspective, he is revered as a "Father of the Church." Sadly, he also steered Jewish–Christian relations in an unfortunate direction. In several homilies that date from his time as bishop of Antioch, John Chrysostom fulminated against Jews, blaming them for killing the Christian Messiah.

"Do you realize that those who are fasting [among us] have dealings with those who shouted 'Crucify him! Crucify him!' and with those who said 'His blood be on us and on our children'? … Is it not folly for those who worship the crucified [Jesus] to celebrate festivals with those who crucified him? This is not only stupid – it is sheer madness" (*Homily against the Jews* [*Ioudaioi*] 1.5, trans. by R. Wilken, *John Chrysostom and the Jews: Rhetoric and Reality in the Late Fourth Century* [Berkeley: University of California Press, 1983], pp. 125–126). In another homily, John preached against the Jewish people this way: "You did slay Christ [the Messiah], you did lift violent hands against the Master, you did spill his precious blood. This is why you have no chance for atonement, excuse, or defense" (*Homily against the Jews* [*Ioudaioi*] 6.2, trans. by Wilken [1983], p. 126).

John wrote and preached in Greek, but in the later fourth and early fifth centuries CE, Christians heard similar messages in Latin from church leaders, such as Ambrose and Augustine.

One thorny problem in interpreting this oratory or writing is figuring out how best to translate the words being used. Were Greek and Latin writers who used the Greek noun *Ioudaios* (plural, *Ioudaioi*) and Latin noun *Iudaeus* (plural, *Iudaei*) referring to "Jews" or to Christians who were acting too suspiciously Jewish? If it is the latter, the "Jews" in John Chrysostom's homilies would best be translated as "Judaizers." That is, they were Christians who – disappointingly, to John Chrysostom – hadn't adequately parted ways with Jesus' Jewish heritage or with his movement's Jewish roots.

The stakes in this debate are high. At issue is the extent to which many Late Antique Christian intellectuals contributed to the rise of anti-Semitism in medieval Europe and the Middle East. If John Chrysostom was referring to "Judaizers," for example, and not to actual Jewish people, his role in stoking anti-Jewish sentiment might be exonerated. Words like *Ioudaioi* or *Iudaei* would simply have "rhetorical" flair. That is, these references were being deployed in a way that was meant to frighten other Christians, not harm Jews.

Advocates of this position must answer a serious objection. For it is undeniable that this kind of loose rhetoric gradually did shape Christian perceptions of their Jewish neighbors. John Chrysostom's "Messiah-killing" message, even if it was intended to be "rhetorical," came at the same time as many documented instances of Christian violence against Jews.

by a natural disaster. People lived amid its ancient streets until the ninth century CE, when a new, smaller settlement with a new name was founded on the Tiber banks.

Because of its long history of residential occupation, Ostia offers an excellent case study for exploring how daily life in the shadow of Rome stayed the same, gradually changed, or was radically transformed from the empire to Late Antiquity. Thus, even though Minucius Felix is a Christian writer with an evangelizing agenda – to explain why Christianity should be seen as superior to Rome's own traditions – if we read his dialogue alongside Ostia's excavated remains, we can begin to trace the outline of a larger story he left out. For Romans throughout the Mediterranean, life in the third-century city was characterized by worship of the traditional gods, emperor worship, mystery cults, family and household gods, and magic.

Traditional worship

Third-century Ostia was a pastiche of old and new temples, shrines, and sanctuaries, and many of the town's gods had been mainstays of Roman life for centuries. Jupiter, Hercules, Juno, Vulcan, Diana: the Olympian gods and heroes had been important to the civic identity of Ostia since the Roman Republic. A Temple to Jupiter stood in the city's Forum, just as it did in many civic centers throughout cities in Roman North Africa, the Roman East, and Roman Europe. These are the classical cults usually described as "pagan" although this book encourages students to avoid that term, in this context, since it was not used by Romans themselves to describe their own worship practices.

At Ostia, as elsewhere, it's crucial to note that there were local variations in the kinds of worship which people considered "traditional." The cult of the god Vulcan was the most important one at the Roman harbor. Vulcan's priests were responsible for overseeing all repairs to sacred buildings. Not all Roman cities shared Ostia's devotion to the Olympian god of the foundry, metal-working, and fire. Other cities built their civic identity around different gods. The mother-goddess Artemis was worshipped at a temple which counted among the seven wonders of the ancient world at Ephesos. Aphrodite (Rome's god, Venus) was the namesake of the important Late Antique city in Asia Minor called Aphrodisias.

Despite these kinds of regional differences, the signs of "traditional" worship in a Roman town were such that Romans could recognize them wherever they went. Worship of the gods was led by local priests who were called, in Latin, *pontifices* (the singular form is *pontifex*, as seen in the two-word name for the chief of all Rome's priests, the emperor; he was called the *pontifex maximus*). Priests performed their roles at temples and oversaw animal and incense sacrifices at the city's altars, located outside these sacred buildings. For in antiquity, people did not worship inside temples; these buildings housed the cult statue and the donations to the gods. Sacrifices took place outside.

Animal sacrifices themselves were enacted as part of a public meal. This grand feast, which gave both priests and city patrons an opportunity to show off their wealth, strengthened the bonds between the city's residents because it brought many people – of elite and non-elite status alike – together for a common meal. No one was required to recite a creed; no one announced the intricate beliefs of their faith. This strong, civic component of Roman sacrifice explains why Minucius Felix's non-Christian character, Caecilius, makes a passionate defense of traditional cult sites throughout Ostia. "Turn your gaze on the temples and shrines of gods," he reminds his recalcitrant friends in his opening speech. These sacred buildings were the source "by which the commonwealth of Rome is protected and adorned" (Minucius Felix, *Octavius* 7.2, LCL trans. by T. Glover and G. Rendhall [1931]). Sacrifice had functioned this way for hundreds of years prior to the third century.

What the streets of Ostia also show us, however, is that Roman "tradition" could and frequently did evolve and change. In fact, the worship of the gods on behalf of the city was not limited to Olympian deities or its famous heroes like Hercules or Vulcan. In the southern neighborhoods of the town was a large sanctuary dedicated to the goddess Cybele, also known as Magna Mater ("the Great Mother"). The large sanctuary had become an important site in town by the second century CE. The goddess had been brought to Rome four centuries earlier from western Asia Minor during Rome's wars against the menacing general Hannibal of Carthage.

By Minucius Felix's time, the memory of Rome's Hannibalic wars was five hundred years old, but the extent to which the "foreign god" Cybele had gradually been embraced as part of Ostia and Rome's civic identity speaks to the flexible nature of Roman tradition (Minucius Felix, *Octavius* 7.1–3, where Cybele is called the "Idaean Mother" because of her cult's origins at Mt. Ida in Asia Minor). Statues, altars, and other dedications would be erected at Ostia's Sanctuary of Magna Mater from the early empire into the late fourth century CE (*Working With Sources* 5.1: Interpreting the Images on the Parabiago Plate; Figure 5.2). In this way, even though the sanctuary had originally been set aside for the worship of a non-Roman god, the cult of Magna Mater at Ostia illustrates how "non-traditional" worship could gradually become equated with the very nature of being Roman. That is, even in Rome, traditions could change. That process depended on who had the resources to pay for the cults and who had the money to make the worship of the gods visible for the people.

Working With Sources 5.1
Interpreting the Images on the Parabiago Plate

In 1907, workers in Parabiago, northwest of Milan, chanced on a stunning find: a large silver plate, measuring 14.5 inches, shaped like a classical *patera*, or offering dish. Created by pouring silver into a now-lost wax mold, the expensive dish was made sometime during the second half of the fourth century CE and has fascinated historians.

The imagery on the center of plate is relatively straightforward to interpret. The woman riding in the lion-driven chariot is the goddess Cybele. She is seated next to the god Attis, a farm boy who, in myth, fell in love with her. Attis holds a set of pipes, associated with the goat god Pan, and a shepherd's crook. His hat is the same style of floppy headgear Romans associated with the "exotic" east.

Around these figures is a truly operatic scene. Three priests of Cybele, called *corybants*, accompany her chariot, one in the rear and two in front. Above the central figures is the personification of the Sun god, driving his own chariot and led by a representation of the morning star. To the top right is the Moon and the evening star. On the plate's lower half, meanwhile, from left to right, are two water nymphs; a personification of the ocean waters; and a female representing the Earth. Four miniature figures are included to represent the four seasons. Finally, at the far right, Atlas holds up the goddess of Eternity, Aion, surrounded by a band of zodiac signs.

Why was this plate made? Who was Cybele? And what is its significance for understanding how Romans worshipped their gods in the second half of the fourth century CE?

The second question is the easiest to answer. Cybele was the god whom Romans called the Great Mother, *Magna Mater*. They had brought her cult from Phrygia in Asia Minor to Rome during the Second War with Hannibal. After setting up her temple on the Palatine Hill, Romans celebrated festivals to Cybele as one of their city's protectors. These festivals became increasingly elaborate over the course of the late Republic and early Empire. And by the middle of the fourth century CE, according to a Roman calendar produced at the time, Cybele's and Attis' holidays occupied almost a week and a half in March. They lasted from March 15 to March 28. City parades, games, and rituals for those being initiated into Cybele's mysteries were some of its popular aspects.

As for who commissioned the plate, that is no longer known. Questions about how to interpret the plate's social significance also remain open-ended. Some scholars claim that, at the time the plate was made – that is, in the middle to late fourth century CE – the people of the Roman Empire had overwhelmingly begun to embrace Christianity. For researchers who ascribe to these views, the plate speaks to a revival of quaint beliefs that had long ago gone out of fashion.

Given the abundant evidence for temple and statue dedication throughout the third and fourth centuries, however, this view now seems hard to sustain. It does not appear that Romans abandoned their worship of the traditional gods so quickly, and the Parabiago plate may be a sign of this ongoing cultural tradition. It could even have been owned by a fifth-century Christian who used it to show off their fondness for some of the most recognizable aspects of traditional Roman culture.

Mystery cults

The widespread visibility of traditional worship also did not prevent Romans from worshipping other gods. "Mystery cults," dedicated to gods like Demeter, Isis, or Mithras, were some of the most popular. Scholars of the early twentieth century like the historian of religions Franz Cumont once referred to these as "Oriental cults," as if they could be grouped together because they came from the foreign, culturally different "East." But that label is no longer appropriate or even accurate. Coded words like "Oriental" try to make specious distinctions between "Western" customs

Figure 5.2 A silver plate with the Roman goddess Cybele from the city of Parabiago, outside Milan, Italy. It has been dated to the end of the fourth century CE, the time when Nicene Christianity was established as the only legally acceptable faith throughout the Roman Empire. Cybele was a goddess who had been important to the protection of the Roman state for six hundred years, and the traditions associated with worshipping her remained a popular part of many city's festival calendars throughout the fourth century CE. As a product of these highly contentious times, the daring display of non-Christian imagery on this silver plate raises intriguing questions about the faith of its owner, who else would have seen it, and how often it would have been displayed or used. The plate is now in the Museo Archeologico, Milan, Italy. Measurement: diameter 40 cm (c.16 in.). Photo credit: Universal Images Group/Art Resource.

(rational, ordered) and allegedly irrational, overly spiritual, or exotic "Eastern" ones. As we saw in the last chapter, though, the rise of many cults like those of the "Persian" Mithras were highly influenced by Greek, Hellenistic, and Roman customs, making any claims about their "foreign" qualities rather difficult to substantiate. Similar problems arise when trying to apply the label to the mystery cult of Isis, which emerged under the Hellenistic rulers of Egypt, the Ptolemies; or to the mystery cult of Demeter. She was one of the twelve Olympian deities of Greece – hardly "Oriental."

So why did scholars like Franz Cumont try to make these cults seem different? There is one key reason. Contrary to the way that the traditional cults worked, mystery cults demanded that the individuals who participated in them undergo an initiation ceremony. No other traditional, civic cult asked worshippers to take this important step. For that reason alone, initiates into the mysteries were often mocked by their peers for having joined organizations with unknown or "sketchy" morals. Salty rumors of what happened on the other side of these closed-door meetings – like stories of sexual perversion – were consumed with voracious pleasure. If we peer in on one group, however, Mithras' initiates, the realities appear a bit more mundane.

Mithras was worshipped far and wide throughout the Roman Empire. Mithraea have been found along the Danube River and in Germany. One Mithraeum has been excavated at Hawarte, in Roman Syria. At Ostia alone, sixteen meeting spaces have been discovered, by far the largest number known from any one city outside Rome. (The latest was discovered in 2014 in excavations along the ancient seashore.) The archaeology of these spaces gives us an important insight into the worship of the god and the community that participated in the mystery cult.

This archaeological evidence is particularly crucial for historians because textual sources for the worship of Mithras are extremely rare. Many of these meeting halls were built into the first floors of Ostia's apartment complexes or in rooms associated with bath houses, suggesting that a local patron arranged for the donation of the space or the community itself was wealthy enough to purchase the property. It is sometimes claimed that Mithras was a god particularly embraced by soldiers and that, consequently, his cult was only accepted on the fringes of the empire. Unfortunately, these attempts to marginalize the Mithras cult, limiting its appeal among a specific social group, do not account for the widespread, well-funded, urban evidence from Ostia and Rome. However the cult spread, however its membership grew, by the third century CE, Mithras had come to be embraced by many more people than those enlisted in the Roman army.

What did initiates do in the Mithraeum? Mithraic worship involved a ritual banquet, which the archaeological evidence makes clear. Many sites are lined on either side with benches where the initiates would have reclined and eaten. It also is apparent that the initiates likely reclined in a specific order, according to seven "grades," or levels. At Ostia's Mithraeum of Felicissimus, named for the donor, a man named Felicissimus, a third-century CE mosaic floor shows the seven symbols associated with these levels. They are the Raven, Bridegroom, Soldier, Lion, "Persian" (depicted with the stereotypical "Persian" hat), the Sun-Runner, and the Father. Although traditional scholars would claim that each "grade" correlates to a level of higher spiritual knowledge – representing a deeper initiation into the Mithras cult – there is a much less innocuous explanation for them. It is equally plausible that the names represent financial levels for the cult's donors. The highest level, called "Father" (*pater*, in Latin), was the standard term used for many financial patrons, appearing in Latin, Greek, Roman, Christian, and Jewish inscriptions. This evidence should not be taken uncritically to suggest that all of Mithras' worshippers were male, either. Scholars are currently investigating whether there is evidence for women initiates.

In the end, what did Mithras' worshippers believe? How were their beliefs different from the people who followed Rome's traditional cults? These questions are difficult to answer although not for lack of evidence. Many Mithraea, not just at Ostia, preserve traces of a common scene, in either painted or sculpted form. It is the scene depicting "the slaying of the bull," or *tauroctony*, by the god Mithras.

The ubiquity of this scene at Mithraea in Rome, Germany, and in Syria seems to suggest it was an important mythical story, one which Mithras' worshippers cherished – like Christians prize the tales of Jesus' birth in the manger. Yet not even that interpretation is certain.

One scholar of Mithras' cult, Roger Beck, has proposed an interesting theory that the "bull-slaying" scene actually commemorates an important astrological event. In Beck's interpretation, Mithras' slaying the bull is not a sacred story whose biographical details new worshippers were forced to memorize as part of their initiation, the way a Catholic learns the catechism of the church. Mithras' slaying the bull, rather, was one way of personalizing the movement of constellations and of showing the triumph of the "Unconquered Sun," as Mithras is frequently called – an astrological event around which the initiates built their own sense of community.

Emperor worship

Even though Ostia is filled with examples of Mithraea, Minucius Felix doesn't mention Mithras' worshippers in his dialogue. That's one reason to be suspicious of using this Christian text to try to reconstruct how all Romans worshipped in the third century. Text and archaeology need to be read side-by-side to be historically and mutually informative. There were other ways of creating community in the Roman world which Minucius Felix doesn't mention, either. The worship of the divine Roman emperor was one of the most important.

Since the time of Julius Caesar's death in 44 BCE, Romans had been familiar with a cult to the Deified Julius (*Divus Iulius*). Caesar's heir, Octavian Augustus, would famously promote the cult of the Deified Caesar – with its own temple, priest, and altar. Later, upon Augustus' death, the practice of honoring successful leaders by worshipping them as gods continued. Over the course of the first and second centuries CE, well-regarded rulers like Augustus, Trajan, and Hadrian were granted the title *divi*, "divine." Many were given temples in Rome and throughout the empire. At times, these honors conformed to local practice, such as the Greek custom of calling the emperor *theos* (the Greek word meaning "God") or using the Latin term *deus* (also meaning "God," as opposed to *divus*, meaning "Divine"). Coins and inscriptions from across the Mediterranean show a variety of terms at various times and various places. The provincial priests of the imperial cult were called *flamines* (the Latin singular is *flamen*). Municipal or local town priests of the emperors' cult were called *sacerdotes* (*sacerdos*, in the singular).

The majesty of emperor worship can be observed at Ostia in the form of a monumental domed building that once stood in the city center. It has been dated to the early third century CE. This building, called today the "Round Temple," once housed colossal portraits of several third-century rulers. Although the remains are bare brick and mortar, we can get a better picture of what may have taken place here if we journey far across the Mediterranean. In the Syrian city of Dura Europos, a well-preserved wall painting shows local citizens and Roman soldiers participating in an incense sacrifice in front of statues of the Roman emperors. Their performance of a cult act for the emperors probably looked very similar to the way people would have honored the Roman emperors at Ostia's "Round Temple."

Dedications and honors for the imperial family were a common feature of local cities by the third century, not just at Ostia. One inscription from the city of Volubilis in Roman Morocco tells us about an important local woman, Flavia Germanilla, who served as an imperial cult priest in the early third century. The inscription calls Flavia a "flaminica provinciae," provincial priestess of the imperial cult (*AE* 1921, no. 19). A sculptural relief from Italy, now in Copenhagen, also shows a third-century Roman woman acting in a highly visible civic capacity. She is shown on an altar in the traditional Roman act of *pietas*, covering her head in order to partake in the sacrifice of a bull (Ny Carlsberg Glyptotek inv. 858).

What can we take away from these scenes of imperial cult participation in the third century, then, and deduce about the cult of the emperors more broadly? The first key point is to recognize that, from its first appearance in Italy in 44 BCE to the time that Flavia Germanilla was appointed provincial priestess at Volubilis, the system was never regulated by either the Senate or the emperors themselves from the central authority of Rome. By contrast, a *laissez faire* approach was common, ensuring that local communities had a degree of flexibility in how – or even whether – they wanted to participate in honoring the imperial family. Second, the precise, "divine status" of specific emperors was never pre-determined in this system. Local communities could choose to worship a *deus*, a *divus*, or a *theos* and then debate the distinctions. Lastly, the leadership of the cult in local cities could include both men and women.

Summary

Roman worship involved many facets: traditional gods, who were constantly changing; the mystery cults, which provided a more intimate sense of community for their initiates; and emperor worship, which bound the empire's center and its periphery together by promoting a set of shared values. There were still other ways Romans worshipped their gods: at home, where ancestral deities were important; or by practicing curses and magic, two avenues of communicating with the divine forces which the authorities did not condone. Magic itself was banned.

The short-lived third-century emperor Decius tried to navigate this complicated social world. He did so against the backdrop of an expanding body of Roman citizens, which Caracalla had brought into the empire. Christian writers like Minucius Felix or Eusebius can be colorful companions for looking in on this third-century political landscape; but ultimately, their voices prove to be much more limiting than they might first appear. Later rulers would engineer their own strategies for unifying the empire. Some of these policies would soon prove disastrous to the civic fabric of Rome.

Study Questions

1. In Roman cities, who were the *flamines*?
2. Describe a picture of what daily life was like in a third-century city. Fill it with as many different people as you can.
3. Did Emperor Decius persecute Christians?
4. Can historians assume that all Christian apologetic writing (*apologia* is an effort to "make a defense of the faith") was intended to convert non-Christians? Provide evidence to support your conclusions.

Suggested Readings

Jan Bremmer, *Initiation into the Mysteries of the Ancient World* (Berlin: De Gruyter, 2014).

Emily Hemelrijk, *Hidden Lives, Public Personae: Women and Civic Life in the Roman West* (New York: Oxford University Press, 2015).

Jörg Rüpke, *From Jupiter to Christ: On the History of Religion in the Roman Imperial Period*, translated by D. Richardson (New York: Oxford University Press, 2014).

Michele Salzman, Marianne Sághy, and Ritta Lizzi Testa (eds.), *Pagans and Christians in Late Antique Rome* (New York: Cambridge University Press, 2015).

6
Social Change

Decius' call for civic sacrifice caused an uproar among certain Christian individuals and communities who felt they were being "persecuted" for their beliefs. Ancient church historians like Eusebius and modern church historians, like the acclaimed twentieth-century scholar Henry Chadwick, chose to write history from their vantage. In *The Early Church* Chadwick described Decius' policy as "a systematic persecution" and "a deliberate attempt to catch people" (London: Penguin, 1993, p. 188). As we saw from evidence in the last chapter, Decius' policy was much more open-ended. There is no evidence to suggest the emperor maliciously designed it to entrap citizens.

Nevertheless, by the second half of the third century CE, two of Decius' successors – Emperor Valerian (r. 253–260) and Emperor Diocletian (r. 284–305) – would begin to force Christians, by law, to participate in civic events. These decrees did specifically target Rome's Christian community. They are the first and only historical instances in which the Roman government deliberately and with malice used the legal mechanisms of the state to discriminate against Jesus' followers.

Only in the most general terms can the policies of Valerian and Diocletian be seen as an attempt to unify Rome's cities. For at their heart, by explicitly identifying one minority group as the source of the empire's larger social problems, these laws stained Rome's long-standing tradition of pluralism. This pluralism had, at times, been granted begrudgingly by Romans who feared the makeup of their changing cities, the foreign identity of merchants, or the advancement of non-Roman groups. Yet for centuries, this system had worked, inspiring forms of civic participation that had allowed foreigners, initiates of mystery cults, even followers of an alleged *superstitio* – like Jews – to find their home in the empire. By the third century, in particular, many Jews had begun to build synagogues with the help of wealthy donors and patrons. From Ostia, where a dedication records the creation of a Torah

A Social and Cultural History of Late Antiquity, First Edition. Douglas Boin.
© 2018 John Wiley & Sons, Inc. Published 2018 by John Wiley & Sons, Inc.

Shrine "on behalf of the Roman Emperors," to Dura Europos in Roman Syria, where Jews transformed a house into a worship space with colorful paintings, third-century Rome witnessed an exciting rise in the visibility of many groups that otherwise are unattested in the archaeological record for previous centuries. To tell the history of the third century as one of widespread decline overlooks these smaller but no less important triumphs.

After a century that had seen emperors attempt to keep Roman society from fracturing, however, and against the backdrop of a state that was hemorrhaging leaders, Emperors Valerian and Diocletian had resorted to extreme steps to persuade the Christian population to join in the enterprise of being Roman. In doing so, they doubled down on the worst of many Romans' cultural fears: by crafting legislation to punish Christians specifically for their beliefs. These laws were disastrous for the empire's morale. They also succeeded in driving a wedge between the empire's Christian communities who were, just as they had been from their first generation, divided amongst themselves about how to live in the Roman Empire. This Christian "identity baggage" would only grow more pronounced throughout the fourth century CE and, later, change many Roman towns.

To understand how and why these changes happened, we need to conclude our narrative of the third century with close-up attention to events at the top of society combined with a wide-angle view of what was happening at the bottom.

6.1   Rome's Laws Against Christians

Emperor Valerian, 257–258 CE

Textual sources suggest that Emperor Valerian issued two decrees against Christians. The first, announced in 257 CE, is known from a third-century Christian account modeled on contemporary trial records, the *Proconsular Judicial Proceedings*. According to this Latin text, Valerian ordered everyone in cities throughout the empire who did not recognize "the worship practice [*religio*] of the Roman people ... to acknowledge Roman rituals" (*Acta Proconsularia* 1.1, trans. by H. Musurillo, *Acts of the Christian Martyrs* [Oxford, 1972]). Based on its imprecise language, this decree appears consistent with Decius' own policy and would not, therefore, have posed an existential problem for all of the empire's Christians – unless they specifically chose to claim a special social status.

In 258 CE, however, Valerian's hostility grew more pronounced. A second decree, known from a Christian source, describes the emperor's revised edict in this way. According to the writer, Valerian now decreed that:

> [B]ishops, presbyters, and deacons should immediately be punished; [and] that [Christian] senators, men of importance, and Roman knights should both lose their dignity and, moreover, be deprived of their property. Furthermore, if, when their means were taken away, these people should persist in identifying as "Christians," then they should also lose their heads. Wealthy women should be deprived of their property and sent into banishment. Finally, Christians in the imperial household ...

should have their property confiscated and should be sent in chains by assignment to Caesar's estates. (Cyprian, *Letter* 81.1, trans. by R. Wallis in the series *ANF*, slightly modified [1886])

This legislation, directed specifically at the Christian hierarchy, as well as financially well-connected Romans, both male and female, must have had a profoundly disruptive effect on the Christian community. Unlike the decree of the previous year, which gave some latitude to Christians to make their own choices about sacrifice, now Christians had no legal recourse or room for creative manoeuvring. Their institutional structure was under assault, as was their donor class.

The situation ended thanks to Sasanian Persia. When Sapur I captured Emperor Valerian in 260 CE, the emperor's discriminatory policy was no longer enforced. Christians must have been joyous. Later, by the early fourth century, they were passing down stories that Valerian's capture had been divine punishment for his ill-conceived campaign against Christians (Lactantius, *On the Death of the Persecutors* 5).

Christian sacrifice in context on the eve of the Rule of Four

In the long history of Christians living in the Roman Empire up until the third century, Valerian's laws stand out as an aberration, but they can often distract scholars from seeing the broader picture. Throughout the empire's cities, many intensely personal dramas were playing out both before and after the political programs of Decius and Valerian as Christians were making complicated decisions about whether to participate or not in Rome's civic sacrifices. Many chose to do so for a variety of reasons, including, perhaps, the need for the approval of their family, friends, and clergy.

Some likely weighed the potential for personal and political advancement. When the government turned against them, in 258 CE, the range of emotions among them – especially among Christians who worked "in the imperial household" (a fact we just learned) – must have run the gamut: from betrayal to resignation to disappointment with their political leadership. One Christian writer working in the early to middle third century CE, Origen of Alexandria, gives us some sense of the panicked conversations that must have been filling the taverns and laundry mats and markets during this turbulent time.

Origen (b. *c.*185–d. *c.*255 CE) reports on a conversation he had with a non-Christian, a man named Celsus, who expressed skepticism that Christians could ever really be good citizens of the empire. "To this [assertion]," Origen explained to his Christian readers, "our answer is":

[W]e do give divine help to the emperors, if I may say, by putting on the whole armor of God when occasion requires. And this we do in obedience to the injunction of the apostle [who said]: "I exhort you, therefore, that first of all, supplications, prayers, intercessions, and thanksgiving be made for all men, for emperors, and for all who are in authority" [quoting 1 Timothy 2.1–2]. (Origen, *Against Celsus* 8.73, trans. by F. Crombie in the series *ANF* [1885], slightly modified)

The fact that a third-century Christian like Origen could appeal to "Paul," "the apostle," ("1 Timothy") to support his argument that Christians were not a threat to the empire shows the malleability of Christian tradition in the hands of Late Antique thinkers. It conforms, too, with the broader picture we can piece together from material culture, such as at the excavations at Dura Europos, Syria, where a well-integrated Christian home-owner succeeded in renovating his house – turning it into a Christian worship space – without neighbors handing him over to the authorities. This Christian church, the earliest worship space ever excavated in a Roman city, dates to the decades prior to 256 CE before a Sasanian army destroyed the town. The construction of the church in the age before Valerian suggests that not all Christians in the third century feared either being seen or heard in their local towns.

It is indisputable, of course, that other members of the Christian faith stood up and stood out during this same time as loud champions of resistance. These Christians did so by suggesting that to call oneself a "Christian" required a non-negotiable commitment to blood and martyrdom. Cyprian, the bishop of Carthage, advocated exactly that position by appealing to the language of militancy, arguing that Christians everywhere were required to act as "God's soldiers" (*Letter* 8). The Roman government may have tried to punish Christians or even torture them, Cyprian wrote, but it was Christian blood which was the real "spectacle ... to the Lord. How sublime, how great, how acceptable to the eyes of God," he claimed, "[was] the allegiance and devotion of His soldiers" when they stood up and opposed the Roman state (Cyprian, *Letter* 8, trans. by R. Wallis in the series *ANF* [1886]).

Bishop Cyprian's words are similar to those of an earlier third-century writer, Tertullian, who claimed that "the blood of the martyrs" was the "seed" that led to the demographic growth of the church (Tertullian, *Apologeticus* 50). This imagery also would have harmonized, to many Christians, with the words of the writer of Revelation, who – in a cosmic drama fought by angels and demons – framed "Rome" as a corrupt, decadent, and depraved new "Babylon" (Revelation 17.5). That was a gloomy tune the writer of the text called 1 Peter had sung, as well (1 Peter 5.13). All these texts may have taught Christians to see a value in cultural separation. And yet they are not the whole story of early Christianity, either.

In the records of a church meeting at Elvira, in Roman Spain, c. 305–306, the hierarchy turned its attention to several challenges facing Roman Christians on the Iberian peninsula. The obsessive list of complaints which they drew up in Latin, which survives as the *Canons of the Council of Elvira*, is a quizzical look at what church leaders feared at the turn of the fourth century. "Persecution" was decidedly not one of them. Among the first five recommendations which the council passed, three addressed the status of Christian *flamines* – priests of the local imperial cult – who were also active members of the Christian community. These canons, or "rules," were designed to limit Christian participation in this important public office. The mere fact that the church leadership had to articulate these rules suggests the ease with which many Christians fulfilled their high-profile duties as Roman politicians, even before Christianity was officially legalized.

There is no reason for historians to try to blur, collapse, or artificially harmonize this conflicting evidence. In the third century and the early fourth century, just as in the first and second centuries, Christians did not see eye-to-eye with their own peers on how to participate in Roman city life. Whether Rome's emperors ever recognized this fact is entirely unclear. What is clear is that by 303 CE, the policy drafted in the palace would be the most discriminatory against Christians yet.

6.2   The End of the Third Century and the Rise of the Rule of Four

By the 280s, Rome's empire had weathered a tempestuous century, militarily, politically, and economically. Gaius Valerius Diocles, a soldier from the city of Salona in Roman Croatia (b. 244–d. 312 CE), engineered the foundations of a new stable state. After being proclaimed emperor by his troops in 284 CE, Diocles began a dedicated campaign to keep the empire from slipping back into civil war and military and political turmoil.

It was a challenging task for anyone, let alone a man from the provinces whom one fourth-century writer reports was the son of a freed slave. In fact, perhaps because of the stigma Diocles felt as an outsider, he soon adopted a more stereotypically Roman – which is to say, Latin-sounding – version of his name: Diocletian. (For these details, we can thank the fourth-century Latin writer Aurelius Victor [*On the Emperors*] 39.1.)

Diocletian's vision ensured that the fifty years of political turnover in the palace soon came to an end. Immediate rivals were quickly eliminated. By 293 CE, a form of power-sharing was instituted among senior-level leaders and junior counterparts. This new constitutional system, in which two senior "Augustuses" (Latin plural, *Augusti*) oversaw the political formation of two junior "Caesars" (Latin plural, *Caesares*), may have helped Diocletian identify future, capable administrators and bring them into the governmental system without risk of civil war or overt political conflict. This Tetrarchy, or "Rule of Four," was implemented across the empire, with the Augusti and Caesares residing in capitals in the eastern and western provinces. Trier in Roman Germany, Antioch in Roman Syria, Nicomedia in Roman Turkey, and Thessaloniki in Roman Greece all emerged as important government centers during the administration of the Tetrarchs. (*Exploring Culture* 6.1: The Many Lives of Rome's "Colosseum.")

Exploring Culture 6.1   *The Many Lives of Rome's Colosseum*

In 70 CE, the Emperor Titus marched a Roman army into Jerusalem. By year's end, the Second Temple would be in ruins. When the war ended, in 74, the province of Judaea would be punished; Jewish prisoners would be paraded through Rome; and the state's finances would be replenished with the spoils of war. Flush with new money, the Flavian family would build an amphitheater that would henceforth define the look of Rome.

Since the Middle Ages, this building has been called the Colosseum, a name taken from its proximity to a "colossal" statue (Cassius Dio, *Roman History* 65.15).

Although it was long suspected that spoils of the Jewish war had been used to fund its construction, within the last twenty years, a study of one Late Antique inscription has cautiously confirmed that assertion. The inscription is an example of the care which later city prefects of Rome lavished on this dear monument. This fragmentary Late Antique text reads:

> During the reign of our two emperors, Theodosius and Placidus Valentianus, Rufius Caecina Felix Lampadius, a most distinguished and [illustrious prefect of the city repaired] the sand-floor (in Latin, *harena*) of the Flavian amphitheater along with its imperial box … and doors but also the stadium seating. (*CIL* 6.32086)

Based on the identity of the ruling emperors and the city prefect named here, historians have dated these repairs to 443–444 CE. The stone itself, conspicuously pockmarked with holes, hides traces of another time, too.

Bronze letters, likely dating from Flavian era, were originally fixed into these holes. According to one professional, this earlier text, included the telling Latin phrase "ex manubiis," a standard formula used to commemorate dedications made "from the spoils of war."

Four hundred years later, when the memories of that Jewish war were distant Roman history (for some), the Flavian Amphitheater would still be standing. It would also continue to lure Romans eager for blood sport, animal or human. Christians and Jews counted among the spectators who filled its seats.

For centuries, emperors and populace had flocked here to be entertained, and the stadium had been frequently repaired. In 230 CE, Alexander Severus allegedly taxed pimps and prostitutes to raise revenue for restoring it (*SHA*, Severus Alexander 24.3). A century later, in 357, Constantius II marveled at the amphitheater's "huge bulk, strengthened by its framework of travertine, to whose top human eyesight barely ascends" (Ammianus Marcellinus, *Roman History* 16.10.4, LCL trans. by Rolfe). Almost one hundred and fifty years after him, yet another official – a Roman consul – would pay "at his own expense" to repair "the arena and the podium around the arena after they were destroyed by a terrible earthquake" (*CIL* 6.32094). That last repair dates to 508 CE.

Gladiatorial combat had long been banned by this time. In 404 CE, the Emperor Honorius had stopped these grizzly matches (Theodore, *Church History* 5.26). Animal hunts had continued.

Only in the eighth century was the building stripped of its entertainment function. In fact, new excavations in the twenty-first century are revealing that the Colosseum's corridors and arena were transformed into housing during the early medieval period. By the Renaissance, the travertine was being carted away for other projects.

For the citizens of the late third-century empire, who watched the profile of these cities grow, the new attention must have made a powerful statement: The Tetrarchs were investing in the future of Rome, the stability of its government, and the security of its people. We should look at the building program in one of these cities.

6.3   A View from Thessaloniki, Roman Greece, Late Third Century CE

Thessaloniki was a city of tradesmen and guilds strategically located on the Via Egnatia, the east–west road that helped travelers cross from Europe to Asia Minor (and vice versa). Because the city was so well integrated into the empire's roads, for example, it is, perhaps not surprisingly, the first city from which we have any written evidence for Paul, one of Jesus' first followers who stopped here in the late 40s and early 50s CE on his way south to Athens and Corinth. Three centuries later, the junior "Caesar" of the eastern empire, Galerius, set up his imperial residence here. Galerius ruled as "Caesar" from 293–305 CE and was promoted to Augustus in 305. He held that senior title until his death in 311.

Galerius' urban investments

With Diocletian's help, Galerius began a new building program in the city. It included a race track. (The Greek-derived word for "race track" is a hippodrome; the Latin-derived word, "circus." Galerius' entertainment structure can be referred to with either term.) Galerius and Diocletian also paid for the construction of a new palace, as well as a mausoleum, or monumental tomb, that was supposed to be the final resting place of Galerius and his family. Thessaloniki's palace had many of the amenities an emperor would have found on the Palatine Hill in Rome: secluded courtyards for whispered meetings, audience halls to host public receptions, dining rooms to entertain clients. There were also comfortable living quarters. These details are known from careful study of the remains of Galerius' palace, which exists today as a mass of truncated brick walls.

Archaeologists still don't have the complete picture of Galerius' palace, but one of its most lasting features, its main entryway, is still standing. This large monument is a four-sided arch, erected at the intersection of two roads. It originally stood at the very crossroads of the Via Egnatia, the entry to Galerius' palace, and the path to the emperor's mausoleum; Galerius had picked prime real estate for his residence. The Arch of Galerius, as it is called, is for historians one of the most important pieces of material culture from the period of the "Rule of Four." For everyone coming into and out of Thessaloniki would have seen it. It communicated the impressive reach of Galerius' authority (Figure 6.1).

The political messages of Galerius' arch and palace vestibule

Unfortunately, the arch is only partially preserved, but several of its sculptural reliefs are still in place on the northwest and southwest piers. These panels celebrated the Tetrarch's deeds and accomplishments and depicted selected events from Galerius' life, such as his military victory over the Sasanian Persians and the peace treaty he

Figure 6.1 This view of the city of Thessaloniki, Greece, looking northeast, shows two important Late Antique monuments: the arch and the rotunda built by the Roman ruler Galerius. The Arch of Galerius, *c.*298–303, commemorated the Roman Empire's recent victories over the Persians. It crossed one of the most important Roman roads in Thessaloniki, the Via Egnatia, which led to the Black Sea and onward to Asia Minor. The arch also formed part of the vestibule, or entrance way, for Galerius' palace. In the distance is the rotunda, or round building, which was likely planned as Galerius' mausoleum. After being promoted from the rank of Caesar to Augustus in 305 CE, he would rule for six years but was eventually buried in modern Serbia, rendering the rotunda a vacant imperial property. By the fifth or sixth century CE, it would be transformed into a church for Saint George, called Agios Georgios in Greek. Photo credit: © Pete Titmuss/Alamy Stock Photo.

signed with them in 298 CE. As a whole, the panels speak to the Tetrarchs' commitment to the social cohesiveness of the empire.

Each scene was divided into registers, or panels. One shows Galerius on a magistrate's chair. In it, dignitaries come to him as supplicants, offering prayers and honors on his behalf. Another shows the emperor in a *paludamentum*, the popular military cloak of the third-century rulers (such as Valerian wears in the Persian cameo [Figure 4.4]). Galerius himself is protected by foreign bodyguards at his side – their hairstyle has been taken to signify their idenity as "German" – and the emperor is shown welcoming a foreign embassy (Figure 6.2). Sasanian ambassadors kneel before the emperor. This reverential act was called a *proskynesis* from the Greek verb *proskuneo* [προσκυνέω], meaning "to kneel down in an act of worship."

Figure 6.2 A close-up view of three sculpted scenes from the Arch of Galerius at Thessaloniki, Greece (c.298–303). In the top panel, which art historians call a register, Caesar Galerius addresses his troops and is surrounded by foreign bodyguards, who are distinguished by their non-Roman dress. In the middle register, Galerius receives an embassy of Sasanians, whom he has just conquered; the three Persian men kneel before the Roman ruler to recognize his power and authority. In the lower register, a traditional Roman sacrifice is taking place. The arcade, at right, acts as an urban backdrop, showing how the sacrifice brought leading figures of the town together to give thanks for Galerius' victory. Some attendees wear togas with their heads covered as a sign of Roman piety. Galerius, in his military uniform, stands at center and offers incense at the altar. Photo credit: © Danita Delimont/Alamy Stock Photo.

By Late Antiquity, "obeisance" to the ruler was a regular political display. In the third century BCE, while traveling and fighting in Persia, the accomplished Macedonian general Alexander the Great had seen it performed by Persians, who used it to show deference to their ruler, treating him in a divine way. In accounts of his campaigns, Alexander and his advisors argued over whether such an act of godly deference towards another human being might be appropriate for Alexander himself (Arrian, *Campaigns of Alexander* [*Anabasis*] 4.10–12). The idea was scuttled as being too scandalously strange for Alexander's subjects, too culturally tainted by its Persian origins. Centuries later, as the Arch of Galerius shows, this form of ancient Persian honor had become a widely recognizable aspect of Rome's imperial cult.

Whether the Roman citizens of Thessaloniki cared about the Persian origins of "proskynesis" during a time of Roman–Persian conflict is uncertain, but by the time of the "Rule of Four," Romans were regularly using a Persian practice as part of their own repertoire for worshipping the Roman emperor. A ritual which had its roots in fifth-century BCE Persia was now being used by the Sasanian's own rivals to emphasize the glory and divine grandeur of their own ruler. Regardless of the irony, the public advertisement of Galerius' triumphs on the arch must have been a welcome message for the people of Thessaloniki. Like many others throughout the Roman world, they may have heard horror stories of recent emperors captured or killed in battle on the banks of the Tigris and Euphrates. The arch was a sign that Rome's greatness had returned.

Other scenes on the arch announced important changes, such as the new constitutional system of the empire and the order that Diocletian had brought to the state. In another panel, the two ruling senior emperors, Diocletian and his colleague Maximian, are enthroned atop the personification of the Heavens, the Roman god *Caelus*; and a personification of the Known World, known in Greek as the *Oikoumene*, the root of our word *economy*. This visual arrangement – of having the emperors buttressed by the heavens and the personification of the universe – promoted a powerful ideology: that the two senior Tetrarchs were "rulers of the known world." That is, they were, in the language of the day, *cosmocratores* (from the Greek words *cosmos*, meaning "universe," and κρατέω [*krateo*], meaning "to rule").

Two junior partners, Constantius Chlorus and Galerius, were seated at the sides of this pair of chief executives. They are surrounded by several deities from Mt. Olympus, the home of the traditional gods. In all, the panels' message reinforces the divine source of the emperors' power. Two additional figures are also present on the arch. They are each winged, female figures who represent the divine idea of *Victory* (*Victoria* is the goddess's name in Latin; in Greek, she is called *Nikē* and was an important local goddess, incorporated into the name of Thessaloniki itself).

In sum, Galerius' building projects at Thessaloniki – at a major intersection promoting the imperial house and located on a main road which united the empire – communicated, like a billboard, the stability of the new government. The scenes from the palace's vestibule, or arch, are also particularly significant for recognizing how the members of the "Rule of Four" promoted their diplomatic and military relationship with Sasanian Persia. New imperial capital cities like Thessaloniki, then, were not tangential to the story of later Rome. At the end of the third century CE, they witnessed first-hand new, important developments and stepped proudly before the townspeople as a herald announcing the strength of Rome's empire (*Key Debates* 6.1: Catastrophe or Continuity? Or a False Choice?; Figure 6.3).

Key Debates 6.1 *Catastrophe or Continuity? Or a False Choice?*

Athens. Site of Pericles' Parthenon, economic powerhouse in the classical era, a city-state governed by the rule of its free male citizens ("democracy"), the home of a creative community where many poets and playwrights won lasting fame. Athens is usually thought of as a classical city, but it is also a Late Antique one whose fortunes raise many questions about urban life in the later Roman Empire.

From the classical to Hellenistic to Roman periods, the agora was one of the most vibrant parts of the city. By the second century CE, almost every square foot of this roughly triangular plot of land, located just beneath the Acropolis, was crammed with temples, altars, fountain houses, meeting halls, a library, an indoor concert venue (the *odeion*, built by the Roman general Agrippa), and several covered porticoes, called stoas. City life pulsed as people flowed through its streets.

What happened to Athens' beating heart in Late Antiquity? Tackling that question involves more than collecting the evidence from this one city. It means wading into a debate that has traditionally divided scholars into two ideological camps.

One side believes that, in Late Antique cities, catastrophe reigned. With the political disintegration of the Roman Empire in 476 CE, the benefits of urban living declined precipitously throughout the Mediterranean. As a result, city life became markedly worse than it had been in earlier periods. Countering this view are a group of scholars who maintain that the feel of city life remained vibrant and appealing, in both the eastern and western Mediterranean.

As textual and archaeological material from Athens shows, however, it's hard to shoehorn the historical evidence into these kinds of rigid ideological frameworks. In the excavated material, there are signs of obvious economic change. Beginning sometime in the third century CE, the market for a major Athenian export – carved marble sarcophagi, used for entombing the dead – severely contracted. There are also clear instances of archaeological destruction. In 267 CE, Germanic invaders, named the Heruli, attacked the city. They burned many buildings, and excavators have found the charred remains of this conflagration in Athens' agora.

What excavations have also revealed is that this attack did not lead to the end of Athens' rich urban life. In the second half of the third century, a new city wall was erected, extending from the Acropolis. For reasons unknown, the area of the agora – which had been included inside the boundary of Athens ever since the fifth century BCE – was now left out of this new protection. In fact, many of the building blocks in the new city wall were harvested from the agora's old buildings.

These signs of architectural cannibalization are easy fodder for historians who wish to find societal gloom in the material evidence, but the picture from Athens is more complex still.

By the fourth century, other regions of the city were thriving, as expensive houses were being built high above the old agora. A hundred years later, after Athens had weathered another attack, the situation changed again. In the center of the agora, around 400 CE, arose a large villa, which may have been the residence of a key government official. Some smaller houses nearby, like one on the Areopagus, would thrive until the late sixth century. Only at the turn of the seventh century – around the time of a Slavic invasion in 582 CE – do archaeologists find traces of abandonment and squatting in previously important neighborhoods.

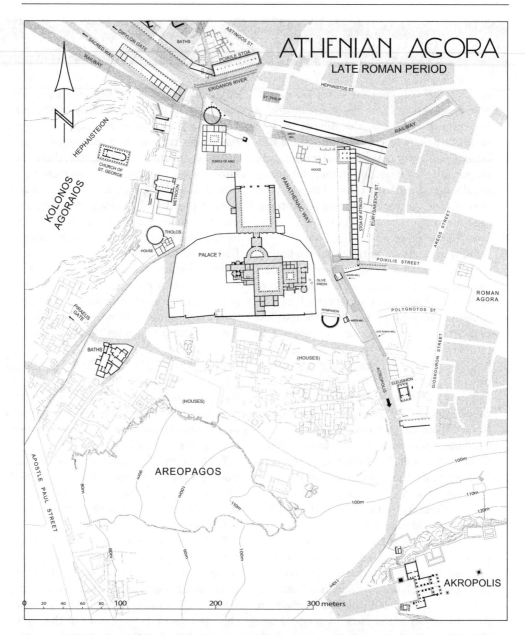

Figure 6.3 A plan of the old agora, or market center, of Athens, Greece, c.400–700 CE. For centuries, its stoas (shaded porticos), temples, shrines, fountains, and wells had seen countless lively characters walk in their midst, from philosophers like Socrates to anonymous wives and daughters of Athenian families out for a day's chores. Even under Rome, emperors and citizens continued to live in the shadow of Pericles' Parthenon and Athens' historic monuments. That story began to change in the middle of the third century CE. When a tribe of foreigners, the Heruli, attacked Athens c.267 CE, the Romans of Athens decided to build a new set of defenses. These walls can be seen on this plan to the east and southeast of the old agora. They were built along the road to the Acropolis, site of the city's precious Temple of Athena, and even incorporated older monuments in the agora, like the Stoa of Attalos. The central area of the old agora would be excluded from the much smaller walled city at this time. Plan courtesy of John Camp, *The Athenian Agora: Excavations in the Heart of Classical Athens* (London: Thames and Hudson, 1998), p. 199 with author's modifications.

6.4 Diocletian's Edict against Followers of Mani, 296 CE or 302 CE

While military campaigns continued on the borders, particularly against the Sasanian state, the maintenance of traditional worship, incorporating animal and incense sacrifice for Rome's gods, including the deified emperors, was seen as the best strategy for promoting cultural cohesion and articulating shared Roman values. The Arch of Galerius draws attention to this point, as the sculptural panels show several scenes of Romans partaking in incense sacrifice at public altars. Diocletian himself was not content to leave civic sacrifices to the whim of the Roman people, however. Like Decius, he too would summon the apparatus of the state to enforce participation. And like Valerian, he would address his decrees to two specific communities whom he felt needed to be policed: the followers of Mani, on the one hand, and the followers of Jesus, on the other.

Mani (b. 216–c.275) was born in Parthia, became a follower of Jesus, and later founded his own prophetic movement. It was at once dualistic yet largely pessimistic about the material world and human bodies. Mani was executed by the Zoroastrian Sasanian state for his teachings.

Much of what historians know about his life can be reconstructed from an extraordinary artifact: "a lump of parchment fragments the size of a matchbox" ("Cologne Mani Codex," *EI* vol. 6.1, pp. 43–46) which contains, in Greek, a fifth-century CE biography of the prophet. The text, written in 1 mm high letters, tells of Mani's calling; how he "was led astray in this disgusting flesh," a detail that refers to his negative view of the human body; and how he was given visions of "boundless heights and the fathomless depths" of his soul's existence (translations of the Cologne Mani Codex from A. D. Lee, *Pagans and Christians in Late Antiquity* [London: Routledge, 2000], pp. 176–177). A second document, written in Coptic, gives more detail about Mani's worldview. "This whole world stands firm for a season, here ... So soon as that builder will finish,/the whole world will be dissolved and set on fire..." (excerpts from *The Manichaean Psalmbook*, Psalm 223, trans. in Lee [2000], pp. 178–179). This text also helps us see that Mani saw creation as a battle between forces of Good and Evil, Light and Darkness. In this unending battle, learning to become aware of the properties in matter – such as how many particles of light may have been contained in plants and other foods – was a vital step for measuring one's success against the demonic cosmic forces. Foods with more light particles steeled the believer against them. Based on the teachings contained in both these documents, it is extremely likely that Mani's followers would have harbored a strong apocalyptic worldview.

What the evidence does not support is the notion that Mani consciously or deliberately founded a separate "religion" called "Manichaeanism." On this point, the evidence would suggest that Mani considered himself to be a believer in Jesus. He was someone who borrowed freely from Christian, Jewish, and Zoroastrian ideas; and he was a creative thinker who transformed these ideas into a community of like-minded believers. It won a wide following.

After Mani's death, his teachings spread to Asia. By 296 CE or 302 CE, they had come to the Roman Empire. We know because at that time the Emperor Diocletian issued a decree categorizing Mani's followers as adherents of a *superstitio*. Furthermore, although Mani had been executed by a Persian king, the prophet's teachings were now spoken of by the Roman government as if they were culturally equivalent to the "accursed customs and perverse laws of the Persians" (*Comparison of Mosaic and Roman Law* 15.3, trans. in N. Lewis and M. Reinhold, *Roman Civilization* 2 [1990], pp. 548–550). Did Emperor Diocletian believe that Mani's followers were secretly transmitting Sasanian values into the heart of his empire? We cannot say for sure, but looking at this period from the ground-up, we do get a different perspective.

In Solona in Roman Dalmatia (modern Croatia), a tombstone with a Greek inscription records the burial of a woman named Bassa. She was a young girl, a virgin, and a native of Lydia in Asia Minor who died in the late third or early fourth century CE, probably around the time that Diocletian was issuing his decree. On Bassa's tomb, she was specifically remembered as a member of a "Manichaean" community (*Texte zum Manichäismus* [*Texts for the Study of Manichaeanism*], ed. by A. Adam [Berlin, 1954], no. 67). We should try to imagine her reaction to the world of Diocletian's anti-Manichaean policy. To her, Diocletian's conviction that he could use the power of the state to unite the Roman people would not have been an abstract political campaign. It was a plan that would have directly affected her life and the lives of other real citizens, at least one of whom, Bassa, died in the very city where Diocletian had been born.

6.5   The Rise of Christianity: Assumptions and Starting Points

By 303 CE, a similar set of legal proscriptions would be enacted against Christians. The story of Diocletian's persecution, its repeal, and the rewriting of the constitution to include a legally recognized place for Christian worship is one that will be taken up in the next chapter on law and politics. Before we do so, we should conclude this chapter by looking carefully at three assumptions that have driven research on the rise of Christianity in the Roman Empire.

"Christianization" and evangelization

Much work on Late Antiquity involves investigations into what historians have traditionally called the "Christianization" of Rome's cities. This shorthand is used to describe how Christians changed urban life and Roman society over the course of the third and fourth centuries CE after their community was granted legal status. As an umbrella term for cultural change, however, "Christianization" carries too much baggage to be useful.

For one, it is too imprecise. Sometimes scholars have used "Christianization" when the phenomenon they are really interested in describing is the spread of the Christian message, a phenomenon more properly called "evangelization." Second, even when historians qualify their use of it in a broader sense – to refer generically to the spread of Christian ideas, imagery, and laws – the use of the term still places researchers "inside the ring" during the middle of an important fight. Since the founding of the movement in the first century CE, many followers of Jesus had adapted perfectly well to life in their local Roman cities and had accommodated their worship and beliefs to the practices of their non-Christian family, friends, and neighbors. Other Christians did not.

The job of the historian is not to take sides in this debate. It is, rather, to stand outside this conversation and play the role of an impartial umpire. That means starting from well-grounded first principles. The first principle would be this: For three hundred years, it is documented fact that many Christians didn't want to "Christianize" anything about the Roman world they lived in. So why should historians assume they had to do so starting in the late third century or early fourth century? (*Political Issues* 6.1: Emperor Constantine in Jerusalem.) For these reasons and more, Christianization as a word will always be a sloppy way of talking about historical change because it shows a stubborn refusal to engage with Christian politics.

Political Issues 6.1 *Emperor Constantine in Jerusalem*

In 135 CE, after three years of war had taxed the patience of Rome, Emperor Hadrian cruelly removed any reference to the Roman province of Judaea from imperial records. A relatively young Roman province – it had only come into existence in 6 CE – the land of Judaea would now be added to parts of the older Roman territory of Syria. Together, the new entity would be called Palestina.

Life for Jews had suddenly changed. Jerusalem, the city revered as the location of the Second Temple, would now be called Aelia Capitolina. This new designation was an homage to Hadrian's family name, Aelius, and to the most prominent cult in Rome, the worship of Jupiter, Juno, and Minerva on Rome's Capitoline Hill. Hadrian altered life in Jerusalem in other ways, too, building a temple to the important Roman goddess Venus (known in Greek as Aphrodite) in the center, or forum, of his new Roman colony.

Hadrian's Temple of Venus would stand for two centuries until Rome's first Christian emperor, Constantine, demolished it. Constantine's biographer, Eusebius, tells the story this way. "The pious emperor addressed himself to another work truly worthy of record in the province of Palestine," Eusebius explains.

> For it had been in time past the endeavor of impious men ... to consign to the darkness of oblivion that divine monument of immortality to which the radiant angel had descended from heaven and rolled away the stone for those who still had stony hearts ... This sacred cave, then, certain impious and godless persons had thought to remove entirely from the eyes of men, supposing in their folly that thus they should be able effectually to obscure the truth ... by building a gloomy shrine of lifeless idols to the impure spirit whom they call Venus and offering detestable oblations therein on profane and accursed altars [erected at the site]. (Eusebius, *Life of Constantine* 3.25–26, trans. by E. Richardson in the *NPNF* series [1890])

The "divine monument of immortality" to which Eusebius refers is "the cave" where Jesus had allegedly been buried. According to Eusebius, it was located beneath the site where

Hadrian had built his Temple of Venus. In this retelling, Constantine clears away the "gloomy" temple to build a church commemorating the Anastasis, the Greek word for "Resurrection."

Today's pilgrims, tourists, and residents of Jerusalem know this building as the Church of the Holy Sepulcher. It was the first imperially funded church in Jerusalem. With it, Constantine made two powerful statements. First, Hadrian's Temple of Aphrodite had been removed. Second, he had kept the Jewish Temple Mount barren. Both were divisive political decisions. Within three generations of Constantine's order, Christians would use the example of the empty Temple platform to argue for their supremacy over the Jewish people and their faith.

As John Chrysostom would preach, "Even now, if you go into Jerusalem, you will see the exposed foundations [of the Temple Mount].... Consider how conspicuous our victory is.... Do you wish me to bring forward against you other prophets who clearly state the same fact: that your religion [Judaism] will come to an end, that ours will flourish and spread the message of Christ [the Messiah] to every corner of the world?" (*Against the Ioudaioi* 5.11–12, trans. adapted by A. J. Wharton ["Erasure"] from P. Harkins, *John Chrysostom: Discourses against Judaizing Christians* [Washington, DC: Catholic University Press, 1977], p. 140).

Constantine's decision about what to build – and what not to build – in Jerusalem led some Christians to the mistaken view that their Jewish Roman neighbors were people of an obsolete faith.

Maps which purport to illustrate the "Christianization" of the Roman Empire are particularly unhelpful for historians since they never explain what, exactly, they are registering as an example of "Christian" identity or "Christian" behavior. In this regard, the dangers of using the word "Christianization" in the writing of history can best be grasped by looking at the way some political commentators have written about the "Islamization" of contemporary Europe or America. As used in these current contexts, the word "Islamization" implies a cultural threat from the Muslim community; and it is based around the assumption that Muslims are incapable of living peacefully alongside their neighbors without radically wanting to impose "their" law or "their" customs on "traditional Western values."

The belief that all members of a monotheistic faith are unable to live in diverse social settings without wanting to change them is a shaky foundation for doing historical research. In this same manner, to tell the story of Late Antiquity as if it were the gradual, inevitable march of Christian customs across the landscape of traditional Roman values perpetuates gross stereotypes about Christians as a group.

Christian demographics and faith-based narratives of rapid conversion

Other questionable presumptions have guided scholarship on Christians and city life in the Roman Empire. A second one is that the ranks of the Christian faithful must have swelled over the course of the third and fourth centuries CE because

Romans of this time were gradually becoming more disenchanted with their own faith traditions, abandoning their temples and letting the sacred spaces of their cities decay. Christianity succeeded, in this scenario, because Rome's worship failed. This approach gained its strongest support in the 1980s and 1990s when one sociologist, Rodney Stark, tried to connect Christianity's allegedly meteoric rise in Rome to the exponential growth that was then being predicted for the Mormon community in America.

In the last few decades, however – notwithstanding an increase in the group's social visibility – membership in the Church of Latter Day Saints in the U.S. has not risen as exponentially as sociologists once forecasted. It now appears, by contrast, that minority religious groups in a pluralistic society can *remain* demographic minorities for much longer than scholarly models once predicted. This reality does not deny that certain individuals within a minority group can find a level of integration which is ultimately disproportionate to their group's population. Contemplating the case of the 2008 U.S. Republican presidential campaign, which featured a member of the Church of Latter Day Saints, might be a useful comparative exercise. Although a milestone in American politics, the rise of this one Mormon presidential candidate cannot be used to explain, across the United States, a new tide of new conversions to the Church of Latter Day Saints. Public visibility and conversion are two social phenomena that are not necessarily correlated.

With this case study in mind, we should be extremely cautious about connecting the rise of early Christian *visibility* with notions of widespread Christian *conversion* throughout the Roman Empire. Even attempts at measuring Christian demographics in Rome may be a bit of misdirection.

Many historians, for example, still assume that Christians *did* succeed in growing their numbers through sermons, outreach, good works, and Bible education. That's how a small 10 percent of the empire eventually converted the remaining 54 million people of the Roman world over time. In these reconstructions, researchers *need* Christian numbers to grow over the course of the fourth century, for only then can they truly begin to explain why Christianity was declared the official "religion" of the empire in the late fourth century. If Romans overwhelmingly embraced Christianity by the middle of the fourth century CE, this argument goes, Christian politicians would have been perfectly within their rights to outlaw older "pagan" practices.

There are problems with this model of history, too. To begin, it assumes that Christianity's rise in Rome was the result of a quasi-democratic political process by which everyone in the empire gradually came to recognize the superiority of the new faith. Comforting as that vision may be to some Christians today, it nevertheless silences the voice of Rome's non-Christians during some of the most intense political debates of Late Antiquity. Second, it also lumps all "the Christians" into one undifferentiated group and presumes that every self-professed "follower of Jesus" would have made the same political choices – that is, to outlaw other people's religious options and to establish Christianity as the official worship of Rome as their faith allegedly required them to. Many of these approaches silently drive many scholarly studies today. Sometimes, they are even regular starting points for scholars working on Late Antique Christianity, but it is important for us to recognize that, as approaches to historical questions, most of them are faith-driven. And all of them are swimming in a stew of highly questionable notions about how monotheistic faiths must necessarily feed intolerant behavior.

Recognizing political disagreement among Rome's Christian community

How the Roman Empire became a Christian state remains today an unsettled question. The widely accepted view is that, at most, 10 percent of the population was Christian in 313 CE, and there may be little use in trying to compile any more precise data. Relevant evidence is slim. That's why, rather than starting our conversation from the assumption that the majority of the Roman world was flocking towards Christianity by the end of the fourth century CE, we should leave room to entertain other models.

One alternate approach would be to consider the idea that Christianity's imposition on the Roman world was exactly that: an imposition. Today, some scholars are likely hesitant to support this view because it will sound, superficially, like a return to the eighteenth-century bigoted idea that Christians advocated an "intolerant zeal." (Indeed, that's how Edward Gibbon characterized Christianity in his famous *Decline and Fall of the Roman Empire* [1776].) We don't need to fall into Gibbon's trap, however, assuming that all Christians subscribed to the same political behavior, to recognize the benefits of taking a top-down approach to this important question. As a decision imposed on the Roman people, the establishment of a Christian state – through legal mechanisms by which traditional worship was outlawed and stigmatized – may have been the product of competing Christian political visions for the Roman state. Consequently, the decision to outlaw traditional worship practices may have been one that not every Christian citizen of the Roman Empire would have chosen to support.

This model has at least one strong benefit. It suggests that counting the number of Christians in the empire, although a noble endeavor, is not crucially important for understanding Rome's social change. To the contrary, the transformation of Rome into a Christian empire would be dependent on the ideologies of its Christian politicians and their advisors, not on the democratic or spiritual wishes of its citizens (*Working With Sources* 6.1: Descriptions of the City of Constantinople).

Working With Sources 6.1
Descriptions of the City of Constantinople

In the seventh century BCE, Greeks established a colony on the western side of the Bosporus Strait, one of the bodies of water that separates Europe and Asia. They called this city Byzantion. Throughout its early history Aegean and Black Sea sailors would stop here to trade. In 493 BCE, the Persian King Darius I crossed the Bosporus in his bold attempt to subjugate the Greek city-states, or *poleis*. The Persian invasion ultimately failed; but by the second century BCE, another army and its generals had marched into the territory: Rome's.

Over the next several centuries, Byzantion would watch as Rome's power and influence grew. Emperor Hadrian established an aqueduct in the city, which was distinguished with a race track, theater, and agora. These amenities gave Byzantion and its people the feel of being a part of the broader Roman cultural world. Later, Byzantion's residents would have to pick sides during Rome's intense struggles for power. Misplaced allegiances doomed the city.

In 193 CE, the people of Byzantion (known as Byzantium in Latin) supported the general Pescennius Niger for the imperial throne – against the rising commander Septimius Severus from North Africa. Niger moved to capture Byzantium, and the historian Herodian, writing in Greek, gives us a glimpse of Niger's motives.

> Located at the narrowest part of the Propontis [the ancient name for the Sea of Marmara, including the Bosporus Strait at the northern end], Byzantium grew immensely wealthy from its marine revenues, both tolls and fish; the city owned much fertile land, too, and realized a very handsome profit from all these sources. [Pescennius] Niger wished to have this city under his control because it was very strong but especially because he hoped to be able to prevent any crossing from Europe and Asia by way of the Propontis. (Herodian, *Roman History* 3.1.5–6, trans. by E. Echols [Berkeley: University of California Press, 1961], with slight modification)

Septimius prevailed, however, and he enacted a harsh retribution against Byzantium. The city was largely razed to the ground: "stripped of its theaters and baths," Herodian writes, "and, indeed, of all adornments." Byzantium was "now only a village" (*Roman History* 3.6.10).

Byzantium did not stay a village for long. By the early third century, Septimius Severus paid to repair the city, its baths, and, most importantly, its walls. Finally, on November 8, 324 CE, the Emperor Constantine decided to rededicate it by naming it after himself. Byzantion now became Constantinopolis, that is, Constantinople, "the city of Constantine." It would grow into the government capital of what later sixteenth-century writers termed the "Byzantine Empire."

Unfortunately, the sources for the urban history of this important Greek colony on the Bosporus, later transformed into a Roman city, are not easy to sort through. Knowledge of the city's earliest history is largely drawn from textual, not archaeological, sources.

Some of these writings, like the histories of Herodian, date from a century before Constantine. Other texts were written later and look back with a nostalgia on Constantine's capital. The eighth-century gazette, written in ancient Greek, called *Brief Historical Notes* (*Parastaseis Syntomoi Chronikai*) preserves many details, for example, of Greek and Roman statues and temples once located in Constantine's city. Not all of these survive. The archaeology of Constantinople – modern Istanbul – has only recently begun to illuminate the history of the city.

Summary

For four hundred years, Christians were a tiny fraction of the empire's 60 million people. As such, they faced the same stigmas – bigotry, public and private hostility, and stereotyping – that other minority groups had faced throughout the empire. What we also saw in the beginning of this chapter is that, like Jews, foreigners, and other minority groups, Christians could also use similar strategies for managing their stigmas. They could participate in civic sacrifice, like they did during Cyprian's day. And they could make connections to patrons in their cities, as they did in Dura Europos. These acts took place in the context of a growing, almost manic desire on the part of many third-century emperors to find a way to legislate social and political cohesion.

The evidence seen here also tells us that the rise of Christianity is probably more complex than a simple tale of how Jesus' followers converted their friends and neighbors through acts of "martyrdom." For, notwithstanding Valerian's or Diocletian's attempts at legalized discrimination, the political successes of the empire's Christians may have been dependent on long-term strategies for acceptance that Christian individuals and groups had been undertaking for centuries. Balancing the long, complicated legacy of Christians finding ways to embrace Roman values with the more widely known history of Christians who rejected any cultural compromises is essential for writing the history of the empire and its cities in the fourth and fifth centuries.

Study Questions

1. Who was Mani? Who was Cyprian of Carthage?
2. How did Emperor Galerius change the city of Thessaloniki?
3. In the age before Diocletian's legal persecution, what was it like for Christians to live in Roman cities?
4. In your own words, state some of the reasons why the word "Christianization" might be problematic for historians to rely upon when describing the fourth century CE.

Suggested Readings

Douglas Boin, *Coming Out Christian in the Roman World: How the Followers of Jesus Made a Place in Caesar's Empire* (New York: Bloomsbury, 2015).

Laura Nasrallah, Charalambos Bakirtzis, and Steve Friesen (eds.), *From Roman to Early Christian Thessaloniki: Studies in Religion and Archaeology* (Cambridge, MA: Harvard Theological Studies, 2010).

Michael Peppard, *The World's Oldest Church: Bible, Art, and Ritual at Dura-Europos, Syria* (New Haven: Yale University Press, 2016).

Christine Shepardson, *Controlling Contested Places: Late Antique Antioch and the Spatial Politics of Religious Controversy* (Berkeley: University of California Press, 2014).

7

Law and Politics

Diocletian's decision to attack Rome's Christian community, which he pursued zealously between 303 and 311 CE, is a powerful example of how Roman laws could be used to muscle citizens' behavior. During this crucial decade for the empire, according to contemporary accounts, the Roman government passed legislation "commanding that churches be leveled to the ground and [Holy] Scriptures be destroyed by fire" (Eusebius, *History of the Church* 8.2, trans. by A. McGiffert in *NPNF* series [1890]). Furthermore, men and women of high class who held positions of authority in the church had their social status stripped (Eusebius, *History of the Church* 8.2).

Fortunately, we have a general idea of how at least some Christians reacted at being made the targets of imperial bigotry. In Nicomedia in Roman Turkey, the city where Diocletian had established his own capital, the emperor's laws were written up and published on the streets. As soon as they were hung, they were being ripped down in protest and disgust. One culprit, says the church historian Eusebius, was not a low-class rabble-rousing peasant, either. A "certain man, not obscure but very highly honored with distinguished temporal dignities, moved with zeal toward God and incited with ardent faith, seized the edict as it was posted openly and publicly, and tore it to pieces as a profane and impious thing" (Eusebius, *History of the Church* 8.5).

A contemporary Latin writer, Lactantius, also evokes the general spirit of civic disobedience that arose in response to Diocletian's legislation. When the emperor's first edicts were announced "depriving the Christians of all honors and dignities," Lactantius explained, "a certain person tore [it] down and cut it in pieces ... with high spirit, saying in scorn, 'These are the triumphs of Goths and Sarmatians'"

A Social and Cultural History of Late Antiquity, First Edition. Douglas Boin.
© 2018 John Wiley & Sons, Inc. Published 2018 by John Wiley & Sons, Inc.

(Lactantius, *On the Death of the Persecutors* 13, trans. by W. Fletcher in the *ANF* series [1886]). The protester's language would not have been lost on his Roman audience. Emperor Diocletian's priorities were being compared to the behavior of two "barbarian" tribes, the Goths and Sarmatians. The commentary was scathing; real Romans were not supposed to act like this against their own citizens.

It was Caracalla's decree of universal citizenship, in many ways, that had led the empire into this quagmire. The result was a difficult decade for the Roman people. Now, after fifty years of political and military instability had come to a close, during which foreign entities like the Sasanian state and Gothic tribes had functioned as easy enemies around which Romans could build their own secure sense of identity, unresolved questions of what constituted a real Roman were now testing every level of society. Emperor Diocletian himself would put up a passionate fight for his own political convictions, but his legislative program had much larger implications for Rome, too – far beyond the sincere but perhaps parochial concerns of many Christians that the law required them to hand over their scriptures to the Roman authorities.

Diocletian's broader vision struck at the heart of what it meant to be Roman. He himself was intent on stripping Roman citizenship once and for all from the empire's Christian community, and that included limiting Christian access to the basic guarantees of legal protections. Lactantius makes this point clear when he explains that the emperor was uncompromising about barring Christians "from being plaintiffs in questions of wrong, adultery, or theft" in their local cities and advocating that the right of voting in Roman municipal elections be taken away from any Christian (Lactantius, *On the Death of the Persecutors* 13). Diocletian's divisive policy, unleashed at the start of the fourth century, nearly ripped the empire in two.

In 311 CE, the year that Diocletian died, it would be Galerius who recognized the need for political reconciliation. On May 1, at the palace at Nicomedia, an announcement was made. Diocletian's decrees would be repealed. Galerius' edict permitted Christians to rebuild their places of worship and restored to them the legal protections of Roman citizenship (Eusebius, *History of the Church* 8.17; Lactantius, *On the Death of the Persecutors* 34–35).

7.1   Roman Law: History From the Ground-Up, Top-Down, and Sideways

The narrative of the late third and early fourth centuries CE can lure one into associating all legal questions with the personalities who occupied the highest chambers of the state. But as we saw in our examination of Diocletian's edicts against Christians, there were larger issues at stake in these conversations. One issue was the extent to which a segment of Romans throughout the Mediterranean would continue to have access to the Roman legal system.

Before continuing with a top-down view of Rome's constitutional developments – a story which famously includes the dramatic meeting in 313 CE between Augustus Constantine and Augustus Licinius at the Tetrarchic capital in Milan – we should give attention to some broader details of Roman legal culture. What was so important about Roman law in people's daily life? What evidence is there to help us research that question?

Petitions from Roman Egypt

Aurelia Ataris was a Roman woman from Egypt, a landowner in the city of Hermopolis, and the daughter of a man who had served in the Romany army. She lived in the fourth century CE and, although a resident of a city in the Egyptian desert, was probably grateful for her access to the Roman legal system.

Hermopolis is located near the modern town of El-Ashmunein, on the west bank of the Nile between Upper and Lower Egypt. In antiquity, it was the capital of its nome, one of the smaller governmental units into which Egypt had been organized by the Hellenistic kings, the Ptolemies. Romans continued this practice of subdividing Egypt in this way, and by the third century CE, there were approximately 60 nomes in Roman Egypt. Hermopolis, the administrative center of its nome, played a strategic administrative role for the government, whose local officials were responsible for communicating with the top-level military and civic governors of Roman Egypt. These officials were the *praeses*, the civilian governor of the diocese; and the *dux*, its military authority. In the time of Aurelia Ataris, the presence of these officials in Roman Egypt was a relatively recent development, however. The separation of provincial authority along civilian and military lines had been initiated by the Rule of Four.

By 346 CE, Aurelia Ataris knew enough about the workings of the Roman government to appeal for legal help when she needed it. And that year, according to a petition that she submitted, events led her to the authorities, specifically, to the local liaison of the Roman *dux*. Her petition, which survives on papyrus, was found as part of an archive of the local official whom she sought out. His name was Flavius Abinnaeus, and his official papers have been published (*The Abinnaeus Archive: Papers of a Roman Officer in the Reign of Constantius II*, ed. by H. Bell, V. Martin, E. Turner, and D. van Berchem [Oxford, 1962]). Copies of Aurelia Ataris' consultation with the authorities were found in this archive. Here is a record of what she reported:

> On the third intercalary day [of the week] at the tenth hour, I do not know why, and acting in the manner of thieves, when I was collecting a debt which he owes me, Pol, surnamed Obellos; and the son of Horion, Apion by name; and his sister Kyriake shut me up in his house. I escaped from his house ... [but] I [now] am laid up, sitting at death's door. Therefore, I ask you this and beg your benevolence: Arrest these people and send them to our lord, the *dux*, for it is his job to punish those who dare to do such things. (Papyrus from the Abinnaeus archive [*P. Abinn.*] 52, trans. by A. Bryen [2013], pp. 264–265, whose study of this papyrus and others is listed in the Suggested Readings at the end of this chapter)

The second papyrus record in the archive elaborates on the details of the kidnapping. There, Aurelia Ataris suggests she was "practically beat[en] to death" by her assailants (*P. Abinn.* 51, trans. by A. Bryen [2013], p. 264).

Roman legal texts in Late Antiquity

Aurelia's case gives us an important insight into the social world of Roman Egypt and the legal culture of the fourth-century empire. The petition is significant for obvious economic and social reasons. It attests to the high financial status of a local woman and the fact that several local men were dependent on her for loans. It also attests to Aurelia Ataris' ability to read and communicate; she signed the last lines of the document. This petition opens a window, more broadly, however, onto the customs of the law that people like her, as citizens, had access to throughout the empire.

The two petitions we possess are dated the day of her attack and the very next day. As historian Ari Bryen has observed in his recent study of these texts, "[I]t would appear [Aurelia Ataris] was aware of her options for finding her way to justice" (2013, p. 93). The language that she used in her report is also revealing. Even though she had a personal and business relationship with the assailants, she described their attack as a surprise ("I do not know why" they assaulted me, she says) and characterized their behavior as if they were an anonymous group of "thieves." We don't need to question the details of the attack to realize how effectively Aurelia Ataris has used the legal system to her advantage as a plaintiff. She has placed the onus on the people she has accused to come clean and to testify as to their motives and their intent.

It is an extraordinary testament to the work and intellectual labors of Roman lawyers that they were able to provide a flexible, lasting legal framework for officials to handle cases like these. Many of Rome's law codes had been written at a time when citizenship was not universal. Gaius was one important legal thinker who laid the groundwork for this lasting system. He lived in the middle of the second century CE, almost fifty years before Caracalla's citizenship decree. One of his most famous works, the *Institutes*, was a handbook surveying legal questions and cases.

Many of the statements included in Gaius' *Institutes* concern stolen property and physical injury. In it, Gaius also discusses the history of punishments that were associated with the cases, oftentimes going back to legal documents written in the Roman Republic:

> The penalties for injuries provided by the Law of the Twelve Tables [originally compiled in the fifth century BCE] were as follows: 'For a broken limb, retaliation; for a bone broken, or crushed, three hundred asses, if the party was a freeman, but if he was a slave a hundred and fifty; and for all other injuries, twenty-five asses.' These pecuniary penalties seemed to be sufficient compensation in those times of great indigence. At present, however, we make use of another rule. For we are permitted by the Judge [*praetor*] to estimate the damages ourselves, and the Judge may either condemn the defendant for the amount of which we have estimated it, or for a smaller sum, as he may think proper. (Gaius, *Institutes* 3.223–224, trans. by F. de Zulueta, *The Institutes of Gaius* [Oxford: Clarendon Press, 1946])

As Gaius' study shows, Roman legal claimants were not married to a strict, inflexible application of previous law or custom. Resolutions, like the amount owed in a property dispute, could be set by judges, which would shape later precedent. In this way, the Roman legal system navigated between tradition and innovation and, as citizenship grew, the number of Romans who could appeal to the law to protect them increased.

Gaius' *Institutes* proved so influential, in fact, that by 533 CE, a lawyer in Constantinople named Tribonian, working on the orders of the Roman Emperor Justinian (r. 527–565 CE), was asked to update it. Justinian's *Institutes* were the result of this process. Along with the emperor's *Digests* and his *Codex* of laws, these three sixth-century documents soon became the foundation of legal culture in the later Roman Empire. All three preserved many of Gaius' earlier, second-century case studies. In this way, the legal culture of the sixth-century Roman Empire – whose capital was at Constantinople, not Rome – represented the continuity of almost a thousand years of Roman legal history (*Exploring Culture* 7.1: The Emperor's Residence in Constantinople; Figure 7.1). Even as the Roman Empire lost territory and its customs changed – by the sixth century CE, citizens were required to identify with one specific version of Christian faith – legal tradition connected the present to the past.

Exploring Culture 7.1 *The Emperor's Residence in Constantinople*

Our archaeological understanding of the palace in Constantinople (modern Istanbul) is woeful. Although we have some idea of its footprint – the palace faced the hippodrome, located on its western side – material from Constantine's or even Emperor Justinian's residence is almost non-existent. Textual sources provide some of our most evocative descriptions.

Corippus, a poet who worked in public relations for the court of Emperor Justin II (r. 565–578 CE), is one of the key witnesses to give us information. Corippus composed his poem to celebrate the arrival, in the mid-sixth century CE, of a foreign embassy. The chief ambassador, named Tergazis, had been sent to Constantinople by the ruler of a kingdom based on the northern Black Sea: the Avars. Telling the story in a way that would impress the emperor, Corippus waxed eloquent about the splendid moment when Avar diplomats entered the palace.

> The imperial palace with its officials is like Olympus. Everything is as bright, everything as well ordered in its numbers, as shining with light: just as the golden shining stars in the curving sky accomplish their courses poised on their own measure, number and weight and remain firm in fixed retreat and one light shines over all; all the stars yield to its superior flames and they feed on the fire of their monarch by which they lie eclipsed. In this way the power of Rome over all that is great keeps itself over all kingdoms in the midst of the people and shines, subject only to the clear sky. (Corippus, *In Praise of Justin II* 3.179–190, trans. by Averil Cameron, *Flavius Cresconius Corippus* [London: Athlone Press, 1967])

Corippus goes on to tell how the Avars "marveled as they crossed the first threshold and [entered] the great hall." Before them, they saw Justin's bodyguards, decked out in helmets with red plumes, standing at attention with golden shields and javelins, tipped with sparkling iron. The impression was stunning. "[T]hey believed that the Roman palace was another heaven" (Corippus, *In Praise of Justin II* 3.236–245). The Avar diplomats who accompanied Tergazis may be the surest we're able to come to envisioning Justin II's palace.

There is at least one other – admittedly less certain – source that may provide relevant information. Between 1930 and the 1950s, several large chunks of mosaic floor were excavated southeast of the hippodrome. Some sections depict hunting scenes, a favorite elite pastime; others show tender moments of everyday life. A man stoops to give food to his mule; a likely squealing child chases a goose. These mosaics have been dated to the first half of the sixth century CE.

Based on what we suspect about the palace floor plan, these mosaics should have come from a wing of the emperor's residence, but no consensus has been reached yet about what building they may have belonged to or even their date.

Figure 7.1   Unlike at Rome, where excavations on the Palatine Hill provide a rich amount of material evidence about the emperor's residence, the palace at Constantinople is not well known archaeologically. This artifact, known as the Great Palace Mosaic, was found in the area east of Constantinople's hippodrome, where the palace was located. It depicts a scene of animal husbandry. In this close-up, two men dressed in colorful tunics, an unpretentious garment worn by laborers, attend to horses and goats. Although a seemingly innocent, rustic scene, the proper cultivation of the land had long been used by Roman poets, like Varro and Virgil, as a metaphor for good governance. That message would have had a powerful resonance in the imperial palace, particularly if the mosaic were visible to diplomatic guests, august senators, and distinguished dignitaries. From the Great Palace Mosaic Museum, Istanbul, Turkey. Dated roughly between the fourth and sixth century CE. Photo credit: © Dennis Cox/Alamy Stock Photo.

The history of Roman law as a story of "horizontal relations"

There is one last reason why legal texts, like Aurelia Ataris' petitions, are so helpful for social and cultural historians of Late Antiquity. As documents that report on the scandalous, *outré* events that took place in Roman cities, the legal texts allow us to see a kind of interpersonal relationship that doesn't fit neatly into models of "top-down" or "bottom-up" history. These texts are fascinating because they preserve snapshots of "horizontal relations" (Bryen 2013, p. 269) – of friends and neighbors whose relationship with each other has gone comically, sometimes even horribly wrong.

That's what happened in May 336 CE when two pigs escaped from the farm of a woman named Aurelia Allous (*Oxyrhynchus Papyrus* [*P. Oxy.*] 54.3771, trans. by Bryen [2013], p. 262). After wandering off Aurelia's property, the lost animals eventually stumbled into a waterwheel near Aurelia's neighbor's land. The owner of the land, a man named Pabanos, had been so enraged that he came after Aurelia with a chisel after trying to slaughter the pigs. According to the petition filed with the local magistrate, Pabanos even tried to drown Aurelia in one of the water conduits.

Although the precise circumstances that led to the escalation of the violence here are missing from the textual reports, as they are from the kidnapping case of Aurelia Ataris, the fact that Aurelia Allous went to the magistrate to pursue her case – leaving a papyrus petition behind in the archaeological record – shows us one of the most important roles that the legal system played in fourth-century Roman Egypt. Both these petitioners saw the law as a protection from a spike in the kinds of violence that could and did disrupt the more mundane rhythms of life on their farm or in their city. Waiting in line to see a local official, reading the complaint, witnessing and signing the petition, then waiting for a response: these were the everyday signs of law that went hand-in-hand with the top-down world of imperial edicts, social policies, and politics.

7.2   The "Edict of Milan," 313 CE

Milan in the early fourth century resembled most large imperial cities. Like Thessaloniki, whose buildings are attested archaeologically, and Nicomedia, whose ghostly presence haunts many fourth-century texts, this city of northern Italy (in Latin, *Mediolanum*) was a cosmopolitan environment outfitted with all the amenities expected by Late Antique Roman citizens. There was a large circuit of walls surrounding the city; an amphitheater for animal hunts and gladiatorial games; baths with statues of the Roman gods, like Hercules; a race track for chariot matches; and broad, column-lined city streets, perfect for staging imperial ceremonies. Milan owed much to the investment of the Tetrarchs. It would also soon become famous as the site of an important "constitutional convention," a meeting between the Augusti of the eastern and western regions of the empire. The two protagonists in this meeting were Licinius (r. 312–324 CE) and Constantine (r. 312–324 with Licinius; 324–337 CE as sole emperor of Rome).

In 312 CE, General Constantine had been proclaimed emperor by his troops at York, in Roman England. In the aftermath of this proclamation, he had decided to march his army against the current Augustus of Rome, Maxentius. It was a daring decision because it undermined the validity of Diocletian's political reforms and challenged the notion of shared rule. In October 312 CE, Constantine successfully seized the capital. The Augustus, Maxentius, drowned in the Tiber Riber.

One year later, in 313 CE, in the aftermath of his stunning victory, Constantine arranged to meet his eastern colleague, Licinius – perhaps to allay fears that Diocletian's system was not in danger of falling apart. The meeting was scheduled for Milan. There, the two men would sign a joint statement clarifying the role and meaning of the practice of *religio* throughout the empire. It is this document, drafted at Milan but announced at Nicomedia, which is known as the "Edict of Milan." It was an imperial decree that had a transformational effect on Roman society.

The Roman constitution in context

The Roman people had no written constitution, but the absence of a formal document does not preclude us from speaking about a "constitution" in more general terms as the legal culture, the formal governmental structure, and the social traditions that undergirded the state. Since the time of the Republic, the mechanisms that allowed the Roman state to function involved a balance between codified rules and an appreciation for traditions and values.

For that reason, Rome's "constitution" from its earliest days can be said to have depended on a combination of specific regulations, such as who could hold a magistracy and when; but also on a set of more loosely defined rituals, such as the performance of a triumph, an honor which allowed a successful general to parade through the streets of Rome and grow his political base. This system was supported by the consensus of the Senate, the men who played an advisory role, and by Rome's priests and priestesses, who were tasked with ensuring that the government's decisions conformed to the will of the gods. *Religio*, in this arrangement, functioned as a branch of Rome's Republic.

The rise of an autocracy in the first century BCE, commonly regarded as Rome's "Empire," was the direct result of a breakdown of this cooperative, consensual system. Yet without reading the ancient sources too naively, it is important for us to realize that the arrangement which came about during these formative years was, in many ways, the product of a creative constitutional renegotiation – one that took hold of Roman society gradually. The "Empire" did not emerge as the result of a radical governmental overhaul, certainly not by one authoritarian man.

Just the contrary. The gradual process by which a single man, such as a highly respected politician like Augustus, was given authority to oversee the entire government ran on a certain cognitive dissonance. Romans could convince themselves that they were staying faithful to their history of living in a "Republic," even as their state grew more and more to resemble a monarchy. The fact that Augustus assumed the role and title of *pontifex maximus*, "Chief Priest" of the government, ensured a particular new level of stability because priests who chose to use ill omens to object to

Augustus' policies would have been seen as deliberately undermining the authority that the Senate and people had invested in him. In extreme circumstances, however, as a vote of no-confidence, the people or the army could always choose to remove those leaders who they saw as failing to live up to their expectations. The history of the third century CE can be seen as a time when even this system was tested.

The larger point is that the broad ideology of Rome's "Republican" system proved remarkably resilient. Throughout Late Antiquity, the Senate continued to work in its accustomed deliberative role; the emperor commanded respect through his personal authority; and the people themselves functioned as an important check-and-balance, calling out political ineptitude or sometimes calling for new leadership in public venues where they met the emperors, such as at the circus games. This constitutional system, in which very little about the actual running or management of the government was ever codified – let alone written down – provided the underpinning for the Roman Empire, both when Rome was a part of the state and even when Constantinople was its sole capital (A. Kaldellis, *The Byzantine Republic: People and Power in New Rome* [Cambridge, MA: Harvard University Press, 2015]).

Expanding the idea of being Roman

Constantine's conference with Licinius' in 313 CE leaps out from history for two reasons. It's not just that the emperors' decisions would affect the political trajectory of Christianity, although 313 CE remains the year which Christians use to commemorate the moment when their faith was legally recognized. (Galerius' edict of 311 CE does not traditionally receive the same recognition.)

There is a second, subtler reason why that Milan conference is important, though. The idea that any Roman ruler would take the time to define, explicitly, what and who constituted a Roman *religio* – by writing their opinions down and distributing that language to the citizens of the empire – represents an entirely new development in the story of Rome's constitution. Where tradition and custom had been the norm for centuries, leading to the difficulties with civic sacrifice in the third century CE, this new formal, fixed legal language now provided a safe harbor for all the empire's 60 million citizens. Christians, according to the language of Constantine and Licinius' edict, were now to be accorded the official status of a *religio* (Lactantius, *On the Death of the Persecutors* 48). And unlike Galerius' edict, this decree would never be challenged or repealed.

The idea of what it meant to worship as a Roman citizen (*religio*) had just been expanded to include all the empire's diverse Christian individuals. Meanwhile, the fortunes of other Christian communities, outside the Roman Empire, would follow different paths (*Key Debates* 7.1: Being Christian in the Sasanian Zoroastrian State: A Case of Constant "Persecution"?). In Rome, the protection of Christian worship had now been written into Roman law. It was a decision that would have unforeseen implications for many priests and bishops, as well as for many ordinary Christian individuals, as they all would now grapple with the responsibility of having been classified as one of the *religiones* of the Roman state.

Key Debates 7.1 *Being Christian in the Sasanian Zoroastrian State: A Case of "Persecution"?*

Emperor Constantine saw himself as "a bishop to people on the outside." That, at least, is the portrait painted by the emperor's Christian biographer, Eusebius (*Life of Constantine* 4.24). Eusebius marshaled powerful evidence to support his claims. In his biography, he included a letter sent by the emperor, *c.*324 CE, to the head of the Zoroastrian Sasanian state, Sapur II (r. *c.*310–379 CE). In it, Constantine advocated forcefully on behalf of the Christian community in Persia and requested Sapur II treat them with respect. "[B]ecause your power is great, I commend these persons to your protection; because your piety is eminent, I commit them to your care" (Eusebius, *Life of Constantine* 4.13, trans. by E. Richardson from the *NPNF* series [1890]).

Whether Constantine really sent such a letter cannot be proven, but the social status of Christians in the Sasanian Empire is a fascinating topic to explore. In many ways, it could easily be told as a story of "martyrdom" and "persecution" similar to pious "church histories" of Christians in Rome. A closer look at Persian politics reveals a different picture. Christians negotiated their place in the Sasanian world in much the same way that we know they did in Rome.

A Middle Persian text written on the so-called Ka'ba of Zoroaster at Naqsh-i Rustam would seem to support the traditional story of Christian persecution. On one side of the monument, the chief priest of the Sasanian Empire, Kerdir, bragged that – under three successive administrations, from 241–274 CE – he strictly enforced Zoroastrian belief throughout society. Worship of the god of Light, Ahura Mazda, also known as Ohrmazd, "held great authority in the empire," Kerdir wrote. "The doctrine of

Ahreman [the god of darkness, Ohrmazd's evil opponent] and the demons was expelled from the empire" (Inscription of Kerdir, trans. by Richard Payne, *A State of Mixture: Christians, Zoroastrians, and Iranian Political Culture in Late Antiquity* [Berkeley: University of California Press, 2015], p. 23). Yet many Christians continued to live in Persia both during and after this time.

Was Kerdir implying that Christians were secretly or openly aligned with the forces of darkness? According to Zoroastrian theological texts, Ahura Mazda and Ahreman were locked in a cosmic battle for control of the universe. Believers thought that this cosmic war would last for three one-thousand-year-long periods, at which time a savior would arrive (named Sōšyāns) and the forces of good would finally triumph over the forces of evil. In the interim, all the elements of the natural world participated in the struggle. Some humans, like Zoroastrian believers, were indisputably on the side of the good. Non-believers were considered either half-human or half-demon; neither was considered as good as the Zoroastrians, but the former could be enlisted as allies in the struggle.

From the founding of the Sasanian Empire to its dissolution in the seventh century, Christians were thought to hold this middle position. Stories about a "Great [Christian] Persecution" written in Syriac and circulated later – during the fifth, sixth, and seventh centuries CE – ignore this complex social reality. Instead, they reinforce a "myth of Zoroastrian intolerance." Like the narratives of widespread "persecution" in Rome, however, these Syriac stories likely functioned as "an effective instrument of Christian institutional building" (Payne 2015, pp. 27–35).

Neither in 313 CE nor at any time during his long reign (d. 337 CE) did Constantine or any other Roman politician make Christianity the official "religion" of the Roman Empire.

7.3 Individual Laws and the Collection of Legal Texts

As we have already seen, Gaius' *Institutes*, written in the middle of the second century CE, provided later jurists with an important model. It taught them how to think, write, categorize, and order Romans laws. The sixth-century CE compilations undertaken by Justinian and his legal team were but the end of a long process, one that involved many other individuals between Gaius and Justinian. This section provides an overview of some other sources for Rome's legal history, particularly sources that relate to the period of Diocletian, Constantine, and later fourth-century emperors.

In general, laws in antiquity took several forms. First, they could be issued as edicts, which the emperors or their spokesmen read publicly to the people. Second, they could be expressed in the form of letters (*epistulae*, in the Latin plural), which were written from the emperor to other members of the imperial administration, who then had the responsibility of disseminating them. Lastly, an imperial law could be announced during an *oratio*, that is, an emperor's speech before the Senate. (A fourth category, called a "rescript," referred to cases in which the emperor had specifically taken the time to answer the legal concerns of a private individual, which technically resulted in a law; this form of legal writing was popular during the third and early fourth centuries but was later phased out.)

In all the cases just described – and for reasons that should be quite apparent in the pre-modern world of limited, immediate communication – the law's announcement was a crucial step in generating public awareness of the emperor's policies. Publication could take several forms. The law's text could be chiseled on stone ("an inscription") or – more commonly – it could be written on parchment, papyrus, or wood and then distributed or displayed throughout town in high traffic areas like in a city's forum or at its temples. Because of the lasting nature of inscriptions, however, the text of several important laws from the time of Diocletian and the Rule of Four still survive.

The Edict on Maximum Prices, 301 CE

One surviving law is Diocletian's "Edict on Maximum Prices," an emergency economic measure known from several fragments of Greek and Latin inscriptions that have been found overwhelmingly in the eastern Mediterranean. These texts on stone make tantalizing statements about the nature of the late third-century and early fourth-century economy. For, as the modern name of this one text suggests, Diocletian's price decree set the maximum amount that merchants could charge for goods and services, starting in 301 CE. The preamble to the law makes clear that it applied throughout the entire empire (*CIL* 3, p. 801). Although it does not seem to have worked, Diocletian's law was an audacious attempt to regulate the economy during a time when prices for nearly every staple of the Roman pantry and kitchen – grain, beans, different types of wine, olive oil, honey, lamb, goat – were rising. Wages for everyone from the mule drivers to barbers and to tailors needed to be legislated from the palace. For that reason alone, as the sign of top-down interventionism, the "Edict on Maximum Prices" remains one of the most intriguing pieces of the economic puzzle of the late third century CE.

The Edict against Christians, 312 CE

A second law to survive on stone was issued by the Tetrarch Maximinus (r. 305–313 CE), the nephew of Galerius who does not seem to have shared his uncle's later preference for toleration. This inscription is a letter from Maximinus to the city of Colbassa, located in southwestern Asia Minor, encouraging them to continue their discrimination against local Christians. It dates to April 6, 312 CE (*AE* 1989, no. 1096). Written a year after Galerius' death but before the "Edict of Milan," the Colbassa decree reveals the extent to which conservative Roman mores – and an irrational fear of Christians – continued to grip many citizens during this period. It also shows the extent to which Diocletian's successors were prepared to keep using the power of Roman law to discriminate against the empire's minority groups. Eusebius claims to have seen a copy of a similar decree Maximinus had sent to and set up in the city of Tyre (*History of the Church* 9). Eusebius' account of that inscription, although written in Greek, matches in many ways the Latin text of the Colbassa decree.

The creation of the Theodosian Code, 429–438 CE

Needless to say, laws that were written on more perishable materials, like parchment or wood, and then tacked up or nailed up around town, have not fared as well. That does not mean we lack the texts of all laws which were never inscribed on stone. The archives for the study of legal history in the fourth century, more broadly, would be empty indeed were it not for the fact that many fourth-century laws were later collected and edited, preserving them for posterity. This project was undertaken on the orders of the Christian emperor Theodosius II (r. 402–408 with Arcadius; 408–450 CE as sole ruler of the eastern empire).

The assembly of the *Theodosian Code* was a grand, collaborative campaign designed to collect laws from Constantine's time to the fifth century CE. Thanks to the dedicated men who worked on it, we have an abundant collection of edicts, orations, and letters that date to the fourth century CE. We can only speculate how much information was lost during this arduous and patently political editing process. When it was finished in 438 CE, however, the *Theodosian Code* was one of the most up-to-date compendia of Roman law for its age and included sections on every aspect of daily life. In sixteen chapters, or books, it outlined and codified topics related to magistrates, marriage, property, slavery, heresy, taxes, *religio*, and *superstitio*.

7.4   Law and Politics in the Fourth Century CE

Now that we have looked at legal culture more broadly, we should return to the world of fourth-century laws and politics. The fact that Christians around the Roman world were not united, socially or politically, before 312 CE would make the following century a particularly difficult one for those both inside the group and outside it. The "Edict of Milan" had been designed to address Christians' legal status in the empire; it had not legislated how Christians should behave as Roman citizens (*Political Issues* 7.1: Gladiators, Chariot Races, and the Laws of the Christian Emperor Constantine). Even as the "Edict of Milan" gave them a new form of social security, however, it was Christians' own spirited conversations – about how much or even whether they should embrace long-standing Roman values, like participating in sacrifice, serving in the imperial cult, or attending Roman festivals and games – which had not been resolved.

Political Issues 7.1   *Gladiators, Chariot Races, and the Laws of the Christian Emperor Constantine*

Did Constantine, the first ruler to self-identify as a Christian, ban gladiatorial games and other wildly popular forms of Roman sport? It's a provocative notion, based on the assumption that all of Jesus' followers looked on the world around them as morally bankrupt and spiritually depraved. Gladiator matches left the arena sand soaked in gore. Breathtaking races in the circus were held on festival days for the gods. Even theatrical performances – comedy, tragedy, mime – were staged in venues the gods protected. Sometimes, based on the script of the play, gods even appeared on stage.

Tertullian, a Christian writing a century before Constantine, was horrified by Roman culture. "What are the things which eye has not seen, ear has not heard, and which have not so much as dimly dawned upon the human heart?" he asked. "Whatever they are, they are nobler, I believe, than any circus, theater, or stadium" (*On the Spectacles* 30, trans. slightly modified from S. Thelwall in the *ANF* series [1885]).

Tertullian did not stop with a simple rhetorical question. He used these well-liked entertainments to warn about the coming of the apocalypse. He described to Christians his terrifying vision, predicting:

[a] last day of judgment ... that day unlooked for by the nations ... when the world hoary with age and all its many products shall be consumed in one great flame! How vast a spectacle then bursts upon the eye! I shall have a better opportunity of hearing the tragedians; louder-voiced in their own calamity; of viewing the play-actors, much more "dissolute" in the dissolving flame; of looking upon the charioteer, all glowing in his chariot of fire; of beholding the wrestlers, not in their gymnasia but tossing in the fiery billows – unless even then I shall not care to attend to such ministers of sin, in my eager wish rather to fix a gaze insatiable on those whose fury vented itself against the Lord. (*On the Spectacles* 30)

For Tertullian and the Christian community who listened to him, there was no delight to be found in these exciting Roman pastimes, "ministers of sin."

Fast-forward a hundred years, when Christians had won the right to set the legislative agenda for the empire, and we find only the slightest hint that any of these social issues were a source of concern. Many Christians attended these events quite openly now, as they learned for themselves how to juggle their faith and their culture in creative ways. In Greek and Latin, they drew the ire of their peers, just as many had from Tertullian (John Chrysostom, *Homily on the New Year Festival* [Kalends] 1–3; Maximus of Turin, *Sermon* 98 on the New Year Festivals).

Even Constantine continued to endorse the games. His one reservation was that criminals no longer be punished as gladiators. In a law issued October 325 CE, the emperor announced: "Bloody spectacles do not please us in civil ease and domestic quiet. For that reason we forbid those people to be gladiators who by reason of some criminal act were accustomed to deserve this condition and sentence. You shall rather sentence them to serve in the mines" (*Theodosian Code* 15.12.1, trans. by D. Potter, "Constantine and the Gladiators," *Classical Quarterly* 60 [2010], p. 597).

The fact that Christians could now argue, speak, and meet openly, without fearing legal punishment, however, did ensure that their own internal, sometimes parochial conversations gained a degree of attention that they had not previously enjoyed. Two heated topics arose in the fourth century that were particularly divisive to the empire's minority Christian community.

One was a dispute over organizational leadership in North Africa. It had ignited in the aftermath of Diocletian's legislation, as Christians began to debate whether people who had handed over the scriptures during the persecution could even be considered "real Christians" any more. (The Christian bishop who took a strict, uncompromising position in this debate was named Donatus.) The second dispute arose out of Alexandria and concerned the relationship of Jesus' humanity to his divinity. (The bishop of Alexandria who argued that Jesus had been created by God, rather than coexisting with God since eternity, was named Arius.) Both men, Donatus and Arius, would eventually have their names defamed, smeared into *-isms* by Christians who found that the best way to disagree with them was through open caricature. (Many triumphalist books have been written about the history of "Donatism" and "Arianism" in Late Antiquity without any attention to the complexities of all sides of the participants in these debates.)

Both these controversies, especially the one surrounding Arius, can still seem more like abstract theological lessons than necessary moments in Rome's history; but by the late fourth century, debates like these were vitally important to bishops who had a vested interest in making sure their party platform – not that of their opponents – earned government support. The following writer, addressing his Christian congregation in 381 CE, was one of those with a vested interest in this topic raised by Arius:

> If you ask for change [in the market], [people in Constantinople] wax philosophical about the Begotten and the Unbegotten. And if you ask the price of bread, they answer,

"The Father is greater, and the Son is subject to him." And if you say, "Is the bath ready yet?" they declare the Son has his being from non-existence. I'm not sure what this evil should be called – inflammation of the brain or madness or some sort of epidemic disease which contrives to derange people's reasoning. (Gregory of Nyssa, "On the Divinity of the Son and the Holy Spirit," in the collected writings of Christian Greek authors [*Patrologia Graeca* 46, column 557], trans. by A. D. Lee in *Pagans and Christians in Late Antiquity* [London: Routledge, 2000], p. 110)

The bishop's concern to regulate and control daily small talk in the marketplaces of Constantinople was the sign of a Christian intra-squad dispute which would only grow louder and more pointed in the fifth century. Church councils would be called to adjudicate these disputes. The effects on the Christian community would be politically and even geographically polarizing.

As for the mass of Romans who did not identify as Christian, one might assume that conversations of this sort – whether surrounding Donatus or Arius – really did seem like an "inflammation of the brain" with little relevance in their day-to-day lives (*Working With Sources* 7.1: The Talmud as Evidence for the History of the Jewish Community). Besides, there was a more pressing legal question for all the empire's citizens during the fourth century. Would Christians, now that they had gained legal status, tolerate Rome's older worship practices or would they try to eliminate them by force of law, making Christianity the only official *religio* of the state?

Working With Sources 7.1

The Talmud as Evidence for the History of the Jewish Community

A hundred and thirty years after the Second Temple's destruction, after a tense time that had witnessed two more failed Jewish revolts against Rome (115–117 CE and 132–135 CE), the Jewish community began to shows signs of healing and rebirth. A collection of "repeated traditions," called the *Mishnah* in Hebrew, was written down by the start of the third century CE. Its teachings had previously been passed down orally. The *Mishnah* is the earliest document that shows us how the Jewish community struggled with the complexity of living in a world without a Temple.

The world of the *Mishnah* and its "supplement," called the *Tosefta*, was a time of rabbis and study houses, called in Hebrew *bet midrash*. In these houses, throughout the Mediterranean and in the lands of the Tigris and Euphrates Rivers ("Babylon"), Jewish law would be taught, interpreted, and debated. During the third and fourth centuries CE, the rabbis, the leaders of these study houses, grew in status. They acted as judges, tax collectors, and leaders of the wider Jewish community.

In the Roman world specifically, they functioned as a parallel government – or at least, self-regulated community – living among the state authorities. The chief diplomatic liaison between the Jewish and Roman authorities was the Jewish "patriarch" (*ha-Nasi*, in Hebrew). The patriarch maintained relations with emperors and other high-placed officers (Emperor Julian, *Letter* 51 [ed. Wright 1923], referencing a matter raised by the Jewish patriarch; and Libanius, *Letter* 160, to the patriarch himself).

This limited form of self-rule would not last. In 429 CE, the Roman emperors eliminated the position of Jewish patriarch (*Theodosian Code* 16.8.29).

It was at precisely this time, *c.*425 CE, that a new set of laws was compiled to provide guidance to Jewish leaders: the *Talmud*. Because these documents were written by Jews who lived close to the Temple, they are called the *Jerusalem Talmud* (*ha-Talmud ha-Yerushalmi*, often abbreviated "Y."). This name distinguishes them from a second collection, written in Persia during the sixth and seventh centuries CE: the *Babylonian Talmud* (*ha-Talmud ha-Bavli*).

The product of many authors and editors, both collections speak to the day-to-day concerns of Jewish people in Late Antiquity. Here is an excerpt from the Jerusalem Talmud:

> A young man sold his property. The case came before Rabbi Hiyyan ben Yosef and Rabbi Yohanan. R. Hiyyan b. Yosef said: On the assumption that he was a reasonable person [i.e., an adult] they signed [the document]. R. Yohanan said: Since he [the purchaser] took it upon himself to remove the property from the family, he must bring proof [of purchase]. (*Jerusalem Talmud, Bava Batra* 9.6/8, 17a, trans. by Catherine Hezser, "Roman Law and Rabbinic Legal Composition," *The Cambridge Companion to the Talmud and Rabbinic Literature*, ed. by C. Fonrobert and M. Jaffee [New York: Cambridge University Press, 2007], p. 159)

This text follows a pattern that was familiar to many Roman jurists. It introduces a case study, then a question, and concludes with an expert's response. Roman laws written as late as the sixth century CE used this formula (Justinian, *Digest* 21.2.11). For historians, this similarity is a sign of overlooked Christian, Roman, and Jewish dialogue in the later empire.

Summary

At the start of the fourth century CE, Emperor Diocletian used state power to coerce Christians to hand over their scriptures, creating an environment where churches could be legally burned and Christians themselves could be threatened with the forfeiture of their Roman citizenship. This policy of dividing citizens and families from each other, separating Christians and non-Christians into two legal camps, was born out of a long-running concern to unify the empire around traditional Roman values. Since the time of the Republic, proper worship, or what Romans called *religio*, was an essential part of this legal framework. There was no concept of secular society in the Roman world.

When Constantine and Licinius met at Milan, the constitutional underpinnings of the state were modified to include Christianity as one of the empire's official *religiones*. This decision did not make Christianity the official religion of the Roman

Empire, but it did guarantee Christians new legal protection in the way they worshipped. This political triumph was something many people throughout the Roman Empire could appreciate, as access to the courts and the use of the legal system were crucial to the way all citizens – not just Christians – resolved conflict in their daily lives.

Study Questions

1. Summarize some of the cases that came to the attention of magistrates in Roman Egypt.
2. What do scholars mean by doing history "horizontally"?
3. Describe the process by which Roman laws were made.
4. How did the Edict of Milan reshape the Roman constitution?

Suggested Readings

Ari Bryen, *Violence in Roman Egypt: A Study in Legal Interpretation* (Philadelphia: University of Pennsylvania Press, 2013).

Jill Harries, *Law and Empire in Late Antiquity* (New York: Cambridge University Press, 1999).

Caroline Humfress, *Orthodoxy and the Courts in Late Antiquity* (New York: Oxford University Press, 2007).

John Matthews, *Laying Down the Law: A Study of the Theodosian Code* (New Haven: Yale University Press, 2000).

8

Urban Life

Material culture has featured in each chapter up until now. We have studied archaeological objects, like flashy cameos, to talk about cultural dialogue and the exchange of craftsmen and ideas between empires outwardly at war. We have traced some the bare outlines of buildings on the ground and contemplated grander remains which opened our eyes to the physical world of Late Antique cities. We have also read imperial laws, written on stone, and everyday petitions, written on papyrus, which have given us a feel for the tangible presence of Roman power in people's lives. Material culture is an inescapable, indispensable, and, above all, necessary part of doing history.

This chapter shows why by looking at material culture and the archaeological remains from two of the empire's most important cities: its beating cultural heart, Rome, and its rising political center, Constantinople. We will also look at material culture from other sites, in Roman Egypt, for example, to help us hear and feel the rhythms of life among the empire's citizens in the decades after Christianity's legalization. This period, the fourth century CE, would be a crucial one for the political narrative of the empire, too.

The century which had opened with Constantine and Licinius' dramatic publication of the "Edict of Milan," in 313 CE, would be bracketed by an even more momentous announcement, in February 380 CE. That year, the three joint rulers of the Roman world, Emperors Gratian, Valentinian, and Theodosius, would release the text of their "Edict of Thessaloniki." Announced in Constantinople but addressed to "all the various nations which are subject to [the emperors'] Clemency and Moderation," the Thessaloniki edict instructed everyone throughout the Roman world to profess "the worship practices [*religio*]" associated with the Christian faith. More importantly, it advocated that all Romans now believe in "the Father, Son, and Holy Spirit, in equal majesty and in a holy trinity." Followers of this law, the

A Social and Cultural History of Late Antiquity, First Edition. Douglas Boin.
© 2018 John Wiley & Sons, Inc. Published 2018 by John Wiley & Sons, Inc.

emperors explained, were to use the name "catholic [universal] Christians." Everyone who did not subscribe to the new, mandated, official *religio* of the Roman world would be henceforth stigmatized as "foolish madmen."

The text of the Thessaloniki decree has been preserved in the *Theodosian Code* (16.1.2, trans. by C. Pharr, *The Theodosian Code and Novels, and the Sirmondian Constitutions* [Princeton: Princeton University Press, 1952], with modifications). Virtually overnight, it changed the power dynamics throughout the Roman Empire, as everyone who had followed Rome's traditional worship practices now confronted a government that was hostile to their beliefs and rituals. Naturally, the logistical intricacies and complications of publishing this law and raising public awareness for it guaranteed that its enforcement would never nearly match the zealousness with which it was drafted. Laws could be ripped down; others could simply be ruined in bad weather. For that reason, how quickly the 60 million citizens of the Roman Empire, post-380 CE, accepted they were now required to identify as "catholic Christians" is impossible for a historian to measure. Temple doors may have been closed throughout Roman cities, charred altars may have lain void of any new animal sacrifice, but one Roman law did not suddenly change what people believed – at least, not immediately.

8.1 Daily Life in the Fourth Century CE and Beyond: Starting Points and Assumptions

Even though all Roman citizens of the late fourth and early fifth centuries CE would soon be required to be "Christians," a historian faces a truly Sisyphian task when trying to push the massive pieces of the fourth century into the fifth. How many "real Christians" were there during this time? And why *did* Christian politicians choose to outlaw traditional worship practices? If it is true that we can't know the precise demographic breakdown of specific faith groups throughout the empire – if our task really is a precipitous uphill climb – then this uncertainty needs to be acknowledged right away, not ignored or replaced with theologically driven assumptions. Evidence, not our own religious beliefs or our own anti-religious preferences, needs to drive our approach to the past.

And yet we do need to pause, to step back and ask whether the emerging framework we've put in place might change the questions we are asking about the evidence. Here are some examples to consider. Should we write the story of the fourth century CE as if it were a world sharply divided into two camps, "pagans and Christians"? Or might that dichotomy imply a dangerous false equivalency – as if the cultural conversations of the fourth century were taking place between two equal sides – which might be historically misleading? Another question to ask might be this one: Were cities, in Constantine's age and afterward, "bipolar" places, as one scholar has characterized them, urban worlds where these two faith groups now hammered out their differences in a debate which eventually led to the "triumph" of Christianity (Peter Brown, *Through the Eye of a Needle: Wealth, the Fall of Rome, and the Making of Christianity in the West, 350–550* AD [Princeton: Princeton

University Press, 2012], p. 47)? Or might it be, rather, that the empire's Christian community itself was bipolar – not the empire's cities – because even on the cusp of the fourth century, Jesus' followers remained sharply divided about what it meant to be a Roman citizen? These are important, big-picture questions which every historian who writes about the fourth century needs to consider before analyzing specific pieces of textual or material evidence.

In this chapter, we will start by exploring some of the complexities within the material record. To begin, not every Christian text or church building erected in the fourth century might have been part of an ideological campaign to convert people to Christianity, as sometimes assumed. In the tumultuous years that followed Galerius's edict and the "Edict of Milan," many Romans remained unconvinced (to put it mildly) that Christians really could be successful partners in the enterprise of running the government; Maximinus' edict to the Roman cities of the east, which we looked at in the last chapter, is one example of the intransigence which many members of the fourth-century Christian community faced in their day-to-day interactions with family, friends, and neighbors.

In this context, we should caution against thinking that Christian buildings, Christian art, or Christian inscriptions – all of which do show a spike in the material record of the Mediterranean during this time – somehow did the hard work of recruiting people to the Christian faith. Like mosques built in culturally conservative cities of modern America, Britain, or France, some of which have been greeted with open hostility, even violence, a greater visible Christian presence in Rome's neighborhoods and the cities of the empire at large cannot be assumed to have been a cultural phenomenon that was wholeheartedly embraced by every Roman citizen. And yet that is exactly how many scholars continue to write about the significance of the admittedly undeniable fourth-century building boom in Christian architecture. Luring the Roman people from their own stale worship traditions, the empire's churches are said to have functioned as "safety valves for well-to-do persons who found the pace of life too fast and too expensive – driven too relentlessly by considerations of honor and reciprocity" (Brown 2012, p. 47). By the mid-fourth century, it has even been suggested, these buildings were advertising "the air of a dignified, morally bracing, and even exciting experiment in countercultural living" (Brown 2012, p. 47).

What we have seen in our discussion so far, however, suggests a more reserved approach. This particularly evangelical aspect of fourth-century Christianity may only be one part of a wider cultural landscape. Because of the complexities of being Christian, which included the fact that many Christians adapted to mainstream Roman values, it becomes difficult to support the argument that all fourth-century material culture was now deployed in an effort to "Christianize" the empire.

In fact, if we remember that Christians remained a marginal community throughout the third and fourth centuries, that, too, will shape the way we interpret the available evidence, both textual and material. Christian buildings and Christian art can just as equally be signs of Christians talking amongst themselves as much as we think they were now trying to speak to the larger urban environment to recruit others to the faith.

In this way, the social aspect of material culture, more broadly – not just the traditional study of aesthetic styles and trends in Christian architecture and

Christian art – can lead us to details of daily life that might have otherwise escaped our notice. In what follows, we will see how the material culture of two cities, far from window-dressing the story of Late Antiquity with interesting pictures, can give us an entirely different way of writing about life in the fourth-century Roman world (*Exploring Culture* 8.1: Silver Gifts and the Roman Emperor on the Crimean Peninsula; Figure 8.1). This evidence comes from two key cities of the fourth-century empire: Rome, the older, more historic capital; and Constantinople, a city inaugurated in May 330 CE.

By the end of this chapter, we will also begin to step beyond the horizon of the fourth century into the fifth and sixth centuries to notice both the continuities and changes in material culture that characterized Mediterranean life before and after Christianity's establishment as an official *religio* – and before and after Rome vanished from its own empire, in 476 CE.

Exploring Culture 8.1 *Silver Gifts and the Roman Emperor on the Crimean Peninsula*

The Straits of Kerch connect the Black Sea to the Sea of Azov. To the west is the Crimean peninsula; to the east, the Taman peninsula of modern Russia. This area may seem far from the classical world of the Roman Empire. But at the turn of the twentieth century, in the city of Kerch – located on the west side of the strait – a puzzling piece of material culture was discovered that raises questions about the reach and the workings of Roman power in the fourth century CE.

The artifact is a medium-sized silver bowl with a detailed engraving. It measures c.25 cm in diameter, about 10 inches, and shows three figures. In the center the Roman emperor in military dress rides horseback. He is carrying a lance, and his head is ringed by a *nimbus*, or "halo." To the emperor's left (the viewer's right) is the winged female goddess known in Latin as *Victoria* or in Greek as *Nikē*. She carries a crown and palm branch. On the emperor's right is a Roman soldier whose shield is engraved with the *chi-rho*. This bowl was found with two others; excavation reports suggest all three were buried during the late fourth century CE. One of its companion pieces shows Emperor Constantius II (r. 337–361 CE).

The silver dish from Kerch is a fascinating object, in part, because diplomatic relations between Constantius II and the rulers of the Crimean peninsula are otherwise unattested.

The dish itself is not one of a kind. Eighteen other silver bowls, all dated to the fourth century CE, have been found across the Mediterranean. One, discovered in southern Spain, is gigantic (74 cm, or almost 30 inches in diameter). It shows Emperor Theodosius surrounded by his court and commemorates the tenth anniversary of his rule (388 CE). Scholars believe all these silver dishes were presented as imperial gifts (Ruth Leader-Newby, *Silver and Society in Late Antiquity* [Burlington: Ashgate, 2004]). Although his identity remains unknown, it appears a distinguished local resident in Kerch was the recipient of an imperial present, too.

The people of the northern Black Sea had known about Mediterranean customs before the rise of Rome. As early as the sixth century BCE, Greeks had founded colonies there; its land proved rich for growing grain. Chersonesus, a Greek city on the southwest side of the Crimean peninsula, was established during this time. Two centuries later, close ties among Greek cities at home and abroad ensured an abundant food supply in Athens. It came from this region.

The situation in the fourth century CE was much different. Rome maintained no direct control over the northern shore of the Black Sea. For centuries, the responsibility for managing this territory had been outsourced to client kings, local residents who worked with the Roman army to maintain control. In the first century BCE/CE, one city even renamed itself "Agrippeia" to retain the support of the general Marcus Agrippa (*Collection of Inscriptions from the Bosporan Kingdoms* [*CIRB*], ed. by V. Struve [Moscow, 1965], number 983, line 6). The Crimean peninsula would not officially be declared a Roman province until the reign of Emperor Justinian.

Figure 8.1 This silver plate shows the Roman Emperor Constantius II, one of the successors of Constantine. He ruled from 337–361 CE. The plate is embossed and engraved with an eye-catching mixture of copper, silver, and black lead, called niello, and gilded. It was discovered in Kerch, near the Sea of Azov in the Bosporus necropolis on the Gordikov estate, on the northeastern slope of Mt. Mithridat, in 1891. Strikingly, no Roman writer ever mentions that Constantius II visited this distant area of the Black Sea – which lay far beyond Rome's borders. For that reason, this piece of material culture is an important historical piece of evidence. It attests to and evokes cultural connections between the people of the northern frontiers and the Roman government which may not have been recorded in contemporary written sources. The dish is now in the collection of The State Museum, Hermitage, Russia (Inventory number 1820-79). Measurements: diameter 25 cm (c. 10 in.). Used by permission of the Hermitage.

8.2 The Archaeology of Rome

A city as large as Rome can only be visited here in small scale, and there is no better way to think about the city than at the level of the neighborhood. Here, we will look at three neighborhoods that give us a rich picture of the fourth-century city. These include the downtown, or Forum, district, an important venue for imperially sponsored projects during the earlier Roman Empire; the Aventine Hill, one of the most celebrated hills of the capital, whose streets reveal a diverse neighborhood of houses, temples, and, later, Christian churches. Third, we will look at an area of urban sprawl outside Aurelian's city walls on the Via Appia, a road where many Roman families went to commemorate the burial of their loved ones. In this way, we will not try to list or categorize every detail about the fourth-century city. But we will try to see how, as a capital and the site of the Senate, the experience of Rome's streets contributes to our understanding of its people.

The city center and the imperial fora

Residents of Rome in the early fourth century had lived through history. Constantine's defeat of Maxentius, in 312 CE, had taken place at one of the northernmost bridges to cross the Tiber, the Milvian Bridge. Constantine's victory would be memorialized in the city center in multiple ways. A victory arch, the Arch of Constantine, was built near the Flavian Amphitheater to celebrate the emperor's military triumph. On it, the Senate and the People of Rome – "SPQR," in the abbreviated public language of Rome's inscriptions – praised Constantine for his successes. These they attributed to the "inspiration of a divinity" and "the greatness of [Constantine's] mind" (*CIL* 6.1139).

Although the text of the dedication does not elaborate on these statements, the sculptural panels on the arch do. To construct this monument, the Senate's workmen used panels from earlier imperial monuments featuring dearly popular emperors like Trajan, Hadrian, and Marcus Aurelius. Scenes of the sun god, Apollo, in his chariot and the moon goddess, Diana, in hers appear on either side of Constantine's monument. The arch itself was built in the shadow of the city's most famous "colossus," a gigantic bronze statue of Apollo which had once stood in the foyer of Nero's Golden House. It had been moved to the Flavian Amphitheater in the second century CE and would later inspire an affectionate medieval nickname for the stadium – "place of the colossus," or Colosseum.

Constantine himself would be given a colossal statue of his own. It would be installed in a law court, or basilica, in the old Roman Forum. This over life-size statue of wood and marble showed the emperor as the king of the Olympian gods, Jupiter, ruling over the known world. The statue was displayed in one of the grandest new halls in the old Forum, the "New Basilica," which Maxentius had begun and Constantine finished.

Constantine's arch, dedicated in 315 CE, and Constantine's colossus in the monumental "New Basilica" were important additions to downtown Rome; but the people who watched them being built and installed witnessed other significant events that were not always fixated on Constantine's larger-than-life personality. Archaeology of the imperial Forum spaces, located in the same neighborhood, gives us a more intimate picture of Rome's fourth-century urban history (Figure 8.2).

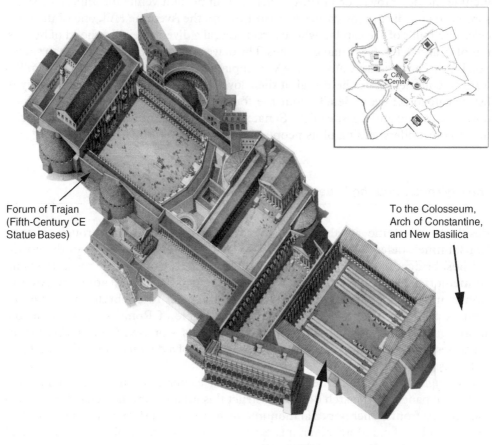

Forum of Trajan
(Fifth-Century CE
Statue Bases)

To the Colosseum,
Arch of Constantine,
and New Basilica

Forum of Peace
(Fourth-Century CE Demolition)

Figure 8.2 The Roman Forum was the commercial and political heart of the city. By the late first century BCE, politicians had begun expanding it with their own projects, under their own names. Many emperors would follow suit. This reconstruction shows these "imperial fora" of Rome, the emperors' grand additions to the city center. From top left to bottom right (roughly northwest to southeast) are: the Forum of Trajan, the Forum of Augustus, the Forum of the Emperor Nerva, and the Forum of Peace. By the fourth century CE, the Forum of Trajan was one of the most popular areas for displaying statues of Late Antique politicians. By contrast, parts of the nearby Forum of Peace had been dismantled and razed. Residents in fourth- and fifth-century Rome lived their life like this, one building at a time, constantly readjusting their expectations about the city. Plan, with annotations by the author, after the digital reconstruction by Inkling. From R. Meneghini and R. Santangeli Valenzani, *I fori imperiali. Gli scavi del comune di Roma (1991–2007)* (Rome: Viviani, 2007), p. 30. Used with the permission of Roberto Meneghini and La Soprintendenza Capitolina ai Beni Culturali, Rome.

Just down the street from the site of the Arch of Constantine and the Flavian Amphitheater, just behind the "New Basilica," was Rome's historic Forum of Peace. It had been built by Emperor Vespasian to commemorate the war against Judaea and had remained an important green space throughout the second through third centuries CE. By the first decade of the fourth century, however, sections of this open plaza – which had once featured a long charming pond – were being demolished. And a group of small buildings, constructed out of the recycled marble and brick, was inserted into the once-tranquil urban oasis. Although the wealthy people or persons who paid for this project are unknown, archaeologists have been able to specify the date of their intervention, the early fourth century CE, based on the discovery of bricks that had been stamped with the year of their manufacture. At this stage the buildings likely functioned as a warehouse or pop-up market space.

The project must have changed the feel of the once-grand urban plaza almost beyond recognition. The contrast with the developments down the street must have been striking. In the heart of old Rome, Vespasian's victory monument had been dramatically disassembled at the same time that shiny monuments for Constantine were being erected. This evidence is an important reminder that the heartbeat of cities, although these spaces did see significant changes in Late Antiquity, cannot be charted as a healthy line leading to sudden death. In this case, it is likely that the warehouses and markets displaced by one of the grandest projects of the early fourth century, Maxentius and Constantine's "New Basilica," had the unexpected development of displacing merchants and workmen who now needed a new home for their businesses. Two centuries later, even their new buildings would be leveled and changed. By the sixth century CE, the Forum-turned-warehouse district would be the site of several burials.

The practice of burying the dead within the city walls, although it would have been virtually unheard of in Constantine's time, is one of the first signs that expectations of what constituted city life were not static values. The idea of what it meant to live in a city could change quite dramatically from the fourth century CE – at least in this one neighborhood of the old capital.

The communities of Rome's Aventine Hill

South of the city center, on one of modern Rome's most residential hills, the Aventine, another story was playing out over the course of the fourth and fifth centuries. The Aventine Hill had been an important site throughout Rome's history. The Circus Maximus, Rome's Greatest Race Track, had been built in the valley between the Aventine and Palatine Hills. During the Republican period, the hill itself had become famous for the resistance of the plebeian class, who organized on the hill to demand greater access to the legislative veto power. In the early Empire, it overlooked a series of emporia, or warehouses, along the Tiber, where a range of commodities from ceramic shipping containers to imported marble was offloaded after arriving from Ostia. These trades gave the hill an identifiably commercial character.

By the fourth century CE, the character of the Aventine Hill had changed again, becoming a place of wealthy homes (Figure 8.3). It was a diverse neighborhood of

The Aventine Hill, Rome

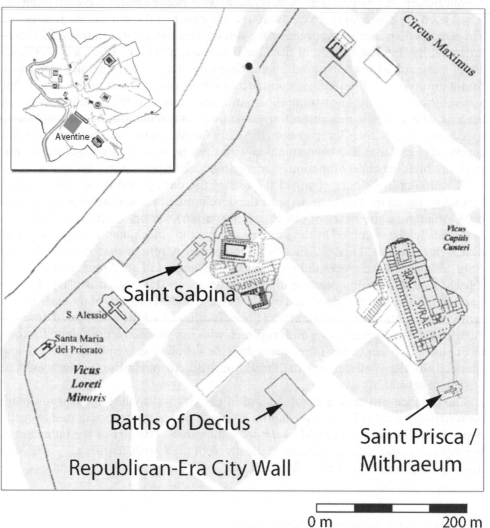

Figure 8.3 Ancient Romans prided themselves on their city's famed seven hills, although they often disagreed about which hills counted; the reason for their disagreement is that there are, in reality, fourteen hills in or near the city of Rome. This plan shows one of the most central and most storied: the Aventine Hill. Romans believed that Romulus' lesser known brother, Remus, had been its first settler. Remus was largely forgotten, but over time, his hill grew into an important part of Rome's identity. By the early fifth century CE, as this plan shows, the Aventine was the site of impressive baths, a local Mithraeum, and early Christian churches. Even portions of the old Republican-era city wall continued to be visible in the Late Antique neighborhood. Author's plan modified from Filippo Coarelli, *Roma* (Bari: Editori Laterza, 2008), p. 449.

temples, baths, churches, and also at least one Mithraeum. The hill was a veritable palimpsest of different epochs, in whose streets one could read the ever-changing story of Rome. The visible traces of the first true wall of the city, built in the fourth century BCE, could be found on the Late Antique hill. Six hundred years after that wall was erected on the Aventine's slopes, a temple would be dedicated to the Syrian god, Jupiter Dolichenus, in the second century CE. These gradual but steady changes continued even during the turbulent political years of the middle of the third century. Emperor Decius, for example, invested in a large public bath complex, or *thermae*, located here. The footprint of Decius' baths is still identifiable, and the dedication of the building is known from inscriptions. A statue of Hercules was even found among its halls, as the gods formed part of the standard repertoire of Roman baths. The building was restored in the middle of the fourth century and again in 414 CE, after the "sack" of Rome by the Gothic leader Alaric.

Perhaps the most intriguing story that the streets of the Aventine tell, however, concerns the different worship communities located here and how they gradually made themselves known – and what happened to their meeting spaces over time. One of these groups was a community of Mithras worshippers. By 202 CE, based on the discovery of an ancient graffito, we know that they had been given permission to renovate one of the rooms in the lower levels of a Roman home, turning it into a Mithraeum (*CIMRM* 476). This worship space was then covered in remarkable, colorful wall paintings, which still survive, showing scenes important to the Mithras worshippers.

The paintings on one side of the Mithraeum's banquet hall show the seven distinctive levels available to initiates. Scenes on the other side show a procession of worshippers leading a bull, ram, and pig to an animal sacrifice. This widely popular scene was well known from Roman civic monuments and may have been painted in the Mithraeum to remind the mystery initiates not to leave their commitment to the civic life of Rome behind. The Mithraeum itself remained in use until the first decade of the fifth century CE when it was filled with rubble. It was during this construction project, which filled the basement space entirely, that the paintings were damaged. A church, dedicated to Saint Prisca, was built on top.

Because the building constructed on top of the ruins was a Christian worship space, some scholars have inferred that the Mithraeum's destruction must have been a malicious act – one that attests to the animosity and intolerance of the Christian community on the Aventine towards their Roman neighbors. The contemporary writer Jerome, for example, who was working and writing at exactly the time that the Aventine space was transformed, alludes to a Christian attack on Mithras worshippers in Rome in one of his pieces of correspondence (Jerome, *Letter* 107). Unfortunately, there is no evidence to connect his letter with the site underneath the church of Saint Prisca; nor is there any indisputable evidence that the Mithraeum was vengefully destroyed. Whoever buried it in the first decades of the fifth century CE may have simply realized that joining a non-Christian group was not a viable cultural choice anymore, after the Edict of Thessaloniki.

The church of Saint Prisca itself holds the distinction of being the earliest Christian building on the Aventine Hill, but it was soon joined by other Christian worship spaces. The church of Saint Sabina (built 422–432 CE) was a second. It, too, like the Mithraeum underneath Saint Prisca, preserves an extraordinary example of Roman material culture. At the entrance to Saint Sabina, two large wooden doors were fashioned with scenes from Jesus' life, stories from Jewish Scripture, and one still puzzling, unidentifiable scene of a gathering of Roman magistrates. These carved panels still stand at the entrance to the church and are one of the Aventine Hill's most treasured cultural artifacts. One scene, located on the upper reaches of the door, may even be the first piece of Christian material culture to illustrate the scene of Jesus' crucifixion. No crucifixion scene made for a church dates earlier than the first decade of the fifth century CE.

Funerary banquets on the Via Appia

The burials in the city center at the Forum of Peace, which date to the sixth century CE, are unique in Rome because the custom of the imperial period was to bury the dead outside the city walls. For that reason, almost all of the roads leading out of Rome during the Republic and Empire were lined with tombs. Many of these were large family tombs, with spaces set aside for the household's slaves. They could be lined with niches to hold cremated remains; or, for those who desired more overt displays of wealth, they could be lined with finely carved marble burial boxes (in the singular, a sarcophagus).

On the Via Appia, which led to southern Italy, another kind of burial practice arose during the early empire: interment in a network of subterranean caverns. These caverns were quarried from the local stone, a soft volcanic rock called tufa, and the deceased's bones would be placed on a shelf carved from the rock. This compartment, or *loculus*, was then sealed. Hundreds of rows of *loculi* could be contained in one underground network. Many Christians, non-Christians, and Jews were buried together in these networks. One catacomb on the Via Appia, at the third Roman milestone, offers a fascinating look at how Christians commemorated their dead in the period before and after Constantine.

This site on the Via Appia is the location of a fourth-century church, dedicated to Saint Sebastian. This church is historically and archaeologically important because it was built near a well-known large tufa quarry, or "cavity" or "cup," called in Greek a *kumbe*. The caverns located in the vicinity of this tufa "cavity" were soon being described as lying "next to the cavity," or in Greek, *kata-kumbas*. The subterranean burials at the third milestone on the Via Appia are not the only "catacombs" in the Roman world, but the local geography gave rise to the word which we still use today to refer to these underground tombs.

The catacombs at Saint Sebastian, on the Via Appia, are important for a second reason. Throughout the year, friends and relatives would visit tombs – whether above ground or below ground – to celebrate the custom of the *refrigerium*, or funerary meal, by which Romans honored their dead. The area underneath the church of Saint Sebastian has been carefully studied and shows archaeological traces of this practice. In a small space which was once open to the sky, before the fourth-century church was built on top of it, hundreds of graffiti, scratched on the wall, record the names of visitors who came to the site to partake in honoring the dead. Some of these graffiti make reference to the magistrates or emperors who were ruling Rome at the time, a key detail that has helped archaeologists date the gatherings here. As this evidence makes clear, the people who were coming to celebrate the *refrigerium* did so during the middle of the third century CE. One set of names explains why the catacomb site of Saint Sebastian is so illustrative for the Christian community specifically.

All of the testimony left behind by the Christian visitors is dedicated to the memories of "Peter and Paul." In effect, the archaeology of the catacombs under-neath Saint Sebastian shows that Peter and Paul were buried and honored here throughout the third century CE. This tradition does not harmonize with other Christian stories told about the burial of Peter at the Vatican Hill, across the river (*Key Debates* 8.1: Faith, Texts, Archaeology, and Today: The Example of St. Peter's Basilica; Figure 8.4); or the burial of Paul, which would later be associated with the Ostian Road. But it does suggest that, just as neighborhoods of Rome could change over time, so, too, could the customs and traditions of the Christian community throughout the city.

Key Debates 8.1   *Faith, Texts, Archaeology, and Today: The Example of St. Peter's Basilica*

In 64 CE, in the aftermath of a fire that affected life in ten of the fourteen regions of Rome, Emperor Nero executed several indi-viduals. The site of these executions was the city's newest sport facility: the Circus of Caligula and Nero. Begun by the Emperor Caligula, also known as Gaius, in 37–41 CE, the track was finished at the beginning of Nero's rule (54–68 CE). Very little of this race track remains archaeologically. An obelisk, brought from Egypt and used to decorate the spine, still exists. It stands in the center of St. Peter's Square, Piazza San Pietro.

When did Nero's gruesome site became associated with Peter? A team of Baroque architects built the current church over an earlier, fourth-century one, but what's bur-ied exactly underneath the fourth-century

church? Excavation has helped clarify the picture.

Directly beneath St. Peter's Basilica is a street of Roman tombs. Romans buried their dead here in a necropolis, or "city of the dead," outside the city center, starting in the first century CE. Then, in the early fourth century, the tombs themselves were "entombed" – during a ground-raising campaign – so that a new building could be supported on top of the site of the old necropolis. This building was a church dedi-cated to St. Peter.

Archaeologists have been able to study the Vatican necropolis to learn more about the burial practices of the Roman world before the rise of Christianity. What they found also sheds light on the Christian development of the site, the center of the Roman Catholic faith today.

Excavators labeled all the tombs they found underneath the church, starting with A and ending with Z and using Greek letters for the remaining tombs. One of these sites, labeled P on plans, caught archaeologists' attention. It was a shrine built in front of a brick wall on an open plot of land. This type of shrine is called an "aedicula" shrine because it resembles a "small building." The brick wall in front of which this aedicula was built was painted red. Archaeologists have given it the unimaginative name: the red wall.

The shrine in area P by the red wall has become one of the site's most important, debated features. Based on a comparison of the top-plan of the necropolis with the location of the Baroque church, one can see why. The red wall is located squarely underneath the altar of St. Peter's, as though the Baroque church had been designed to preserve the memory of the person buried in area P. The discovery of writing scratched on the red wall, found by an archaeologist working with papal sponsorship in the 1960s, makes the story even more intriguing. Only five letters of this Greek graffito remain visible, but according to one interpreter, it says: "Pet[er is] in[side]." (According to scholarly convention, the square brackets indicate which letters are missing from the ancient text.)

Is Peter really buried in area P at the red wall beneath the altar of St. Peter's? A careful study of the construction technique used to build the red wall, as well as an analysis of construction marks stamped onto the clay bricks, has allowed archaeologists to date the shrine. At the earliest, it was erected in the late second century CE. There is no physical evidence that takes us back any further in time to connect Peter's supposed death in 64 CE with this late second-century tomb.

8.3   The Archaeology of Constantinople

After 330 CE, Rome was not the only capital of its empire. At the end of a bent tip of a promontory that reaches out from Europe towards the continent of Asia, Constantine would build a second. Unlike the cities of the Tetrarchs, like Galerius' Thessaloniki or Diocletian's Nicomedia, Constantinople would have its own Senate, a second advisory body to the Roman emperor, drawn from wealthy local citizens of the eastern Mediterranean. It was a bold vision but perhaps an appropriate one for a man who had defeated Licinius in 324 CE and had emerged as sole ruler of the Mediterranean.

It was also an extraordinary distinction for this one city in the east although the reality behind its rising stature was far less hyperbolic than people today might characterize the emperor's decision. By investing heavily in Constantinople, Constantine did not move the capital of the empire from Rome. In the simplest terms, the fourth-century Roman Empire now had two capitals. What can the archaeology and history of Constantinople (modern Istanbul) tell us about daily life in the empire's second center of power?

The Vatican Necropolis (St. Peter's Basilica)

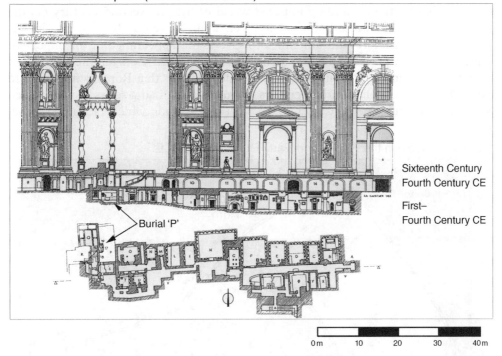

Figure 8.4 This illustration shows St. Peter's Basilica at the Vatican in two forms. Below is what archaeologists and architects call a "top-plan." It shows a bird's-eye view of the burial street, or necropolis, underneath St. Peter's. The necropolis was in use from the first century to the early fourth century CE. The second view, above, is a longitudinal elevation drawing of the seventeenth-century church; it shows a view of the site from the perspective of someone standing at ground level. In this drawing, the lowest ground level corresponds to the levels of the first century CE; followed by the fourth century CE; and then the Baroque church. By studying the elevation, archaeologists can better visualize how Constantine's church of "Old St. Peter's" demolished the ancient necropolis and how the later construction of "New St. Peter's" replaced Constantine's. The burial area marked on the plan by the letter "P" dates to the late second century CE. Plan of the necropolis and longitudinal section of the "Sacre Grotte Vaticane" and Basilica di San Pietro by K. Gaertner. Used with the kind permission of the Fabbrica di San Pietro in Vaticano.

A new city but with a forgotten history

To begin, Constantine's city was not the first on the site. Greeks had settled a colony here in the seventh century BCE. They called their settlement Byzantion. It stood at the intersection of a tri-water area – the Bosporus Strait, the Sea of Marmara, and the Golden Horn – and was a vital way station for Greeks sailing from Athens and the Peloponessus to the Black Sea. Byzantion played an important part in the history of Greece's military encounters with Persia.

The Persians were eventually driven back, but the city of Byzantion continued to grow. During the expanding imperial world of the late second century CE, the Roman emperor Septimius Severus had taken credit for refounding the city, investing in its infrastructure and amenities to give it the appearance of an important center of Roman power. So it was that, by 324 CE, when Constantine first began planning to rename it, the city had many of the elements that Romans had come to expect from cosmopolitan urban centers (Figure 8.5). It had a series of walls which Septimius Severus had constructed. It had several roads which facilitated travel

Constantinople in the Fourth and Early Fifth Centuries CE

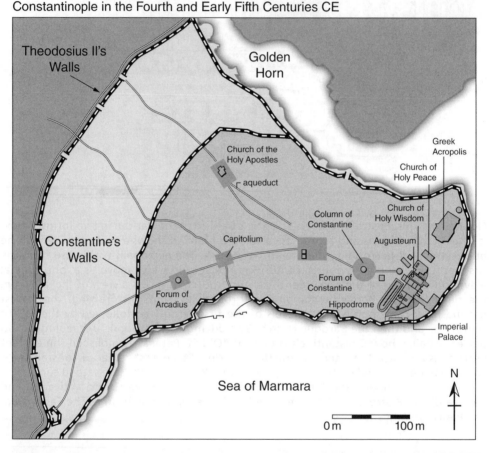

Figure 8.5   The city of Constantinople in the late fourth century and early fifth century CE. Often claimed to be the site where Constantine moved the capital of the Roman Empire, Constantinople was, in reality, a second capital. The site itself had first been settled by Greeks, then expanded by Romans in the second and third centuries CE. All throughout this long history, it had been known as Byzantium. In 330 CE Constantine celebrated the momentous change in the life of the city; in line with popular displays of imperial power, he chose to re-found it and rename it after himself. With a new forum, a new palace, a race track, and – most importantly – its own Senate, citizens of the empire began to imagine Constantine's city as a "Second Rome." Only when the Roman world fractured, in 476 CE, did Constantine's city emerge as the empire's sole capital. Plan by Wiley's illustrators.

across its European peninsula. It had a Roman basilica, a temple to the goddess Cybele, and one dedicated to the goddess Fortuna, called by her Greek name, Tyche (the Goddess of Chance or Good Luck). If textual sources can be trusted, the city also boasted a Temple of Jupiter, Juno, and Minerva, the trio of gods worshipped on Rome's famous Capitoline Hill. Unfortunately, much of modern Istanbul still hides the physical appearance of Septimius Severus' and even Constantine's Roman city, and scholars are dependent on textual descriptions to reconstruct the feel of the fourth-century city.

Some sites are known archaeologically. The hippodrome, or race track, is one of the most visible. Located on the far eastern end of the peninsula, the track was a functioning part of Septimius Severus' Roman city but may not have been a fully polished building until the age of Constantine. The race track itself adjoined the imperial palace, following the urban model of Rome, where the emperor's residence overlooked the Circus Maximus. A public bath, the Baths of Zeuxippos, was also a popular venue in this region of the city. It contained the traditional set of hot and cold rooms, a soothing respite for Romans all throughout the empire, and also included an exercise ground, a gymnasium – a part of the landscape of Hellenistic cities since the time of Alexander the Great. The Baths of Zeuxippos were another pre-existing Roman construction that was completed by Constantine.

Constantine's Forum

In finishing many of Septimius Severus' projects, a task which could mean little more than adding a splash of expensive marble, Constantine equipped the empire's second capital with the kinds of spaces an urbane citizen would have expected to have down the street from their homes. Like other Roman rulers before him, the emperor used these projects to advertise his political legitimacy and increase public support for his rule. One important project in this regard was Constantine's Forum.

For centuries, emperors had built new forum spaces to promote the messages of their political campaigns. In this way, from Julius Caesar to Vespasian and Trajan, the downtown district of Rome grew as the emperors added new spaces for law, diplomacy, and business. Trajan's Forum, built in the second century CE, was one of the busiest places in the capital and included a multilevel shopping mall. For politicians, it also remained one of the most important venues in Late Antique Rome (*Political Issues* 8.1: Justinian's Nea Church and the Architectural Audacity of Roman Emperors). Constantine's own decision to build a forum in Constantinople was consistent with the broader set of cultural expectations that emperors provide new civic spaces for their citizens; and that they use these spaces to increase their standing among the city's residents.

Constantine's Forum in Constantinople did both these things. Designed as a circular plaza, it was located at an important transition point in one of the city's major east–west roads, the Mese, which connected the palace to the far western reaches of the peninsula. Its appearance was also filled with potent messaging.

Political Issues 8.1 *Justinian's Nea Church and the Architectural Audacity of Roman Emperors*

In the Roman Empire, audacious building projects could make or break a politician's career. When Nero (r. 54–68 CE) decided to create a man-made lake in the center of Rome, as part of his scheme for a large private palace, judgment against him was swift. "There was nothing," Nero's biographer Suetonius wrote, "in which the emperor was more ruinously prodigal than in his building" (*Life of Nero* 31.1, LCL trans. by J. C. Rolfe [1914]). Nero's reputation has suffered, but his creative vision – experimenting with concrete, pushing the limits of engineering – set a high bar for innovation. It also may have dared his successors to continue to think big.

Emperor Trajan, overwhelmingly praised throughout Late Antiquity as the model of a respected ruler (r. 98–117 CE), also tested the limits of engineering in a way that won him fame. To create his Forum, he ordered his builders to cart away a significant part of the city's Quirinal Hill. The feat was so impressive, the Senate erected a sign to boast about the accomplishment. This inscription explains, in Latin, that Trajan's column was erected "to demonstrate how high the mountain was and the extent of the site which had to be cleared away" to bring such a great work to completion. In the fifth century CE, business was still transacted in the shadow of Trajan's towering legacy.

Dreams of daring feats of architecture inspired leaders of the eastern Roman Empire even after emperors gave up control of Rome. Many of Justinian's buildings (r. 527–565 CE) set new, high bars for what was possible. In Jerusalem, one project was the New Church of Mary, the Bearer of God (*Theotokos*).

Unfortunately, only the most frustrating archaeological foundations remain of Justinian's church. But Procopius provides details about its grandeur and about the challenges which the emperor's team faced while designing it. Battling the natural topography of Jerusalem was a major obstacle. "This city is for the most part set upon hills. However, these hills have no soil upon them but stand with rough and very steep sides, causing the streets to run straight up and down like ladders," Procopius explains in his treatise *On the Emperor's Buildings*.

The site where Justinian envisioned building the New Church also caused headaches for the design team. "The Emperor Justinian gave orders that it be built on the highest of the hills … [But as a result of the emperor's vision], a fourth part of the church, facing the south and the east, was left unsupported" (*On the Emperor's Buildings* 5.6.2–5, LCL trans. by H. Dewing [1940]). What did the engineers do?

Procopius explains how the engineers solved this architectural problem.

> They threw the foundations out as far as the limit of the even ground, and then erected a man-made substructure which rose as high as the rock. When they had leveled this substructure with the natural rock, they set vaults upon the supporting walls and joined it to the other foundation of the church. Thus the church is partly based upon living rock and partly carried in the air by a great extension artificially added to the hill by the Emperor's power. (*On the Emperor's Buildings* 5.6.6–8, trans. by H. Dewing [1940], slightly modified)

This ingenious solution for erecting a church would likely have impressed Emperors Trajan and Nero alike.

As a homage to the widely adored Trajan, Constantine included a large victory column at the center of his Forum (Figure 8.6). It was quarried from purple Egyptian porphyry, one of the most expensive building materials available known anywhere in the Roman world. A statue of the triumphant emperor, wearing a crown with the rays of the sun, stood on top of the column. This imagery was borrowed from Hellenistic rulers, like Alexander and his successors, who used the sun to play up the cosmic dimensions of their political authority. The use of that Hellenistic imagery here helped Constantine tell a powerful story about his own rule; it was rooted in the past and drew upon both Hellenistic and Roman precedents.

Figure 8.6 Like other Roman emperors before him, Constantine (ruled jointly 312–324 CE; 324–337 as sole Augustus) used his money and stature to put his unique stamp on city life. One way he did so, at Constantinople, was to create his own forum. An expensive porphyry column stood at its center. Little remains of this Forum of Constantine, which is now part of the Çemberlitaş neighborhood of Istanbul, except portions of this damaged column. This digital reconstruction, based on textual reports of what it looked like, shows the Emperor Constantine making reference to the sun god Helios, or Apollo. The sun god had been a figure popularly embraced by Hellenistic rulers, centuries earlier, in the age of Alexander the Great. These rulers had used it to allude to their own divinity. Roman rulers, including Constantine and his successors, would embrace that same tradition. Reconstruction © Byzantium 1200.

Emperors living in Constantinople, both before and after the vanishing of Rome from the Roman Empire, would undertake similar projects. New Forum spaces would be built in the late fourth century CE for Emperor Theodosius; and later, in the fifth century CE, for Arcadius and Marcian. Even Justinian, in the sixth century CE, would erect an equestrian statue of himself in Constantinople's city center. In doing so, Justinian was following a precedent going back centuries to rulers like Augustus. A statue of the "first citizen" of Rome, riding a chariot, pulled by four horses, stood at the center of Augustus' Forum in Rome.

Urban infrastructure and neighborhood residences

Constantinople was more than a flat billboard for an emperor's message, however. Bordered on its western peninsula by a strip of city walls – completed by Constantine, then pushed further out by the Emperor Theodosius (r. 379–392 CE, emperor of the eastern Mediterranean; 392–395 CE, sole ruler of the Roman world) – the second capital of the empire was also a working city and a place many people who did not have palace jobs simply called their home. As such, its citizens had basic needs which Constantine and his successors also met. One necessity was fresh water. The people of Constantinople received theirs from an aqueduct which brought water into the peninsula from a source 100 kilometers away in the mountains of Thrace. This aqueduct fed the Baths of Zeuxippos, and its overflow was channeled into large reservoirs under the city, called cisterns, for later use.

Constantinople was also a city of shippers, sailors, bakers, and trades. On the peninsula's southern side, two harbors were constructed during the middle to late fourth century CE to accommodate grain shipments from Roman Egypt. Unlike Rome's supply, which was stored at Portus and Ostia, Constantinople's food supply was offloaded, managed, and stored directly on the peninsula itself. The shipping industry's presence in the city must have given the neighborhoods there a commercial feel.

A late fourth-century CE government document, a terse list known as the *Notitia* of Constantinople, records the number and kinds of buildings found in each region of the city. It reveals that most laborers did live around the city's harbors although it doesn't elaborate why. Perhaps they liked the location, offering a convenient walk to work. Or maybe the day-in, day-out noise of crates and jugs made rents cheap. Whatever the reason, wealthier citizens, by contrast, had their abodes – richly furnished estates, called in Latin singular and plural *domus* – in the far western regions of the city and closer to the palace. The *Notitia* also does not, unfortunately, give us any details of domestic life that might let us into the homes of those Romans who lived in the fourth-century capital (*Working With Sources* 8.1: Tableware and Kitchenware: From Artifact to Museum Exhibits and Private Collections; Figure 8.7), although it does leave us with at least some hint – or whiff – of life on the city streets at the turn of the fifth century CE.

One region of the city, near the Forum of Theodosius, was packed with warehouses and bakeries. According to the *Notitia*, it was also one of the least populated neighborhoods in town, maybe because the stiff smell of baking bread made it undesirable place to call home.

Working With Sources 8.1

Tableware and Kitchenware: From Artifact to Museum Exhibits and Private Collections

"'Food, when it's taken, usually makes people quiet; wine makes them talkative.'" So pronounces the wealthy dinner host in an early fifth-century CE Latin text, the *Saturnalia*. Describing a ritzy gathering celebrated during Rome's raucous winter "Festival of Saturn," the *Saturnalia* was written by a man intimately familiar with the world of elite Roman mores: Macrobius, a senator and one-time praetorian prefect of Italy and Africa (lived *c.*400 CE).

Parties like those described by Macrobius and their humbler counterparts – peasant meals in an upstairs apartment or a dinner of snacks at the local tavern – were times for talking and conversing. And subjects could vary wildly based on the people gathered around the table or bar. In the *Saturnalia*, which explicitly evokes Plato's symposium, the host laments that no one is really saying anything substantial at all: "We're silent even while we're drinking! As though a dinner party like this should abstain from treating serious or even philosophical topics" (Macrobius, *Saturnalia* 6.1, LCL trans. by R. Kaster [2011], slightly modified). Not everything was always serious, of course. Even Macrobius' soiree is filled with attendees cracking jokes.

Eavesdropping on a dinner party outside these highly styled, literary vignettes is a bit more challenging, but archaeological evidence can help. Dining rooms, mosaics, and paintings can help set the scene. The implements used to display a hot platter or hold the wine set the table.

Today, most students of the ancient world encounter ceramics in a museum, displayed behind the glass of an exhibit; a few luckier ones will be able to hold a "sherd" (or pottery fragment) for themselves, wash it, and catalogue it. Sherds may not be the most newsworthy artifacts, and the value of ceramics at large may seem slight. (Some whole ceramics do show up on the art market and come without any provenance; ethically minded scholars are wary of writing about them.) Still, ceramics tell a story or two.

One type widely found at Late Antique contexts is "African Red Slip Ware." Varying in color from burnt orange to brick red, with a matte finish, African Red Slip Ware enjoyed a wide popularity on Roman tables and in kitchens from the third through seventh centuries CE. Molded out of local North African clay, it was regularly in demand as far away as the Black Sea. Its surfaces could be plain and austere or stamped with decorative, floral designs; some were covered with figures and animals.

One African Red Slip Ware bowl, now in Germany, shows a much grizzlier conversation topic than we may deem appropriate for a dinner party: It shows a bear ready to maul a criminal, stripped and tied to a post for execution. Based on materials which archaeologists found near this artifact, we know this piece of tableware was being passed around in the mid-fourth or early fifth century CE.

Bowls with similar scenes, showing gladiators, circus races, and even executions were common in the Roman world and remind us that Romans didn't need to have a seat in their local amphitheater to be able to stare, face to face, at the performance of gruesome public spectacles.

Figure 8.7 This example of African Red Slip Ware shows a criminal tied up for torture and death in the jaws of the beasts of the amphitheater. Found in Sicily, it has been dated to the second half of the fourth century CE. This peculiarly grizzly punishment, known as "*damnatio ad bestias*," often appears in stories about Christian "martyrs," those followers of Jesus who – either during periods of documented legal discrimination or in other circumstances – found themselves facing public execution. This dish would likely have been passed around the room at an expensive or at least moderately wealthy dinner party. Now in the Badisches Landesmuseum, Karlsruhe, Germany (inventory number 68/28).

Summary

This chapter has used two of the empire's capital cities, Rome and Constantinople, to develop snapshots of urban life in the fourth and early fifth centuries CE. In doing so, it has deliberately avoided narrating the history of these spaces through a dry, chronological account of building projects. In Rome and even in Constantinople, the new capital, older monuments could exist alongside new ones, and long-held values and cultural traditions – like the ideologies associated with Hellenistic kings or deified Roman emperors – remained ever-present in the atmosphere. All the residents of Rome and Constantinople, the emperor, Senate, and people, breathed this air.

Not everything about the past survived, of course. Buildings and whole neighborhoods could change, as we saw with the Forum of Peace in downtown Rome and in the example of the Mithraeum on the Aventine Hill, which was buried underneath a later Christian construction project. These instances of destruction cannot be written out of the history of any city. And yet, when trying to assign significance to them, caution is also warranted. Many times, as in the case of the Mithraeum under Saint Prisca, material culture does not tell us what we want to know: about how it was buried, by whom, and why.

Finally, by emphasizing the way that churches formed but one part of these multi-layered cities, we have been able to capture a wide-lens view of city life that was not centered around insular questions of Christian worship or the history of the Christian church. Constantine, for example, did sponsor new church building in both Rome and Constantinople. But the material culture of these cities, which includes baths, statues, and race tracks, shows that the development of Christian meeting spaces was not necessarily the most important aspect of life in the fourth-century city.

Study Questions

1. When was the city of Constantinople dedicated? What was its administrative relationship to Rome?
2. Take your friends for a tour of the Aventine Hill in Rome in the early fifth century CE. What would you tell them about the history of the neighborhood?
3. Does it matter whether Saint Peter is really buried underneath the Vatican? Why or why not?
4. Using examples from Rome and Constantinople, illustrate how Roman politicians used building programs to promote their ideas and their visions for the empire.

Suggested Readings

Sarah Bassett, *The Urban Image of Late Antique Constantinople* (New York: Cambridge University Press, 2007).

Neil Christie, *From Constantine to Charlemagne: An Archaeology of Italy, AD 300–800* (Aldershot: Ashgate, 2006).

Lucy Grig and Gavin Kelly (eds.), *Two Romes: Rome and Constantinople in Late Antiquity* (New York: Oxford University Press, 2012).

Nicola Denzey Lewis, *The Bone Gatherers: The Lost Worlds of Early Christian Women* (Boston: Beacon Press, 2007).

9

Community

The Mediterranean is a diverse place. Desert valleys unfold around the hills of Jerusalem. The lush, green carpet of Egypt welcomes people from the sandier parts of Africa. Olive groves in North Africa and Greece lend the land a silvery flicker, a kind not seen in colder northern regions, like Thrace, where olive trees don't grow. Amid these geographic differences, however, common ideas could still take root in Late Antiquity. An almost countless number of cities watched as Christian churches were erected on their streets and neighborhoods during the political whirlwind of the fourth century. And yet the fact that churches sprung up virtually everywhere is not surprising. For a community that had been given legal permission to worship openly and the injunction to do so in a way that promoted "the well-ordered state and the tranquillity [*quies*] of our times," as the so-called Edict of Milan had expressly stated it (Lactantius, *On the Death of the Persecutors* 48, trans. by W. Fletcher in the *ANF* series [1886]), Christian buildings gave the empire's minority Christianity community an important opportunity to demonstrate their allegiance to Roman ideals.

In the early fourth century, Emperor Constantine himself had set the pace and shown the way. In Rome, a church for the city's bishop would be built on the model of a classical law court, or basilica. Often erroneously described as a "secular" building, or described as a uniquely Christian house of worship uncontaminated by the legacy of Rome's gods, a basilica, by contrast, had long been a symbolic site, a place where the divine authority underpinning the empire's law and order was made manifest. Inscriptions found throughout the Roman world, inside non-Christian basilicas, attest to the ways in which Romans associated their own gods and their own divine ideology with these civic buildings. According to a text from one city in Roman Gaul, a *basilica* was located within that town's popular sanctuary (*AE* 2001, 1383).

A Social and Cultural History of Late Antiquity, First Edition. Douglas Boin.
© 2018 John Wiley & Sons, Inc. Published 2018 by John Wiley & Sons, Inc.

According to another inscription, we learn that a priestess of the imperial cult dedicated a statue for the emperor, which she set it up inside a basilica (*AE* 1982, 682).

Given the indissoluble nexus between *religio* and the management of the Roman government, it should not be surprising to learn that some of the first churches built in the post-Edict of Milan political landscape were either modeled on Roman basilicas or were dedicated out of a concern for shared Roman values. In Rome, one important basilica was located in the capital's eastern neighborhoods, the Esquiline, on land that had once belonged to the Lateranus family. This "Lateran basilica," later known as the church of Saint John, would become the seat of the bishop of Rome. On the other side of the empire, in early fourth-century Constantinople, on land located north of the palace and near the city's hippodrome, a church would be dedicated to Holy Peace, in Greek *Hagia Eirene*. She was a divine quality that was revered by long lists of Roman and Hellenistic rulers. Statues of Eirene were popular in Hellenistic art. In Rome, her Latin equivalent, *Pax*, had been worshipped at an Altar of Peace since Augustus' age.

Not all churches would follow the basilica model, however. Nor was every Christian individual and community ready, willing, and eager to participate in Constantine's vision for a "well-ordered state." The movement led by followers of Bishop Donatus in North Africa suggests that some Christian communities remained committed to separating themselves socially, particularly from contact with other Christians who were judged to have made too many compromises with Roman culture. The remains of churches throughout the Roman world, even though they are found across the empire, thus reveals a level of diversity and experimentation that makes it difficult to generalize about Christian architecture or Christian communities.

The fourth-century church of Saint Agnes in Rome, for instance, resembles a circus, or race track. Its main focus was probably a burial in the center of the building. We will look at the community who gathered there later in this book. At Tebessa, meanwhile, in Roman Algeria, the church there combined elements of a Roman basilica with a tri-conch, or clover-shaped, domed hall. These two distinct building types, although connected by their common origins in Christianity, created spaces that pulled worshippers and visitors in multiple directions, not just towards an altar at the front. The church at Tebessa was built in the late fourth and early fifth centuries CE.

In brief, even as one set of Christian beliefs was established as the empire's official worship and portions of Italy itself fell under the leadership of Ostrogothic kings like Theoderic, Christian communities never settled on one specific form for their community spaces. The church of Saint Vitalis in Ravenna, an Italian city that remained under the control of the sixth-century Roman government in Constantinople, was octagonal. It was built in 526–549 CE.

As this overview of Christian architecture reveals, from the fourth century onward, we see many Christian communities designing and building worship spaces that were driven both by local, inward-looking concerns – such as the need to construct an assembly space around the burial of an important local person, for example – and by the growing social pressure to articulate their Roman bona fides. All these new spaces helped Christians find their individual and communal voices (*Exploring Culture* 9.1: Shenoute's Monastery in Egypt). But as we will explore throughout this chapter, their communities were not the only ones that enlivened the dynamic of a Roman city.

Exploring Culture 9.1 *Shenoute's Monastery in Egypt*

Picture a desert landscape. At its center, the leader of a new, charismatic movement. He has just declaimed passionately against the customs of the people around him, even going to a nearby village "to throw down the idols which were there." The oddly familiar elements of the scene may trick us into believing we know it. But the man at the center was not Jesus or Muhammad of Mecca (c.570–632). He was a monk, Shenoute (c.355–c.466), the head of a monastic community at Atripe.

Atripe was in southern Egypt, near the modern city of Sohag. Shenoute's community worshipped at Deir Anba Shenouda, the "White Monastery," called so today because of the hue of its walls. The village to which Shenoute had traveled was named Pleuit. It was on that journey, according to the monk's biographer, Shenoute "entered the temple and destroyed the idols, smashing them one on top of the other" (Besa, *Life of Shenoute* 83–84, trans. by D. Bell [Kalamazoo, MI: Cistercian Publications, 1983]). Shenoute's zealous acts helped him become leader of the community.

Shenoute had been drawn to the monastic life in his thirties. By then, c.380 CE, monasteries for both women and men, separated into different buildings, had been set up in every corner of the Roman world. Customs and practices inside these communities varied from region to region, but in principle, monasteries offered Christians a space set apart from the complicated outside world – a place where Jesus' followers could dwell comfortably with like minds. The leader of the monastery was responsible for drafting a rule, or structure, for communal living. The Christian Pachomius (d. 346) had founded an important monastery in southern Egypt in the fourth century CE and authored one such "rule book."

Shenoute did the same for Atripe's monks, authoring letters, sermons, and guidelines (called "Canons") – all written in Coptic, a local language of Roman Egypt. His earliest letters set a radical tone since Shenoute was neither the monastery's founder nor its leader at the time he was writing them. In them, Shenoute disapproved of the current administration:

> There is a great evil upon you, which is to say that not only did you – in your envy and your hatred and your disobedience and your pollution and your defilement which you committed – not fear God, but a group of evil people formed another gathering with each other among you. … They fled like dogs into the refectory in order to eat and drink on that day, even though it did not please [the father of the community]. (Shenoute, *Canon* 1.22–23, trans. by C. Schroeder, *Monastic Bodies: Discipline and Salvation in Shenoute of Atripe* [Philadelphia: University of Pennsylvania Press, 2007], p. 31)

It was quite challenging for a monk to live in these kinds of cloistered communities. Some monks had broken into the kitchen for an after-hours drink and snack, against the rule of fasting. Shenoute uses this episode to insert a wedge between the monastery's virtuous monks, monks of questionable mores, and the monastery's leader, who seems to have little control over his community.

9.1 Mystery Cults

Nicagoras, a citizen of Roman Athens, was a man with a mission. In 326 CE, Emperor Constantine had sent him to Egypt to assemble an art collection that could be displayed in Constantine's new capital. We know about Nicagoras' business trip because he scratched two messages on the wall where he visited. What these texts record tells us about yet another important community in the fourth-century Roman Empire.

The cult of Demeter and Persephone at Eleusis

In the Valley of the Kings, near Thebes, Nicagoras proudly gave thanks to the Christian ruler who had tasked him with the important responsibility of coming to Egypt on official business. Passing the burial place of King Tutankhamun, Nicagoras took out a sharp stylus and used the opportunity to deface the tomb of Pharaoh Ramses VI (r. 1145–1137 BCE). Among the details he scrawled on the wall, among all the accomplishments Nicagoras must have been proudest of, he took a brief moment to tell posterity, in Greek, that he had been "an office holder [specifically, a torch-bearer] in the most sacred mysteries of Eleusis." (For Nicagoras' graffiti, see the two texts in the edition of Greek and Latin inscriptions from Thebes, ed. by J. Baillet, *Inscriptions grecques et latines des Tombeaux des Rois ou Syringes à Thèbes* [Cairo, 1920–1926], nos. 1265 and 1889.) Nicagoras of Athens had a good reason to want to tell people about his initiation into the mystery cult at Eleusis, outside his own hometown. He was a member of a historic club.

Since the seventh century BCE, people in the Greek world, Roman citizens and even emperors like Augustus had journeyed to the plain of Eleusis to be initiated into the cult of Demeter and Persephone. The rituals here were structured around the mythical story of these two Olympian goddesses. In this famous Greek myth, Persephone is abducted one day and taken to the underworld. Demeter grieves at her daughter's loss and contrives a famine to punish all of humankind for not helping Demeter learn the whereabouts of her daughter. In the end, Persephone is recovered although she must spend a portion of every year in the underworld on account of the food she ate while there.

In the performance of the cult at Eleusis, initiates physically recreated this emotional journey. It began with a public procession that started amid the classical temples of Athens. Then, the future initiates would depart for Eleusis, where Demeter was believed to have founded a sanctuary to ensure that humans did not transgress her anymore. Once they arrived, initiates were then guided – under the cover of darkness – into the main hall of Demeter's sanctuary. There, surrounded by torch-bearers, they became initiates into the mysteries. These rituals proved so popular that they were performed for nearly eleven hundred years until, in the late fourth century CE, the sanctuary was forced to stop initiating people after the Edict of Thessaloniki.

Anthropological perspectives on initiation

What exactly happened to men like Nicagoras when they were initiated has proven hard to answer, but that doesn't mean mystery cults like those of Demeter and Persephone, Isis or Mithras can be dismissed as tangential to Late Antique history. Earlier scholarly opinion once believed that the popularity of the "mysteries" laid the foundation for the rise of Christianity because they gave people a more "spiritual" outlook on life. Many scholars, especially churchmen, pointed to the story of Persephone's "dying" and "rising," and the experience of being "reborn" as crucial ingredients in this recipe for social and cultural change.

The research of anthropologist Victor Turner, who worked in the twentieth century, seriously undermined many of these straightforward, "spiritualizing" interpretations of the mystery cults. Turner set forth his research in an important book, *The Ritual Process: Structure and Anti-Structure* (Ithaca: Cornell University Press, 1966, pp. 96–97). In it, he collected case studies documenting how rites of initiation can be used to build and foster group identity. By being led away from the regimented structure associated with everyday society and passing through a state of disorientation, people can be gradually reoriented to a new way of seeing their relationships to each other.

Turner called this new way of being *"communitas,"* Latin for "community." He himself preferred the Latin term because it spoke to the lasting social dimensions of the process he was studying. Indeed, to him, the more common word "community" suggested that these new bonds were too limited to a specific place when, in fact, one of the most important aspects of them was that they were portable. They created a sense of belonging which stayed with people after the initiation event had ended.

In essence, then, while it is true that mystery rituals like those at Eleusis were structured around a journey from darkness into light, in a story that paralleled the mythical exploits of gods who "died" and then "rose" again, Turner's work cautions us that there is no necessary reason for concluding that initiates themselves were "spiritually reborn" as a result of this process. The larger point, for him, was that group initiation, when organized around powerful rites of passage, helped individuals build relationships that they could not make elsewhere. Most important of all, this urge for "communitas" did not overturn society's traditional way of structuring relationships; it existed alongside it. In this way, Turner's work helps us see why even smaller groups of Christians, like monastic communities, also may have become fashionable in the fourth and fifth centuries. These individuals were building new, like-minded relationships for themselves in an ongoing dialogue with, not a dramatic break from, the Christian Roman society that was emerging around them.

Nicagoras, the fourth-century traveler who carried with him the lasting memory of his initiation at Eleusis, all the way to the Valley of the Kings in Egypt, helps us see the phenomenon that Turner was trying to capture.

9.2   Christian Communities and Christian Law

As churches began to appear in Mediterranean cities, it was a transformative time, in many cases radically so. By the fifth century CE, sites associated with mystery cults, like private Mithraea or the public sanctuary of Demeter at Eleusis in Greece, would no longer be repaired. Roman cities themselves would witness a second round of Christian economic investment, as the construction of more prominent baptisteries began to appear. The fact that the overwhelming number of these large urban buildings appear for the first time in the fifth century, not the fourth century, is intriguing. These were places where the Christian rites of initiation took place, a necessary part of joining the Christian community. Built in the decades following the Edict of Thessaloniki, many of these showy new structures may have helped cement Christianity's position as the official worship of the empire.

By the fourth century, many bishops had also begun petitioning the government to hold their own separate legal proceedings in their basilicas. These "Christian courts" functioned on principles of Christian law and were guided by the reading and interpretation of scripture, not Roman case studies or Rome's legal history. The Christian author Sozomen, who lived in Constantinople and wrote a history of the church in the middle of the fifth century CE (c.440 CE), gives us some of the details of this legal arrangement. It was the Emperor Constantine, he says, who "exempted the [Christian] clergy everywhere from taxation and permitted litigants to appeal to the decision of the bishops if they preferred them to the state rulers" (Sozomen, *Church History* 1.9, trans. by C. Hartranft in the *NPNF* series [1890]). By appealing to this Christian "episcopal audience" (*episcopalis audientia*, as it became known in Latin), plaintiffs agreed to let their church leaders, not the Roman government, settle their legal complaints.

The establishment of this quasi-parallel legal system, designed to implement "Christian law," may seem disruptive to the proper functioning of Rome's government. In many ways, it was. It also cast an unnecessary pall of suspicion on those Christians who, in the decades after Constantine, worked as committed magistrates and lawyers within the Roman legal system. Christian plaintiffs who chose to appeal to their bishop, not their local magistrate, were making a political statement that Rome's law was not as important as Christian law. Perhaps because of the divisive effect this arrangement had on Rome's civic community, Emperor Julian (r. 360–363) – the last descendent of Constantine's family, a man who had been raised in a Christian household – overturned it. "It is ... evident," the emperor wrote in 362 CE from his mansion in Antioch, "that the populace ... have been led into error by those who are called 'clerics'." The immediate result of Julian's edict was that clerics were "no longer allowed to sit as judges" (Julian, *Letter* 41.437A, LCL trans. by W. Wright [1923]). It was a decision that later Christian emperors and their legal staffs would wrestle with during the fourth and fifth centuries. And over time, the rights of "episcopal audience" crept back into Roman society.

Whatever the benefits of this deal and whatever else may have motivated Julian's repeal, some long-term context is also essential here. In brokering this arrangement, Christians had not been legal innovators. Nor had their desire to police their community within the confines of Christian law set them on a path that separated them irrevocably from Roman civic society (*Key Debates* 9.1: Who Were the "Pagans," and What Is the Origin of This Word?). In fact, in establishing the right of "episcopal audience," Christians had borrowed a page from the playbook of the empire's Jewish communities. In the late Hellenistic and early Roman world of Asia Minor, one community of Jews had petitioned the authorities in Sardis, modern

Key Debates 9.1 *Who Were the "Pagans," and What Is the Origin of This Word?*

"Pagans" are people who come "from the crossroads of farmland and from rustic places on the outskirts of town" (Orosius, from the preface to *Against the "Pagans"*). So claimed a Spanish Christian, writing in Latin at the start of the fifth century CE. He believed that non-Christians had deserved this label because many of them lived in the backwaters of the Roman Empire. The Latin word for describing the rustic outskirts of a major city is *pagus*; one who lives there is a *paganus*.

Orosius' beliefs, planted in the fifth century, certainly took root. In modern accounts of Christianity's rise, it is city folk, we are often told, not country folk, who first flocked to the Christian church. The "pagans" were the stubborn hicks who refused to convert. There's a comforting faith-history here. This scenario conjures up an image of masses of cosmopolitan Romans "waking up" to the power of Christianity while the more ignorant, unsophisticated dragged their feet. But is Orosius' comment fable or fact?

In Latin, the word *paganus* did not always mean "rustic." It could also mean "civilian." In this meaning, common throughout the Roman Empire, *paganus* functioned as an antonym for "soldier," *miles*. (Our word "militant" is related to *milites*, the plural form of the same word.) A "soldier" was someone who had enlisted in the Roman army; a "civilian" was someone who had not taken up that call of duty. As a result, some scholars believe that Jesus' followers originally used the word *paganus* to refer to non-Christians, those who had not yet enlisted in "the army of the Messiah [Christ]."

Which explanation is correct? The answer may be neither. Both of these approached start from the same assumption: that Christians would have used the word "pagan" to describe outsiders. New research, on the other hand, has demonstrated that *paganus*, meaning "civilian," was used by Christians to mock the behavior and beliefs of their own Christian peers.

"Real Christians" saw themselves as "soldiers." They were the uncompromising believers who were strong enough to wage a cultural war on God's behalf. Other Christians, who may not have shared their radical social ideas, were targeted for "civilianism." The use of the word in this way is documented as early as the middle of the fourth century CE, precisely the time when it became legal for Christians to move freely about Roman cities and to be open about their faith. The question of whether Christians should continue to adapt to Roman culture by attending circus races or going to the theater became a strong point of contention – for militant Christians who saw Roman culture in black and white.

In this interpretation, the rise and spread of the word grew out of a heated conversation that took place among the empire's Christian community. It was not the sign of a frustrated evangelization campaign to convert "non-Christians." Only later, in 409 CE, would "pagan" come to acquire the meaning it now has; in that year a Christian emperor redefined the word to mean "non-Christian" by law (*Theodosian Code* 16.5.46). Orosius' imaginative speculation about rustics who hadn't yet converted to Christianity was written after this.

Turkey, to adjudicate their own disputes according to Jewish law. The Roman magistrate wrote back:

> Jewish citizens of ours have come to me and pointed out that from the earliest times they have had an association of their own in accordance with their native laws and a place of their own, in which they decide their affairs and controversies with one another; and upon their request that it be permitted them to do these things, I decided that they might be maintained, and permitted them so to do. (Josephus, *Jewish Antiquities* 14.235, LCL trans. by R. Marcus [1943])

The Jewish writer Josephus preserves other such documents, and although they date from the second and first centuries BCE, their relevance for Late Antiquity should not be overlooked. This legal history provided a precedent to many Christians who, knowing their movement had been an offshoot of the Jewish community, viewed their identity as different yet similar enough to ask for the same rights.

9.3 The Jewish Community: Shared Values and Social Diversity

The petitions preserved in Josephus, granting Jewish communities the right to "decide their affairs and controversies with one another," did not create a divided, bipolar society, however. Notwithstanding the difficult periods of military aggression and revolt that had characterized Roman and Jewish interactions in Jerusalem, especially around 70 CE, Jews and Romans throughout the wider Mediterranean world had not lived segregated lives. In cities like Priene and Sardis in Roman Asia Minor, for example, Jews were some of the most highly visible, integrated members of the community. The material culture of these cities is crucial for telling their stories.

Synagogues

Both Priene and Sardis preserve the remains of Jewish meeting spaces, or synagogues, a term that was derived from the Greek word for "coming together." Jews in antiquity did not always use this word to refer to their assembly spaces, however. In Hellenistic Egypt and on the island of Delos, Greek inscriptions and texts refer to Jewish worship spaces as a *proseuchē* (προσευχη), or "prayer hall." Surprisingly, very few of these spaces have been identified archaeologically. In the Jewish homeland, buildings that can incontrovertibly be identified as synagogues are, although not unknown, certainly a rarity before 70 CE. The identification of one, at the mountain of Masada, was aided by the discovery of fragments of Hebrew Scripture that, by chance, were found within the meeting space. Only in the third century CE, at the earliest, do synagogues begin to emerge more clearly from the archaeological ruins of Mediterranean cities by and large.

The synagogue at Priene is one of these spaces. It was built by a local Jewish community who adapted a Hellenistic house for their worship needs. Although the date of this renovation is still not clear, scholars have plausibly suggested that it took place in the late second or third century CE, at the earliest. The presence of the Jewish community in this house was confirmed by the discovery of a stone fragment with a menorah on it. In addition, during the renovation, a niche for the Torah had been added to the house's east wall so that the community would recall the memory of the Temple during its gatherings. The fact that members of the Jewish community in Priene lived and worshipped in the middle of the city suggests many of its individuals were well known, maybe even recognizable participants in Priene's city scene.

The city of Sardis tells a similar story. It, too, preserves the archaeological remains of a synagogue in a building that was not originally designed for the Jewish community. There, the community assembled in one of the side halls within one of the city's bath complexes. This bath complex, with Hellenistic-style gymnasium, had been a beloved urban amenity since the second century CE (Figure 9.1). The fact that one portion of it was transformed into a synagogue speaks to the ease with which the local Jewish community moved among the wider populace and were accepted by them. (In this context, it is worth recalling, as a crucial aside, that not all Jews were willing participants in the shared culture of their Hellenistic and Roman worlds. In the second century BCE, during the period of Maccabean resistance to the Hellenistic rulers, many Jews advocated a *rejection* of these customs because they were seen as compromising their Jewish faith and identity. Attending the Hellenistic gymnasium was one of the most egregious behaviors that was stigmatized by the anonymous Jewish writer of the text known as 2 Maccabees, for example [2 Maccabees 4.9].)

The text of 2 Maccabees, written in Greek, never became a part of Jewish Scripture, however. And six centuries later, the Jewish community at Sardis showed that it had little to fear about meeting in a room that was connected to such an important cultural and civic institution as the city's local gymnasium and bath. Here, too, as at Priene, depictions of *menarot* (the Hebrew plural of *menorah*) adorned the space; and niches for the Torah guided individuals' minds in the direction of their lost Temple. According to excavators, this building was transformed for Jewish use in the fourth century CE. A recent proposal suggests it was transformed during the sixth century CE. Whichever the precise date, the synagogue at Sardis was an enormous meeting hall, measuring almost 80 meters long, built in a room adjoining one of the city's most fashionable spaces.

The importance of Jewish place and time

The extent to which Jewish communities used their local connections to build their worship spaces – by transforming a house in Priene or the bath complex in Sardis – should not suggest that these communities were compromising every and all aspect of their Jewish identity. The material culture from other synagogues shows

Figure 9.1 Jews had been living outside the Jewish homeland well before the Jewish diaspora – since at least the Hellenistic period – and the city of Sardis in Asia Minor was one site that had a long-established Jewish community. This image shows a view of the synagogue at Sardis, which served local Jews during the fourth through sixth centuries CE. Urban context is crucial for understanding the life of Jews at Sardis in the Roman Empire. From this angle, you can see across the synagogue hall towards the lawn of a Roman bath complex and gymnasium. In antiquity, a wall would have separated these two spaces, but this photograph illustrates a key social-historical detail. The Jewish community at Sardis had received permission to use and renovate a room in the city's bath complex to create a worship space for their own community. The circumstances that led to this architectural project suggest that, for the members of this one minority faith living in Roman-era Sardis, civic engagement and social integration were important values. Image © Archaeological Exploration of Sardis/President and Fellows of Harvard College.

us that all of these communities were intent on finding a creative balance that would help them express their own history and traditions at the same time that they built connections to their non-Jewish neighbors and other residents. Many of them used a distinct sense of time to foster their own awareness of a Jewish identity.

The Jewish calendar was and is a lunar calendar, based on the phases of the moon, but adapted to the solar year. (The solar year is the sequence of seasons which result from the path of the earth and the position of the sun; in this system, a year is divided into twelve months, and each month is divided into either 29 or 30 days.) In the Jewish calendar, the lunar units generally overlap with the solar seasons. Thus, the first month of the Jewish spring is Nisan, which coincides with March and April, while the winter month of Adir overlaps February and March.

The date of Jewish rituals, around which Jews gather to worship, is based on dates in this calendar. As a result, Passover always begins on the "15th of Nisan"; Hannukah on the "25th of Chislev"; and Rosh Hashanah, the New Year, on the "1st of Tishrei," which overlaps with September or October. Because there are more days per year in the solar calendar, however, than in the lunar one and because Romans used the solar year to tell time, the precise date of these Jewish holidays was never fixed. Like Jewish holidays in America, for example, important ancient festivals associated with Hanukkah, Rosh Hashanah, and Passover could often give the appearance – at least to those outside the Jewish community – of always jumping around the calendar in an unstable, quixotic way.

In antiquity, Jewish communities used material culture to support their distinct sense of time and place. In many synagogues, intricately laid mosaics, carved stone reliefs, or colorful paintings depicted ritual objects which alluded to these significant moments in the Jewish year, or which directed the community to the memory of the Temple.

The *menorah*, the seven-branched lamp stand, is the most well known of these objects. In the third century CE, it became one of the most popular depictions of a Jewish identity and was seen in synagogues, as at Priene and Sardis, but also in tombs and on ceramic lamps. Today's *menarot* have nine branches which commemorate the miraculous burning of oil, for eight days straight, which took place after the Maccabean family had gained possession of the Second Temple in 164 BCE. In antiquity, a seven-branched *menorah* had been a part of Jewish Temple rituals since Moses had been instructed to make it, on Yahweh's command (Exodus 25.31–40). During the Second Temple period, this *menorah* was kept in Jerusalem. Its oil was lit on a daily basis as part of the Temple rituals. Jewish individuals who chose to depict the *menorah* were evoking a time long gone when their rituals took place in Jerusalem.

In addition to *menarot*, Jews used other symbols to evoke their Jewish identity, many of which were rooted in their calendar. The *lulav, ethrog*, and *shofar* are three objects that also appear frequently in synagogues. These objects were not required for Temple worship in Jerusalem, but they each figured in Jewish rituals. The *shofar*, or ram's horn, was blown every Rosh Hashanah to mark the Jewish New Year. It was also blown on the Day of Atonement, Yom Kippur. Other objects were drawn from still other festivals. The *ethrog*, a type of citrus fruit, and the *lulav*, a date-palm branch, were used in the festival of Sukkot ("Tabernacles," or "Booths") to mark the end of the year – commemorating the forty years of wandering which the Jewish community suffered after their exodus from Egypt. Those who celebrate it are instructed to take a palm branch, a willow, a citrus fruit, and myrtle branch (Leviticus 23.40), bind them together, and wave them during the festival.

It is not surprising to see that representation of objects like these became popular in the century after the destruction of the Second Temple. Throughout the year, they helped give Jewish communities a feel for their history that was distinct from the ordinary march of Roman time. And yet even here, the way each community chose to balance their Jewish and Roman commitments was complex and resisted easy categorization. A synagogue at Hammat Tiberias, in Israel, will help us see the diversity that existed within the empire's Jewish communities.

The synagogue, located near the Sea of Galilee, has a particularly striking mosaic floor (Figure 9.2). Constructed in the fourth century, the main hall of the building is a square room which was damaged in the fifth and was later rebuilt in the sixth. As a community space, it would last until the eighth century CE. An apse in the assembly space oriented the community toward Jerusalem, as in other synagogues. The depictions on the mosaic floor at Hammat Tiberias are anything but standard, though.

In the floor's center is a personification of the Greek and Roman sun god, Helios. Here, Helios is shown holding a globe and a staff, representing his dominion over the known world, which was precisely the way Roman emperors were depicted. Around Helios are the twelve signs of the Zodiac, from Aries and Aquarius to Sagittarius and Scorpio; and each has been labeled in Hebrew. The four corners of the floor were filled with personifications of the four seasons. There was also a panel with the *lulav*, and elsewhere on the floor, the names of its donors, written in Greek and Aramaic.

What did this piece of synagogue artwork mean to the community? Because the imagery is so unique, it has been difficult for scholars to agree upon an interpretation. Some see the Helios figure as the representation of the Roman emperor, the *cosmocrator*, or ruler of the known world. For others, the notion that the Roman emperor, a Christian, would be depicted in a Jewish worship space is difficult to accept. A different interpretation would suggest that Helios, the sun, was meant to underline the importance of the solar calendar to Jewish time. In this approach, the Zodiac can be seen as a symbol of the lunar cycle, and Helios of the solar one. Whichever the interpretive path one chooses to follow, the mosaics at Hammat Tiberias, like the synagogues at Sardis and Priene, confirm the distinctness of Jewish time in an empire where many Jews comfortably lived and worked among an overwhelmingly non-Jewish population.

9.4   The Communities of Roman Egypt, Fourth–Fifth Centuries CE

One territory in the empire, Roman Egypt, offers a rich case study for the wide-ranging forms that Late Antique community could take. Egypt's cities were sites where Roman soldiers were stationed. Its cities, oases, and desert roads and hills were places where churches and monasteries developed, such as Mt. Saint Catherine's on the Sinai peninsula. Roman Egypt was also home to one of the empire's most cosmopolitan cities, Alexandria, where social and theological tensions were festering during the fourth century CE (*Political Issues* 9.1: Theological Creeds as Party Platforms). One of these groups, nourished on a militant form of Christianity, would later be responsible for burning to the ground an architectural gem and cultural beacon of the Roman world, Alexandria's Temple of Serapis. This catastrophe stunned many Christians, Jews, and non-Christians at the time. It also illustrates, for us, many of the unresolved tensions which the empire's Christian community at large had not yet addressed about how Christians should live as citizens in the Roman Empire. Let's look at these groups.

Figure 9.2 The floor of a synagogue at Hammat Tiberias, near the Sea of Galilee (modern Israel), was laid with bright, lively mosaics. This photograph shows the design. At the top of the photograph are two *menarot* (singular, *menorah*) on either side of a building, a structure which is intended to symbolize the lost Jewish Temple in Jerusalem. Beneath this panel is a scene of the sun god Helios – or possibly the Roman emperor – commanding a four-horse chariot. In a circle are the twelve signs of the zodiac, each labeled in Hebrew, while in the corners are personifications of the four seasons. It's easy to look at this image today and study it as one would a photograph, although it is worth remembering that, in antiquity, visitors would have walked across the face of this picture. As a whole, the mosaic shows us that Jewish communities in the fourth- through sixth-century Roman Empire both maintained and developed their own traditions, in part, by relying on a ritual calendar that was distinct from their non-Jewish neighbors. Photo credit: © www.BibleLandPictures.com/ Alamy Stock Photo.

Political Issues 9.1 *Theological Creeds as Party Platforms*

By Shenoute's time, laws had been used to stigmatize most non-Christian religious traditions, and bishops had begun to set parameters for proper Christian belief. The Nicene creed, formulated in 325 CE, had been articulated as the only state-sanctioned expression of Christianity. At issue was an important matter of belief: Had Jesus been born the Messiah ["Christ"] or had he become the Messiah? According to the council of Nicaea, Jesus had been both human and divine, co-eternal with God, at his birth. Anyone who believed otherwise – supposing, for example, that there once had been a time in the earth's history when Jesus hadn't existed – would be excluded from the community.

"Nicaea" was a carefully worded document which outlined the group's most important beliefs. How people lived these beliefs on a day-to-day basis is another question. Neither a party platform nor a theological creed pre-determines the way that people behave in their daily life. That said, the effects of Nicaea would ripple through the empire for centuries.

Nestorius (386–451), bishop of Constantinople from 428–431, and Cyril, bishop of Alexandria (412–444), were two of the men it ensnared. For them, the debate about Jesus' human and divine nature had raised several complications which demanded revisiting. If Jesus had been the Messiah at the time of his birth, then Mary, his mother, had given birth to a god. The idea of a divine offspring sprouting from a human family tree was not unheard of in antiquity – Hercules was the son of Zeus and the human Alcmene – but for fifth-century bishops, the concept of a divine offspring needed more clarity if it was going to be applied to Jesus.

By 431 CE, at Ephesos, leaders would convene a council to try to resolve the matter. The Council at Ephesos awarded Mary an important Greek epithet: *Theotokos*, meaning "God-bearer." Nestorius, uncomfortable with the term, tried to argue that "God-bearer" unduly privileged Jesus' divinity over his humanity. But in this dispute he lost – both the argument and his title. Defeated at the Council of Ephesos, Nestorius left for Persia to spread his message. Nestorius' beliefs would become the basis for many Christian communities in Sasanian Persia, Central Asia, and China.

Cyril, too, quibbled with the Ephesos language. He would assert that Jesus had only one nature (*physis*), uniting the human and the divine. Although not technically at odds with the council's decisions, Cyril's belief in Jesus' "one nature" – like Nestorius' belief in two natures – would shape the story of Christianity. By 451 CE, a follow-up council at Chalcedon (the modern Kadıköy neighborhood of Istanbul, on the Asiatic side of the Turkish capital) was summoned to resolve the matter. In the Chalcedon revisions to their platform, bishops would reaffirm that Jesus had two natures, human and divine, both of which had been united in one essence. This language proved unacceptable to many of Cyril's supporters in Alexandria, who believed Jesus had one, not two, natures.

Cyril's beliefs, nevertheless, fostered a strong sense of community among those who supported him. Today, the Armenian Apostolic Church and the Coptic Orthodox Church in Egypt identify with his belief in "one nature," called *miaphysitism*, from the Greek word for "one" (*mia*).

Antony and the monastic communities

Antony (*c.*250–356 CE) was a lively model for many Christians in and beyond Roman Egypt. They told stories about him, preserved letters that were thought to have been written by him, and looked up to him as the founder of an ascetic, monastic way of Christian life that others began to emulate. In the middle of the fourth century, the bishop of Alexandria, Athanasius, would compose a *Life of Antony* that ensured the man's lasting, saintly reputation. Later Christians, in the eastern and western Mediterranean, revered Athanasius' biography because the story seemed to convey "in the form of a narrative, the laws of the monastic life" (Gregory Nazianzus, *Orations* 21.5, trans. by C. Browne and J. Swallow in the *NPNF* series [1894]). Augustine of North Africa would express admiration for Antony's *Life* (*Confessions* 8.6).

Regrettably, not much is known about Antony that is verifiable. Athanasius' *Life of Antony*, however, is not the only source we have to depend upon. Other fourth-century documents give us a picture of a man which, like a view through a prism, changes depending on which one we pick up. These texts speak to three characteristics that may have helped Antony gather and grow his devoted community. In one document, preserved in Syriac and Armenian, the author (Serapion of Thmuis) emphasizes how Antony had assumed the role of patron and protector in divine matters, able to defend many Christians who knew him against the attack of harmful demons. In another source, a collection letters which is traditionally attributed to Antony himself, Antony emerges as a wise teacher. Here, he is a figure who reveals his "secret knowledge" to Christians ("*gnōsis*," in Greek), different from the sort of learning one could get through a traditional Roman education or the study of philosophy. The third of the sources for Antony's life, written by an Egyptian monk (Pachomius), lionizes Antony for being the founder of a monastic movement (*Working With Sources* 9.1: Buried Coptic Writings and "Gnostic" Gospels from Nag Hammadi, Egypt).

Which set of sources preserves the "real" Antony is impossible to say, particularly because Athanasius' later biography showcases all three different characteristics. What does emerge from Athanasius' story is that Antony was presented to others as a holy figure who gave up sex, encouraged fasting, and renounced wealth, all decisions which contemporary Christian readers were encouraged to emulate. In this respect, it seems clear that Athanasius, who was the bishop of Alexandria at the time he published his *Life of Antony*, was using Antony's memory to promote his own individualistic idea of what it meant to be a member of the Christian community at Alexandria.

Roman army members and military families

In the same way that not every Christian community was built around a renunciation of sex, food, or wealth, not every community in Roman Egypt was necessarily united around the bonds of worship and belief. Members of the Roman army

Working With Sources 9.1
Buried Coptic Writings and "Gnostic" Gospels from Nag Hammadi, Egypt

Books are more than a collection of words or a demonstration of one's literary pretensions. They are also pieces of material culture. As archaeological objects, they come from specific contexts – in a library, in a house, on a street, in a town – all of which are significant details which historians have to consider when assembling the social profile of their owners. Where and how a piece of writing was found is just as important as what the piece of parchment or papyrus says.

That warning is particularly important to keep in mind when reading and discussing the Nag Hammadi codices. Found by accident in 1945, the Nag Hammadi codices are a collection of thirteen books which had been stuffed in a jar and buried in Upper Egypt in the late fourth century CE. When they were rediscovered, the codices ignited a debate about Christian origins and Christian orthodoxy because they contained many "lost Christian writings" such as a *Gospel of Mary* and a *Gospel of Thomas*.

All the texts were written in Coptic, a language that had emerged in the third century CE. Combining an everyday form of Egyptian (the "demotic," or spoken, language, as opposed to its more elaborate "hieroglyphic" form) with letters borrowed largely from the Greek alphabet, Coptic became an important means of literary expression for the Christian communities in Roman Egypt. Shenoute, head of the monastic community at Atripe, is one of the only known authors of an extensive Coptic body of work.

Why were the Nag Hammadi texts buried? Based on the sometimes shifting facts that surround their discovery, there has been endless speculation. Some scholars see the late fourth century as a period of theological oppression; they believe that these alternate histories of Christianity were deliberately buried in Roman Egypt during a campaign to enforce orthodoxy. The jar itself, they note, was found outside an important monastery where such writings were not likely to be appreciated. Others, pointing to the broader cultural practices of burial in Egypt – in which the deceased were buried with "books of the dead" to ensure safe travel to the afterlife – suggest that the jar had originally been located near a tomb.

The partially documented discovery of the codices and the corresponding lack of any excavation report means that the debate about where they were found will likely continue. For that reason the texts will also likely remain at the center of a conversation about the diversity of beliefs in early Christianity. Although the books are pieces of Late Antique material culture, many of the texts are believed to be translated copies of earlier, Greek writings.

The *Gospel of Thomas* is one of these. A collection of quotations attributed to Jesus, it lacks the familiar narrative structure of the more well-known gospels and does not even mention the crucifixion. Scholars speculate that it was compiled at a very early date in the formation of the Jesus movement, perhaps the middle of the first century CE. Who were the people who read these alternative stories about Jesus, and how reflective were their beliefs of the broader Christian community?

stationed in Egypt, although they may not have undergone the same rites of initiation as Nicagoras, the official of the Eleusinian mysteries, or the followers of Mithras, show us how military service could create the same kinds of deep, personal links that civilian Romans formed in other settings.

The story of Flavius Taurinos is particularly illustrative. We can trace four generations of his family's fortunes (five, if we consider the fact that we know the name of Flavius Taurinos' father), thanks to papyrus documents from Hermopolis. These documents form an essential collection for following the tightly knit fortunes of one Roman military family during the late fifth and early sixth centuries CE.

Flavius Taurinos was born sometime around 405 CE. Son of a local Egyptian named Plousammon, by adulthood, Flavius was already serving in the Roman army. Enlisted in the cavalry unit known as the Mauri, alongside Moorish soldiers from the Maghreb of North Africa, he died in 455 CE, just as a Vandal brigade was attacking Portus, the industrial harbor of Rome. The shock of this attack may have shaped the decision of Flavius' son to enter the army, too. Flavius Ioannes the first (435–500 CE), born in Egypt, also served in the military, but he shows signs of pursuing a much more ambitious career path than his father. Ioannes quickly advanced from his unit to serve in the emperor's palace, where he held the post of notary, or *scrinarius*, before being transferred back to Egypt. He named his own son for his dad, Flavius Taurinos the second (*c.*465–512/513 CE).

Continuing the legacy of father and grandfather, the boy also found his voice by serving in the Roman army. But by the end of the fifth century CE, he had parted ways dramatically with family tradition. Taurinos became a priest. Finally, the last of the Flavius family, Flavius Ioannes the second, is known to have worked in the administration of the emperor. He probably died in the mid-sixth century CE. (Family details have been reconstructed from papyrus records; the lineage has been pieced together by B. Palme in *EBW* [2007], pp. 244–253.)

The fortunes of this family, rooted in the world of Roman Egypt although not entirely limited to it, show how military service could lead to promotion and advancement over time. Expectations within the family may have been conservative, and options for a son's or grandson's future may have been limited financially. But the legacy of Flavius Taurinos illustrates for us that some fathers could be rewarded greatly – and their sons could gain much – by being active members of a community of soldiers. The lives of families like these, although some of the hardest stories of Late Antique history to reconstruct, are important for seeing how blood connections bound people together as much as a membership in an association, guild, or army unit.

Disaffected communities: "God's soldiers," c.391–392 CE

In the late fourth century, the Roman military in Egypt – many of whom may have been Christian – were grappling with a different kind of "soldier" in their midst. These citizens, who also identified as Christians, came from Alexandria and its surroundings. Motivated by their own unique understanding of their faith, they saw themselves as enlisted in God's heavenly army.

Once home to Cleopatra, Alexandria in Late Antiquity was still a queen's city. A document written in the language of Syriac, the *Alexandrian City Survey*, catalogues the number of its houses, temples, churches, baths, taverns, and even porticoes. Although preserved in a later manuscript, this methodologically compiled list was likely composed between the mid-second century and late fourth century CE. A densely packed, throbbing sea-side city springs to life from its dry accounting.

Each of the five quarters of Alexandria is inventoried, each designated in antiquity with a Greek letter. All together, there were 47,790 houses across the five neighborhoods, 8,102 courtyards, 2,478 temples and shrines, 1,561 bath complexes, 935 inns and taverns, and 456 porticoes (P. Fraser, "A Syriac '*Notitia Urbis Alexandrinae*'," *Journal of Egyptian Archaeology* 37 [1951], pp. 103–108, at p. 104). The last detail might seem a trivial kind of public feature to include, but in the sun-drenched Nile Delta – the hill country of Texas is roughly on the same latitude as Alexandria – these types of covered walkways were highly prized. And, like the colonnades at Thessaloniki and Constantinople, hallmarks of imperial greatness, the colonnades at Alexandria transformed this waterfront city into a glamorous stage suitable to host Roman emperors.

Over this crowded landscape was perched the Serapeum, or "Sanctuary of Serapis," the largest, most popular, most prominent temple in the city. In 391 or 392 CE, armed with the teachings of their faith, a band of Christian militants plotted to attack it. These disturbing events are recorded in Latin by an early fifth-century Christian writer, Rufinus of Aquileia (*Church History* 11.4, 11.23). They form one of the darkest chapters in fourth-century history.

In 388 CE, Christians had attacked a synagogue in Raqqa, Syria. In 415, the Christian community of Minorca would burn a Jewish worship space on the island (Severus of Minorca, *Letter on the Conversion of the Jews* 13–14). A graffito from Rome, dated to perhaps the middle of the fourth century CE, shows an imperial statue being toppled to the ground. These examples remind us that Late Antique Rome was an empire home to many kinds of communities, not all of whom were enamored with the values of toleration, the legitimacy of Roman government or the urban presence of Jewish neighbors. The destruction of the Serapeum is not the only known example of Christian violence directed against non-Christians after the Edict of Milan, but it was the most catastrophic. In many quarters of the empire, not just in Alexandria, it negatively defined Romans perceptions of Christianity for years, if not generations.

Summary

This chapter, which discussed people and events from the third to the sixth century CE, illustrated the ways individuals chose to participate in communities. Christians and Jews were two natural groups for us to examine, as their monotheistic beliefs distinguished them from the other citizens of the Roman Empire. In subscribing to a belief in one God, Jews and Christians were thus distinct, but the distinctiveness of their faith didn't automatically make them socially different.

We also looked at people who were initiated into ancient mystery cults and, using anthropologist Victor Turner's work, discussed how rites of initiation create a sense of "communitas," a bond that, nevertheless, exists alongside the more ordered social structures outside the group.

Finally, we considered evidence from one region of the empire, Egypt. This case study introduced us to a complex picture of Late Antique society, where some Christians were encouraging the formation of their own niche, micro-communities, like monasteries. Other citizens were serving in the army and benefiting from their networked connections. Still other communities – of disaffected Christians – were plotting ways to express their discontent with Roman society. This last episode in Alexandria helped us see that, at the end of the fourth century CE, the Roman Empire faced significant challenges, many of which were rooted in the fact that the empire's Christian community had vastly divergent ideas of what it meant to be a Roman citizen – ideas that some believed were worth fighting and dying for.

Study Questions

1. Who is Victor Turner? What discipline was he trained in? How would you define his concept of "communitas"?
2. Name three Roman cities which had a strong Jewish community. How do you know?
3. What words would you use to characterize the Christian community of Roman Egypt in the fourth century CE?
4. Can you think of another example, ancient or modern, which illustrates how people use time and calendars to promote a sense of community?

Suggested Readings

David Brakke, *Athanasius and the Politics of Asceticism* (Oxford: Clarendon Press, 1995).

Lee Levine, *The Ancient Synagogue*, second edition (New Haven: Yale University Press, 2005).

Karen Stern, *Inscribing Devotion and Death: Archaeological Evidence for Jewish Populations of North Africa* (Leiden: Brill, 2008).

Ann Marie Yasin, *Saints and Church Spaces in the Late Antique Mediterranean: Architecture, Cult, and Community* (New York: Cambridge University Press, 2012).

10
Economy

In the last chapter, four generations of Plousammon's descendants told us about the lasting ties of family, home, and community in Roman Egypt. From the early fifth century CE, the time when Emperor Theodosius oversaw the establishment of Nicene Christianity throughout the empire, members of Plousammon's family served in the Roman army, traveled outside the borders of the Egyptian town where they had grown up, and worked in the emperor's palace. By the early sixth century CE, when the Roman Empire's only capital was at Constantinople, the last known member of the family had settled back near home as a Christian priest. The circuitous tales of this one family, set against the competing lives of urban bishops and desert monks, exposed the complexities of life for citizens of Roman Egypt. Texts written on papyrus helped us piece this picture together, indicating the family's movements over space and time.

Papyrus can also tell us about travel patterns that were a necessary part of people's everyday work. The movements of one Roman army unit in Egypt offer an instructive example. According to papyrus fragments found at the "City of Sharped Nose Fish" (Oxyrhynchus), we know that one elite cavalry unit – called in Latin a *vexillatio* – was stationed there at the beginning of the fourth century before they were eventually divided up and sent on separate missions. This unit's name was the Mauri. It is the unit to which Plousammon's son, Flavius Taurinos, belonged, and around 339 CE, he and his fellow service members were given marching orders to disperse. One group was sent to Lykopolis; the other to Hermopolis. Because of the way Mauri soldiers show up on papyrus documents scattered throughout Egypt, not just in Oxyrhynchus, we can plot their rough itineraries over the span of two hundred years until roughly 539 CE when the records disappear.

The Mauri are the best documented unit in the empire's Late Antique military. Between 339 and 539 CE, these men saw almost every corner of Roman Egypt.

A Social and Cultural History of Late Antiquity, First Edition. Douglas Boin.
© 2018 John Wiley & Sons, Inc. Published 2018 by John Wiley & Sons, Inc.

Reports indicate that, by the sixth century, they had even seen the first cataract of the Nile, where they would have spied the southern frontier cities of Syene and the island of Philae, site of an important Temple of Isis. (The first Nile cataract is one of six units of the river where the water turns into shallow rapids. Today, only one cataract is within the country of Egypt: at Aswan. The other five are further south, in modern Sudan.) Over the course of two hundred years, members of this elite unit also show up in Elephantine, near Syene; and at the western oasis in Lysis. (To learn more about the substance of these documents, see *EBW* [2007], p. 258.) By plotting this range of ancient cities on a map using geospatial tools, we can visualize how much mileage the Mauri were accruing (Figure 10.1). Taking data and translating it to a visual form shows that a soldier's assignment in late Roman Egypt did not tie him to a specific city or region, even during peacetime. Over the course of a career or the course of a unit's deployment, these men traveled considerably away from their home base in the "City of Sharped Nose Fish."

This chapter looks at a few other people's jobs, where their work took them, and at the entertaining ways they passed the time. What these individual stories will also help us describe is some sense of the nature of the economy before, during, and after the "vanishing" of Rome.

10.1   Egypt beyond Its Borders

There's a good reason we've spent time looking at daily life on the ground in Roman Egypt in this and the previous chapter. "Egypt," as a place, as an idea, held many Romans throughout the empire captive, even among people who had never disembarked at Alexandria or seen the Nile. This Roman fascination can be dated back as early as the first century BCE, the time when Augustus put an end to Hellenistic rule in Egypt and appropriated the land as his personal province. Egyptian-style paintings, tombs built in the shape of pyramids, obelisks with hieroglyphics – all these began pouring into the Roman world and were devoured by Roman consumers.

Porphyry and the economy of marble

Specific locations in Egypt were especially prized for their luxury exports. That's why, ever since the first and second centuries CE, the Roman government had taken imperial control of the quarries at Mt. Porphyrites, near modern Ghebel Dokhan. The stone mined from this mountain, porphyry, was a deep purple which, to Romans, evoked extravagance, power, and prestige. It appears in the floor of Rome's Pantheon, built in the second century CE. By the third century CE, statues erected for members of the Rule of Four would be carved from it. In the fourth century, members of the imperial family would be buried in sarcophagi made of it. Constantine would set a porphyry column at the center of his Forum in Constantinople as the ultimate urban crown jewel.

Papyrus, Roman Egypt, and the Army, c.339–539 CE

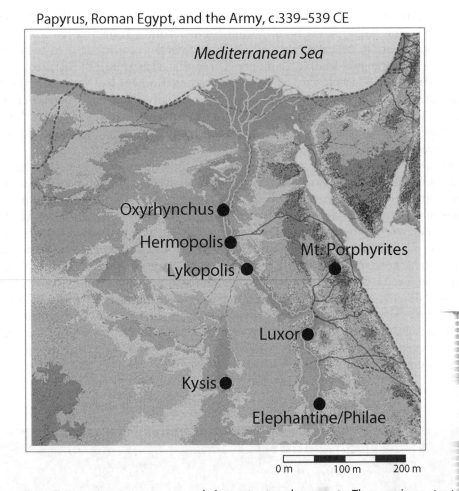

Figure 10.1 Texts on papyrus are not only important as documents. They are important as objects, and where a scrap of papyrus was found can often give us fascinating information that might otherwise not be contained in the text itself. This map shows the distribution of papyrus records related to the Mauri units of the Roman army in Egypt, *c.*339–539 CE. As the data reveal, these soldiers were stationed far from the traditionally cosmopolitan cities of the Mediterranean coastline, suggesting that residents and villagers all throughout Late Antique Egypt knew the presence of Rome in their daily lives. By combining a detailed analysis of the documents with geospatial tools, historians can draw a more complex picture of Roman society and culture in Egypt, one that might not be immediately apparent when looking at just one or two scraps of evidence, especially outside Egypt's more well-known cities, like Alexandria. Open-access mapping tools like the Ancient World Mapping Center, UNC-Chapel Hill, make this task easier. Author's map based on data from the Ancient World Mapping Center, UNC-Chapel Hill.

Porphyry was not the only speciality stone used in construction, however. Since the first and second centuries CE, emperors controlled access to quarries in Roman Tunisia, where another uniquely colored marble called giallo antico was found. This yellowish stone, sometimes found in shades of orange and brown, also became one of the most prized elements in imperial buildings. Still others – like the purple-veined though largely white marble from Roman Turkey known as pavonazzeto, or the dark green stone called serpentine from Sparta – contributed to a boom in Rome's wide-ranging marble economy. These materials were not just luxury construction goods. They played a role in conversations Romans had about their empire. Pavonazzeto had been used to depict statues of "barbarians" in Trajan's Forum in Rome, for example. By using one of the finest imported marbles to depict "uncivilized," conquered foreigners, the emperor was making a promise to his people about the greatness of the Roman military and the superiority of Roman culture.

By Diocletian's time, the price of working in these marbles was astounding. And, thanks to the Edict of Maximum Prices, specifically, we have some *relative* sense of the cost involved. Serpentine from Sparta cost 250 denarii per foot. Giallo antico and pavonazzeto, 200 denarii per foot. Those planning to build in basic white would have been working on a slightly more modest budget. The maximum price for white marble, according to Diocletian's Edict, was set at 75 denarii per foot. These prices would have created a two-tiered system of construction costs, but that doesn't mean the more expensive marbles were unavailable to moderately wealthy Roman homeowners or patrons of synagogues or churches. In Late Antiquity, a popular floor and wall style, called *opus sectile*, used shaved pieces of colorful marble to create a pastiche design that, while certainly elegant, must have been a fraction of the cost of buying each stone by the foot (*Key Debates* 10.1: A Marble Burial Box with a Heroic Tale: Signs of a "Middle Class"?).

Key Debates 10.1 *A Marble Burial Box with a Heroic Tale: Signs of a "Middle Class"?*

The phrase "middle class" makes pre-modern historians bristle. "Class," they point out, is a concept that originated in the nineteenth century, and it gained widespread use after the studies of Karl Marx and Friedrich Engels, two men interested in describing how a group's access to the means of production shaped their self-perceptions. Later, sociologist Max Weber would expand these ideas, emphasizing the importance of studying "social status" as well as economic "class." Today, scholars are quite attuned to how culture shapes what it means to be "middle class." Playing Friday night football or going to summer camp can be expressions of "class" values, too.

Workers in Rome recognized that they belonged to a commercial group, something akin to our notion of "class." But that doesn't necessarily mean they had shared values, culture, and aspirations like we know them today. For traditional scholars, "middling class" is their preferred term to describe these non-elite groups.

But is all this fuss really necessary? Marble burials dating to the early third century CE suggest that there may be at least some benefits in using the modern term to talk about the ancient world. The clue comes from the practice of carving mythical stories on their faces.

There were many ways to dispose of a beloved's body in the Roman Empire. Cremation was one; ashes would be put on display in a family mausoleum. Inhumation was another, either through burial in a box, called a sarcophagus; or underground, sealed on a shelf in a network of caverns, called catacombs. There was no one way to be buried, and a deep, personal, spiritual meaning does not fully explain why some people made the choice the burial which they did. Status and one's social networks – what your neighbors did, what was thought popular, what was trending – these factors that shaped burial customs, too. By the third century CE, intriguing patterns emerge.

Sarcophagi were decorated with scenes of heroes and gods: the story of Orestes, who avenged his father's gruesome murder; the story of Niobe, whose children are savagely killed by Apollo and Diana. Some scholars believe this repertoire of Greek myths gave people a chance to show off their knowledge of the plots, characters, and setting. In this interpreta-

tion, the sarcophagi speak to an elite, hyper-educated class. (The fact that so many of the myths involve details ill-suited to commemorating beloved family members is never addressed.)

Could these sarcophagi be signs of "middle-class culture," however? Twenty-nine sarcophagi from Rome have inscriptions confirming they belonged to senators. Of these, only five are decorated with myths. One conclusion to draw from this fact is that the people who bought these memorials did not do so because they were eager to show off their education. They did so because the pictures spoke to generic values they held dear: Orestes was a model son, Niobe was a grieving mom.

If true, then the sarcophagus industry is one of the strongest indicators that there were "middle-class values" in the third century CE. Workshops took "hackneyed motifs … long used in Rome's art industry" and turned them into ready-made objects for people who liked what they meant (Emmanuel Mayer, *The Ancient Middle Classes* [Cambridge, MA: Harvard University Press, 2012], p. 164).

Egyptomania in Rome and Constantinople

Egypt exported more than its luxury purple stone. Papyrus was also popular, and the land's cultural heritage – old sphinxes and obelisks from the age of the pharaohs – were some of the most visible artifacts in the empire's capitals. At both Rome and Constantinople, the major race tracks of the cities were decorated with Egyptian pieces. Two of these artifacts were placed there in the fourth century. In the middle of the fourth century, Emperor Constantius ordered the erection of an Egyptian obelisk on the spine of the Circus Maximus. By the end of the fourth century, Emperor Theodosius had arranged for an obelisk to be brought to the hippodrome of Constantinople. These sites were two of the most popular entertainment venues of the Late Antique empire (*Exploring Culture* 10.1: The Grain Industry, Free Bread, and the Bakers at Ostia; Figure 10.2). The presence of Egypt in the center of each race track must have made every game day feel like a trip to another world, especially for men, women, and children who had never set foot in Egypt.

Exploring Culture 10.1   *The Grain Industry, Free Bread, and the Bakers at Ostia*

Since the Roman Republic, the people of the city of Rome imported more grain than they produced at home. Egypt's annexation in 27 BCE ensured that there would be a steady supply of ships bringing this raw material to the capital. The Prefect of the Grain, the *praefectus annonae*, managed the government office overseeing its distribution. But there were also lesser officials, stationed throughout the empire, who oversaw the local transport of this vital commodity.

A receipt from Egypt, dated to the period of Diocletian (284 CE), reveals the seriousness with which three mid-level workers in the empire's food department took their job. Having successfully delivered their goods, Aurelius Isidorus, Aurelius Asclepiades, and Aurelius Plutinus wrote to the Roman oversight official in Oxyrhynchus: "We present to you the aforesaid authentic receipt and a copy of it which we beg you to sign in order that we too may have the security of the said authentic receipt" (*Select Papyri*, no. 426, LCL trans. by A. Hunt and C. Edgar [1934]).

With the founding of Constantinople in 330 CE, all grain shipments from Egypt would be sent, for logistical reasons, to the capital on the Bosporus. Rome's grain supply, by contrast, would be hauled from the shores of North Africa. It entered the capital at the imperial harbor, Portus, and its sister-town, Ostia, where it would be sorted, stored, and taken to the city.

At the warehouses and wharves of Portus and Ostia, some grain would be set aside for a lottery, to be distributed to citizens fortunate enough to hold a ticket. This system likely supplemented, not covered, a family's food expenses for a month. If the *Writers of the Imperial History* [*SHA*] can be trusted, it was Emperor Aurelian (r. 270–275 CE) who became a political hero to those who depended on the lottery. "Among the various ways in which, with the aid of the gods, we have benefited the Roman commonwealth, there is nothing in which I take greater pride than that by adding an ounce I have increased every kind of grain for the city" (*Life of Aurelian* 47.2, LCL trans. by D. Magie [1932]). The balance of Rome's imports were sold on the private market.

By the late third century, bread – not grain – was being distributed in these lotteries. The change must have been a boon for a working-town like Ostia whose bakers benefited from the policy change. Archaeologists have identified one neighborhood in the southern section of the city that must have been thriving in Late Antiquity. Two houses occupied almost half of a city block; both were used as homes into the fifth century CE. Across the street was a bakery, also in use in the fifth century CE.

Ostia's bakers must had an especially lucrative business during holidays and on festival days. Several terracotta bread molds have been found throughout the ruins of the city. These show bears mauling gladiators and lions devouring helpless prey. They also show chariot racers posing with their victorious horses and holding victory palms. The style indicates these date to the fourth century CE, a perfect take-away to enjoy on game day.

Figure 10.2 Founded in the third century BCE, Ostia was Rome's harbor town, its connection to the Mediterranean, and a cosmopolitan city. Even as Rome built new shipping and warehouse infrastructure north of the city, at the site that would become Portus, Ostia remained a diverse town where the Late Antique elite lived alongside bakers, merchants, and other guilds of workmen and day-laborers. Residents of Ostia knew how to enjoy themselves, too. The city was filled with taverns, many of which have been dated to the third century CE. These two rare artifacts also offer a glimpse at daily life. They are clay molds used for baking bread. Each is stamped with a design celebrating racing culture. The left shows a horseman and a four-horse chariot, or quadriga (Ostia inventory number 3645). The right depicts a victorious racer on a chariot drawn by ten horses (Ostia inventory number 3530). Courtesy of the National Italian Photographic Archive, ICCD (Photo E27259A).

10.2 The Arena and Racing Culture

The broad appeal of gladiatorial matches, animal hunts, and chariot races vaulted many gladiators and race-track drivers to the level of cultural superstars. Throughout the Mediterranean, in homes and taverns, archaeologists have found mosaic floors which depict episodes of hunting, boxing, and chariot racing. Oftentimes, the names of the athletes are set in stone along side these scenes. Sometimes, in chariot scenes, even horses are labeled. A mosaic from Emerita, the city of Mérida in Roman Spain (ancient Lusitania), for example, depicts one race-driver, named "Marcianus," with an exhortation to "Victory" (*Nica*, for the Greek *Nikē*). Marcianus commands a four-horse chariot whose ace racer is also named: "Inluminator" (Figure 10.3).

This scene has been dated to the second half of the fourth century CE, and others like it have been found throughout the Iberian peninsula. On the one hand, these pieces of material culture show us the fame such men and their horses could acquire.

Figure 10.3 During the early empire, the southern Iberian peninsula had been a mining region, where metals like gold, copper, and tin were extracted by slave labor. By the second century, Spanish olive oil had become a popular commodity offloaded at Rome's wharves. During the "Rule of Four," the provinces of the Iberian peninsula were reorganized into the diocese of Hispania. Mérida (ancient Emerita), in modern Spain, in the province of Lusitania, was one of its important cities. This expensive mosaic floor comes from a villa at Mérida and is a sign of the high-level wealth that had been generated throughout the Iberian peninsula by Late Antiquity. It depicts a racer named Marcianus and his star horse, whose Latin name is also given: "Inluminator." The palm leaf in the center and a Latin version of the word "*Nikē*" – the Greek word for "Victory" – imply that these two athletes were local heroes whose accomplishments were worthy of being set in stone. Second half of the fourth century CE. Now in the Museo Nacional de Arte Romano, Mérida (inventory number CE26389). Photo credit: © David Keith Jones/Alamy Stock Photo.

They also tell us something about the economic world of racing culture more broadly. Although we know nothing more about people like Marcianus or their horses, vivid mosaics like the one in Mérida – commissioned for display in wealthy Roman homes – must have been counted among the owners' most cherished conversation pieces. Perhaps they even worked to highlight their role as financial sponsors, or maybe they just spoke to their status as zealous fans of a particular team. (In Late Antiquity there were four: the Greens, Blues, Whites, and Reds.)

This culture spanned the entire Mediterranean; and, even after 476 CE, when places like Rome and Spain were cut off from the Roman Empire, it can still be seen in the Roman Empire centered around Constantinople. Around 500 CE, the emperor honored one of the most popular race drivers, named Porphyrius, with seven monuments originally displayed in the hippodrome. Today, only two of these monuments survive. On them, Porphyrius stands at the helm of his four-horse chariot and receives a crown of victory from the goddess Tyche. The texts inscribed on the lost five monuments are also known from a Greek manuscript:

> This Porphyrius was born in Africa but brought up in Constantinople. Victory crowned him by turns, and he wore the highest tokens of conquest on his head, from driving sometimes in one color and sometimes in another. For often he changed factions and often horses. Being sometimes first, sometimes last, and sometimes between the two, he overcame both all his partisans and all his adversaries. (*Greek Anthology* 15.47, LCL trans. by W. Paton [1918])

This text tells the story of an athlete who was passionate about his sport but not so single-minded about his team that he couldn't recognize a good opportunity if and when it was offered to him. If there was a chance to win with another horse (or if the owners of another color paid him more), Porphyrius followed the money. Many of his adoring fans likely followed him.

10.3 Economic Realities, Third–Sixth Centuries CE

Porphyrius may not have cared where his money came from. He raced for whichever owner gave him a greater cut of the winnings, but other people were not so fortunate. They owned farms and worked the land, scraping by financially and sometimes at a season's whim. Many rented land on large estates that belonged to wealthier landlords. The residents of the empire's cities knew the comforts of a life built on consumption and trade. Here, in the empire's more urban centers, lived people of varying degrees of wealth, and there was social and economic opportunity for those who were connected or took financial risks. Clearly the economy was built on the general concept of exchange, but can we say anything more specific about how it worked?

Economic historian Chris Wickham has been at the forefront of studying this pre-modern system and has cautioned students and specialists about how difficult it is to generalize about it. Sometimes, a system of economic exchange – in which people trade goods, food, or money – is not necessarily driven by fixed rules.

Wickham asks students to imagine the complexity of exchange in this way: "One can buy apples from a shop, or get a gift of apples from a friend, but one can also buy apples from a friend, perhaps at a special price for friends ... Is this 'really' sale, or [is it a] gift-exchange?" (Chris Wickham, *Framing the Middle Ages* [New York: Oxford University Press, 2007], p. 695). Wickham's concern is that we should not expect the ancient evidence to conform to one set category. Parts of the ancient economy may have been built on values of consumerism and profit; others, on agricultural production and the redistribution of goods among people who needed them. Still others, on the allure of an old-fashioned barter.

Some aspects of this system were assuredly greased by interpersonal connections. The fourth-century writer Libanius, a lawyer in Antioch, was a teacher who was called upon to make this networked system work for his students. One of his pupils, Apringius, was planning to pursue further legal training in Berytus, Roman Beirut. He had asked Libanius to help him secure a position in town, based on Libanius' professional connections. Libanius knew exactly whom to contact:

> To Dominus: Thus, you inspire men of maturity to pursue occupations of the young. Apringius, our friend, after several trials before the bar (tribunal), has come to you to study law because it is from you alone that he can acquire knowledge ... Try to shorten the time of his studies so that he can put his knowledge to practice. I will also entreat you insofar as tuition is concerned. He is a good man but poor and although he cannot give as much in payment now, he remembers favors. (Libanius, *Letter* 1171, trans. by L. Hall, *Roman Berytus: Beirut in Late Antiquity* [London: Routledge, 2004], p. 209)

As Libanius' letter on behalf of his impoverished student makes clear, the Roman economy could always be made to work in favor of those who knew the right people, regardless of how it worked for someone else (*Political Issues* 10.1: Cemetery Workers and a Guild Recruited for Mob Violence).

The two economic corridors of the state

Exchange, whether in money, favors, or a mixture of the two, was the central feature of this economy. As archaeological excavations show, objects made in one city or food harvested in another could travel considerable distances between the third through fifth centuries CE. At this stage, then, we should try to describe how and why the expectation of connectedness took root and what happened to it after the fifth century. The first two questions may seem basic to a student of the ancient Mediterranean; why *wouldn't* Rome's empire have been economically integrated? But here, too, historian Wickham offers a caveat:

> It is not inevitable that the Mediterranean, or half the Mediterranean, should be as closely integrated as it was in 400 [CE]; it is not even "natural" given the similarity of resources in most Mediterranean regions. It is even less inevitable that interregional products should get substantially inland from coastlines and waterways ... These processes were largely the products of the political and fiscal underpinnings of the Roman world-system and, when that went away, so in the end did exchange. (Wickham 2007, p. 718)

Political Issues 10.1 *Cemetery Workers and a Guild Recruited for Mob Violence*

Guilds, or "colleges" (in Latin, a *collegium* or *corpus*) were social clubs for people who worked in trades. Shipbuilders, rope and leather merchants, even funerary workers could belong to a college. They would dine with other members in a guildhall, or *schola*. Many guildhalls also had temples that were dedicated to trade's divine patron.

These colleges met in spaces that were usually set aside by a wealthy owner. In the late second century shipbuilders at Ostia dedicated a statue for their "best patron" (*optimus patronus*), Publius Martius Philippus (*AE* 1955, no. 177). Philippus' donations likely helped the college expand and attract new members. By the third century CE, they had built a temple on the north side of the street and a larger meeting hall, with a banquet hall, on the south. Guild life was diverse and an important part of Roman city life. In the middle of the third century, in Roman Spain, one of the Christian bishops, Martial, and his sons worked in a local funerary guild. They even attended the feasts, held in honor of the college's patron god (Cyprian, *Letter* 67.6). A half century later, by Constantine's time, Christians would be running many of their own funerary guilds.

The *parabolani* at Alexandria were one such college. Likely named because they took up the risky job of managing corpses – the Greek word *parabalos* refers to someone "exposed to danger" – these Christian funerary workers were part of a well-established system that oversaw burial for people in town. Burial in antiquity was a private affair, not paid for by the state, and the *parabolani* are attested in Egypt through the early seventh century CE (Giessen Papyrus Collection, Germany, *Papyri Iandanae* [*P. Iand.*] 8.154; see also Sarah Bond, "Mortuary Workers, the Church, and the Funeral Trade in Late Antiquity," *Journal of Late Antiquity* [2013], pp. 140–143).

Alexandria's Christian funerary workers branched out from their day jobs in "creative" ways, too. By the fifth century CE, the *parabolani* had become infamous as one of the most cut-throat urban mobs whose thuggish behavior was at the disposal of Alexandria's bishop when he needed it. Some scholars suspect that Bishop Cyril himself deployed this guild in his conflict with the Christian government officer Orestes in 415 CE during which Hypatia was killed.

What we know for sure is that the Christian emperor in Constantinople was not amused by their reckless behavior. In 416 CE legislation addressed "the social terror of those who are known as the *parabolani*" (*Theodosian Code* 16.2.42, preface). The law decreed that membership would be capped at 500 people, and its ranks could only be drawn from Alexandria's poor (*pauperes*), not from wealthy residents or from anyone who attempted to pay or bribe their way in. All names would now have to be submitted to the local prefect for approval (*Theodosian Code* 16.2.42.1).

Other restrictions were put in place to regulate these riot-prone Christian funerary workers. They were forbidden to attend "any public spectacle whatsoever or enter a local town council or go into a courtroom," unless, of course, they had actual business there (*Theodosian Code* 16.2.41.2).

These are critical considerations to keep in mind when talking about what happened to the Mediterranean economy in the fifth through seventh centuries CE. The first step in the process of exploring the ancient economy, however, is determining what evidence to use. What do we have that is useful, and where do we find it?

By the early fourth century, the most important aspect of the Mediterranean economy was the emergence of two trade routes which pumped goods and money through the state like a twin set of arteries. These corridors were the two state-managed sea passages that brought food from North Africa to Rome, in the west, and from Egypt to Constantinople, in the east. Both grain-producing regions were heavily taxed, and as a result, government policies helped grow and sustain the trade between these provinces and the capitals.

Although the government did not itself determine what was traded, many enterprising merchants – in North Africa, for example – cleverly exploited both the state-protected shipping routes and the availability of the steady stream of sailing ships to send their own goods to Rome. Fashionable ceramics from Tunisia, for example, could be packed on board in the left-over cargo holds, offloaded at their destination, then sold in the Italian markets. It was a boon for everyone involved. Baked clay containers may be one of the most unassuming, ubiquitous class of artifacts discovered on archaeological sites, but for historians, these vessels hold more than the residues of olive oil and wine. Even in their broken pieces, they tell a story about the ancient economy.

The importance of ceramic evidence

Archaeologists find ceramics and sherds (not "shards," a term which refers to glass) nearly everywhere. Marble could also travel great distances, but it was a luxury good. Ceramics were more widely used across a much more economically diverse set of the population.

Tableware, cookware, and kitchenware were made of clay and fired in a kiln. Once fired, these bowls and cups – although they could potentially be damaged in shipping, in the kitchen, or in a domestic fit of rage – were virtually indestructible. Because clay composition can be studied and traced scientifically, many ceramic production centers are known from the Mediterranean. Roman Tunisia was home to one of the most popular. Its kilns were famous from the fourth through eighth centuries CE for manufacturing vessels with a distinctive orangish-red glaze, called "African Red Slip Ware." During the third and fourth centuries CE, many North African merchants were filling the extra space in the state-run grain shipments with extra pieces of African Red Slip Ware.

Ceramics help historians literally connect the dots of the Roman economy. By compiling the data for what kinds of ceramics have been found in which cities, specialists have been able to assemble profiles of the import–export trade across the Mediterranean. Between 300 and 500 CE, for example, most tableware found in the eastern Mediterranean is predominantly Late Roman C and D, a style of container manufactured on the island of Cyprus and in the Levant. African Red Slip Ware, by contrast, shows a greater distribution in cities and regions closer to Tunisia, like Roman Libya. This comparative evidence offers a helpful reminder that, even in the fourth-century empire, when the state had two capitals and encompassed the entire Mediterranean basin, not everything about the economy was driven by the sweeping movements of trans-regional trade (Wickham 2007, p. 707). Tableware in the Levant was supplied largely by an intra-regional economy. Large parts of the Roman world were dominated by local economies.

The importance of the wooden legal texts from Vandal North Africa

A slightly different picture emerges from cities in the western Mediterranean. In 439 CE, when Vandals took control of Carthage, the cozy relationship between the state-backed food trade and the enterprising merchants who had negotiated to have their own goods shipped in the extra space on board – a partnership which had lasted for two hundred years – was shut down. The Vandal political upheaval (Vandal Kingdom of North Africa and Sicily, r. 439–534 CE) did not halt all trade between North Africa and Italy, but the end of state-sponsored grain shipments did disrupt a system that had benefited cities on both shores of the Mediterranean.

The situation for people living in North Africa during Vandal rule was also probably mixed. Farmers who had once been required to pay extravagant rent to their landlords, who, in turn, used the money to pay Rome's taxes, now found themselves without the burden of an extra bill. As a result, more money in the Vandal period was likely pouring into the accounts of already wealthy citizens of North African cities. For those at the lowest end of the economic ladder, the situation does not seem to have improved. One extraordinarily rare set of documents, legal texts written on wood and found by chance in a storage jug, show us one farming family in Vandal North Africa that had hit hard times. These legal texts, written in Latin, are known as the Albertini Tablets, after the name of the French scholar, Eugène Albertini, who published the first transcription of them.

The Albertini Tablets call forth an intimate picture of the partnership that could exist between landlords and farmers in late fifth-century CE Vandal North Africa. Many of the contracts specify that they came from the estate of Flavius Geminius Catullinus, which was being overseen by his family's freedmen, at Tebessa in Roman Algeria. The names of two local peasants, Processanus and his wife Siddana, show up frequently in this collection. This couple owned the right to farm a small part of Flavius Geminius Catullinus' large estate. And between 493 and 496 CE, Processanus and Siddana – "because [neither of them] knew how to read and write" (Albertini Tablets 13, line 33; Tablet 3, line 45) – worked with Catullinus and his freedmen overseers to sell back the rights to farm the land they rented.

In the course of these negotiations, the couple divested themselves of, among other crops and tools, a grove of fig trees and olive trees, and an olive press. All said and done, husband and wife eventually sold off almost six or seven plots of land. The final sum of money earned from these sales was one gold coin, or *solidus*. However much the people on the top rungs of the economic ladder may have been celebrating their freedom from the Roman tax system, the Albertini wooden tablets show that at least some people at the bottom were still "struggling to make ends meet" (Andrew Merrills and Richard Miles, *The Vandals* [Oxford: Wiley Blackwell, 2010], p. 160). The end of the Roman tax system, which had linked the societies and economies of North Africa and Italy in a strong bond, thus led to both a downturn and an upturn for the people of Vandal North Africa.

A hundred years later, the situation was thrown into tilt yet again. In 534 CE, the Roman Emperor Justinian recaptured North Africa from the Vandal government and reopened the long-defunct state-sponsored food routes. During Justinian's reign, these ships no longer left Carthage for Italy, however, a land which the Roman Empire no longer controlled. They were setting sail towards an entirely new destination, the empire's only capital, Constantinople. The newly recovered Roman control of North Africa, and the economic link between its cities and Constantinople, would last until the seventh century CE.

10.4   The Crypta Balbi Excavations, Rome: The Story of a Social Safety Net, Third Century–Sixth Century CE

What was happening to the city of Rome itself during this time? In 476 CE, the capital had been placed under the political management of Ostrogothic kings. Thanks to important new excavations from the city center, we can reconstruct the changing fortunes of the old capital and its people during this time. This evidence comes from the site of the "Crypta Balbi" in Rome's lower Campus Martius.

Built in 13 BCE by a man from Roman Spain, Lucius Cornelius Balbus, the theater and crypt (or subterranean portico) which bear his name are fascinating sites in the history of the Late Antique city. The Crypta Balbi provides information that sheds light on the economy far beyond the limits of the city of Rome, too.

Visitors to the site sometimes don't realize how unique it is. Roman archaeologists face a dilemma every time they begin an excavation. The amount of material that has accumulated, layer after layer over seasons and centuries, can make it difficult for researchers to decide which artifacts will be granted top billing in the final report and which ones will be relegated to fine print. In a modern capital like Rome, a city that has been inhabited for thousands of years, these decisions have acute consequences for our understanding of history. For the city of Michelangelo and the Renaissance popes sits on top of medieval limekilns and pilgrim churches, which, in turn, were built on top of Roman warehouses and ancient temples.

For much of the late nineteenth and twentieth centuries, the lure of the layers of "classical Rome," the period associated with big names like Julius Caesar, has meant that archaeologists made a choice to look for material that related to the first and second centuries CE, the period in which the Roman Empire expanded to its greatest geographical extent. Evidence from the in-between times of history was often tossed aside during these campaigns or packed in a crate and sent to a storeroom. Sometimes, the circumstances of Late Antique discoveries were never recorded at all.

In the 1980s, archaeologists in Rome decided it was time to address this historical imbalance. During one of the largest excavations undertaken in the city since the time of Benito Mussolini in the early twentieth century, they made it a specific goal to find and record the entire stratigraphic story of one neighborhood: from antiquity to the present. These excavations took place on an ancient street a stone's throw from where Julius Caesar had been murdered: the lower Campus Martius near the Theater of Pompey.

Ceramics from the Crypta Balbi excavations

For almost all Rome's history, the lower Campus Martius had been located outside the walls of the city. It was not a suburban area, though. Rome's first permanent theater, dedicated by Pompey, was located here, as were many temples vowed by victorious generals during the Republic. There was also a large open sanctuary, called the Porticus Minucia, where grain would be distributed to citizens who were fortunate to have a lottery ticket granting them a food supplement. By the first century CE, the area north of this distribution center would be occupied by Rome's first Pantheon, an audience chamber built to honor Augustus.

Cornelius Balbus contributed to this development (Figure 10.4). In 13 BCE, he added a second theater and the subterranean portico which bore his name. Less than a century later, a fire would devastate much of the surrounding area (c. 80 CE), but Balbus' projects remained an integral part of the Campus Martius into the third century CE (*Working With Sources* 10.1: Coins as Evidence for Ancient Inflation?).

The excavations of the 1980s have been particularly beneficial in helping scholars reconstruct the history of the site beyond the third century. During those campaigns buckets and eventually crates of ceramic material came to light that have shed light on our understanding of the Late Antique economy. By the end of the excavations, 100,000 sherds had been collected that illustrate the nature of the goods coming into Rome between the third and sixth centuries CE.

Ceramic specialists identified 47 percent of the collected material as having once belonged to amphorae, or shipping containers for liquid like oil or wine (singular, amphora). Of these amphorae sherds, nearly half of the material was classified as African Red Slip Ware, coming from North Africa. One fifth of the amphorae transport containers were imported from the eastern Mediterranean. A tenth of the amphorae had been shipped from southern Italy. The source of the remaining vessels could not be identified.

Additional data from Rome's harbor town, Ostia, compiled from the study of nearly 4,000 sherds unearthed during excavations in the late 1990s and 2000s, confirms the general outlines of this picture in Rome. It also allows us to see the historical picture with a little more specificity. Transport vessels for wine and olive oil are particularly well attested at Ostia. Between 280 and 350 CE, Ostia was importing approximately 64 percent of its wine from eastern Mediterranean markets. These products came from the Aegean Sea and Black Sea. By contrast, about half of Ostia's olive oil was being imported from North Africa during this same time. If we look at

The Lower Campus Martius, Rome (Third–Seventh Centuries CE)

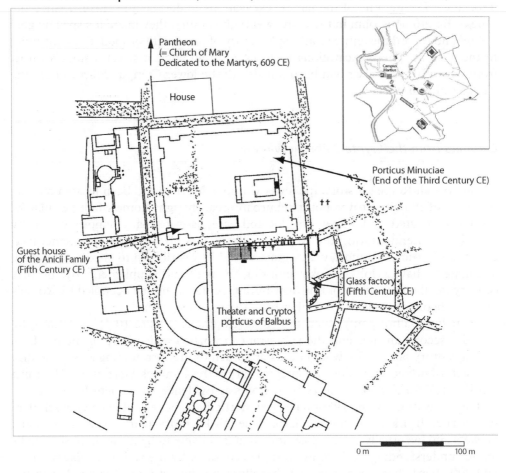

Pantheon
(= Church of Mary
Dedicated to the Martyrs, 609 CE)

House

Porticus Minuciae
(End of the Third Century CE)

Guest house
of the Anicii Family
(Fifth Century CE)

Glass factory
(Fifth Century CE)

Theater and Crypto-
porticus of Balbus

Campus
Martius

0 m   100 m

Figure 10.4 When the Emperor Aurelian paid for the construction of Rome's new walls at the end of the third century CE, some neighborhoods which had once been outside the city's boundaries were suddenly located within it. The Campus Martius, or Field of Mars, was one such region. In 13 BCE, Cornelius Balbus, whose father had been born on the Iberian peninsula, had dedicated a theater here to honor the rise of Augustus. This plan of the lower Campus Martius shows the urban area around Balbus' theater in Late Antiquity. During the empire, citizens received their state-sponsored grain distribution at the nearby Porticus Minucia; it fell out of use in the late third century CE and, by the fifth century, had become a Christian guesthouse (called a *xenodochium*) and a church. Plan by D. Manacorda, *Crypta Balbi, Archeologia e Storia di un Paesaggio Urbano* (Milan: Electa, 2001), p. 44. Used with the permission of D. Manacorda, with author's modifications.

the evidence that can be accurately dated to the period between 350 and 475 CE – the time period just before Ostrogothic rule was established in the city of Rome – this robust data line shows surprisingly little signs of falling. Wine imports into Rome during this period are actually more geographically diverse than in earlier periods. About 55 percent of the imported wine was originating in the Levant.

Working With Sources 10.1
Coins as Evidence for Ancient Inflation?

Some showed the emperor as Chief Priest of Rome. Others depicted personifications of divine qualities, like *Felicitas* (Happiness), *Securitas* (Security), or *Pax* (Peace). They could glorify the leader of the Roman world for his military prowess and could bear eagles to announce when those leaders had been taken up to the skies – turned into *divi*, gods. They came in sizes large and small and were composed of varying metals and alloys. Coins were more than money. They were tokens of a political ideology that kept the empire together.

When we think about the historical value of coins, however, we are probably more accustomed to wonder how they might shed light on narrow economic questions. In the early fourth century CE, for example, a new coin – the gold *solidus* known as a *nomisma* in Greek – was introduced to pay Roman officials, including the army. This coin's introduction has been seen as an important move in stabilizing the economy as it emerged from the third-century economic crisis.

To many historians, coin evidence, in particular, testifies to the seriousness of that crisis. Numismatists, scholars who specialize in the analysis of coins, including their weight and metallic composition, have detected what they see as disturbing trends in silver coins issued during the third century. Gradually, the amount of precious metal used in them was lowered. The signs of this "currency debasement," seen across the third-century Mediterranean, have been used to support the case for a widespread economic crisis in the third century. As coins lost value, their purchasing power decreased. Prices were soon raised so that merchants could continue to make a profit. Soon, the economy was beset with hyper-inflation. It spiraled dramatically out of control.

This narrative will seem like an open-and-shut argument because it uses the familiar language of modern economics and theories of inflation. But there are significant reasons to question it. To begin, inflationary theories depend upon quantifiable data points which are lacking from antiquity. These include "the actual money supply in circulation and its relation to the number of inhabitants and the supply of goods" (Christian Witschel, "Re-Evaluating the Roman West in the Third Century A.D.," *Journal of Roman Archaeology* 17 [2004], p. 258). Without any empire-wide census figures or even archival records from a "federal" Roman bank, which might have helped us calculate the amount of money in circulation, historians of the ancient economy are left playing guesswork. The extent to which the entire Mediterranean world depended on coins as bullion (that is, they were worth the value of their metal content) or as a token currency (that is, the coin's value was greater than its metal content) is also, surprisingly, an open historical question.

Coins may be a dime a dozen as artifacts. But just because they were once used as money doesn't mean they give us the best snapshot of the economy – during the third century or at any other time. There may have been much more fluidity to how people used coins than we suspect.

As for olive oil amphorae, ceramics from Ostia suggest nearly 91 percent of the old harbor town's supplies were coming from North Africa. (For an in-depth look at these numbers, including the significant sample sizes, see the report by ceramics specialist Archer Martin, "Imports at Ostia in the Imperial Period and Late Antiquity: Evidence from the DAI-AAR [German Archaeological Institute-American Academy in Rome] Excavations," in *The Maritime World of Ancient Rome*, ed. by R. Hohlfelder [Ann Arbor: University of Michigan Press, 2008], pp. 105–118.)

When the material from Ostia and the Crypta Balbi are taken together, then, a snapshot of the Late Antique economy does begin to develop.

While other cities throughout the Italian peninsula may have seen a drop-off in goods from North Africa with the end of the imperial food deliveries, Rome, at least, maintained a thriving import economy between the third and late fifth centuries CE. In other words, we might say that underlying economic features of the capital of Ostrogothic Italy proved quite resilient, even during a change in government from empire to kings.

Two final details from the Crypta Balbi excavations

There are two other features of the Crypta Balbi neighborhood which are significant. One relates to the changing patterns of Rome's urban history, the other to events in contemporary Constantinople.

Food handouts would cease at the Crypta Balbi sometime at the end of the third century, as portions of the Porticus Minucia were abandoned. Over time, this large open public space would be gradually raised by rubble. And by the sixth century CE, a *xenodochium*, or Christian hostel, had been built on the site of the former food distribution center. We know because a Latin inscription records the act of a late fifth-century Roman aristocrat, Anicius Faustus, who paid to have the space trans-formed back "into its earlier use" (*CIL* 6.1676).

Anicius Faustus was a member of one of the wealthiest families in Rome, the Anicii. Later bishops of Rome, like Gregory I, make reference to a "guesthouse of the Anicii family" as a famous center of Christian philanthropy and care for the urban poor (Gregory, *Letters* 9.8). This "social service" institution is also mentioned in the Latin biography of the ninth-century Pope Leo III (*Liber Pontificalis* [Book of the Popes] 98.80) as being located near the monastery of Saint Lucia, which was built inside the Porticus Minucia. All this evidence suggests that, even as state-sponsored food distribution was stopped with the Vandal occupation of North Africa, wealthy Romans picked up the reigns of this long-standing city tradition. Anicius Faustus seems to have reinstituted it on the same site – this time, as his own private gift.

The last important detail to emerge from the Crypta Balbi pertains to life not Rome but in fourth-century Constantinople. On May 18, 198 CE – according to two Latin inscriptions that have been known from Rome since the sixteenth century – the guild in charge of measuring grain at the Porticus Minucia was honored with statues of the twin gods Castor and Pollux (*CIL* 6.85a–b). The date for this dedication was not chosen at random; it was the day in which the sun passes into Gemini, the constellation named for "the divine twins." The two statues thus functioned as a generous acknowledgment to the work of the grain measurers but also called upon Rome's divine protectors of seafaring to ensure the safe arrival of food in the future.

A century and a half later, after the Christian emperor Constantine founded his new city on the Bosporus, workers in the second capital were still following this Roman model. On May 18, 332 CE, the people of Constantine's new city celebrated the festival of the *Annonae Natalis*, which honored the successful delivery of food from Egypt (*Chronicon Paschale* at 332 CE) – the exact same day Romans gave thanks to Castor and Pollux for ensuring food delivery in Italy. That holiday correspondence tells us, once again, that some customs and festivals in fourth-century Constantinople were not immediately different than the ones celebrated in Rome itself. Traditions could be imported, too.

Summary

Studying the economy demands careful attention to assumptions, working definitions, and method. During the period in which the Roman Empire had two capitals, the main economic corridors were the state-sponsored food delivery routes that linked North Africa and Rome, in the west, and Egypt and Constantinople, in the east. Luxury goods, like marble, played an important role in the economy. But smaller, more everyday objects, like ceramics, give economic historians more useful data for reconstructing imports, exports, and trade across the Mediterranean.

As this data reveals, many merchants, particularly those in North Africa, capitalized on the state grain shipments to ship their wares to Italy and cities far beyond Roman Tunisia and Algeria. Apart from the continued presence of African Red Slip Ware in Rome, however – seen in the Crypta Balbi excavations and at Ostia – Italian demand for African Red Slip Ware withers in the fifth century CE. From this phenomenon, economic historians like Chris Wickham have deduced that intra-regional trade, not trans-regional shipping, was a more important, more resilient feature of the Roman economy than we sometimes assume. Thus, although goods like marble could travel great distances, long-distance trade eventually became less prevalent in the late fifth-century western Mediterranean when the Roman food system – which had long sustained these twin shipping routes – was finally shut down. In the eastern Mediterranean, the greater number of sea routes for bringing food from Egypt to Constantinople sustained the Roman Empire in the east for two more centuries up until its loss of Egypt to Arab armies in 641 CE.

Study Questions

1. Identify the following marble types by their color and geographic origin: giallo antico, porphyry, serpentine.
2. What evidence do historians use to estimate the cost of marble construction projects?

3. Why are ceramics such an important body of evidence for archaeologists and historians?

4. The Crypta Balbi excavations present a slice of daily life in Rome before and after 476 CE, when Christian emperors were replaced by Christian kings. How did society and culture change during this transition?

Suggested Readings

Alan Cameron, *Circus Factions: Blues and Greens at Rome and Byzantium* (Oxford: Oxford University Press, 1976).

Leslie Dossey, *Peasant and Empire in Christian North Africa* (Berkeley: University of California Press, 2010).

Ine Jacobs (ed.), *Production and Prosperity in the Theodosian Period* (Leuven: Peeters, 2014).

Chris Wickham, *Framing the Early Middle Ages: Europe and the Mediterranean, 400–800* (New York: Oxford University Press, 2007).

11

The Household and Family

Across the Mediterranean home was the defining unit for many Romans and non-citizens alike: father, mother, sons, daughters, and slaves. Some would try to leave this world behind. Others would try to bring parts of it with them as they sought opportunities elsewhere. Augustine, born in 354 CE in the town of Thagaste in Roman Algeria and later priest and bishop in the town of Hippo until his death in 430 CE (bishop 395–430 CE), illustrates the path that someone could take to get away from their family yet keep close its dearest members simultaneously.

Raised by a father named Patricius and by his mother, Monica, in modern Souk Ahras (Algeria), Augustine pursued a Roman education in Madauros, about fifteen miles away. By around seventeen, he had wound up in Carthage, where he finished his studies and became a teacher. It was after several years of teaching in Carthage that he decided to leave his family's roots in North Africa for Rome. Augustine was not, however, leaving his family. Although his father had died, sometime before Augustine's departure in 383 CE, Augustine left North Africa with the help of a financially well-placed supporter and accompanied by his mom. Two years later, by 385 CE, mother and son had traveled to Milan, then the resident city of the emperor.

The story of Augustine's journey from North Africa to Rome, Milan, and eventually back again shows us a late fourth-century family on the move. In many ways, however, this family was missing one of its most defining members. The male head of the household, or *paterfamilias*, traditionally exercised authority over all members of his estate, including slaves, and oversight over all its financial dealings. In this way, the management of a *domus*, as Roman writers referred to the household in Latin, was one that came with both social and economic responsibilities. During the fourth through sixth centuries, this domestic world and the values it was built on would be passed down, renegotiated, and changed as Christianity became the official identity of the state.

A Social and Cultural History of Late Antiquity, First Edition. Douglas Boin.
© 2018 John Wiley & Sons, Inc. Published 2018 by John Wiley & Sons, Inc.

The values associated with running a Roman household would also provide much inspiration to bishops in Rome, who used its ethical framework to grow their authority over other Christian leaders. By the middle of the fifth century CE, the bishop of Rome – once an equal among the emerging church hierarchy – had acquired a new identity: pope. Understanding how the Roman household works and the gender roles it assumed is integral to understanding the rise of a Christian authority structure outside of it. These are the topics of this chapter (*Exploring Culture* 11.1: The "Third Gender").

Exploring Culture 11.1   *The "Third Gender"*

In antiquity, gender identity was defined in binary terms: male in one category, female in another. There was one group, however, that challenged such neat and tidy polarities. They belonged to a "third gender" (*tertium genus*, in Latin). Although it does not appear to be a term with which they self-identified, its use by ancient writers gives us a chance to look more closely at the phenomenon behind it.

According to the anonymous *Writers of the Imperial History* [SHA], Emperor Severus Alexander (r. 222–235 CE) used the term to denigrate members of his imperial staff, the palace eunuchs. Eunuchs were self-castrated men who had entered into government service; their lack of a family or any sexual partner gave them a higher-level security clearance. The benefit of having a staff of eunuchs had been recognized as far back as the Persian Empire of the fifth century BCE. Three hundred years later, eunuchs were employed throughout Roman cities as family guardians (Terence, *The Eunuch*). That did not keep Emperor Alexander from despising them.

> [The emperor] used to say that eunuchs were a third sex of the human race, one not to be seen or employed by men and scarcely even by women of noble birth. He removed all eunuchs from his service and gave orders that they should serve his wife as slaves. And whereas Elagabalus [the previous emperor] had been the slave of his eunuchs, Alexander reduced them to a limited number and removed them from all duties in the Palace except the care of the women's baths. (*SHA, Life of Alexander Severus* 23.5–7, LCL trans. by D. Magie [1924])

By the time of Diocletian's constitutional reforms a century later, one writer considered eunuchs to be among those who "had chief authority at court and with the emperor" (Lactantius, *On the Death of the Persecutors* 15, trans. from the *ANF* series). They would hold this important power in the eastern Roman Empire, too. Narses, a Christian from Armenia, would serve Emperor Justinian as a court eunuch in Constantinople in the mid-sixth century CE (Procopius, *History of the Wars* 1.25).

Palace eunuchs were not the only ones pushing the boundaries of gender expression. The priests of a popular Roman cult, the cult of the goddess Magna Mater, were included in this group, too. Known as *Galli*, they embraced a style of dress that conservative Romans deemed much too effeminate (Apuleius, *Golden Ass* 8.27–28). In this case, however, gender transgression likely worked as a positive feature of the cult; it marked the priests as patently different yet bestowed on them an elevated status that was closer to the Great Mother (*Magna Mater*) than ordinary worshippers.

Anthropologists and sociologists have studied how gender transgression can often work in this dual way: causing fear and promoting awe, simultaneously. An appreciation for the role of gender expression in ancient cults may even explain why some fourth-, fifth-, and sixth-century Christians began depicting Jesus in an androgynous way. Scholar Thomas Mathews has given the most provocative presentation of this material in *The Clash of Gods: A Reinterpretation of Early Christian Art* (Princeton: Princeton University Press, 1993).

11.1   Home as a Place

Where people called home obviously varied depending on their wealth, their aesthetic preferences, and their taste. Several cities have provided evidence for the kind of spaces people lived in. These examples will not only help us see the domestic sphere in concrete terms. They will provide a good starting point for helping us imagine the way a Roman home worked as a social space.

Apartments

Many families of modest means lived in an apartment complex. Cities like Ostia, Ephesos, Alexandria, or Jeme – in Middle Egypt – have all revealed these structures. These cities' apartments share certain features but also have significant differences.

In Jeme, a city in the Egyptian hills of Thebes, on the west bank of the Nile opposite the ancient dynastic site of Luxor, archaeologists revealed traces of two- to three-story buildings in the cubic shape of a tower. These tower houses had long been popular in Middle Egypt as residential units for middle- and lower-class residents of the city. Their living area was arranged vertically. A view from the street through the door rarely offered a glimpse of the inside.

A shared entry space here also does not seem to have been a priority for the residents. Families or individuals who occupied the flat lived on the upper floors so that smoke from their cooking could be easily vented to the sky. Lower floors were largely uninhabited. The cooler spaces within the apartment complex were largely set aside for storage. On the first floor at Jeme, for example, water jugs might be sunken into the cavernous floors so that refreshment could be offered to passersby. (The apartment towers at Jeme are also fascinating because of where they were constructed. They were built both within and on top of the walls of one of Jeme's ancient Egyptian sanctuaries; the evidence is discussed in *EBW* [2007], at pp. 130–131.)

Even within a region like Roman Egypt, however, there could be diversity. At Karanis in the Fayyum, apartment units are also structured vertically. But there, the upper stories, not the lower ones, were designated as storage space. They were called in Greek *kella* (Latin, *cella*). At Alexandria, meanwhile, a city whose apartments provide a third contrast to the tower homes at Jeme, the ground floor of residences had much more of a social function. In the quarter of modern Alexandria known as Kom el-Dikka, archaeologists discovered a whole block of residences. Each unit was organized around a central courtyard. Some of these courtyards were occupied by a latrine, shared by everyone in the complex. From the courtyard a set of stairs provided access to the upper stories, where there were one- or two-room units for families or individuals to share (*EBW* [2007], pp. 131–132, 231).

Alexandria's open-layout apartments, structured around a common courtyard, are identical to the form of apartments in Ostia. These "islands," as the blocks were called in Latin (*insulae*; Latin singular is *insula*) were built around a shared central courtyard with an open sky. Stairs, usually in a hallway off this courtyard, led to modest apartments on the upper floors. At Ostia, although the evidence is slim, it appears people lived in apartments alongside their fancier, wealthy neighbors through at least the sixth century.

Houses

Like apartments, houses varied widely based on regional architectural styles, customs, and wealth, but – as with apartments – nowhere is the idea of the family as a social space more visible than in the study of a Roman home. With spaces set aside for cooking and for studying, as well as rooms for banqueting and hosting guests or patrons, houses in the Mediterranean were stages for a dizzying area of performances. Some of these activities were public, like the entertainment of friends and professional contacts. Some were private and took place in the bedrooms or personal quarters (*Key Debates* 11.1: Can Texts About Women Help Us Recover the Voices of Real Women?).

For these reasons, throughout much of the Roman Empire, whatever the precise architectural plan of the property being investigated, it is nearly impossible to identify public and private rooms. Social life in the house followed different patterns depending on the time of day and depending on a visitor's degree of access to power. Even the exact function of a room might have changed throughout the day. This level of activity can often be detected through careful excavation and recording of the artifacts found in a specific space.

One third-century CE house at the harbor city of Ephesos in Roman Asia Minor, for example, has been particularly well studied. Known as Hanghaus 2.4

Key Debates 11.1   *Can Texts About Women Help Us Recover the Voices of Real Women?*

Women made up roughly half the ancient Mediterranean population. When one considers the paltry number of surviving texts written *by* women, however, that population balance explains why ancient history may have been written by, for, and about men.

Specialists in ancient historians are not the only ones grappling with how to right this gender imbalance. Since the 1970s, many other fields have tried to find a way to address it, too. Joan Wallach Scott, author of a widely influential volume, *Gender and the Politics of History* (New York: Columbia University Press, 1988), played a leading role in these efforts. Wallach Scott challenged researchers in all disciplines to uncover stories about the lives of women who had been ignored. With a memorable play on words, she advocated for adding "her-story" to history.

In the field of ancient history, this mandate was easier read than done. Some scholars – many of them female – pushed back against the idea that any text written about women *by men* could ever be trusted. The characters who appeared in these male-authored sources, although they may have really existed, functioned more like literary inventions. This way of reading the ancient sources was frustrating and chilling. Women's real day-to-day actions – their own voices, the complexity of their choices – seemed doomed to obscurity all over again.

Recent years have seen welcome new directions, as scholars turn to contemporary and comparative examples of feminist histories, such as the meaning of Islamic headscarves, to consider the lives of ancient women in thought-provoking ways. One tool is to look at ancient women's clothing choices as complex and, above all, creative social performances (Kate Wilkinson, *Women and Modesty in Late Antiquity* [Cambridge: Cambridge University Press, 2015]).

Demetrias, the Christian granddaughter of a wealthy Roman matriarch, Faltonia Anicia Proba, can help us see the potential of this new approach. After fleeing Rome in 410 or 411 CE with her Christian mother and grandmother, Demetrias chose to live as an ascetic. It was a radical decision, breaking three generations of family tradition. One male writer describes Demetrias' modesty in the following way:

> Her precious necklaces, costly pearls, and glowing gems she put back in their cases. Then dressing herself in a coarse tunic and throwing over herself a still coarser cloak she came in at an unlooked for moment, threw herself down suddenly at her grandmother's knees, and with tears and sobs showed her who she really was. (Jerome, *Letter* 130.5, trans. by W. Fremantle et al. in the *NPNF* series [1893])

Demetrias' decision may seem like a highly conservative one to us, a way of unconsciously upholding male power by downplaying her own wealth, jewelry, and glamor – the very things that would have made her stand apart as a powerful woman. If we think about "the creative work of modesty" (Wilkinson 2015, p. 3), however, we can see Demetrias' choices in a more subtle way. She was making a powerful statement about what it meant for her to be part of an ascetic community.

Looking at female clothing as an expression of community formation can help historians break out of the box of debating whether Demetrias' behavior was an act of resistance or a highly traditional decision. In this approach, Demetrias' fashion choice speaks to "who she really was."

("Slope 2, House 4") because it is part of a series of residences built into a gradually rising hill on the southwestern part of the city, it was a two-level house in
which excavators found a motley assemblage of artifacts (Figure 11.1). On its
first floor, a collection of lamps, weights, and cooking pots was found in the
spacious interior courtyard, a place where any guest would have stumbled over
them on their way to visit the owner. Against the walls of the entry vestibule, by
contrast, several shipping containers, or amphorae, had been propped up. The
scattered location of the tools and the piles of quotidian junk undercut the image
of an ancient home as having rooms that were always neatly separated by social
function (see K. Bowes at the end of this chapter).

Meanwhile, upstairs – in a room with a nice mosaic floor, the kind that would
have spoken to the wealth and status ambitions of its owner – archaeologists discovered a hoe for gardening or farming, more lamps, and even fragments of sculpture.
All of it was strewn on the room's mosaic, as if the space were being used as a
convenient storage closet. The lesson from Slope House 2.4 at Ephesos is not to be
foolhardy when trying to determine the function of domestic rooms on an archaeological plan. The dangers are confirmed by additional evidence from the center of
the house, where the chance discovery of a graffito showed that the owner's well-
trafficked courtyard – not his formal dining room – was one of the most popular
places for hosting his summer dinner parties.

When studying Roman houses, one other consideration is important to keep in
mind: people's ever-changing moods and aesthetic preferences. Some residences in
a city like Ostia were built in the second century CE but remained occupied by families and were consistently repaired over time, with trendy new features. The House
of the Fortuna Annonaria (named for the discovery of a statue possibly dedicated to
the goddess Fortuna, associated with the state food supply) was largely a second-
century residence that was occupied well throughout the fifth century CE. By the
fourth century CE, owners had added a *nymphaeum*, or fountain wall, to the house.
Lined with marble, a private fountain was a popular architectural feature in Ostia's
fourth- and fifth-century homes. Not every aspect of Late Antique living was done
in new, contemporary construction.

11.2   House-Churches in the Long History of Christianity

The fact that Roman houses were social spaces is an essential starting point when
discussing the history of Christianity. Wealthy home-owners had played a crucial
role in providing meeting spaces for many of Jesus' earliest followers. The money
that came for transforming, adapting, and renovating these spaces, such as seen
in the archaeological evidence at Dura Europos, shows us that, by the middle of the
third century CE, many of Jesus' followers had made important social connections in
the cities where they lived.

These small communities may have grown more visible because of the way they
reached out to Romans of means and used their wealth in creative ways. Many of

'Slope House 2' at Ephesos, Asia Minor

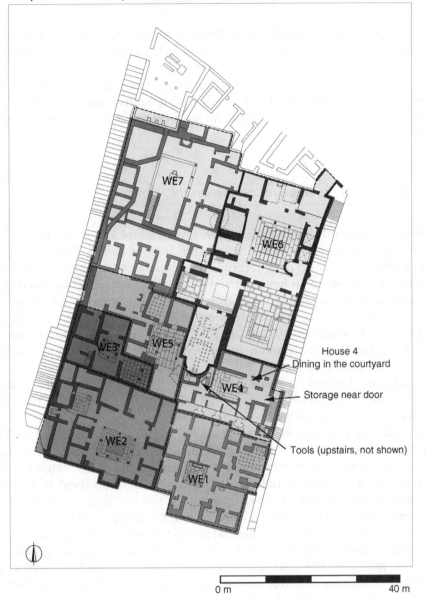

0 m   40 m

Figure 11.1 One of the most important harbors of the Roman East, the streets and houses of Ephesos provided the backdrop for uproarious comedies, such as those written by the Roman playwright Plautus. They had also been the stage for serious personal dramas. Paul, a Hellenistic Jew, had passed through here during his first-century CE travels. Ephesos itself has been extraordinarily well excavated, with much material dating to Late Antiquity. These six houses were built into a terrace on the south side of one of the main city streets. Called by excavators the "Slope Houses" because of where they were built, they reveal, among other things, how modern notions of "public" and "private" living don't map onto ancient households. In Slope House 2.4 (on plan, at the middle right) several tools and ceramic shipping containers were found on the ground floor; some were even stored upstairs. The courtyard, meanwhile, which would appear to be one of the most utilitarian spaces in a house, was known to have been used for elegant summer dining. At the end of the third century CE, an earthquake damaged this entire block. Plan adapted from Norbert Zimmermann and Sabine Ladstätter, *Wall Painting in Ephesos from the Hellenistic to the Byzantine Period* (Istanbul: Ege Yayinlari, 2011), p. 43.

these home-owners may have directly influenced the rites practiced on their property or the beliefs held by the community meeting in the home. This long backstory in domestic living and private worship is important because not all Christians migrated from "private" houses to "public" churches in the years after the Edict of Milan. Material and textual evidence from across the Mediterranean confirms that many wealthy Christians in the fourth, fifth, and sixth centuries CE continued to worship in their houses.

Tituli *and the transformation of the Caelian Hill, Rome*

The best way to study this phenomenon involves looking at the history of the Christian *tituli*, twenty-two of which are known from Rome. The *tituli* of Rome have often been conceived of as forerunners of Catholic parishes, which is to say, they were once believed to have functioned as their local neighborhood church. The Latin word *titulus* (plural *tituli*) from which these worship spaces take their name, however, was a legal term meaning "inscription" or "title." And it is now thought that the word *titulus* was used to signify how the property had been acquired and from whom; a *titulus* was thus not necessarily the same as a basilica or church. According to Roman law, it simply designated the land or property which had been donated for someone else's use. The name of the benefactor was given after the "title" (*Political Issues* 11.1: Wealth, Patronage, and the Voice of Influential Women; Figure 11.2).

The *titulus* Pammachius, located on Rome's Caelian Hill overlooking the Flavian Amphitheater, is one of the twenty-two *titulus* properties known from the city. Although the identity of Pammachius is not certain, the archaeological evidence from the site shows how a traditionally residential neighborhood of upper-class houses and perhaps middle- to lower-class apartments and shops could be gradually transformed over time to become a large Christian worship center.

By the late second century CE, there were two buildings in this neighborhood: an apartment, or *insula*, with shops and, across a small garden to the north, a large two-storied house. By the third century CE, the residents of the house had acquired the apartment complex and used it to pursue an expansive renovation of their home. During this time, a household shrine was installed in the garden courtyard at the base of a stairway which led to the home's upper stories. Based on traces of the wall paintings which survive, this shrine was dedicated to Venus or Isis.

A century later, in the middle of the fourth century CE, the owners added a new painted landing at the top of their courtyard stairway. Now, instead of leading to the upper stories of the home, it terminated in a small enclosure, like a closet, which was transformed into a chapel for the home-owners. Frescos painted on the wall show scenes of martyrdom and Christian prayer. It was built above the first-floor household shrine to Venus or Isis.

The final stage in the neighborhood's transformation occurred in the first decades of the fifth century CE. At that time, the whole area – old apartments,

Political Issues 11.1   *Wealth, Patronage, and the Voice of Influential Women*

Georgia was a resident of Jerash (in modern Jordan). As with so many other women who called the ancient Mediterranean their home, details about her life – beyond the name of her nearest male family member, Theodorus, her husband – are scant. We do have an important piece of material culture that gives her a concrete social presence. As it turns out, Georgia was a Christian with a sizable fortune.

In 533 CE, she and her husband donated money to build a local church, dedicated to Saints Cosmas and Damian. To make sure people knew where the project's funds had come from, the couple had their portraits and names put on display. In two separate panels set into the floor near the front of the church, "Georgia, wife of Theodore" and Theodore greet the members of the congregation. The mosaic is still in situ, or on site, in the church of Saints Cosmas and Damian.

Georgia's display of wealth wasn't unique for her day, nor is it unique in the annals of Christianity. Since the time of the very first documents left behind by the followers of Jesus, in the middle of the first century CE, women of means were providing financial or logistical resources for the early community. In fact, they can be found in almost every generation of early Christian history.

The apostle Paul's letter to the people of Rome is one of the earliest documents attesting to this fact, written around 56–58 CE. At the time it was composed, Paul was staying in Corinth, Greece – specifically at its harbor city, Cenchreae, waiting for a journey to Rome. In his letter to the community at Rome, in advance of his arrival, Paul asks that they extend every hospitality to the advance members of his team. He also thanks several women for being "patrons," or "benefactors," of the Jesus movement. Asking for help from the community, Paul says:

> I commend to you our sister Phoebe, a deacon (or "minister") of the church in Cenchreae. I ask you to receive her in the Lord in a way worthy of his people and to give her any help she may need from you, for she has been the benefactor of many people, including me. (Paul, *Letter to the Romans* 16.1 [*NRSV*])

Elsewhere in the same letter, Paul mentions a husband and wife team, Priscilla and Aquila (Romans 16.3) who provided similar resources to him in his preaching. This arrangement for private funds was quite common in antiquity. Personal patronage and social connections paid for many of the amenities that individuals, communities, and even cities took for granted.

In Ostia, outside Rome, Faltonia Betitia Proba and her husband paid for the water supply to their local neighborhood bath complex. Archaeologists discovered their names stamped on a lead pipe, dated to the mid- to late fourth century CE, when Anicia Faltonia Proba's husband was Prefect of the City of Rome.

Figure 11.2 Although far removed from the grandiose cityscape of Rome, the cities of the Roman provinces were places of architectural innovation and experimentation. Gerasa (Jerash, modern Jordan) illustrates that point nicely. This photograph is a view, seen facing north, of Jerash's marketplace, a distinctive oval forum. The idea of having a circular city center, although not popular in the wider Roman empire at the time, would, nevertheless, be adapted to cities like Ostia and Constantinople by the fourth century CE. Jerash itself would remain a place where local citizens used architecture to advertise their own status and ambitions. In the early sixth century CE, a wealthy couple donated money for a local church to be dedicated to Saints Cosmas and Damian. The names of the husband and wife were set into tiles on the church floor so that worshippers would know it was the laity – not the priests – who had provided such an expensive gift for the community. Photo credit: Ann Morgan, with permission.

garden courtyard, fancy multi-story house – was given to the church as a *titulus*. The house was then partly demolished and buried. A church dedicated to Saints John and Paul would be built on the site. This church would be called a *titulus* in subsequent Christian documents.

House-churches and church leadership

The issue of who controlled or managed these kinds of worship spaces once they were donated to the church is not entirely clear, and that is ultimately why they are both historically puzzling and so significant. In fact, it is very likely that the owners of the house underneath the fifth-century church of Saints John and Paul retained, not forfeited, their leadership role in the church community when they donated it. This arrangement, although beneficial from a property standpoint to the church as an institution, could have also caused countless headaches for church leadership if the patrons of the property did not share the bishop's vision for the spiritual direction of the Christian community.

Thus, although the role that patrons played in the construction of Christian churches was entirely consistent with practices going back to the time of Jesus' followers, by Late Antiquity the logistics of this continuing partnership were gradually beginning to frustrate many bishops. As leaders of the church, in the age after Constantine, many bishops felt empowered to assert their own control over the extended Christian family. Heated debates soon arose between the bishops and the wealthy financiers, conversations which became particularly acute in the fourth and fifth centuries. One result of this dynamic was that many bishops themselves began hunting for sympathetic donors so that they could finance their own church communities, no strings attached.

Consequently, although it is tempting to read this period as one in which the powerless Christian laity began clashing with an increasingly powerful Christian hierarchy, all parties involved – the home-owners, the property donors, and the bishops – were awash in money. And all parties were mindful of the ways that patronage could grease a palm or unlock a door. Continued church attendance at home after the age of Constantine gave rise to an intense Christian conversation about whose money should speak more loudly within the institution of the church.

11.3   Family and Household Relations, c.405–551 CE

Among the cacophony of a Roman home, run by its *paterfamilias*, it can be hard to hear other voices. This situation is especially true given the gender ideologies which dominated Roman society. The voices of women, for example, although the wealthier ones could manage their own inheritances and make a powerful contribution to the life of a city, can be difficult to hear in their own terms. Material culture can help. One female mummy from the city of Antinoöpolis in Egypt has become known as "The Embroiderer" because she was buried with the tools of her craft (*EBW* [2007], pp. 173–175). Although anonymous, she speaks beyond the grave through the love of her work.

Other women were not so fortunate. They passed through history silently or entered the history books because men spoke about them and for them. Two examples from the early fifth and early sixth centuries CE show us how the ideologies of the household were built around properly defined gender roles. Here, two male writers, Jerome and Procopius, describe women who threatened or subverted those roles.

Jerome and the lives of two Christian women in Gaul: c.405 CE

In the early fifth century CE, the Christian writer Jerome (*c.*437–420 CE) was based in Bethlehem. He had been working on new Latin translations of selected Jewish and Christian scriptures by drawing upon his knowledge of Hebrew and Greek.

Even if Jerome felt separated from his old friends and family in the western Mediterranean – he had been born on the Adriatic in modern Croatia – geographic distance was not going to keep him from intervening in their affairs if the case demanded it. In 405 CE, a Christian monk came to him with one such concern:

> A certain brother from Gaul told me that his virgin sister and widowed mother, though living in the same city, had separate apartments and have taken to themselves clerical protectors either as guests or as (financial) stewards; and that by associating with strangers in this way, they have caused more scandal than by living apart. (Jerome, *Letter* 117.1, trans. by W. Fremantle et al. in the *NPNF* series [1893], slightly modified)

This letter reveals the circumstances under which the monk felt compelled to reach out for Jerome's help. The monk's sister and mother had taken advantage of the death of the family's male authority figure, the *paterfamilias*, to move out of the family home and take up residence in two separate properties. As a result, neither woman was any longer under the constant supervision of a male, apart from the relationship which each had with their Christian "clerical directors" (*clericus*, meaning "clergy"). The fact that these clergy "managed [both the mother's and daughter's] small properties" suggests that they may have been associated with a household-church, or *titulus*, in Gaul.

Whatever the exact circumstances of the mother and daughter's daily routine in their own apartments, their unnamed brother-son was scandalized by their relative freedom. He asked Jerome to write a letter to them to rebuke them for their decisions, as if the choice of mother and daughter to live alone threatened to undermine *his* social status as the male member of their family. Jerome took up the case willingly. To the daughter he wrote that her status as an unmarried young Christian woman – living outside the protection of a monastic community, although with a male Christian friend – was exposing her to dangerous forces that might derail her vow of chastity:

> At dinner whether you like it or not, you will be forced to eat meat (and that of different kinds). To make you drink wine, they will praise it as a creature of God. To induce you to go with them to the baths, they will speak of dirt with disgust.... Meanwhile, some singer will perform for the company a selection of softly flowing airs; and as he will not venture to look at other men's wives, he will constantly fix his eyes on you who have no protector. (Jerome, *Letter* 117.6, trans. by Fremantle et al. [1893], slightly modified)

To the mother, Jerome crafted a message that appealed to her status as a respectable woman of means. "You have a son and a daughter," Jerome pleaded with her, mentioning her two Christian children. "[But you also have] a son-in-law – or at least one who is your daughter's partner," he added, trying to shame her to put an end to the fact that her Christian daughter, although chaste, was sharing an apartment with an unmarried Christian man (Jerome, *Letter* 117.6, trans. by Fremantle et al. [1893], slightly modified).

Although Jerome's letter to the two women in Gaul gives us his perspective on these matters, not theirs, the document does raise questions about the social expectations and burdens placed upon Christian women by Christian male friends and family.

As is clear here, many of these expectations conflicted with how Christian women themselves conceived of the social options open to them. Many women, that is, following the customs of the wider Roman world, did not see their personal decisions as a problem affecting anyone else – until they looked through their mail and found a letter from Jerome.

Procopius tells of a scandalous Christian empress, c.550–551 CE

Three generations after the imperial settlement with the Ostrogothic kings, during which parts of the Italian peninsula had been erased from the map of the Roman Empire, similar expectations for proper female behavior at home and in public can be found in Procopius. His target was the Roman empress. A Christian living in a Christian Roman Empire, Procopius was scathing in his indictment of the Emperor Justinian and his wife. He clearly found the emperor's policies of political intolerance – by which different faith traditions, even different Christian theological beliefs, were deemed heretical and outlawed – appalling. Empress Theodora was not immune to Procopius' criticism, either. In a text published c.550–551 called *The Secret History* (called in Greek the *Anecdota*), he casts the sixth-century empress as a woman of loose morals, degenerate behavior, and as a sex addict who, "though she was pregnant many times, yet practically always she was able to contrive to bring about an abortion immediately" (Procopius, *The Secret History* 9.19, LCL trans. by H. Dewing [1935]).

The intent behind Procopius' scandalous portrayal was not to question the legitimacy of the female leader, however. In his discussion of the Ostrogothic Queen Amalasountha, daughter of King Theoderic (r. 489–526 CE), Procopius showed that he could respect a female politician when she displayed "the dignity befitting a queen" (*History of the Wars* 5.2.21, LCL trans. by H. Dewing [1916]). The acerbic, almost slanderous comments about Empress Theodora, by contrast, suggest that Procopius was not impressed by the emperor's life partner, a female whom he caricatured as breaking all social conventions. Bringing Theodora into the ring helped Procopius land a powerful punch. If Emperor Justinian was struggling to manage his own household, how could he be trusted to govern the Christian Roman state? (*Working With Sources* 11.1: The Dramatic Life of the Mathematician, Scientist, and Philosopher Hypatia of Alexandria.)

11.4 Slaves and Slavery

The emperor and his estate managers were the most prominent of the landholders throughout the Mediterranean, but one didn't have to be a member of the imperial house to sell, trade, and manage a portfolio of farms and properties. Nor did one have to be male. All farms, estates, and households – from the houses of Rome's Caelian and Aventine Hills to the villas of Spain and the emperor's palace in Constantinople – ran on slaves. Moreover, no faith community in Late Antiquity,

Working With Sources 11.1

The Life of the Mathematician, Scientist, and Philosopher Hypatia of Alexandria

She helped her friend design an astrolabe, a device that measured the height of stars. Her father, a famous mathematician, trained her in the sciences. By the time she was an adult, she had taken her love of inquiry and transformed it into a career as a teacher and philosopher. Her name was Hypatia (c.355–415 CE), and she was one of the most accomplished mathematicians, scientists, and philosophers of antiquity. She also happened to be a woman.

Tragically, nothing that Hypatia wrote or made has come down to us, but countless others memorialized the story of her life and dramatic death. The first substantial account appeared in the middle of the fifth century CE. A Christian writer named Socrates of Constantinople, also known as Socrates Scholasticus, included her biography in his lengthy *Church History*. In the male-dominated world of the Roman Empire, Socrates admired the way she held her own:

> On account of the self-possession and ease of manner, which she had acquired in consequence of the cultivation of her mind, she not infrequently appeared in public in presence of the magistrates. Neither did she feel abashed in coming to an assembly of men. For all men on account of her extraordinary dignity and virtue admired her the more. (*Church History* 7.15, trans. by A. Zenos in the *NPNF* series [1890])

Hypatia's outspokenness also may have led, in this male-dominated Mediterranean, to her undoing. When conversations between the leading government official of Alexandria, Orestes, and the bishop of the city, Cyril, broke down – the issue seems to have focused on whether Orestes had been acting "Christian enough" – Hypatia was pegged as the source of the problem because "she had frequent interviews with Orestes" (*Church History* 7.15).

Whoever undertook this libelous campaign against her, we cannot say. But the rhetoric did succeed in lighting the passions of Christians who believed that Orestes was not the "real Christian" he claimed he was. Soon, a Christian mob, stoked by a "fierce and bigoted zeal," took their anger out on Hypatia. Meeting her in the street, they dragged her from her carriage, stripped her, and murdered her (*Church History* 7.15).

How much of this story is true? Did Socrates get the basic outline correct, or does another source challenge his version of the story? Unfortunately, no one after him showed any interest in the facts of the case. Many writers did the opposite. From the mid-fifth century CE to the age of the Enlightenment, people expanded, elaborated, and embellished the story of Hypatia's life and murder for their own purposes. One of the most distorted retellings comes from a Christian writing in the seventh century CE named John. John looked back on Hypatia's death as if it were the final victory in a long set of Late Antique "cultural wars" that had been fought between Christians and non-Christians. In John's retelling, Alexandria's bishop at the time, Cyril, was the one who won the day for, under his opposition, "the last remains of idolatry in the city" were destroyed (John of Nikiu, *Chronicle* 84.103, trans. by R. Charles [1916]).

Even Socrates of Constantinople may have used Hypatia to serve his own needs. Socrates was writing at a time when the bishops of Constantinople and Alexandria had parted ways over how to describe the relationship between Jesus' humanity and divinity. In Socrates' presentation of these events, Alexandria and its people do not exactly come across as models of civic behavior.

regardless of the moral leadership which many faith communities *did* provide in support of the abolitionist causes during the modern era, would ever advocate to break, disrupt, or shut down this entrenched system of slave labor. Between the third and eighth centuries CE, Christians and, later, Muslims never led an organized intellectual, social, or cultural revolution to challenge the fundamental existence of a slave-owning society. (A helpful guide to the Islamic material is Mohammed Ennaji's *Slavery, the State, and Islam*, trans. from the French by Teresa Fagan [New York: Cambridge University Press, 2013].)

The practice of slavery had a long precedent in the Greek and Roman worlds, in both agricultural contexts and in household management. Taken as prisoners in war, slaves could be drawn from any region of the known world; in this way, ancient slavery was not based on race. Many males and females had to endure lives of servitude as a result. They could also be educated and might work as tutors in Greek and Roman households, teaching students their own native language. Many paid for their freedom based on the savings they earned and set aside, called their *peculium*. Others were beaten by farmers or worked long, hard hours in Rome's mines. Still others, as property of the imperial house, managed the infrastructure of the capitals, like the slaves who were tasked with inspecting the aqueducts.

The ubiquity, even the necessity of slaves in the Roman world, may explain why many of Jesus' followers never tried to replace this system. In fact, it was through a process of conforming to Roman cultural values that many of Jesus' followers taught others to perpetuate the injustice of robbing another human of their liberty. These early Christian compromises with Roman culture are preserved in Christian Scripture in several passages which scholars refer to as the "household duty codes" (in Colossians 3.18–4.1, in Ephesians 5.22–6.9, and in 1 Peter 2.18–3.7). These exhortations compelled all of Jesus' followers to conform to mainstream values: Women were told to obey their husbands; children, their parents; and slaves, their masters.

Even in the time of the Christian Emperor Justinian, the division between free and un-free was still being articulated in Roman law. Justinian's *Institutes* set forth the working legal definitions for who constituted a free citizen, a freedman, or a slave:

The chief division in the rights of persons is this: men are all either free or slaves. Freedom, from which men are said to be free, is the natural power of doing what we each please, unless prevented by force or by law. Slavery is an institution of the law of nations, by which one man is made the property of another, contrary to natural right.... Slaves either are born or become so. They are born so when their mother is a slave; they become so either by the law of nations, that is, by captivity, or by the civil law, as when a free person, above the age of twenty, suffers himself to be sold, that he may share the price given for him. (Justinian, *Institutes* 1.3, trans. by O. Thatcher [ed.], *The Library of Original Sources: The Roman World* [Milwaukee: University Research Extension, 1907])

Emperor Justinian's matter-of-fact presentation and acceptance of a society built upon the concept of slavery underlines a key point. In the sixth century CE, even the most zealous advocate for a Christian state never questioned the moral foundations of a world in which some men were free and others were not.

And yet, the most historically empathetic explanation as to why an ancient abolition movement never grew perhaps lies in the fact that, in antiquity, slaves were not existentially or economically bound to a lower social status. With the right patron and the right funds, any slave could potentially become free. Justinian's own policies towards freedmen show that he saw manumission as an important mechanism for sustaining a degree of social mobility in the state. "We have made all freedmen whatsoever Roman citizens," the emperor decreed:

> without any distinction as to the age of the slave or the interest of the manumittor, or the mode of manumission. We have also introduced many new methods by which slaves may become Roman citizens, the only kind of liberty that now exists. (Justinian, *Institutes* 5.3)

The rate and extent to which Romans freed their slaves over the course of the third through sixth centuries is unknown, unfortunately, as it is for earlier periods of Roman history. These social demographics were not the sorts of details the state ever kept records or numbers on, at least as far as have been preserved for us. Nevertheless, selected documents can give a human face to Justinian's impersonal laws.

The most famous is the example of the wealthy husband and wife, Valerius Pinianus and Valeria Melania (383–439 CE). Before moving to Jerusalem to build a Christian monastic community, the couple liquidated their household properties in, among other places, Roman Spain and Gaul. Eight thousand slaves were freed during this sale (Palladius, *Historia Lausiaca* [Life of Melania, in Greek] 61.3). With significant landholdings elsewhere, in Roman Italy and North Africa, the couple was not exactly bankrupting themselves by cutting these men and women loose (Palladius, *Historia Lausiaca* 61.5). In fact, in the Roman world, a patron's generosity could and often did establish a long-lasting connection between freedmen, freedwomen, and their former owners. These tight bonds often paid dividends as freedmen and freedwomen began their own careers outside the estate and further elevated the stature of their patrons. In short, even the reasons that may have motivated Christians like Pinianus and Melania to free their slaves need not have been exclusively attributed to their Christian faith.

11.5   Households and the Emergence of the Papacy in Rome

Because the proper management of one's household was central to Roman life, many Christians in the age after Constantine looked to Roman models to help articulate their vision for the Christian church. In Rome itself, this conversation played out in a complicated social setting. Wealthy Christians were continuing to worship in their own homes, as we saw from the archaeological evidence underneath the fifth-century church of Saints John and Paul, while at the same time wealthy bishops were trying to attract all of the city's Christian community to new worship spaces, the city's basilicas.

During the fifth and sixth centuries, in particular, bishops would make a gambit to steer more Christians in their direction. They did so by pitching a message with three carefully crafted components. First, they claimed to be true and legitimate heirs of Saint Peter, whose tomb was believed to be located underneath the basilica at the Vatican. Second, they began to use the title "Summus Pontifex," or Highest Priest, to emphasize their authority in divine matters, particularly when engaging in theological conversations with Christians in the eastern empire. Leo, the bishop of Rome in the middle of the fifth century (b. 400; bishop 440–461 CE), was the first to have the audacity to appropriate this role, which directly challenged the authority of Roman emperors to act in their government capacity as Pontifex Maximus. (It is during Leo's reign that the bishop of Rome will first be called "Papa," or "Pope," a title that was intended to assert his leadership over the wider Mediterranean Christian community.)

The third way the bishops of Rome sought to increase their power over Christian communities, both in the city and beyond it, was by asking congregations to think of them as household managers of God's estate. That is, the bishops of Rome began to refer to themselves as if they were the people to whom God had entrusted the running of the entire Christian family.

Bishop Gregory (540–604; r. 590–604 CE) preached this idea to his congregation in a homily, telling them, "I am the servant [slave] of the supreme *paterfamilias*" (Gregory, *Homily on the Gospels* 36.2). In this metaphor, borrowed from Roman culture, Gregory was but a lowly slave who had been entrusted with the oversight of the estate. And God, he argued, was the highest authority whom Gregory served. This self-presentation would have sounded paradoxical to many Christians. Was Gregory trying to be a slave, or a powerful leader? But through his rhetoric Gregory was effectively molding the Christian community into one which looked to the bishop of Rome as a leading authority. By identifying with the slave's role, spiritually, Gregory could simultaneously claim a greater right to intervene in the temporal, spatial, and political affairs of every Christian household, whether a resident of Rome or someplace else.

This imagery, in which the bishop of Rome became the chief servant who oversaw the management of God's household, became widespread throughout the fifth and sixth centuries CE. It was an important part of how the bishop of Rome emerged as a trans-regional authority figure.

Summary

The story that Augustine tells of leaving home in North Africa with his mother provided a point of departure for us to explore the place and meaning of home in society. In this chapter, we looked at examples of domestic spaces, from the lower- to middle-class apartments of Egypt and Ostia to the upper-class houses of Ephesos and Rome. Although archaeological plans can be helpful for discussing life in a Roman home, we also saw that, when done carefully, excavations show us that rooms in a Roman house were also much more multifunctional than we might assume. The Slope House at Ephesos, with its garden tools upstairs and shipping containers by the front door, brought the messy realities of day-to-day living back to the fore. The concepts of public and private were also especially hard to apply to these spaces.

The physical world of where people lived was important for a second reason. From evidence within the city of Rome, we saw that many wealthy Christians chose to continue to worship at home in the centuries after Constantine legalized Christianity. The archaeological and textual sources which attest to *tituli* churches were significant in this regard because the legal context of this language suggests that property donors may have remained financially or even spiritually invested in the community which they had funded. This world of churches, ostensibly owned by the bishop but in effect managed by others, gave birth to a competitive environment, where many Christian voices fought for the ear of the larger community. By the fifth and sixth centuries, the bishops of Rome were appropriating the power and imagery associated with the Roman house to suggest that they, not anyone else, were the most effective managers of God's family.

Study Questions

1. What is a Roman *paterfamilias*?
2. In what ways were Roman apartments and houses similar to or different from your apartment or your family's house?
3. By the fifth century CE, Christians had a long history of having met and worshipped in homes. Retell that history. How does it change over time? How does it stay the same?
4. Why do you think the bishops of Rome invoked the values of the Roman household to assert their authority over other Christian communities in the fifth century CE?

Suggested Readings

Kim Bowes, *Houses and Society in the Later Roman Empire* (London: Duckworth, 2010).
Kate Cooper, *The Fall of the Roman Household* (New York: Cambridge University Press, 2007).
Kyle Harper, *Slavery in the Late Roman World, AD 275–425* (Cambridge: Cambridge University Press, 2011).
James O'Donnell, *Augustine: A New Biography* (New York: Ecco Press, 2005).
Kristina Sessa, *The Formation of Papal Authority in Late Antique Italy: Roman Bishops and the Domestic Sphere* (New York: Cambridge University Press, 2012).

12

Ideas and Literary Culture

A few famous race drivers, some scandalous burial workers, and the details of the ceramic industry have helped us see how people occupied their time through work and trade between the third and sixth centuries. In this context, we also indirectly glimpsed the ways in which people of all classes passed their leisure hours: cheering for their favorite chariot team or enjoying a dramatic performance. As we begin this chapter, which looks at the wide-ranging literary culture of the Mediterranean, we should start with one community of the Roman world for whom the life of the mind – not necessarily sport or spectacle – was one of their most pressing concerns. These men and women valued deep intellectual inquiry and a rigorous, rational pursuit of the origins of the known world. They were philosophers, but they weren't opposed to attracting an audience and growing their own brand, either.

Starting in the age of Archaic Greece, thinkers in Asia Minor began pursuing a "love of wisdom" (*philos* [love] + *sophia* [wisdom]), which they used to build their own intellectual reputations and recruit like-minded followers. Competition was important, as different thinkers began suggesting competing ideas for what might explain the workings of the physical universe. By Classical Greece, two of these intellectual communities had become famous in Athens. They were organized around the teachings of Aristotle and Plato. Plato's Academy, as his school was called, would remain a vital center for those wishing to pursue the life of the mind up until the early sixth centuries CE.

Then, both schools faced an existential threat. We know what happened because of the report of a Greek lawyer named John (*c.* 480–*c.* 570 CE; his nickname, "Malalas," is the Syriac word for "lawyer"). John the lawyer wrote an eighteen-volume history of the world from the birth of Jesus to the age of Justinian, called the *Chronicle* [*Chronographia*]. In it, under an entry for the year 529 CE, he records that the Roman

A Social and Cultural History of Late Antiquity, First Edition. Douglas Boin.
© 2018 John Wiley & Sons, Inc. Published 2018 by John Wiley & Sons, Inc.

Emperor Justinian ordered the philosophy schools of Athens to be shuttered (*Chronicle* 18.47). One of the classical world's most fiercely intellectual communities, groups which had thrived for the last two hundred years under Christian rulers of the fourth and fifth centuries CE, was now forced to disband.

12.1   The "One" and the Many: Philosophical and Anthropological Perspectives

Those who cultivated a passion for wisdom had never been compelled to study in Athens. Alexandria was famous for thinkers like Hypatia, who lived in the late fourth and early fifth centuries CE. Almost a hundred years before her time, however, the halls and classrooms of Alexandria had educated one of the most influential thought-leaders of the Late Antique world, Plotinus (205–270 CE). Born in Egypt, a student in Alexandria, Plotinus later moved to Rome, where he published his ideas and built his own philosophical community. Almost single-handedly Plotinus reinvigorated the study of Plato. In doing so, he laid the groundwork for an explosion of interest in Plato's teachings and Plotinus' elaborations of them during the fourth, fifth, and sixth centuries and beyond. We call this movement Neoplatonism.

Much of what we know about Plotinus comes from one of his students, Porphyry of Tyre, who edited Plotinus' writings, the *Enneads*, and released a biography, the *Life of Plotinus*. Plotinus' own intellectual pursuits were motivated by the desire to explain the underlying metaphysical unity of the dizzyingly diverse natural world in which he lived. He did so by taking Plato's idea of non-material forms and positing that everything we see around us is an illustration of one unitary principle. Plotinus called this principle the "One":

> [I]f people are going to say that nothing prevents one and the same thing from being many, there will be a one underlying these many; for there can be no many if there is not a one from which or in which these are, or in general a one, and a one which is counted first before the others, which must be taken alone, itself by itself. (Plotinus, *Enneads* 5.6.3, LCL trans. by A. Armstrong [1984])

Plotinus' challenging ideas would provoke many conversations and literary works in the decades and centuries after his death. Next-generation thinkers like Proclus (*c.*410–485 CE) would pick up the baton and explore the ramifications of Plotinus' teachings. Others, like Augustine, writing in his early fifth-century CE work *City of God*, would claim that "Plotinus, whose memory is quite recent, enjoys the reputation of having understood Plato better than any other of his disciples" (*City of God* 9.10, trans. by M. Dods in the series *NPNF* [1887]).

Loyal followers aside, we should remember that not everyone in the Mediterranean would have necessarily subscribed to Plotinus' ideas. Historians themselves need to be wary of letting their own intellectual preferences guide their interpretation of what evidence has been left behind. One case study from Late Antique material culture, from a burial context, will demonstrate why.

Scenes of the hero Hercules' returning from the underworld are well known from the Roman catacombs. Sometimes, these illustrated tales often appear next to specifically Christian scenes. Does that mean that the deceased – or perhaps the people who visited the grave – were questing after the one, unified spiritual reality which lay behind their complicated lives? (In this interpretation, Hercules' return from the dead is seen as a Neoplatonic allegory for the hope of Jesus' resurrection.) This rather specialized way of understanding Late Antique material culture became popular in the twentieth century because it gave scholars a way to explain the rise of Christianity in peaceful, non-violent, terms. As more Romans came to embrace a Neoplatonic worldview, people began embracing the more culturally appealing elements of Christianity by adding them to their own belief systems. Later, when they reached a higher level of philosophical sophistication – recognizing the true "one" behind Rome's many gods and heroes – they converted to Christianity. Or so the story goes. These feel-good theories grew out of a scholarly fascination with the concept of "syncretism," a word that describes the blending of different beliefs (*Exploring Culture* 12.1: The Mash-Up Poem).

Exploring Culture 12.1   *The Mash-Up Poem*

Standout female writers did not emerge from the Greek and Latin literary scene. Sappho, who sang poignantly about the power of female love in the sixth century BCE, takes the lone prize of a woman who set down her vision in verse – and became famous in antiquity for it. Yet only two complete poems of hers survive.

In order to find another strong, female literary voice, we have to look ahead to the mid- to late fourth century CE when a poet known as "Proba" rocked audiences with an experiment that would win her literary acclaim throughout the Middle Ages. Following in the footsteps of a loose artistic movement that created new works by recycling old verses, line for line, from classic Latin and Greek poets, Proba set to work on composing a life of Jesus. Her artistic creation is one of the best examples of an ancient mash-up text known as a "cento," or "patchwork." It is also the only full-length poem authored by a Christian woman to outlive antiquity.

For her source material, Proba had used the iconic Latin text of the epic poet Virgil (d. 19 BCE). Other examples of the literary mash-up, drawing upon Virgil, survive; Tertullian remarks that such chimerical works were common in his day, the turn of the third century CE (*On the Prescription against Heretics* 34.3–4). Poets working in Greek would use Homer as their starting point. In neither language, however, could the "patchwork" poem ever be called a specifically Christian practice. In fact, far from being the thoughtless exercise which some later commentators made it out to be – the Christian writer Jerome loathed the tediousness of the form, calling it "puerile" (*Letter* 53.7) – it demanded high linguistic creativity.

Proba's talent cannot be dismissed. Latin, like Greek, is a language in which nouns and adjectives have specific genders (male or female) and number (singular or plural), and writers and speakers use word endings to specify the function of a noun within a sentence;

there are distinct ways of identifying a subject and entirely different ways of identifying an object. Poets like Virgil, who wrote his *Aeneid* over the course of a decade, worked obsessively to make sure their sentences not only fit the meter of their poem but that the end product surprised their listeners.

By extracting these lines from their original context, Proba was skirting disaster. Subjects of classical sentences might need to be changed to fit the Christian plot, and each of Virgil's carefully tooled lines might break if forced, against its will, into another rhythmic scheme. The fact she succeeded in combining them into something provocative and new speaks to her artistic prowess.

Her poetry made a forceful political statement. Consider the cento's final lines, addressed to her husband: "... And if we are deserving because of our *pietas*,/then let our virtuous descendants continue worshipping in this way" (Proba, lines 693–694, borrowing *Aeneid* 2.690 and 3.409). *Pietas* is the central value of Virgil's epic. It conveyed a Roman's sense of duty towards his or her family, to the gods, and to the state. By appropriating these ideas for her life of Jesus, Proba showed her readers that being a Christian in fourth-century Rome was entirely consistent with centuries of traditional Roman values.

Today, some scholars are intensely skeptical of "syncretism" as an idea, and historians of Late Antiquity need to be aware of their vocal displeasure with it. As Rosalind Shaw and Charles Stewart have reminded researchers in a volume of essays on the topic, *Syncretism/Anti-Syncretism: The Politics of Religious Synthesis* (London: Routledge, 2014), not everyone at all times wants to blend their beliefs with others or find ways of mixing them into a shared, or common, value system. Oftentimes, individuals can be adamantly defensive about the details of their own beliefs, even a non-Christian one. For people who fit this profile in the fourth-, fifth- or sixth-century Mediterranean, Plotinus' ideas would not have been appealing at all. They probably would have been insulting.

12.2 Literature and Ideas after the "Vanishing" of Rome

For the Roman Empire of the sixth century CE, the geography of power was far reduced from memories of Trajan or Augustus. The people of the city of Rome, which had formerly controlled the entire Mediterranean basin – and then, by the Rule of Four, only one half of it –now lived as exiles from their own empire. The "Roman world," as its citizens knew it, had been reduced to the territory of modern Greece, the Balkans, Asia Minor, the Levant, and Egypt. For the residents of this radically reduced Roman world, political life was now centered in Constantinople.

There were significant continuities, though. During the fifth and early sixth centuries CE, Latin would remain the language of government, just as it had been when the empire was based in Italy. Greek, a language traditionally spoken and used in the eastern Mediterranean, would come to be the official language only in the mid-sixth century CE. The Roman government in Constantinople during this time also remained structured around an authority figure who ruled with prestige and consent. Called in Greek a *basileios*, the Latin equivalent of "emperor," his position can also be translated as "king." The Senate and people of Constantinople ruled with him, in effect preserving the kind of Republican-model of government which Emperor Augustus had tried to institute in the aftermath of the divisiveness of Julius Caesar's day.

For many reasons, however, some scholars prefer to use a new label, "Byzantine," to distinguish this new political and cultural world in Constantinople from its predecessor. It is a word choice that must be justified, not assumed. The people of this metamorphosing Roman world, with their only capital Constantinople, conceived of themselves as "Romans," regardless of the fact that many of them increasingly spoke and wrote only in ancient Greek. They also referred to their state as *Romania*, "the territory of Rome," a label that played off many people's understanding of their capital city, Constantinople, as a "New Rome."

The reasons why many Christians had begun to conceive of this city as a replacement for Rome is a fascinating topic and one which we will treat in a moment. For now, it is important to note that this teleological belief – that the world of "Old Rome" would eventually come to end and a rising "New Rome" would replace it – has biblical roots. In the Book of Revelation, written at the time when Christians were a paltry minority, "Rome" is presented as a den of iniquity, the "whore of Babylon," whose empire must be toppled before God returns to reign on earth. To Jesus' followers of the late first century CE, that worldview may have offered a degree of comfort during a period when their own fate as citizens of the Roman Empire was precariously insecure.

Three centuries later, after Theodosius I had established Nicene Christianity as the official worship of the Roman Empire, that scriptural story about the "whore of Babylon" must have had a much different resonance. Christians were now politically in charge of this new "Rome," a government entity which many within their community had been fulminating against since the first century. The invention of Constantinople as a "New," which is to say now *Christian* "Rome," may have helped ease many Christian anxieties about working with, and collaborating with, a state that had long been defamed as one of the beasts of Revelation.

It may also explain why some modern scholars, using a delicate sleight of hand, subtly change all references to "New Rome" and the "Eastern Roman Empire" to "Byzantium" and the "Byzantine Empire" at precisely this point in their stories. This casual switch wipes out all traces of the end-time thinking, faith-driven cultural anxiety, and apocalyptic preoccupations which were a significant aspect of Christian thought during the fourth through sixth centuries CE (*Key Debates* 12.1: Why Should Historians Read Tales of "Angels" and "Demons"?). Interestingly, however, these symptoms of an apocalyptic worldview would not be limited to the Christian communities of the Roman Empire. Other manifestations of them would soon be revealed elsewhere.

Key Debates 12.1   *Why Should Historians Read Tales of Angels and Demons?*

Evagrius, who grew up in the Roman territory of Pontus, needed a change of scenery. Born around 345 CE, having worked in Constantinople as an assistant to the bishop, he later moved to Jerusalem. There, he fell frustratingly in love with a married woman and suffered a devastating breakdown. When a Christian ascetic recommended he should self-care by retreating to the desert, Evagrius left right away to confront his demons, literally.

In Egypt, Evagrius compiled a study guide for monks who were tormented with demons. In eight books, originally written in ancient Greek, he reflected on 498 Bible passages that could provide spiritual solace to tortured souls. Each was prefaced by a situation that might have been causing a monk some consternation. "Against the thoughts that taunt us because our parents have forsaken us and will not send us gold to meet our needs," one begins, Evagrius recommends reading the Psalms: "'For my father and mother have forsaken me, but the Lord has received me'" (Evagrius, *Talking Back* 3.3, trans. by D. Brakke [Collegeville: Liturgical Press, 2000]). The way Evagrius documents his demonic thoughts and imaginatively matches them with Bible passages illustrates how seriously he and Christians like him tried to ward off the chief demon – "Satan," in Evagrius' worldview – from their everyday life (Evagrius 3.19).

These are certainly not the kinds of protagonists one expects to see in a history book. "Angels" and "demons" are the sort of cast members you usually find in heady, spiritual dramas. They are also such a natural part of the story of religion, we might even be led to assume that all people, at all times throughout history, must have believed in these kinds of mystical beings – or at least some version of them. This is far from true, and it's essential for social and cultural historians to recognize why.

The belief that "angels" and "demons" are waging a cosmic war on behalf of humanity is not found in the Psalms which Evagrius quotes, nor is it found in any of the Hebrew Scriptures written before the Hellenistic age. The origins of this potent pair of spiritual beings come later.

Many people will probably know the basic outline of Satan's fall from heaven and how the good archangel Michael battled to defeat him. Tales of Satan and the archangel shaped later Jewish and Christian belief; they clearly influenced Evagrius. Yet the idea of angelic warriors battling Satan, who is equated with the Devil, does not exist in any piece of ancient literature before the third century BCE. The anonymous Jewish text known as *1 Enoch*, written in the third century BCE and edited over time, is the source for this well-known drama. *1 Enoch* tells of angels who rebelled against God and were punished as a result. The writer presents this battle as a warning to his readers that the suffering of their present, evil times will be overcome and that hope will prevail.

As one of the first expressions of a dualistic worldview found in all of Jewish literature, *1 Enoch* holds a privileged place in collections of apocalyptic writing. Even though it was excluded from Jewish and Christians Bibles, the author's vision of angels fighting demons would also have far-reaching impact, teaching many Jews and Christians to see the world around them in warlike, dualistic terms.

12.3   The Literary Culture of Justinian's Roman Empire

Justinian's Latin Laws

Emperor Justinian would leave his mark on the capital in many ideological ways. Under his reign, he used legal mechanisms to prop up Nicene Christianity. In a law of 544 CE, which forms part of the "new laws," or *novels*, of the collection called the *Justinianic Code*, the emperor set forth the requirements for worship throughout the territory he controlled.

"We believe the first and greatest good for all men to be the right confession of the true and pure Christian faith," Justinian explained, "so that it may be strengthened thereby in every respect and all holy priests may be joined in concord and with one accord profess and preach the right Christian faith." The law continues on this theme, emphasizing Justinian's strict sense of Christian identity and the need to quash all theological opposition: "Every pretext invented by heretics may be destroyed, as is shown by the books and the different edicts written by us." It also attributes the belief of "heretics" to "the work of the Devil" and castigates these suspicious folks for holding assemblies "not in accord with the holy catholic and apostolic church of God" (*The New Laws* [*Novels*] *of Justinian*, no. 132, trans. by F. Blume and T. Kearley). This law was read to the people of Constantinople on April 4, 544 CE.

Justinian's Constantinople, like the shrunken Roman Empire over which he ruled, was not a society that tolerated creative thinking about God. As this law makes clear, the emperor was determined to root out problematic beliefs and practices; the decree itself makes a mysterious reference to the threat of "secret baptism." But policing the public meant having eyes and ears into people's own houses.

"We want everyone to know," the emperor continued, "that if hereafter there are found those who hold unlawful assemblies or come together therein, we shall not suffer that to be done in any manner. But the houses where anything of the kind takes place, shall be given to the holy church, and the penalties specified by law shall in every respect be inflicted upon those who hold unlawful assemblies or who come together therein." Such behavior was deemed to be "heretical insanity" which could "destroy the souls of others," translated by Blume and Kearley, whose work, *The Annotated Justinian Code*, is housed on-line at the University of Wyoming Law Library, 2016.)

Justinian's Greek-speaking Christian state

Justinian's ideological commitment to promote a Christian state can be put in a larger context if we look at the story of the empire's Jewish communities – and the Jewish communities on the empire's borders – during the same time. Inside Justinian's empire, synagogue construction boomed, particularly in cities near the Sea of Galilee, a fact that attests to the vibrancy of Jewish communities in a state that was particularly concerned to legislate a Christian worldview. Many of these synagogues also preserve mosaic artwork and inscriptions written in the dominant language spoken by residents of the East Roman Empire: ancient Greek (*Political Issues* 12.1: The Value of Learning a Second Language in Changing Times).

As it was for many minority groups throughout the empire, language was an important expression of cultural identity. For the Jewish community, the debate over whether to use the dominant language of their cities, Greek in the east or Latin in the west, was one that went back centuries and had little consistency. (Recall that the Jewish author of 2 Maccabees had vilified his fellow Jews for adopting Greek customs by writing a manifesto against them – in Greek.) Under Justinian's reign, these kinds of internal debates continued to drive the community apart. Many bubbled to the surface of political life in Constantinople, demanding the emperor's attention.

Political Issues 12.1   *The Value of Learning a Second Language in Changing Times*

Emperor Majorian (r. 457–461 CE) was eager to reclaim territory in Roman Spain and Gaul that previous administrations had ceded to Goths and Germans. Ultimately, Majorian failed. But for his brave attempt, Sidonius Apollinaris would forever thank him.

A Roman, born c.430 CE at Lyon in southern Gaul, Sidonius Apollinaris had watched the world around the Rhône River valley change quite dramatically in the middle of the fifth century CE. Like Rutilius Namatianus before him, Sidonius had sought a career in Rome. After Emperor Majorian was murdered, in 461, Sidonius returned to his estate in Gaul. By 476 CE, the cities along the upper Rhône River had come under the control of Germanic kings, Burgundians.

Sidonius was at his writing desk during this time, composing Latin letters to family and friends, even if no one ever wrote back right away (or at all). "It was right that my loquacity should be checked by the revenge of silence on your part," he bashfully begins one note to a relative (Sidonius Apollinaris, *Letters* 5.3, LCL trans. by W. Anderson [1965]). "The fact that I received no reply to the letter I sent you seems to be a discredit to your friendship," he starts in another (*Letters* 5.4). Amusing as the apparent snubs and rejections may be, Sidonius' writings, collected in nine books c.477 CE, provide some of the most intimate, important glimpses of life in late fifth-century Gaul – as the Roman Empire vanished and as new opportunities appeared.

Sidonius' letter to his friend Syagrius is one such document. In it, Sidonius marvels how nimbly Syagrius has adapted to the times. "I am ... inexpressibly amazed that you have quickly acquired a knowledge of the German tongue with such ease," he tells Syagrius. "I should like you to tell me how you have managed to absorb so swiftly into your inner being the exact sounds of an alien race" (*Letters* 5.5). The results of this new skill set were manifest immediately. "You are loved, your company is sought, you are much visited, you delight, you are picked out, you are invited, you decide issues and are listened to," Sidonius writes. So impressed was he by Syagrius' meteoric rise in the new court, he compared it to watching "a young falcon [bursting forth] from an old nest (*ex harilao*)" (*Letters* 5.5). With his vocabulary even Sidonius may have been trying to adapt.

Language scholars have long been puzzled by that last word. Translated into English as the word "nest," it is wholly unknown in any Latin writings before Sidonius' time. One social and linguistic hypothesis about its origins is that it may have been a bit of the language spoken by the Burgundians which Sidonius has recently picked up.

The fact that Syagrius was acquiring the language of the new government is revealing for a second reason, however. Not all the new kingdoms of the rapidly changing western Europe were rushing to eliminate Latin from their daily culture. Sixth-century Italy, the kingdom founded by Theoderic, prided itself on its Latin heritage and its Roman traditions. Theoderic's spokesman, the *quaestor sacri palatini* – the same office that had existed in Rome prior to the take-over – was a Latin-speaking official, Cassiodorus. In addition to communicating the king's message, Cassiodorus wrote a history of the Goths in Latin, now lost. His knowledge of this "classical" language ensured that he became a valuable member of the new Ostrogothic government.

In 552 or 553 CE, the emperor was forced to respond to one petition, in particular. A question had arisen amongst the empire's Jewish communities about whether Greek or Hebrew should be used in synagogue service for reading Jewish Scripture. Justinian answered with a law published February 8, 553. In it, he was forced to recognize and to take sides in a thorny internal conversation.

"From the reports made to us," Justinian announced, "we have learned that some, knowing only the Hebrew language, want to use it in reading the Holy Scriptures. Others think that the Greek language also ought to be used, and they have for a long time disputed among each other." The emperor then gave his opinion on the matter. "We, informed of this matter, think that those who also want to employ the Greek language in reading the Holy Scriptures are better" (*The New Laws* [*Novels*] *of Justinian*, no. 146, trans. adapted slightly from D. Miller and T. Kearley). Some will see this law as Christian meddling in a dispute that affected only a small fraction of the empire's non-Christian population, but Justinian's belief – expressed in the law's preface – helps explain why the emperor felt motivated to act on the issue of what language should be used.

"The Hebrews, hearing the sacred scriptures, should not indeed have adhered to the bare letter [of these texts] but should have considered the prophesies contained therein, by which these announce the great God and Jesus Christ the Savior of the human race," the Christian emperor reasoned. Language, in short, was part of the reason the Jewish people had "given themselves over to foolish interpretations" and "wandered away from the correct meaning" of their own sacred texts, or so Justinian was trying to argue (*The New Laws* [*Novels*] *of Justinian*, no. 146, trans. by D. Miller and T. Kearley). The emperor's words barely conceal a scathing indictment of the Jewish people's inability to recognize that Jesus had been the Messiah.

12.4   Literature as a Source for the Study of Medicine and Disease

As we have seen so far, literature and the world of ideas have been important for many reasons. Poetry and prose give us access to people's cultural values. Legal writing allows us to analyze the political priorities of emperors and their advisors. Literature also plays a key role in helping historians reconstruct significant moments of crisis. The plague that devastated much of the Mediterranean world in the middle of the sixth century CE is one of those events. Not described by any ancient medical writer (and thus, not known by any precise diagnosis), the plague is best known from writers who worked in a literary, not scientific, milieu. This fact doesn't necessarily disqualify what they report about the plague, but it does limit the kinds of questions we can ask of them.

Procopius of Caesarea is one of the most important sources for the study of this sixth-century plague. During the events of the year 542 CE, he reports:

> During these times there was a pestilence, by which the whole human race came near to being annihilated. Now in the case of all other scourges sent from Heaven some explanation of a cause might be given by daring men, such as the many theories propounded by those who are clever in these matters; for they love to conjure up causes which are absolutely incomprehensible to man, and to fabricate outlandish theories of natural philosophy, knowing well that they are saying nothing sound, but considering it sufficient for them, if they completely deceive by their argument some of those whom they meet and persuade them to their view. But for this calamity it is quite impossible either to express in words or to conceive in thought any explanation, except indeed to refer it to God. (Procopius, *History of the War* 2.22.1–3, LCL trans. by H. Dewing [1914])

Procopius' testimony about the physical effects of the plague, which is among the most extensive of our ancient sources, will be summarized in a moment. As these prefatory remarks of the author show, however, trying to use a writer with literary predilections to reconstruct the history, spread, or pathology of an ancient pandemic is a journey that can face serious headwinds. Many of Procopius' contemporaries freely speculated about the plague's origins, and some of their explanations struck him as "absolutely incomprehensible," filled with "outlandish theories of natural philosophy." Procopius himself, a Christian writing in a Christian state, attributed the cause of events to God.

Historians, especially those who specialize in ancient medicine, do not need to accept all of Procopius' claims or the claims of other literary documents to be able to reconstruct details of the pandemic. This way of approaching the sources – critically and with an eye to their literary audiences – is a slightly more nuanced method than trying to use these texts to make an accurate medical diagnosis fourteen centuries after the fact.

What we know based on the number of sources who make mention of the disease is that it arrived in the empire around 541 CE. Its scale was enormous. By the end of that decade, it was showing up in places as geographically removed as modern Azerbaijan, where it appears in 542 CE, and the island of Ireland, where it appears in 544 CE. Within two decades, it had also come to Constantinople. By the end of the sixth century CE, it was located in the Black Sea. (For the details behind this time-line, see Peregrine Horden's essay, "Mediterranean Plague in the Age of Justinian," which she contributed to *The Age of Justinian*, a collection of essays edited by Michael Maas [New York: Cambridge University Press, 2005], pp. 134–160.)

What was the plague's genetic make-up? DNA research into the matter is just beginning. But from the reports of ancient writers, it is difficult to say since none of our sources – including the Greek writer Procopius – was trained in medicine, nor did they specialize in writing medical treatises. Having said that, Procopius provides details about the plague's symptoms and the extent of its devastation. It included a fever, which led to swelling of areas such as the stomach, armpit, next to the ears, and in the thighs. Some people went into a coma during this time or suffered delirium (Procopius, *History of the Wars* 2.22.6–39). When the epidemic reached Constantinople, bodies were being disposed of at the rate of five thousand a day. Later, the statistic rose to ten thousand a day (Procopius, *History of the Wars* 2.23.1–2).

This plague was more than a public health crisis. As Peregrine Horden has pointed out in her study of the material relating to this pandemic, "Any disease is at once a biological, a psychological, and a social phenomenon; and the biological must not be privileged in defining it" (2005, p. 143) – however much our scientifically trained minds want to recreate the circumstances of the pandemic and reconstruct the nature of the disease. That said, genetic studies of sixth-century bodies may soon suggest that this plague was *Yersinia pestis*, the "bubonic plague" that struck Europe during the early modern period, the fourteenth through seventeenth centuries.

Whether such a clinical certainty will be established remains to be seen. For now, it might be better to conclude that our written evidence works best when it helps us explore the "psychological" and "social" aspects of this devastating pandemic.

12.5 The Rise of a Book Culture

Over the last few chapters, we have seen how things like ceramics, values, and now diseases could be shared over wide regions. Ideas and texts were spread this way, too. And by the fourth century CE, they were being traded in a form that looked much different than in earlier periods of Mediterranean history. They were being exchanged as bound books.

Books, a natural part of our cultural landscape, were uncommon in Julius Caesar's Rome. For centuries, people had traditionally read on scrolls, pieces of a reedy plant that had been pounded together to form long sheets. These were stored in a rolled-up manner. Books, on the other hand – manufactured from either leaves of papyrus or pages of dried animal skin, called parchment – were rare.

There is little evidence for their widespread use in the first through second centuries apart from the first-century CE poet Martial (a non-Christian). Martial wrote a series of poems, titled *Epigrams*, which he made available in book form (Martial, *Epigrams* 1.2.1–4). These books were later called in Latin *codices* (the singular form is *codex*). By the fourth century CE, books were one of the hottest advances in Rome's technological landscape.

Many codices have survived from this time. A fourth-century copy of Virgil's poem the *Aeneid*, showing scenes of the hero Aeneas sailing away from Queen Dido, is preserved in the Vatican Library. In Vienna, there is a sixth-century copy of a medicinal and pharmacological text. Called *De materia medica*, "On Matters Related to Healing," the text was composed in the middle of the first century CE by a Greek scientist named Dioscurides. The book that exists in Vienna was copied in the early sixth century CE (Figure 12.1). It includes nearly five hundred pictures of plants, animals, and insects that illustrate the detailed points of Dioscurides' text. In its opening pages, it also depicts several men important to the history of medicine, such as the second-century doctor and philosopher, Galen.

Books and patrons

The Vienna Dioscurides manuscript was dedicated to a wealthy Roman of Constantinople, Anicia Juliana (*c*.461–527 CE), an important patron of book culture and of the Christian community in sixth-century Constantinople. Anicia Juliana appears in the opening pages. She is shown seated on a throne surrounded by personifications of Magnanimity (*megalopseuchia*, or "greatness of spirit," in Greek) and Prudence (*phronesis*, "good sense"). These representation allude to Juliana's status as a much loved contributor to life in the capital. Her most visible benefaction had come, in the years prior to 525 CE, when she had paid to construct a church, Saint Polyeuktos, in one of Constantinople's aristocratic neighborhoods, out near the city walls.

Thanks to a few fragments of Greek inscriptions, combined with the preservation of a literary text in the *Greek Anthology*, we can say quite a bit more about Empress Anicia Juliana and the book culture of her day. The text which was erected to celebrate the construction of the church was itself composed as a poem. From it, we learn:

> Juliana, the glory of her blessed parents, inheriting
> their royal blood in the fourth generation, did not cheat the
> hopes of that queen who gave birth to noble children, but raised
> this from a small church to its present size and beauty, increasing
> the glory of her many-sceptered ancestors. For all that she
> completed she made more excellent than her parents, keeping
> the true faith of a mind devoted to Christ [the Messiah].
> Who has not heard of Juliana, that in her care for piety
> she glorified even her parents by finely labored works?
> (*Greek Anthology* 1.10, lines 7–15, LCL trans. by W. Paton,
> rev. by M. Tueller [2014])

It becomes clear why the anonymous artist of the Vienna Dioscurides manuscript pages dedicated his book to this wealthy woman of Constantinople. At the time

Figure 12.1 For avid readers, codices, or books, were much more than carefully sewn-together pages of text. They were treasure chests, potentially filled with all sorts of captivating illustrations drawn from the subject matter – the poetry of Virgil, for example, or a famous scene from scripture. Sometimes, they could even include a portrait of the person who had commissioned such a laborious commodity. This portrait of Anicia Juliana appears in the opening pages of an early sixth-century CE codex. The codex itself is a medical text, authored by first-century CE writer Dioscurides. Anicia Juliana's portrait was included here likely because she had paid to have the codex copied. The privileged daughter of a Roman emperor (462–527/528 CE), she was one of the most high-profile patrons of the residents of Constantinople. Juliana is shown seated between the personifications of Generosity and Wisdom. From the so-called "Vienna Dioscurides," Nationalbibliothek, cod. med. gr.1., fol. 6v. Bildarchiv der Österreichische Nationalbibliothek, Vienna.

Anicia Juliana's church of Saint Polyeuktos was built, it was the most glorious in the capital. Twelve years after its dedication, Emperor Justinian, perhaps feeling a sting of inadequacy, would start work on a building to surpass Anicia's ambitions. Justinian's church of Hagia Sophia, dedicated in 537 CE, would be the result.

Books and beliefs

We should be wary of making theological inferences from the beats and silences in this story, however. The fact that there is no literary and archaeological evidence for the widespread circulation of books during the "pagan" Roman Empire, followed by a rise in book popularity during the rise of the Christian state, does not mean that Christians popularized the book as a writing form. Nor does it mean that Christians of Late Antiquity only used books while non-Christians, like Jews, used earlier, old-fashioned technology, like scrolls.

When seen in its entirety, the evidence suggests that, throughout the fourth through sixth centuries CE, all kinds of faith communities used and passed down texts as codices. In the middle of the fourth century, around 354 CE, a wealthy senator in Rome commissioned a calendar of city festivals. Known as the "codex-calendar" because it was bound in book form, this artifact is one of the most crucial pieces of evidence for the longevity and preservation of traditional Roman worship practices in the Roman Empire. It was hardly what Christians today would classify as a "Christian" object. Along similar lines, the codex known as the Ashburnham Pentateuch, today found in the collection in the Bibliothèque Nationale, Paris, is an important book example of the Pentateuch, that is, the first five writings in the Hebrew Bible. Thought to have been produced in Italy around 500 CE, its surviving pages suggest that Jewish communities, too, recognized the value of the codex.

The "codex-calendar" from Rome and the Ashburnham Pentateuch are two manifest examples which suggest that the rise of this new "book" technology had less to do with people's faith identities than is sometimes assumed. Even examples from material culture, such as scenes on Christian sarcophagi, show that Christians themselves depicted each other reading and using scrolls, *in addition to books*, throughout the fourth and fifth centuries CE. Explanations for cultural change which depend primarily on the "religious identity" of book users, such as the assumption that a Christian preference for the book was somehow a feature unique to the Christian faith, fail to take into account this wider evidence. These theories should be treated suspiciously.

12.6   Latin Poetry and Christian Communities in Rome, c. 366–600 CE

Throughout the Mediterranean, other poems, written in languages like Latin, would be erected for famous Christian men and women. A poem honoring Augustine's mother would be set up at Ostia in the late sixth or early seventh century CE (*Working With Sources* 12.1: A Tombstone for Monica, Mother of Augustine). It was part of a long tradition of funerary poetry, erected in Latin in and around Rome, which went back to one of the most influential bishops of Rome, Damasus.

During his tenure as bishop of the city, Damasus (c. 304–384 CE; bishop of Rome, 366–384 CE) composed many verse epitaphs, or grave markers, for the city's saints. He then commissioned a renowned fourth-century calligrapher, Furius Dionysius Filocalus, to inscribe these poems on marble. All of these texts were erected at the

Working With Sources 12.1

A Tombstone for Monica, Mother of Augustine

In 387 CE, Augustine, fresh off visits to Milan and Rome, was waiting at the harbor with his Christian friends for a boat back home. "We sought for some place where we might be most useful in our service to you, God, and were going back together to Africa," he recounts in his autobiography. "And when we were at Ostia on the Tiber, my mother died" (Augustine, *Confessions* 9.8.17, trans. in the *NPNF* series [1870]).

Monica and Augustine, mother and son, had bonded in the days before her unexpected death. Augustine would later remember how "she and I stood alone, leaning in a certain window, from which the garden of the house we occupied at Ostia could be seen; at which place, removed from the crowd, we were resting ourselves for the voyage, after the fatigues of a long journey. We then were conversing alone very pleasantly," he remarks (*Confessions* 9.10.23). The scene has etched itself in many readers' mind. Even scholars, when they write today about Ostia in the late fourth century, can't avoid the trap of wanting to experience the city just as Augustine and Monica did – even though they were transients, even though they were just passersby.

Archaeology has contributed to these imaginative exercises. In 1945, kids were digging a hole near the basilica of Saint Aurea – the modest cathedral of modern Ostia – when they found the fragment of a tombstone. It had Augustine's name on it. Damaged on the right side and missing half its text, these six lines of Latin became like the tantalizing clue in a hunt for ancient treasure. Scholars soon filled in the missing parts of the text with a poem known from a seventh-century manuscript; someone around that time had seen the inscription and copied it down. What they soon recognized was the epitaph, or memorial, erected for Monica. The complete poem reads:

> Here the most virtuous mother of a young man set her ashes, a second light to your merits, Augustine. As a priest, serving the heavenly laws of peace, you taught [*or*, you teach] the people entrusted to you with your character. A glory greater than the praise of your accomplishments crowns you both – Mother of the Virtues, more fortunate because of her offspring. (Douglas Boin, *Ostia in Late Antiquity* [New York: Cambridge University Press, 2013])

The discovery of Monica's tombstone set off an explosion of interest in Augustine's Ostia, as scholars vied with each other to deduce who had paid for the monument and when. The answer, it was thought, would bring us closer to that scene in the window and maybe even give us the name of the owner of the house who had hosted mother and son.

Potential candidates were soon lined up for vetting, with many scholars focusing on the pool of Ostia's wealthier residents, men and women who were alive in the decades immediately after Monica's death. In doing so, scholars may have made a fatal error: by overlooking the stone.

A new analysis of the inscription takes this story in a wholly different direction. "Mother of the Virtues" was a popular personification for the Christian virtue "Love" during the late sixth century and early seventh century CE. A funerary inscription written in a script similar to the one used on Monica's has also been found at Ostia in a sixth- or seventh-century CE context. The memorial for Augustine's mom has now been dated to this time. The window has closed on finding "Augustine's Ostia."

cemeteries, catacombs, and churches where the saints were thought to be buried. Many of these survive, in whole or in fragments. The entire collection numbers nearly forty poems.

The poem which Bishop Damasus carved for Saint Agnes was erected at the church of the same name on Rome's Via Nomentana. It was placed in front of Agnes' alleged burial *loculus* in the catacombs underneath the basilica. This composition helped the bishop of Rome craft his own message about women in the early church and their rejection of Roman ideals and values in the age before Constantine: "Freely she trod under foot the threats and madness of the savage tyrant [the Roman emperor]/when he wished to burn her noble body with flames," Damasus explained in his eulogy for Agnes (*CIL* 8.20753, lines 4–5, trans. by Dennis Trout in *Being Christian in Late Antiquity*, ed. by C. H. Harrison, C. Humfress, and I. Sandwell [New York: Oxford University Press, 2014], p. 224). Visitors to Agnes' grave in the late fourth century CE would have come away with a mini-history lesson, written by Bishop Damasus, about the events that had led to the rise of Christianity, as he understood them. Given the fact that Damasus had come to the role of bishop of Rome through a contested election – in fact, there were two bishops in the city until 378 CE – it is likely that this literary campaign also helped him win support from his political backers in Rome's Christian community. (The story of this intra-Christian conflict is recounted in a Latin text by the fourth-century Roman historian Ammianus Marcellinus [*Roman History* 27.12–15].)

Damasus' decision to produce Christian literature also had a second aim. It promoted Rome's pious tourism industry, attracting devoted visitors to popular Christian burials throughout the city and suburbs. Two centuries later, a poem honoring Augustine's mother would be set up at Ostia, whose death her son had memorialized in his *Confessions*, to capitalize on the same phenomenon.

12.7   Looking Ahead: "People of the Book"

"People of the Book" is a label many people today invoke when talking about Jews, Christians, and Muslims because all three faith groups revere a set of sacred texts. By emphasizing a common denominator – books – a cultural object that unites three world religions, we draw attention to their shared cultural heritage and, by extension, to some of the shared values of their believers. By emphasizing these connections and shifting the focus of religious history away from conflict-driven narratives, many commentators are trying to knock down walls that might divide people of different faiths. It's an admirable, ecumenical mission.

For all its modern power, however, "People of the Book" is actually an ancient phrase and one with a much more curious resonance. Drawn from a chapter, or *sura*, in the Qur'ān (Q 4: 171), the phrase was written in Arabic and displayed on the inside of the drum of a beautifully tiled building in Jerusalem known as the Dome of the Rock. This building – a Muslim shrine, not a mosque – sits atop the Herodian platform of the Second Jewish Temple. An octagonal building constructed at its base of gleaming white marble, it was erected in the late seventh century, on a site which had been left barren by non-Christian and Christian Roman emperors alike, ever since the Jewish Temple had been destroyed in 70 CE (Figure 12.2). Begun in 688, finished in 691 CE by the Umayyad ruler 'Abd al-Malik, the Dome of the Rock glittered like a diamond, set into the void which loomed over the city.

The mosaic on the interior dome of the shrine is filled with swirling vines that evoke a garden in paradise. Amid the tendrils are the regal crowns of several Mediterranean rulers, such as the Sasanian Persian diadem. The Qur'ānic chapter from which the phrase "People of the Book" was drawn was spelled out in mosaic tiles that lined the dome's inner ring. It instructs readers not to believe that God was originally a three-person entity, an allusion to the Holy Trinity of Christian theology (God the Father, the Son, and Holy Spirit). "O people of the book," the Arabic inscription reads:

Figure 12.2 After Muhammad's death in 632 CE, leaders of his movement took the title *amir al-mu'minin*, or "Commander of the Believers." Over the next two decades, these commanders led armies into neighboring Roman and Persian territory, eventually conquering and seizing lands from Spain to Pakistan. By the middle of the seventh century (c.661 CE), as deep, long-lasting disagreements were beginning to arise within the community over who would be the true successor to Muhammad's vision, one dynasty emerged as a powerful political voice: the Umayyads. 'Abd al-Malik was the second Umayyad ruler and the first of Muhammad's successors to take the title *khalifa*, or "caliph." He built the Dome of the Rock, seen here, a shrine – not a mosque – begun in 688 CE, finished in 691 CE. The mosaic on the interior features elegant Arabic calligraphy and promotes the oneness of God. Broadly addressed to the "People of the Book," it also shows an awareness of Christian concepts of the Holy Trinity. Under the Umayyads, the Believers' were beginning to articulate a vision of Islam which had more fixed boundaries than their movement may have originally had. Photo credit: Author's photo, 2009.

[D]o not exaggerate in your religion (*din*) and speak of God only the truth. The Messiah Jesus son of Mary was only the apostle (*rasul*) of God and His word, which he cast unto Mary, and a spirit from him. So believe in God and His apostles but do not say "three." Desist! [It is] better for you. For indeed God is one God. ('Abd al-Malik's mosaic inscription from the Dome of the Rock, trans. by F. Donner, *Muhammad and the Believers* [Cambridge, MA: Belknap Press, 2010], p. 234)

This artistic inscription and the Qur'anic quotations woven into it tell us something significant about the seventh-century eastern Mediterranean. By 690–691 CE, the time when the phrase "People of the Book" was put on display inside this important Muslim shrine, it is clear that followers of Muhammad had learned quite a bit about the theological beliefs of followers of Jesus.

Yet as the building and the text show, cultural connections that may have bound Jews, Christians, and Muslims together – their love of books, for instance – did not necessarily create a social environment where everyone felt comfortable with sharing their ideas and beliefs. How and even whether individuals and communities in the past chose to find common ground with each other is more complicated than identifying the one or two aspects of culture they ostensibly shared, such as books.

Summary

The people of the Late Antique world spoke many languages: Syriac, Coptic, Greek, Latin, Armenian, Gothic, Nabatean, Pahlavi (Middle Persian), Arabic, Hebrew, and Aramaic. As a result, the study of the period offers researchers many more voices and perspectives on the time than the classical history of Greece or Rome, which traditionally have been centered about Greek and Latin. What is also truly remarkable about Late Antique history, then, is that the sources preserved in these languages – especially from realms on the empire's frontier, or in places where Roman power withdrew – are more numerous than in earlier periods. The abundance of these texts, in multiple languages, allows us to recalibrate our historical vision, focusing on local environments and creating a more kaleidoscopic view of history instead of one told through a restricted set of lenses.

The growing popularity and exchange of bound books broadened this world.

In this chapter, the sixth century CE, in particular, emerged as a key time period for analyzing literary and intellectual developments. Although Latin remained the language of law in Justinian's Roman Empire, writers and intellectuals had been largely working in Greek throughout this time, as the works of Procopius of Caesarea and the inscription honoring the patronage of Emperor Anicia Juliana revealed. By the middle of the sixth century, however, Greek had become the official language of Constantinople. In the western Mediterranean, meanwhile, a Latin culture flourished. Bishop Damasus of Rome, in the late fourth century CE, is one person who gave this culture a Christian push. Books themselves were valued objects among non-Christians, Christians, and Jews.

Finally, the inscription from the Dome of the Rock in Jerusalem confirms that, by the late seventh century CE, many faith communities throughout the Mediterranean, like Christians, were often identified with their books. The extent to which Christianity caused the rising popularity of books throughout the Roman Empire, however, is far from certain.

Study Questions

1. Name one Late Antiquity community formed around the life of the mind. What did they believe? Who were some of its members?
2. Who was Anicia Juliana? How did she contribute to the sixth-century CE world of culture and ideas?
3. Explain the historical challenge of writing about the sixth-century plague.
4. Was the Emperor Justinian right in trying to prevent Jews from reading their scriptures in Hebrew? If you support his policy, explain why. If you disagree with it, can you imagine what might have led him to this decision?

Suggested Readings

Scott Johnson (ed.), *Greek Literature in Late Antiquity: Dynamism, Didacticism, Classicism* (Aldershot: Ashgate, 2006).

Andrew Smith, *Philosophy in Late Antiquity* (London: Routledge, 2004).

Jeffrey Spier, Herbert Kessler, Robin Jensen, and Steven Fine (eds.), *Picturing the Bible: The Earliest Christian Art* (New Haven: Yale University Art Museum, 2007).

Dennis Trout, *Damasus of Rome: The Epigraphic Poetry* (New York: Oxford University Press, 2015).

Part III
The Illusion of Mediterranean History

Part III

The Illusion of Mediterranean History

13
Geography and Society

In the sixth century CE, contact between the Roman Empire in the eastern Mediterranean and other cities and regions of the globe rises to an astounding level. The western Mediterranean took on a different, more regional political focus. Two examples will help sketch the developments in western Europe before we turn our eyes, historically, in the other direction.

In the kingdom of the Franks, a territory comprising parts of modern France and Germany, a new regal family would establish power in the late fifth century CE. Clovis, founder of the Merovingian dynasty of kings, would be baptized by the bishop of Rheims – just east of Paris – in 496 CE. By the thirteenth century, an important Gothic cathedral would be constructed in this city where subsequent French kings would go to be inaugurated.

In Italy, meanwhile, Gothic kings would establish a dynasty in parts of the old Roman peninsula. Many features of daily life, such as the restoration of the Flavian Amphitheater for animal games, would keep the people of the peninsula anchored during this time of political turnover. But with the new rulers would also come a new language and new traditions. King Theoderic would sport some rather unusual facial hair, a mustache, in public and even on coins. In this way, like his Visigothic counterparts, who were settled in the Iberian peninsula, the Ostrogothic rulers of Italy would strike a creative balance between local and new custom. Many imperial offices, like consul, a position dating back to before the empire, for example, would retain their ceremonial function even as the constitutional framework changed around it under the new kings.

The Frankish, Visigothic, and Ostrogothic efforts at keeping Rome alive spawned a sixth-century European continent that politically and culturally looked much different than it did in the fourth century, when Gothic and Vandal tribes had first arrived in the empire. By the sixth century CE, so much time and distance had come

A Social and Cultural History of Late Antiquity, First Edition. Douglas Boin.
© 2018 John Wiley & Sons, Inc. Published 2018 by John Wiley & Sons, Inc.

between them that the Gothic community in Italy, the "Ostrogoths" ("Eastern Goths"), had even begun distinguishing themselves from Goths in Spain, the "Visigoths" ("Western Goths"). Neither Romans nor Goths had used these labels during the early fourth century. Only after the Gothic populations had moved from the lands above the Danube River to the territories where they settled – whether in the provinces of Roman Spain or in the city of Rome – did their new, distinct identities begin to emerge. Visigothic and Ostrogothic people and their customs would contribute to the social, legal, cultural, artistic, and economic story of western Europe from the fifth through seventh centuries CE.

13.1   Seeing the Sixth Century Through the Eyes of an Emperor and a Traveler

Let's pick out one or two strands from the fraying Roman world and see where they take us. One person who can lead us in fascinating directions is a man, Cosmas, nicknamed "He Who Sailed to India." Cosmas wrote *c*.545 CE during the reign of the Emperor Justinian (r. 527–565). His nickname is the translation of an ancient Greek adjective, Indicopleustes, given to him by medieval copyists who passed down the manuscripts of his texts. Cosmas' writings reveal an important part of the puzzle of the rapidly expanding sixth-century CE globe (*Exploring Culture* 13.1: Literature, History, and Material Culture in Armenia, Crossroads of Empires; Figure 13.1). A look at the lives of both him and the emperor whom he lived under can lead to intriguing ways of thinking about Mediterranean history, seen-from-above and from-below, during the middle of the sixth century CE.

Exploring Culture 13.1   *Literature, History, and Material Culture in Armenia, Crossroads of Empires*

The Black Sea lay to its west and the Caspian Sea to its east. The Caucasus Mountains formed its northern boundary; and Mesopotamia, its southern. This was the ancient kingdom of Armenia. It was a plot of land that would come to occupy slices and slivers of many modern countries: of Georgia, Turkey, Azerbaijan, and Iran. The modern Republic of Armenia is a much reduced footprint of this ancient kingdom, but its land bears many traces of the two empires, Roman and Sasanian, that came to shape its people, its customs, its language, and its architecture.

Armenia was long kept on the Roman state's periphery, governed by client kings who were its strong allies. Under the reign of Emperor Nero (54–68 CE), the King of Armenia, Tiridates I, made the journey to Rome to pledge allegiance to the empire. "While the king made supplication," Suetonius tells us, "Nero took the turban from [King Tiridates'] head and replaced it with a diadem" (*Life of Nero* 13.2, LCL trans. by Rolfe [1913–1914]). The act of investiture established a dynasty that remained loyal to Rome for two hundred years.

By the third century CE, the kingdom's relationship with Rome had grown complicated. The rise of Sasanian Persia to the kingdom's south posed one of the most urgent crises because Sasanian leaders began to claim the territory as their own. Armenia's capture would restore a part of the glorious Persian Empire of the fifth century BCE. From the third through the sixth centuries, soldiers in the Sasanian and Roman army became an unavoidable presence in the region. Armenia's client kings and its people saw their relationship with Sasanian and Roman governments fluctuate greatly during this time.

According to the earliest written history of Armenia, composed by a man who lived in the kingdom, it was King Tiridates IV (r. 298/299–330 CE) who was the first ruler to convert to Christianity. This story comes from the *History of the Armenians*, written in the language of Armenian by a man known as "Agathangelos," or Good Messenger (*aggelos*, in Greek, is pronounced *angelos*; it can mean either "messenger" or "angel"). His text has been dated to the mid-fifth century CE (Anne Redgate, *The Armenians* [Oxford: Blackwell, 1998]). Unfortunately, the circumstances, even the date, of King Tiridates IV's conversion are not easy to fact-check, given that they are recounted in only one source.

Two centuries after King Tiridates IV, however, a dramatic rise in material culture does attest to the growing social profile of Christianity. One sixth- or seventh-century church is exemplary. At the town of Ptghni (ancient Ptlni), a worship space was constructed out of colorful local tufa, or volcanic rock. Above its southern door the artists were commissioned to carve a man on horseback in a hunting scene alongside depictions of the saints and the risen Jesus.

A hunting scene also appears at the fourth-century burial for the Armenian royal family, at the nearby city of Aghstk. Hunting scenes were also popular in Sasanian and Roman material culture. The inclusion of a similar scene at Ptghni suggests that Christians in the kingdom were able to mold their local customs to their Christian beliefs. This process of cultural adaptation opens up new ways of thinking about King Tiridates's conversion, suggesting that his decision to embrace Christianity did not necessarily usher in a period of rapid social change. "Just as it was to do in other societies, the success of Christianity in Armenia was to involve compromises and accommodations with traditional attitudes and behavior which compensated for the tensions between them" (Redgate 1998, p. 122).

Emperor Justinian, 527–565 CE

Justinian ruled from Constantinople, but many of his days were preoccupied with the fate of people and lands elsewhere. In particular, Justinian went to war to take the cities of Italy and North Africa back from Ostrogothic and Vandal control, respectively. He also met Sasanian forces in the military theaters of Mesopotamia to try to expand Roman power and limit the Persians' westward advances.

Figure 13.1 At Ptghni, Armenia, stands a lonely shell of a building that used to be a Christian church. All that remains of it are a set of sturdy walls, remarkably preserved almost roof-high. Stacked from local reddish-black stone, they are punctuated by a series of windows, which once looked in to the single-aisle nave. This photograph shows the south wall of the church at Ptghni, built in the late sixth or early seventh century CE. It is a detail of the stonework on the lintel, the frame around the doors. whose iconography reveals a mixture of local customs and artistic styles found broadly throughout the Late Antique world. At left, we see a man on horseback hunting with his bow, a popular pastime among local elites in sixth-century CE Armenia. To the right are framed portraits of saints, similar to portraits of other holy men and women in churches in western and eastern Mediterranean cities. The ancient kingdom of Armenia was a perennially contested territory in political and military struggles between Rome and Persia. Photo credit: Bertramz at Wikimedia Commons, Creative Commons, Attribution-ShareAlike 3.0 Unported license.

Justinian had a tactical mind. When he became emperor, in 527 CE, the Roman state was at one of its most diminished sizes in antiquity: only modern Greece, the Balkans, Asia Minor, the Levant, and Egypt lay within its political control. By the end of Justinian's reign, his generals had successfully seized back several western lands that the empire had not controlled since the fifth century. The important harbor at Carthage, the cities of North Africa, and even the southern tip of the Iberian peninsula would be triumphantly reclaimed, as were the old imperial heartlands of Sicily, the Italian peninsula, and cities along the Adriatic Sea. To manage many these territories, the emperor installed an exarch, or governor from Constantinople, at Ravenna on the northeastern coast of the peninsula, near Venice.

This shaky recovery would falter. By the late sixth to early seventh century CE, a newly organized group from northern Italy, called Lombards, succeeded in establishing their own state on lands they wrestled from Justinian's empire. Control over Italy's territories were then divided up yet again, this time between Lombard and Roman leadership.

Justinian's Christian architecture

Justinian's Christian convictions led the emperor on a quixotic campaign to enforce proper theological belief throughout the Roman Empire, and he used Constantinople to make powerful claims about his authority. One wondrous piece of architecture spoke to the emperor's vision for the "holy catholic and apostolic church." It is the church of Hagia Sophia, which exists today as a museum.

Teams of brick-layers and masonry men, as well as artists and artisans specializing in mosaic and stone: all began working on the site in 532 CE. Five years later, in 537, a building of domes and half-domes had risen, like a web of delicate bubbles, on the seaside promontory of the Golden Horn. The church had been cleverly designed and engineered by two men steeped in the scientific knowledge of classical antiquity. Isidore and Anthemius, the architect and engineer, both hailed from Ionia in western Asia Minor, Isidore from Miletus and Anthemius from Tralles. Ionia's cities had been producing some of the Mediterranean's top-tier scientists since the sixth century BCE when "wise men" – lovers of rational inquiry called *philosophoi* in Greek, like Anaximander, Thales, and Anaximenes – had set out to investigate the origins of the physical world. Like all rigorous, methodically minded thinkers who have ventured to explore the natural world, not all these men would always get it right. Anaximander (*c.*610–547 BCE) believed the world was shaped like a column drum, with a flat top. Still, seen as part of a demanding intellectual tradition, Ionian minds would come to shape the Mediterranean world in important ways. In the case of Hagia Sophia, it was literally so.

Hagia Sophia, the church dedicated to "Holy Wisdom," was born from both the imagination and careful planning of two wise men working in this same tradition (Figure 13.2), still flourishing in Ionia, almost one thousand years after Anaximander.

In many ways, then, Justinian's world, a world in which only one, limited version of faith was considered politically acceptable and architectural daring was enlisted in the service of the emperor's vision, was a land of puzzling social contradictions. The mathematical ingenuity and creative thinking that were needed to fashion the domes and half-domes of Hagia Sophia had been cultivated since the creation of the Pantheon, in Rome's Campus Martius. And yet this level of innovation was, paradoxically, encouraged at a time when a stricter vision of the Christian state was being promoted and policed, often with detrimental effects on society and daily life.

13.2 Cosmas' Christian World

Cosmas the voyager to India ("Indicopleustes") gives us another perspective. It is not just a view of someone standing outside Constantinople's rarefied world of diplomatic dinners and policy debates. His writings transport us into a different kind of place, of classrooms and living rooms, church halls and taverns, where ordinary but educated citizens grappled with how to think about their role in the world.

Figure 13.2 In Constantinople, north of the palace and the popular hippodrome, Emperor Justinian would commission a magnificent urban church, Hagia Sophia ("Holy Wisdom"). Replacing an earlier church of the same name which had recently succumbed to fire, this new Hagia Sophia would be designed and built by two ambitious engineers and architects, both from Asia Minor: Isidore of Miletus and Anthemius of Tralles. The building seen here is largely their vision, from 532 and 537 CE, with slight modification. After Turks seized control of Constantinople in 1453, four minarets were added to the corners – in the late fifteenth and sixteenth centuries – for the Muslim call to prayer, transforming Hagia Sophia into a mosque. The building stayed a mosque until the twentieth century when, in 1935, Mustafa Kemal Atatürk, founder of the modern state of Turkey, decided that this important treasure from Justinian's time should become a symbol of Turkey's secular ideals. The mosque was turned into a museum, which it remains today. Photo credit: Author's photo, 2007.

Cosmas shows us a sixth-century Roman Empire where scripture governed many people's lives, apocalyptic thinking was commonly accepted, and the day-to-day realities of being a minority were anything but easy.

Geography

As best as scholars can tell, Cosmas lived and worked in Alexandria, an important cultural capital since the Ptolemies. Science, math, medicine: Alexandria had specialized and excelled in them all. By Justinian's time, it had also become renowned for its Christian thinkers, too. The voices of theological commentators like Origen or the bishop of Alexandria, Cyril, would earn an important place in Christian writing. Cyril's influence, in particular – recall how he had believed the human and divine natures of Christ were united in one union (*hypostasis*) – had shaped the beliefs of Alexandria's Christians throughout the fifth and sixth centuries.

Cosmas grew up here, and Alexandria itself may have nudged him into the study of geography. Although it can be debated whether he traveled as far as his writings or his nickname imply, he left behind a book which describes a world far wider than the one which captivated his emperor. His writings, called the *Christian Topography*, survive in three illuminated manuscripts.

Cosmas' *Christian Topography* takes his readers south from the Mediterranean, through the Red Sea, to the southern tip of the Arabian peninsula (modern Yemen), to the Indian Ocean and the modern island of Sri Lanka. This "travelogue" shares many of the contradictory features of Justinian's age. Aiming high, born of an honest desire for intellectual exploration, it is stuck in an unimaginatively literalist Christian worldview, one which keeps its readers bound to scripture.

Here is how Cosmas explains and analyzes the shape of the physical world. He begins by citing a story from Jewish Scripture, specifically, from a passage in the first five books, the Pentateuch:

> [In the Book of Exodus] God [Yahweh] directs Moses to construct a Tabernacle [the dwelling place of Yahweh before the Temple in Jerusalem was built] according to the pattern which Moses had seen in the mountain – this Tabernacle being a pattern, so to say, of the whole world. Moses therefore … gave it a length of 30 cubits and a breadth of ten. Then … he divided it into two compartments. This outer space was patterned after the visible world. (*Christian Topography* 3.51, trans. by J. McCrindle [1897], modified)

Cosmas' literal reading of Jewish Scripture has led him to propose that the earth was shaped in the form of a two-dimensional rectangular plane, like the Jewish tabernacle.

Cosmas' worldview is important not because this lone travel writer's voice stands as an example of the Roman Empire's ignorant multitude, all of whom presumed the earth was flat. As we have already seen, key scientific thinkers like Anaximander, in the sixth century BCE, had held similar views although Anaximander's theories were based on rational inquiry and Cosmas' were based on a literal reading of Jewish Scripture. What is remarkable, rather, is how different Cosmas' ideas were from men and women of his own time.

The centrality of scripture

By the age of Justinian, the overwhelming opinion of classical scientists had moved towards the idea that the earth was round. Aristotle, in the fourth century BCE, had been one of the first to propose a spherical earth, but there were others who elaborated on this idea in crucial ways. The mathematician, astronomer, and observer of the natural world, Claudius Ptolemy, who lived in second-century CE Alexandria, had been one of the first to describe it, in treatises specifically devoted to the topic. Several of his books, including his *Guide to Mapping the World* and the *Almagest* (Arabic for "the great book"), would remain popular in Late Antiquity and into the Middle Ages, across faith communities and in various languages. Late Antique Christians – like Augustine, who admitted the possibility that the earth was spherical, not flat (Augustine, *City of God* 16.9) – likely inherited this idea from the mainstream, widespread popularity of earlier classical thinkers like Claudius Ptolemy.

Cosmas may have been a lonely, idiosyncratic voice, but that does not make him an outlier in all respects. Many of his Christian friends, neighbors, and family would have accepted it unhesitatingly that scripture could and should provide the organizing basis for all intellectual endeavors. This deference to scripture's unerring "truth" shows up in many corners of Late Antique society. Both Christians who read scripture literally and those who read it allegorically found ways to make biblical texts the basis for their ideas, opinions, and arguments.

Augustine, one of the most famous Christian voices to encourage others how to read scripture allegorically, himself did so when he discussed the earth's geography. Christians could embrace the notion that the earth was round, he argued, although there was no reason to "jump to the conclusion that [the other side of round earth] has human inhabitants" (Augustine, *City of God* 16.9, LCL trans. by E. Sanford and W. Green [1965]). Augustine's wariness about populating another side of the planet was based on an assumption he shared with Cosmas: "There is absolutely no falsehood in scripture, which gains credence for its account of past events by the fact that its prophecies are fulfilled," he explained (Augustine, *City of God* 16.9). For Augustine, the Christian Mediterranean was the entirety of his known world.

Even though Cosmas Indicopleustes based his geography on a literal reading of Jewish Scripture and Augustine based his geography on the classical intellectual tradition, both appealed to the idea that scripture could not be wrong when it came to describing the world they lived in. For Christians who read works by both men or for other readers who took the time to compare their ideas, Christians must have seemed the practitioners of a curiously inconsistent faith.

Apocalyptic thinking

There is another, peculiar facet of Cosmas' world which, until recently, scholars have been hesitant to discuss as a historical reality. The reasons for this reticence come from the rather embarrassing nature of the evidence. Some people in the sixth century CE – it is impossible to put demographic figures on this group – believed Jesus' resurrection was near, that the Last Judgment was imminent, and the world would come to an end in the middle of Justinian's reign.

We can chart the level of this anxiety in a number of ways. First, there is testimony recorded by those who heard people fretting about the approaching end times. A lawyer who worked in Constantinople in the middle of the sixth century CE, Agathias (*c.*532–*c.*580), left behind one such record. He wrote an important text, in ancient Greek, called the *Histories*. It continued the narrative which Procopius of Caesarea had begun and describes Justinian's wars in Italy. It also preserved an account of what happened when, in 557 CE, an earthquake shook Constantinople.

According to Agathias, the emperor's own carefully planned and costly church, Hagia Sophia, was damaged during this time; and many Christians throughout the city were fretful about how to interpret that event. Agathias' description of the earthquake is important for several reason. First, he notes that the catastrophe happened during an ancient Roman civic festival, the *Brumalia*. Held over a series of weeks prior to the winter solstice (*brumalis*, in Latin, means "pertaining to the winter"), the festival lasted from the end of November to the middle of December and may have been dedicated to the god Dionysos. The evidence for this holiday, although seemingly tangential to the account of the earthquake, reveals that, even in the sixth century, the civic calendar of Christian Constantinople were not entirely consumed with Jesus' life.

Agathias also gives us some information about how certain Christians reacted to the cataclysmic event:

> The tremors continued for several days; and though they had lost most of their initial fury and were of much shorter duration, they were still sufficiently violent to disrupt any remaining semblance of order. Fantastic stories and extraordinary predictions to the effect that the end of the world was at hand began to circulate among the people. Charlatans and self-appointed prophets roamed the streets prophesying whatever came into their heads and terrifying still more the majority of the people who were particularly impressionable because they had already become demoralized [by the natural disaster].... Others, as might have been expected, pondering over the motions and aspects of the stars, hinted darkly at greater calamities and at what amounted almost to a cosmic disaster. (*Histories* 5.5, trans. by J. Frendo [Berlin: De Gruyter, 1975])

Interestingly, although he never identifies them as Christians, Agathias does not hesitate from passing harsh judgment on these doomsday individuals and the "charlatans and self-appointed prophets" who accompanied them on their ranting. Offering an interesting sociological comment on end-time thinking, he concludes: "Society ... never fails to throw up a bewildering variety of such persons in times of misfortune."

What is remarkable is that these undercurrents of end-time thinking were not limited to Constantinople or the East Roman Empire. Visions of an unknown judgment, looming just off the horizon – perhaps tomorrow, perhaps hundreds of years from tomorrow – were part of the world familiar to many sixth-century Christians. One bishop of Rome would famously drew upon these powerful beliefs to suggest that his flock urgently modify their ethical behavior, even if the second coming of the Messiah could not be predicted.

"Our Lord ... wants the final hour to be unknown to us," Pope Gregory (*c.*540–604 CE) preached to his congregation in Rome, "so that it can always be suspected." Gregory's apocalyptic beliefs may not have been rooted in the same fixed certainty of the people Agathias refers to as "charlatans and self-appointed prophets" of the end time. But his evocation of imagery associated with the last days did serve a useful purpose.

As the pope explained, "while we cannot foresee [the end time], we might be prepared for it without pause. Therefore, my brothers, fix your mind's eye on the mortal condition, prepare yourself for the coming Judgement with daily tears and laments!" (Pope Gregory, *Homilies on the Gospels* 1.13.6, trans. by J. Palmer, *The Apocalypse in the Early Middle Ages* [Cambridge: Cambridge University Press, 2014], p. 61). For many communities throughout the sixth-century Mediterranean, whether in the capital of the old Roman Empire or the current one, a steady stream of apocalyptic thinking trickled through daily life.

In fact, by the end of the century, one monk may have had enough with these doomsday scenarios (*Key Debates* 13.1: End-Time Thinking and the Invention of the "A.D." Calendar). Soon, the "A.D." dating system would come to be the dominant way of recording time throughout medieval Europe. Widely adopted by the eighth century CE, it was first invented in Cosmas' day to address the growing needs of a society that, from the top-down, wanted to structure the whole calendar around the life and death of Jesus, promoting Christian ideals around the clock.

Key Debates 13.1   *End-Time Thinking and the Invention of the "A.D." Calendar*

Since the second century CE, some Christian writers had calculated that life on earth would last for six thousand years. At that point, the world would either come abruptly to an end or Jesus would return as the Messiah to preside over his kingdom. The number six thousand was not decided upon due to any careful, physical observation of the earth's geology, however. It was arrived at through a selective literal and symbolic reading of Jewish Scripture.

In the non-canonical *Letter of Barnabas*, written in the second century CE, the anonymous Christian writer uses the six days of creation, in the Book of Genesis, as a starting point for concocting his history of the earth. Adding a dash of the Psalms – "For a day in your courts is better/than a thousand [days] elsewhere," Psalms 84.10–11 [*NRSV*] – the writer deduced that the present age would last six thousand years.

In and of itself, the countdown to six thousand posed no immediate or widespread concern because no one really knew how old the earth actually was. It could always be debated. By the mid-third century CE, that would change. For one Christian, Hippolytus of Rome, the clock was perilously close to approaching the end. Hippolytus believed that Jesus had been born in the 5,500th year since the creation of the world, which left a balance of five hundred years before stoppage.

Like the writer of the *Letter of Barnabas* before him, Hippolytus did not arrive at this calculation based on scientific methods, like carbon dating any artifacts in the alleged tomb of Jesus, for example. Turning to the Jewish story of Moses in the desert, who made a tabernacle for Yahweh – "It shall be 2.5 cubits long, 1.5 cubits wide, and 1.5 cubits high," Exodus 25.10 [*NRSV*] – Hippolytus used these raw numbers to date Jesus' incarnation as the Messiah. Jesus must have been born in the 5,500th year of the world, he argued, because the measurements of Moses' tabernacle added up to 5.5 (Hippolytus, *Commentary on Daniel*, fragment 2.5). So it was that Hippolytus, writing in the mid-third century CE, concluded that the earth was two hundred years away from the end of time.

This mathematical, theological backstory may explain why some Christians in the sixth century CE believed the apocalypse was near. As the 550th year after Jesus' birth approached, so, too, did panic about what would happen next – for those convinced of the accuracy of Hippolytus' math. Agathias' account of the earthquake in Constantinople is crucial evidence in this regard. It also raises an important question.

How many Christians were embarrassed by these hysterical, end-time speculations, and more importantly, did they do anything about it?

Scholars have not reached a consensus yet on whether the issue of when the world would end was as urgent as it may seem, but one piece of evidence suggests the people of the sixth century were trying to find ways to postpone it. One monk, Dionysius Exiguus ("Dionysius the Short") would propose that Christians start counting time from the birth of Jesus, which Dionysius called year one in the "Year of our Lord" (*Anno Domini*) system. By resetting the world clock to 1 A.D. – in effect, by adding a period of "extra time" to the age of the world – Dionysius may have been at the forefront of a clever campaign to switch off people's apocalyptic fears.

Religious minorities

The divergence of Christian opinion over how to read and interpret Jewish and Christian Scripture – seen throughout Justinian's reign – is an important feature of Late Antique Christian society, but disagreement about scriptural interpretation is a phenomenon with an even longer history. Jewish and gentile followers of Jesus had been disagreeing about how to interpret Jewish Scripture since the earliest generation of the Jesus movement. The issue of whether Christians should read Jewish Scripture literally, however, is made all the more historically intriguing by the fact that Jews themselves had long been reading their own sacred texts in an allegorical way, too. Since at least the time of Philo, also a resident of Alexandria, in the first century BCE, Jews had been exploring allegorical reading of books, like Genesis, about the creation of the world.

Both Cosmas' and Augustine's peculiar understanding of how to read Jewish Scripture seems, then, strangely myopic, given the vibrant intellectual traditions which flourished in the Jewish community itself. When combined with the fact that, from the very top of Justinian's Roman Empire, Jewish people were presumed to need Christian guidance to correct the "mistaken" way they interpreted their own scripture, it becomes clear that, for sixth-century Jews throughout the Mediterranean, the Christian world was an acutely awkward one to participate in.

13.3   Beyond Rome's Christian Empire in the Sixth Century CE

One last remarkable aspect of Cosmas' writing is the breadth of his geographical knowledge. In fact, although he may seem in some regards to show a frustratingly narrow interest in the world outside the Bible, his text, the *Christian Topography*, is one of the most extraordinary testimonies of a Late Antique writer describing the world beyond the Mediterranean Sea (*Political Issues* 13.1: The Arab Client Kings of Sixth-Century Persia and Rome).

The word topography comes from the Greek roots *topos* (τόπος), meaning "place," and the verb *graphein* (γραφεῖν), "to write, or describe." In his text, Cosmas describes the route that a traveler would take departing from Alexandria and journeying down the Red Sea. Along the western edges of the Red Sea, towards its southern end, a voyager would encounter the land of Axum, in modern Ethiopia. Axum, Cosmas tells us, was an important Christian kingdom on the southern border of the Roman Empire.

From the Red Sea, one could continue sailing along the southern shore of the Arabian peninsula, the territory where the countries of Yemen and Oman are located today. In Cosmas' time, the southwestern tip of the Arabian peninsula was occupied by the kingdom of Himyar. It was the site of a thriving Jewish state until 525 CE when it was taken over by Axum's Christian leaders. (For the details of the military attack against the "Homerites," as Procopius called the people of Himyar, see Procopius' *History of the War* 1.20.1–13.)

The further, eastern part of the Arabian peninsula entered into the orbit of the Sasanians, who, as traders and diligent administrators, oversaw ships coming into and out of the Persian Gulf. Cosmas must have been a fascinating tour guide, taking readers to far-away lands which, to many Romans, had existed in a nebulous region of the world, at best. Here is one of Cosmas' travel descriptions:

> [There is a] country of silk situated in the remotest of all the Indies, and lies to the left of those who enter the Indian sea, far beyond the Persian Gulf and beyond the island called by the Indians Selediba and by the Greeks Taprobanē. This country is called Tzinista and is surrounded on the left by the ocean.... Indian philosophers, called the Brachmans, say that if you stretch a cord from Tzinista to pass through Persia, onward to the Roman dominions, the middle of the earth would be quite correctly traced. They are perhaps right; for the country in question [the land of silk] deflects considerably to the left, so that the loads of silk passing by land through one nation after another, reach Persia in a comparatively short time while the route by sea to Persia is vastly greater.
> (*Christian Topography* 2.45, trans. by J. McCrindle [1897], slightly modified)

Cosmas offered this helpful guide to his readers so that they could make an efficient journey. Voyagers who went "by land from Tzinista to Persia," as opposed to making the trip by boat, shortened "very considerably the length of the journey." These written instructions were more than an imagined geography. When we replace Cosmas' ancient place-names with their modern counterparts, the global distance covered by this sixth-century text becomes remarkable.

Taprobanē is, according to most scholars, the island of Sri Lanka; the Indian philosophers to whom Cosmas refers are likely a group of distinguished Hindu priests,

Political Issues 13.1 *The Arab Client Kings of Sixth-Century Persia and Rome*

Significantly, although neither the East Roman Empire nor the Sasanian Empire directly administered any of the land on the Arabian peninsula, the imperial presence of both was unavoidable there. By the sixth century CE, both empires had established informal treaties with local tribes in the north of the peninsula, in territories that bordered Persia and Rome.

In the northwest of the peninsula, southeast of the Roman province of Syria, Roman officials partnered with a politically talented family, the Jafnids, part of the Arabian tribe of Ghassan. This Arab-Roman family governed their own kingdom but, as allies of the Roman emperor in Constantinople, contributed soldiers to the Roman army and provided a trustworthy buffer against any advances from Sasanians through this contested region.

In the northeast region of the peninsula, at the border of the Euphrates River, southwest of Persia, was located a second Arab kingdom. It was ruled by the Nasrids, a family culturally fluent in Persian customs who hailed from the Arabian tribe of Lakhm. These Persian-Arab leaders played an important role governing their territory as a client state of the Sasanians. In this way, the Lakhmid kingdom also functioned as a buffer, protecting the Sasanians from Roman aggression.

Together, these two families, the Jafnids and the Nasrids – from two different tribes – effectively locked their partners, the Romans and the Sasanians, out of any control over the Arabian peninsula. This tense standoff affected life for many other people living on the peninsula. There were key routes and trading posts in the peninsula's sometimes mountainous but overwhelmingly desert landscape, of course, which drew outsiders. But Roman and Persian merchants, both of whom were keen to cultivate connections to Asia, largely found ways to work around them. Romans used the Red Sea to sail around the Arabian peninsula. Sasanians, because of their control of overland roads to and from Asia, were also able to avoid leaving their footprints in the sands of the peninsula. (Cosmas had marveled at the Sasanians' advantage in trade.)

A critical turning point in Roman–Sasanian relations would come in the sixth century, potentially upsetting long-standing arrangements with these Arab client kings.

As Romans increasingly began to sail around Persia, taxes which had once trickled into the Sasanian treasury from overland travellers diminished. Whether for these reasons or to make a forceful response or perhaps because of aggressive measures devised in Constantinople, Sasanian Persians began, during the sixth century CE, to encroach on territory in the southern Arabian peninsula, in areas of modern Oman and Yemen.

The result of this Sasanian expansion was that, by the end of the sixth century, the two empires of Rome and Persia were not only facing each other across the Euphrates River border. They were meeting each other along sea routes on the south side of the Arabian peninsula. The people of the Arabian peninsula were now boxed in by strong imperial powers and, in the north, by the two family-run states which had established political allegiances with them.

the Brahmins; and Tzinista, the land of silk, is a reference to lands held by imperial China, an empire whose first dynasty, the Qin, ruled in the third century BCE. In this way, from the words of one sixth-century writer who lived in Alexandria, the veil that had once shrouded the continent of Asia – clouding it in obscurity for many people who lived in the proudly cosmopolitan Roman world – begins to lift. We should seize this opportunity to see the expanding sixth-century world from as many of their perspectives as possible.

13.4   Sixth- and Seventh-Century South Asia

Sri Lanka and the economy of the Indian subcontinent

Much ancient evidence exists for contact between the people of continental Asia, the Indian subcontinent, and the Mediterranean, but it is often not highlighted in basic narratives of Greece or Rome. The unfortunate result is that students of the Mediterranean world may not be as familiar with it as they should. Examples of exchange between the Hellenistic rulers and the people in the territory of Bactria has already been discussed. For the Roman people, the classical Latin writer Pliny preserves one of the most telling encounters, which dates to the time of the Emperor Claudius (r. 41–54 CE).

A Roman administrator, a freed slave in charge of collecting taxes in the Red Sea region, had set sail into the Arabian gulf – his destination is unclear – but an unexpectedly strong wind blew him off course. The Roman official landed in Taprobanē, Sri Lanka, where a group of ambassadors received him. Eventually, four of the ambassadors would travel back to Emperor Claudius' court in Rome. From their accounts, Pliny learned about the government, trade, and beliefs of the people of the distant island. They were ruled by a king, had an expensive local marble that resembled tortoise shell, worshipped a deity whom Pliny equated to Hercules, and, unlike the people of the ancient Mediterranean, did not practice or endorse the institution of slavery (Pliny the Elder, *Natural History* 6.24).

Pliny's first-century account of the people of Sri Lanka is important, even if it is a piece of far-removed, second-hand testimony. Archaeological evidence, by contrast, has allowed scholars a closer glimpse of life on the island. Nautical archaeologists, working at the modern fishing town of Godavaya, have studied the site of a shipwreck dating to the first century BCE–first century CE, that is, generally, to the period the Sri Lankan ambassadors were sent to Rome.

The Godavaya site is the oldest known shipwreck in the Indian Ocean, and the remains of the wreckage there confirm Sri Lanka's central position in a system of trade that brought goods from India, the inland regions of Gandhara (see Chapter 1), and China. Among the raw materials found in the submerged ship were bars of copper, iron, and ingots of glass. There were also stones with inscriptions on them in a Middle Indo-Aryan language of ancient India, called Prakrit, related to Sanskrit. Other examples of Prakrit have been found, on stone, at cities in Nepal, Bangladesh, Afghanistan, and Pakistan.

As we will see in a moment, these inscriptions, which date to the third century BCE, are critical documents, not the least because they help us understand the spread of Buddhism. For now, it is important to stress that the same language used by Buddhist individuals in the third-century BCE subcontinent was found on stones in the first-century Godavaya shipwreck. Language and ideas, not just objects and luxury goods, were a vital part of Sri Lanka's interconnected world in South Asia.

"Buddhism" and "Hinduism"

We set foot in this region, the northern Kabul valley near the Indus River, at the outset of our book. Specifically, we looked at the ways in which Hellenistic Greeks, in the decades following Alexander's conquests, influenced local residents in Bactria, an ancient kingdom comprising parts of modern Afghanistan, Tajikistan, and Uzbekistan. By the second century CE, a community of monks here had incorporated Hellenistic, Parthian, and Sasanian artistic traditions of sculpting figures out of stone to depict a spiritual leader who was important to their community: the "Enlightened One," or Buddha. One Buddhist community, in Mathura, northern India, created a larger-than-life sandstone portrait bust of the Buddha in the early fifth century CE (Figure 13.3). Other communities, like the Buddhist monks at Bamiyan, Afghanistan, carved giant statues of the Buddha directly from the cliffs.

Since the exchange of ideas, practices, and values between people of different cultural backgrounds is a phenomenon that takes place in two directions, it is worth rewinding our story here to see how the people of this region of ancient Asia influenced the myriad soldiers, settlers, and traders who had come from the ancient Mediterranean.

Looking at the economic system that linked Sri Lanka to the Indian subcontinent and beyond is one way of doing so. Another way would be to investigate individual and communal beliefs and values, how they were expressed in local settings, and how they spread beyond the confines of the communities themselves.

The Buddhas at Bamiyan and the portrait head from Mathura give us an excellent opportunity to discuss the historical development of what we now call "Buddhism" and the social world of the Indus River valley out of which it emerged. Like so many of the religions encountered in Mediterranean antiquity – "Christianity" and "Judaism," in particular – "Buddhism" as a name of a distinct "religion" was not a term that the monks at Bamiyan would have been familiar with. The word was coined by nineteenth-century Christians who were struggling to describe sets of beliefs that were entirely foreign to them. The word "Hinduism," an umbrella term used to describe the diverse beliefs and practices associated with the people east of the Indus River, was invented during the nineteenth century, too. We can use these words as modern shorthands as long as we understand that, for the people of Late Antique Central Asia and India, their self-perception and self-description would have been slightly different.

The history of Buddhism and Hinduism are intertwined. Hinduism is the more ancient of the two, with sets of sacred writings, the Vedas, which date to c. 1000 BCE.

Figure 13.3   The Gupta Empire ruled northern India from the early fourth century through mid-sixth century CE. This portrait of the Buddha ("Enlightened One") was carved during the Gupta period, c.430–435 CE. It comes from the city of Mathura, about 90 miles southeast of the modern Indian capital, Delhi. Larger than life size, it was made from sandstone and is one of several representations of the Buddha from South Asia and the Indian continent that date to Late Antiquity. Some of these were truly monumental, such as those produced in the adjacent Ghandara kingdom. Many pilgrims and tourists intrigued by the story of the Buddha came to these cities and left records of their journey. During the Gupta period, in particular, one Chinese writer, Faxian, turned his experiences into a book, *A History of the Buddhistic Kingdoms*. It was published in the early fifth century CE. From Uttar Pradesh, Mathura. Carved from pink granite. Measurements: 50 x 30 x 38 cm (c.19.6 in. tall x 11.8 in. wide x 15 in. deep). Now in the collection of the Musée Guimet (Musée national des arts asiatiques), Paris (Inventory number MA 5029). Photo credit: Ravaux. © RMN-Grand Palais/ Art Resource, NY.

These texts are a collection of prayers, hymns, rituals, and philosophical reflections, the latter of which are known as the Upanishads. Together, the Vedas describe a world of many gods and set forth the "order," or *dharma*, that should rule one's behavior. Starting from the very earliest period of Hindu history, the interpretation of these texts and how they applied to the Hindu rituals was controlled by a select group of priests known as *brahmans*. These are likely the figures Cosmas alludes to in the sixth century as "Indian philosophers."

The extent to which the brahmans regulated ritual and controlled the interpretation of the Vedas, throughout the first millennium BCE, played an important role in the emergence of Buddhism. The word Buddha itself is an epithet applied to a person.

Coming from the Sanskrit, *budh*, meaning "to awaken," Buddha is a general descriptor applied to individuals who are thought to have broken free of a thirst for material things. Like those who are raised in the Hindu religious traditions, followers of the Buddha also search for the "universal law and order," or *dharma*, that guides the world; but they do not believe in a pantheon of gods.

For Buddhists, the first person known to have achieved an awakened, or enlightened, state was Siddhārtha Gautama. Born in the region of modern Nepal, sometime in the fifth century BCE (*c.*485–405 BCE), Siddhārtha Gautama turned away from his wealthy upbringing to become an itinerant teacher and celebrated monastic leader. Later, other individuals were able to achieve Siddhārtha's level of awakening and carried on the name of "Buddha."

Followers of the Buddha's teachings, to which the term *dharma* can also be applied, lived throughout the ancient Indian subcontinent. In the third century BCE, one famous ruler embraced the Buddha's teachings and inscribed them on stone. King Ashoka (r. *c.*272–231 BCE), whose rule was contemporaneous with the eastward spread of Hellenistic power, set up a series of edicts which announced his support for Buddhist teachings. To date, thirty-three inscriptions have been discovered on stone pillars, rocks, and caves throughout Nepal, Pakistan, Afghanistan, and India, some in the capital, Delhi. Most are written in Prakrit, the language which appears on the stones in the Sri Lankan shipwreck discussed earlier. One edict expresses King Ashoka's sincere desire "that all unbelievers may everywhere dwell unmolested throughout his kingdom), as they also wish for moral restraint and purity of disposition" ("Rock Inscription of Ashoka," edict 7 in the *Collection of Indian Inscriptions* [*Corpus Inscriptionum Indicarum*] 1, edited by A. Cunningham and E. Hultzsch, 1925, p. 121]). Another is bilingual, written in Aramaic and ancient Greek. Found in Kandahar, Afghanistan, it refers to Ashoka's Buddhist beliefs as *eusebeia* ("piety").

These teachings about "piety," *dharma*, would spread far beyond King Ashoka's borders. By the late second century CE, they had spread westward and were known to a bishop in Alexandria. Clement was aware that some people in India followed "the precepts [teachings] of Buddha, whom, on account of his extraordinary sanctity, they have raised to divine honors" (*Various Observations* [*Stromata*] 1.15, trans. by W. Wilson in the *ANF* series [1885]). The Buddha's teachings had also spread to China. By the early seventh century CE, one Chinese monk, Xuanzang, would embark on a journey to India to try to learn more about the Buddha's teachings. He, too, would visit Bamiyan and, like Cosmas, would leave behind an important description of his arrival in India from the north and east. We will look at his world in the next section.

The community of monks who lived in the Bamiyan caves, in the sixth century CE, were witnesses to all the ancient and vibrant tradition of South and Central Asia.

13.5 Sixth- and Seventh-Century China and Central Asia

The writer who set out to learn more about Buddhism in India, Xuanzang, was born at a crucial time in Chinese history (*c.*596–664 CE). From accounts edited by one of his students, we know that Xuanzang (pronounced *shwan-tsahng*) witnessed the end of one imperial dynasty and the beginning of another, the Tang. The Tang dynasty governed China from 618–907 CE from their capital at Chang'an.

Today, Chang'an is a city of almost 10 million people, called Xi'an (pronounced *shian*), and is famous for its archaeological collection of terracotta warriors, which date to the third century BCE. These life-size statues were part of the mausoleum of the first emperor of the Qin dynasty. (The name of this ruling family, pronounced *chin*, is thought to be the origin of the later European word, "China.") Xuanzang studied Buddhism in the capital before setting out for India. The road he took offers several fascinating glimpses of the social and cultural world of Central Asia in Late Antiquity.

For those wanting to head west from Chinese territory, the preferred itinerary led paradoxically through northern China – the Himalaya Mountains posed too formidable a barrier to the south – along a network of routes which have come to be called the Silk Road. This "road" was actually a series of oasis towns in the mountains and deserts of Central Asia. The scattered location of these cities, from China to Iran, meant that travelers had wide latitude to plot their destinations and plan their layovers. The city of Turfan was one of the important connector cities. Xuanzang stopped here on his way to Bamiyan (*Working With Sources* 13.1: Graves in Turfan, Xinjiang, on the Northern Silk Roads; Figure 13.4).

The nature of trade along the Silk Roads

One caveat is important to keep in mind about the nature of trade along and between this constellation of cities. Despite the many fables that have been passed down about a vibrant, long-distance economic system uniting east and west along the "Silk Road," archaeological evidence suggests the contrary. When evidence for the Chinese military is found at these oasis cities, there *are* signs of a healthy, long-distance trade. When evidence for the Chinese military is absent – that is, when imperial funds were not being invested into the local cities – trade was more restricted and local.

Burial evidence from Turfan attests that Sasanian currency was widely prized in the oasis towns of the mountains and deserts of northern China (Figure 13.5). The overwhelming number of the coins which have been found in these cities suggests that Persian merchants, not daring frontier traders from Justinian's "New Rome," may have been responsible for pumping a significant amount of money into the system. Bold European adventurers who dared to cross entire continents would come later.

Coins as evidence for shared customs in Rome and Sasanian Persia

These coins also reveal a telling connection between two empires, Rome and Persia, that were increasingly at war with each other throughout the sixth century. Justinian governed proudly as a Christian leader. The emperor's laws also defined life in his

Working With Sources 13.1
Graves in Turfan, Xinjiang, on the Northern Silk Roads

Turfan meets the complex profile of many Silk Road towns in Late Antiquity. Geographically, it is located in the sweltering Taklamakan Desert of northern Asia. Politically, it is part of an autonomous region of China known as Xinjiang and is home to a large Muslim population of Turkish ethnicity known as the Uighurs, who trace their history back to this region.

Residents of Turfan in the sixth century CE were also ethnically diverse. Archaeologists who have excavated graves in the city have detected a mix of burial customs here, suggesting that settlers from Imperial China lived in Turfan alongside a local population, known as the Jushi. The largest influx of Chinese residents likely came in the third century CE since the earliest document bearing Chinese characters found in Turfan dates it 273 CE. Three hundred years later, the Chinese population was swelling. By 640 CE, the city was declared an official prefecture of the Tang empire (r. 618–904).

Turfan's graves also reveal something else. Because of the city's arid climate, tomb after tomb was filled with fragile pieces of handiwork that would otherwise not have survived in a different location. A headdress of silk flowers was one stunning artifact. Paper is another material that has been found in abundance. Residents of Turfan had used recycled paper to make touching last gifts of clothing – hats, belts, and shoes – for their deceased loved ones, a common cultural practice at the time.

As researchers looked more closely at many of these paper remains, however, they made another discovery: many of the tomb clothes bore traces of writing. By the time scholars had done taking the clothes apart and transcribing what had been written on them, they had assembled approximately two thousand individual documents. They were receipts. Flour, grains, vegetables like onions and scallions, pots for cooking, spices, and animals were all on sale in Turfan, as the tallies on the scraps showed. "These documents offer unparalleled insight into the life of ordinary people living in a Silk Road community between 273, the date of the earliest Chinese document, and 769, the date of the last" (V. Hansen, *The Silk Road: A New History* [Oxford: Oxford University Press, 2012], p. 94).

Also of interest: many of the merchants' names were neither local nor Chinese; they were Sogdians, an Iranian people whose kingdom was based in the Central Asian city of Samarkand (in modern Uzbekistan).

Turfan's graves tell yet one more story about life on the northern Silk Road. Overwhelmingly, the currency found throughout the city's tombs is Sasanian silver. By contrast, coins found in cities to the east of Turfan – closer to the Tang capital at Chang'an (modern Xi'an) – are largely bronze Chinese issues. The fact that Sasanian silver was a popular, perhaps even preferred coin in Turfan suggests the city benefited from long-distance trade, even more so than in the Chinese capital. Roman coinage, the sign of direct economic interaction with people from the Mediterranean, is present but sparse. Sasanian Persia may have been the lynchpin in these transcontinental exchanges.

Figure 13.4   Although its precise findspot is unknown and specific details of its acquisition history, in 1951, are not as well documented as cultural heritage advocates currently propose, this female rider likely comes from the desert city of Turfan. Made from fired clay, the figure was likely deposited in a grave at the Astana cemetery, from which other similar artifacts have come. It dates to the Tang dynasty (618–907 CE). The Tang period was a pivotal age for Chinese expansion into Central Asia, and fashion was at the forefront of this change. Elaborately decorated silk veils became a popular look among women when they were seen in public; this woman rider may, in fact, be missing her silk veil, which would have originally hung from her wide-brimmed hat. The city of Turfan (in Xinjiang, Uighur Autonomous Region) is situated in the Taklamakan Desert and lies along the northern routes taken by traders to and from China. Because of the extreme heat, many graves were discovered with otherwise perishable materials, like silk and recycled paper. Among the latter were pawn receipts, giving the price of goods in the Tang dynasty, even preserving the origins of the traders passing along these desert roads. Measurements: c.14.25 in. high (36.2 cm) x 11.50 in. long (29.2 cm). Open-Access collection, Metropolitan Museum of Art, New York.

Christian empire, reminding citizens that it was protected by the Christian God. In Persia, a similar ideology reigned, even if the divinities were different. King Khusrow II (r. 590–628 CE) publicly appealed for Zoroaster's protection by depicting an altar on new Sasanian currency. The altar, ablaze to honor the god, is attended by two priests. King Khusrow II himself is wearing the winged crown of victory. Together, both sides of the coin promote the divine underpinnings of Khusrow's sixth- and early seventh-century rule.

Figure 13.5 a,b This Sasanian silver coin, showing King Hormizd IV (r. 579–590 CE), was found in a burial at the Astana cemetery in Turfan. Although the Chinese army and Chinese government invested heavily in their frontier trading posts like Turfan, these cities were also important stopping points for foreign traders, many of whom came from Sogdiana in Central Asia or from farther afield. As a result of the diversity of people running these routes, Chinese money was hardly the only currency used in transactions. The high prevalence of Sasanian coins in "Silk Road" tombs, for example, like the one seen here from Turfan, suggests that Persia played a crucial role in this economic ecosystem. Coins from the Roman Empire, by contrast, are rare, even during the sixth and seventh centuries CE. Many of the Roman ones that have been found are counterfeit. British Museum inventory number IA,XII.a.3. Photo credit © The Trustees of the British Museum.

Summary

As we have seen throughout this far-reaching chapter, men like Cosmas and Xuanzang not only ventured far from their homes, in Alexandria and Chang'an, during the sixth century CE. They also left behind, in ancient Greek and Mandarin, important written accounts of their journeys. The two men's destinations may have been roughly the same – a Christian hoping to see Sri Lanka; a Buddhist hoping to learn more in India – but each of their routes posed a unique set of challenges.

For the people of the Mediterranean who were inspired about contact with Central and South Asia, travel options were limited because of the need to travel by sea; the Sasanian Empire blocked easy access to the overland routes between Constantinople and China. For residents of Tang China, like Xuanzang, government officials in the newly acquired territory of Turfan controlled the flow of people in and out of the empire. In between these two men and their capitals the Sasanian state was a pivotal geopolitical player. The illusion of an isolated, self-contained "Mediterranean" is hard to sustain during this time.

Study Questions

1. Who was Siddhārtha Gautama?
2. Describe some of the benefits and limitations of relying upon Cosmas "Who Sailed to India" as a source for understanding the sixth century CE.
3. In what cities or regions of the Mediterranean can we find traces of apocalyptic thinking in the sixth century?
4. What happened to the economy of the Silk Road cities and regions when the Chinese Empire withdrew its army and its investment? What does this scenario tell you about the nature of trade in sixth-century Central Asia? How does it parallel the economic relationship between Rome and North Africa in the fifth century CE?

Suggested Readings

Deborah Deliyannis, *Ravenna in Late Antiquity* (New York: Cambridge University Press, 2010).
Valerie Hansen, *The Silk Road: A New History* (New York: Oxford University Press, 2012).
Scott Johnson, *Literary Territories: Cartographical Thinking in Late Antiquity* (New York: Oxford University Press, 2016).
James Palmer, *The Apocalypse in the Early Middle Ages* (Cambridge: Cambridge University Press, 2014).

14
A Choice of Directions

War arrived with the coming of the seventh century CE. Two Arab families – the Jafnids and the Nasrids – would each watch as their respective allies, Rome and Persia, clashed over access to trade routes between the far east and the Mediterranean. This conflict, although perhaps only tangentially related to the daily life of the Jafnid and Nasrid families on the Arabian peninsula, would, nevertheless, come to affect Late Antique history in a crucial way.

The use of client kings, by Rome and Persia, to stabilize their tense frontier suggests that the situation between these two empires, although delicately managed, was primed for more open hostility. The situation escalated in the early seventh century CE. That's when the Roman Empire, still trying to rebound from Justinian's efforts to reconquer the old western Mediterranean provinces, suffered a surprising, devastating loss closer to home. Sasanian armies would take historic provinces in Egypt, Palestine, and Syria. Then, more problems arose. The administration in Constantinople would watch as, over the course of two years, from 612–614 CE, the city of Jerusalem fell into Sasanian hands.

For many Romans in Constantinople, the loss of these lands was a rude, aggressive disruption of the empire's peace. Since the foundation of Constantinople, in the early fourth century, grain shipments from Egypt had been sent directly to the Bosporus. Egypt, long the bread-basket of distant Italy, had served Constantine's city. So it did for three centuries when the Sasanian attack raised the terrifying prospect that the empire would now lose direct, taxed control over its food supply.

The loss of territories along the south and eastern shores of the Mediterranean made many Christians throughout the empire deeply anxious. Another source of apprehension grew from their beliefs about Jerusalem.

14.1   Jerusalem in the Sixth and Early Seventh Centuries CE

Jerusalem in the sixth century CE was a cosmopolitan city with all of the amenities a resident of the Roman Empire could have expected. It had changed quite significantly from the time of Emperor Hadrian, however. Sixth-century residents and visitors witnessed the construction of a new, more monumentalized urban core. One spectacular street, the city's main north–south axis – called in Latin the *Cardo Maximus* – benefited from this period of new investment.

The *Cardo Maximus* had been an important feature of Jerusalem since Hadrian's time. Its spacious berth, connecting the northern gates of the city to the central heart of Hadrian's Jerusalem, the Temple of Aphrodite, allowed wide, comfortable room for both foot and cart traffic. It had remained a major thoroughfare through Constantine's day, when the Church of the Holy Sepulcher was constructed in the city center at the site where Jesus was alleged to have been buried. Three centuries later, the *Cardo* was extended further into the city's southern neighborhoods. This newly paved and framed thoroughfare dramatically guided residents and pilgrims to and from the doorstep of one of Emperor Justinian's most important buildings: the Nea Church. Remains of this wide, colonnaded street, dated to the sixth century CE, are still visible in modern Jerusalem.

Urban investment in this road attests to the ways in which even the places of daily pedestrian traffic throughout Jerusalem – not just the city's major monuments – gripped Christian imagination throughout the sixth century. Tourism was thriving.

Around 570 CE, an anonymous pilgrim from Piacenza, Italy, came from far beyond the eastern Mediterranean shore to walk the streets of what he or she thought of as Jesus' city. This pilgrim from Piacenza left behind a travel journal, written in Latin, with pictures of the sites that had motivated him or her to visit Jerusalem and the Holy Land. The description of the rituals which took place at the Church of the Holy Sepulcher are particularly fascinating because they show the popular allure of an important relic: a fragment of the cross on which Jesus had been executed (*Exploring Culture* 14.1: Jerusalem and the Lure of the "Holy Cross").

The Temple Mount in Jerusalem at the dawn of the seventh century CE

Jews who saw or heard Christians processing around Jerusalem must have been both fascinated and frustrated. While Christian pilgrims and pious residents were marching from Constantine's Church of the Holy Sepulcher to Justinian's New Church, stopping at other holy sites inside and outside the city walls, the most sacred site for Jews, the ruined Temple Mount, remained an urban eyesore (Figure 14.1). Justinian's own massive New Church, perched on its natural and man-made hill, not only towered over the city. It looked down on this urban scar, an open wound for many members of the Jewish community who stood in the shadow of the Temple platform and Justinian's Jerusalem.

Exploring Culture 14.1 *Jerusalem and the Lure of the "Holy Cross"*

Devout men and women had been making the voyage to see this piece of timber since the mid-fourth century CE. Whether these visitors were being sold a fraudulent experience can certainly be debated since no one in the Roman Empire – Christian, Jew, or other – ever cared to talk about the "true cross" until four hundred years after Jesus' death. In fact, the earliest testimony historians have been able to find which refers to it dates to the mid-fourth century CE. There is every reason to be skeptical about whether Christians actually discovered a real board, a plank, or splinter from the felled first-century tree that had been used in Jesus' crucifixion.

Still, tradition can be a powerful way to create a community among believers, especially those who are scattered over long distances. That is what happened among Christians of the Mediterranean who, after the mid-fourth century, pined to see Jerusalem and worship with fellow Christians at the site where they believed Jesus was resurrected. The faithful who made the journey, must have been overwhelmed with bliss. What we know from our contemporary textual sources is that it could also bring out the worst in people.

According to the Latin travel journal of one wealthy woman, Egeria, who sailed from the western Mediterranean to Jerusalem in the late fourth century CE, deacons at the Church of the Holy Sepulcher had to act as ersatz bouncers to keep pilgrims from pirating pieces of the cross. Egeria notes that, on one specific occasion, "one [of the pilgrims] bit off a piece of the holy wood and stole it away. For this reason," she explained, "the deacons stand around and keep watch in case anyone dares to do the same again" (*Travels* 37.2, trans. by J. Wilkinson [1971]).

By Justinian's time, when the anonymous pilgrim from Piacenza visited Jerusalem, reverence still pulled people to this supposed fragment of the "true cross" – and the nature of the visit had become even more theatrical. "You can see the place where [Jesus] was crucified," our anonymous pilgrim reports, "and on the actual rock there is a bloodstain." The wood of the cross itself was kept in the courtyard of the basilica in a small side room. "We venerated it with a kiss," the pilgrim says. This ritual of adoration extended to "the title [plaque] which [the executioners] had placed over the Lord's head, on which they wrote 'This is the King of the Jews.'" It also included "the sponge and reed mentioned in the Gospel [on which Jesus had been offered a drink of wine]" and "the onyx cup which [Jesus] had blessed at supper" (*Account of the Piacenza Pilgrim* 20, trans. by J. Wilkinson [1977]).

A generation later, in 612–614 CE, when Jerusalem was taken by the Sasanian army, the Christian pilgrim-industry was thrown into disrepair. It also lit a fuse under the Emperor Heraclius (r. 610–640 CE) to plot to recapture the city.

Figure 14.1 The Temple platform, where two Jewish Temples once stood until the second was destroyed by a Roman army in 70 CE. Almost every Christian Roman emperor from the politically accommodating, like Constantine, to hard-liners like Theodosius chose to leave it barren and desolate. In doing so, all asserted the political and cultural superiority of Christianity over Jewish history by leaving this important Jewish worship place in ruins. Beginning with the Umayyad ruler 'Abd al-Malik, Muslim rulers of Jerusalem – looking to distinguish themselves from other "People of the Book" – would communicate the same message taking a slightly different approach. Instead of leaving the platform in ruins, 'Abd al-Malik would erect the shrine, the Dome of the Rock, directly in its center. By the tenth century CE, a mosque would be constructed nearby (off to the right). The site is known in Arabic as Al Haram al Sharif ("The Noble Sanctuary"). Photo credit: Author's photo, 2007.

This urban effect had been carefully stage-managed and planned. Both the Christian emperor Constantine and the Christian Justinian had decided not to invest any of the empire's money in the ruined Temple Mount. In doing so, they argued with their silence, as countless Christian writers would allege in their sermons and writings, that Jesus' death had rendered Jewish worship obsolete and outdated.

In Justinian's time, these were not novel ideas; they already had a long history. Ever since the first Gospel had been composed, sometime around 70 CE and attributed to an author named "Mark," Jesus' followers had wrestled with the Jewish roots of their movement. Debates about how much or even whether Jesus' Jewish and gentile followers should embrace Jewish ritual and tradition led to periods of vicious in-fighting. These conflicts would become particularly acute during the first-century war with Rome. They would also plan the seeds of the pernicious anti-Jewish ideology which would circulate later.

Mark's story about Jesus' arrival in Jerusalem exposes this undercurrent of thinking, one which would swell into more open hostility against Jews in later centuries. "Mark," written about a generation after Jesus' death, describes what happened in Jerusalem this way: After making the tiring journey from the Galilee region, Jesus visits the Temple; but the hour is rather later, and so he plans to return in the morning. The next day, before Jesus ascends the Temple Mount – when he will famously cleanse it of its moneychangers and curse their allegedly corrupt practices – "Mark" recounts the following odd story:

> On the following day, when they came from Bethany, [Jesus] was hungry. Seeing in the distance a fig tree in leaf, he went to see whether perhaps he would find anything on it. When he came to it, he found nothing but leaves, for it was not the season for figs. He said to it, "May no one ever eat fruit from you again." Then they came to Jerusalem. And he entered the temple... (Mark 11.12–14 [NRSV])

Jesus and his disciples leave Jerusalem later that evening, but in the morning, one of them makes a shocking discovery. "Rabbi, look!" Peter calls out. "The fig tree that you cursed has withered" (Mark 11.21 [NRSV]).

Why has Jesus taken out his hunger pains on an innocent fruit tree for not offering him breakfast? The episode is made stranger still – and Jesus' anger, even more irrational – by the inclusion of an authorial comment: "It was not the season for figs." Odd though it is to us, the tale must have comforted Mark's readers and listeners. Mark' story about the death of the tree, cursed never to bear figs again, frames Jesus' climactic encounter with the Temple moneychangers. "Mark" has used Jesus' interaction with the fig tree to "predict" the Temple's destruction – not exactly a difficult bit of mental magic since the Gospel was likely written after the Roman army had already destroyed the building.

For Jewish members of Mark's community, people who lived through the turbulent 70s CE, "Jesus' words" must have been comfortingly reassuring. The message that they heard in the Gospel was that Jesus "knew" the Second Temple had to be destroyed. In fact, it was as if Jesus had eerily foreseen the struggles and wars of the late first century CE, a period when every Jew in Jerusalem – not just Jesus' followers – was now confronted with the horror of having watched a foreign army decimate their holiest site. Mark's conviction, expressed in the vivid storytelling of his Gospel, was that the loss of the Temple was part of God's plan.

Even though Mark's community never referred to itself as "Christians," their unique explanation for understanding what happened to the Temple would morph into an expressly Christian worldview. It would also have deleterious effects on Jewish–Christian relations. In the fourth century CE, Constantine would leave the Temple Mount barren to confirm that its fate was exactly as Mark's "Jesus" predicted it was be. Two centuries later, Emperor Justinian created an newer, grander focal point for the city, doubling down on the specious assertion that the Christian faith had "replaced" Jewish worship.

This long backstory helps explain why, in 630 CE, when Jerusalem was recaptured, the Christian emperor Heraclius maintained the same "Jerusalem policy" as his Christian predecessors. Heraclius had waged a heroic military campaign. Over the course of nearly six years, he and his army had repelled Sasanian forces from lands formerly controlled by Constantinople. The emperor himself is alleged to have marched into the Sasanian capital, at Ctesiphon (outside modern Baghdad), and recovered the fragments of the "holy cross of the Lord" which the Sasanian raiders had pilfered from Jerusalem (Sebeos, *History* 29.99, trans. by R. Bedrosian [1985]). Yet even as these pieces of wood were being gloriously restored to the Church of the Holy Sepulcher – "There was no small amount of joy on the day they entered Jerusalem," the seventh-century writer Sebeos reports, writing in Armenian – centuries of rubble at the old Temple Mount remained.

The opinions of Jews who longed to recover the Temple did not matter to Christian politicians who had been raised to believe that Jesus had "predicted" its destruction all along.

Jesus' end-time preaching and Jerusalem before the seventh century CE

The events of 70 CE would shape Late Antique history in yet other profoundly important ways related to Christian hope for the Second Coming of Jesus.

After the Roman attack, as the Temple Mount collapsed into a wasteland, a desolate site where no one could afford to be caught wandering, Jesus' followers faced a difficult decision: Should they continue to embrace Jesus' Jewish heritage and identify themselves as "Jews," or should they articulate a new name for themselves, something distinct? Not coincidentally, the first appropriation of the word "Christian" by Jesus' followers dates to this period, after 70 CE.

A new name, however, did not soothe the crippling anxiety which many of them had about the missing Temple. "Mark" had tried to ease their concerns by suggesting Jesus had foreseen this period of difficulty, too. In a key monologue, set in Jerusalem, Jesus is alleged to have said:

> "When you hear of wars and rumors of wars, do not be alarmed; this must take place, but the end is still to come. For nation will rise against nation, and kingdom against kingdom; there will be earthquakes in various places; there will be famines. This is but the beginning of the birth pangs.… But when you see the desolating sacrilege set up where it ought not to be (let the reader understand), then those in Judea must flee to the mountains.… So also, when you see these things taking place, you know that he is near, at the very gates. Truly I tell you, this generation will not pass away until all these things have taken place." (Mark 13.7–8, 14, 29–30 [*NRSV*])

The passage is filled with apocalyptic rhetoric. In fact, in many scholars' opinion, it is very close to preserving the very end-time teachings that may have earned Jesus a questionable reputation in the early first century CE. As Jesus' speech appears here in "Mark," however, one detail raises a red flag for historians. "*Let the reader understand*" is the author's interruption, not Jesus'. It cannot be a part of Jesus' speech because Jesus, we know, never wrote anything down.

Why does the author "Mark" interrupt this dramatic story at such a crucial point? One answer is that he wants readers to understand its relevance to their current situation. For although Jesus may have taught his disciples that the end was near in their own lifetime ("Truly I tell you, this generation will not pass away until all these things have taken place"), those who lived after his execution knew differently. Nothing had happened. By choosing to dramatize Jesus' speech *now*, during the war with Rome (66–74 CE), Mark reassures his community that the end was finally coming: amid the "wars and rumors of war" in the late first century CE, as "nation [was rising] against nation."

Whether Mark was quoting Jesus cannot be known. Actual first-hand testimony, written down in Jesus' lifetime, preserving Jesus' own words, does not exist. And yet, even if we admit the limitations of our evidence, we can still draw an important historical conclusion from "Mark's" text. By the late first century CE, some of Jesus' followers believed that the Messiah's return would happen in Jerusalem.

Two decades after the Gospel of Mark was written, the author of Revelation would make a similar claim. (According to the text, the writer was a man named John from Patmos, an island off the coast of Asia Minor.) In his writings, this John describes a powerful vision that came to him:

> Then I saw a new heaven and a new earth; for the first heaven and the first earth had passed away, and the sea was no more. And I saw the holy city, the new Jerusalem, coming down out of heaven from God, prepared as a bride adorned for her husband. And I heard a loud voice from the throne saying, "See, the home of God is among mortals. He will dwell with them as their God; they will be his peoples, and God himself will be with them; he will wipe every tear from their eyes. Death will be no more; mourning and crying and pain will be no more, for the first things have passed away [in advance of the Second Coming of the Messiah].... Write this, for these words are trustworthy and true" (Revelation 21.1–6 [*NRSV*])

As this passage shows, less than a generation after "Mark's" time, still more followers of Jesus were convinced that the Messiah's return was intimately intertwined with visions of Jerusalem, "the holy city." These fantastic scenes, which the writer calls a "prophecy," were revealed to him by God through the work of "an angel" (Revelation 1.1) – a Greek word which means *messenger* (*aggelos* [ἄγγελος] pronounced "angellos"). According to John, God's "messenger" came to him and told him, "Now write what you have seen, what is, and what is to take place after this" (Revelation 1.19).

End-time preaching and Jerusalem during the seventh century CE

This text presents challenges for historians because its visions – of angels and demons and of stories loaded with symbolism – are so utterly unmoored from reality. In one chapter, combining prose and poetry, the writer invokes the help of another "messenger" to predict the downfall of "Babylon." "Fallen, fallen is Babylon the great!/It has become a dwelling place of demons..." (Revelation 18.1 [*NRSV*]), the author wails. The reference is not to the bygone Babylonian Empire but to the world of the early Christians, living in the Roman Empire.

The text of Revelation presents the complicated struggle of Jesus' followers trying to find their way in the cosmopolitan world of Rome as a spiritual battle with end-time dimensions against demonic enemies, who are characterized as being offsprings of the "whore of Babylon."

Six hundred years after Jesus' alleged prediction of an imminent catastrophe ("Truly I tell you, this generation will not pass away until all these things have taken place"), the belief that Christians were witnessing the final times remained a strong one. To Christians of the Emperor Heraclius' reign, for example, the Persian capture of the "true cross" and the taking of the holy city of Jerusalem looked like an incontrovertible sign that the world was rushing fast towards its long-prophesied doomsday.

One writer, Theophylact Simocotta, expressed this very anxiety. Born in the late sixth century CE, in Egypt (very little about him is known outside his monumental work of history, not even his exact birth date or birth year), Theophylact lived at the time when news of the Sasanian army's attack on Jerusalem began to spread. He also lived to see Emperor Heraclius, in 620 CE, wage a successful counter-attack. Writing his *History* shortly thereafter, Theophylact uses the figure of the Sasanian King Khusrow II to reassure Roman readers that the emperor's victory was not only foreordained; it was a heaven-sent sign that would hasten the end. "Be assured that troubles will flow back in turn against you Romans," Khusrow II says. The king continues:

> The Babylonian race [the Sasanians] will hold the Roman state in its power for a threefold cyclic group-of-seven years [ancient Greek can express this unit of measure-ment in one word: *hebdomad*]. Thereafter you Romans will enslave Persians for a fifth group-of-seven years. When these very things have been accomplished, the day without evening will dwell among mortals and the expected fate will achieve power, when the forces of destruction will be handed over to dissolution and those of the better life hold sway. (Theophylact, *History* 5.15.5–7, trans. by M. and M. Whitby [1986])

Theophylact's readers must have delighted in the speech since they knew, from their own vantage in the middle of the seventh century CE, that Khusrow's "prophecy" had come true. The king had died, a Christian emperor had overturned "the Babylonian race," and Sasanian Persia no longer threatened the people of the empire.

The emotional effect of the king's "prophecy" must have also been reassuring, among certain Christians. For, according to Theophylact's script, the emperor's vic-tory and the return of the "true cross" to Jerusalem heralded a crystal-clear message from God: "The day without evening" – the last day – was finally near. Drawing upon belief in an imminent Second Coming, Theophylact cast a golden, almost heavenly glow on the world of the seventh-century CE eastern Mediterranean. That light radiated upon Jerusalem.

14.2 The Social World of the Arabian Peninsula in the Sixth Century CE

As we left the reign of Emperor Justinian, we journeyed with Cosmas Indicopleustes on a voyage to the Indian Ocean. In addition to taking us far beyond the Mediterranean, allowing us to gain a view from the ground of people and customs in South and Central Asia, Cosmas sharpened our understanding of the world closer to his own home, too. During the sixth century, East Roman traders now felt comfortable sailing east through the Red Sea into the Gulf of Aden – in effect, bypassing Sasanian tax stations on the overland route. As a result, the southern Arabian peninsula became a crucial geographic pawn in the games played by these two empires.

The situation in the south peninsula must have been tense, especially as it was set against the backdrop of a fragile peace in the north. There, Arab-Roman and Arab-Sasanian allies had been enlisted to secure the borderlands. By 570 CE, the Sasanian King Khusrow II made a bold gamble: He invaded the territory of modern Yemen and installed a Sasanian governor to disrupt Roman traders. By 610, the two empires were locked in outright war. Virtually two entire dioceses, of the East and of Egypt, would be lost. Emperor Heraclius would respond to the challenge.

Inside the confines of the Arabian peninsula, boxed in by the hard and soft power plays of Sasanian and Roman leaders, another story was already in progress.

The interior of the Arabian peninsula held little interest to rulers of Rome or Persia. That, at least, would explain why each empire enlisted Arab families to police the northern borders and why the center of the peninsula was never a prized land-grab for either state. The two empires' stark political borders were not sealed cultural boundaries, however. For centuries, people of Arabia had been trading with their neighbors on all sides. Leather – for belts, tents, and military use – was a key commodity, valued by Romans and Sasanians alike. Values were another. The ability, indeed, the willingness of the local Jafnid and Nasrid families to work with the Roman and Sasanian government reveals a second, subtler kind of exchange. Certainly there were many local leaders who recognized the benefits of being politically, not just economically, engaged with people beyond the peninsula.

Daily life unfolded across the peninsula in many ways, and geographic and environmental factors played a critical role shaping this social world. Two places where we can detect the rhythms of sixth- and seventh-century daily life the best are merchant oases and desert sanctuaries.

Merchant oases and desert sanctuaries

Blankets of sand cover a large portion of the peninsula, but there are significant respites. A rugged plateau called the Hijaz lines the western peninsula, along the Red Sea. The cities of Yathrib and Mecca are located here, and each in their own way is indicative of the kinds of cities one would find on the peninsula. Mecca was the center of an important sanctuary; Yathrib, a city whose name was later changed to Medina (meaning, "The City" [of the Prophet Muhammad]), the location of a vital oasis. Both shed light on daily life at the dawn of Islam.

Yathrib, in the west, was like sites as far away as the Persian Gulf and the Gulf of Oman. Medina has changed quite dramatically from its appearance in the sixth century, but the fifteenth-century city of Birkat al-Mawz, in modern Oman, can provide a comparative, evocative example of what it might have looked like. Situated in the shadow of the mountains, Birkat al-Mawz is a lush settlement of mud-brick houses surrounded by green date palms and banana trees. Local springs ensured a steady agricultural harvest both for the oasis's residents and for families in surrounding villages who were dependent on it.

Sixth-century Yathrib would have fit this profile. Date groves flourished around the local springs, and the oasis as a whole benefited from its position at the base of the mountainous Hijaz region. We can even sketch a rough profile of its residents. Organized in tribes, as life was elsewhere throughout the peninsula, Yathrib's residents were a diverse group, including many Jewish families who lived at the oasis and in its vicinity.

Mecca may not have been as verdant, but it was equally thriving. Unfortunately, archaeological information about life in the sixth- and seventh-century town is slim, so we need to look elsewhere to create a mental picture of it. One site which might be useful in this regard is the location of a desert sanctuary that has been excavated in modern Yemen, at Ma'rib. The sanctuary of Almaqah at Ma'rib was an important pre-Islamic religious site (Figure 14.2). Archaeological evidence suggests that it remained in use at least through the fourth century CE, if not later. Similar sites, focused on other gods, can be found across the Arabian peninsula.

The deities worshipped at these shrines were diverse. Many were related to the stars, the sun, the moon, and the cosmos, like the god Almaqah, to whom the sanctuary at Ma'rib was dedicated. Sites like these, "cut off" from other places, were considered holy and were called in Arabic *haram*, a word for "sanctuary." Apart from being places where people interacted with their gods, a *haram* also played a key role in daily human interactions on the peninsula. The space inside the boundaries of a *haram* offered a neutral ground where individuals, families, and tribes could come, meet, and resolve their differences. Violence here was socially forbidden; the local families in charge of maintaining the site ensured it.

This background is crucial for getting a feel of sixth-century Mecca, site of the holiest sanctuary in Islam. Today, skyscrapers and other ambitious buildings rise from the desert. But at the turn of the seventh century, Mecca was a desert sanctuary town. Like Ma'rib, it was the site of an important local shrine, the Ka'ba, or "Cube," which housed a sacred black stone. By the sixth century CE, one local family, the Quraysh, maintained and administered this holy site. They proved quite capable stewards, and their leadership drew a mixture of local families and traders to Mecca.

14.3   The Believers Movement

Muhammad (b. *c.* 570 CE) grew up in this world of merchant oases and local shrines. That might be the extent of what we can safely say about his early life. The details of Muhammad's birth, even the year, are not preserved in any sixth-century documents. But the lack of precise information for one man born on the Arabian peninsula should hardly be surprising, especially given how little we know about the lives of Muhammad's contemporaries – the historian Theophylact, for example – whose writings are important for understanding the seventh-century Roman Empire.

Figure 14.2 Among the people living in the southwestern Arabian peninsula were the Sabaeans, who had come to power around the eighth century BCE. The Sabaeans built this sanctuary at Ma'rib, in modern Yemen. It was dedicated to Almaqah and received worshippers for more than a thousand years, until at least the third or fourth century CE. Sabaean architecture helps scholars visualize the landscape of the pre-Islamic Arabian peninsula. These square-shaped pillars formed part of the sanctuary's entrance. Similar cuboid forms appear throughout Arabia, in part because of the long-established custom there of artists working in stone (in contrast to the Roman world where pourable concrete inspired different forms). Managed by a local family, the Ma'rib sanctuary provided a safe space where individuals from different tribes or with competing interests might come together. Both in form and in its custom, the Ma'rib sanctuary evokes the social world of other sanctuaries on the pre-Islamic Arabian peninsula, like Mecca. Photo credit: Eric Lafforgue/Alamy Stock Photo (2006).

Stories that were told about Muhammad's early life cannot be dismissed so readily, however. These are signs of a rich biographical tradition that his followers passed down in the centuries after his death (632 CE). It developed for good reason. The movement that Muhammad founded, which we call "Islam," toppled the status quo in Mecca at the sanctuary of the Ka'ba and radically transformed the social and political relationship between the Arabian peninsula and the Roman and Sasanian Empires. As we will see, the circumstances that led to this transformation was a series of relentless battles waged outside the peninsula.

The success of Muhammad's movement was also dependent on something else: the creation of a new sense of community. Their strong group identity sprang in large part from a seminal collection of Arabic texts, called the "Recitations," or the "Qur'an." According to Islamic tradition, Muhammad had received these revelations directly from a monotheistic deity, Allah. Then, they were written down in Arabic exactly as Allah had revealed them to him. Consisting of 114 chapters, subdivided into verses, the Qur'an remains the holiest text for Muslims today.

An essential starting point for thinking about the Arabian world of the sixth and seventh centuries is that neither the name "Islam" nor the word "Muslim" were ever used by Muhammad's first followers in the way they have come to be used now. The text of the Qur'an makes this point abundantly clear, largely referring to the people of the earliest community as *mu'minum*, or the "Believers." This Arabic word (singular, *mu'min*) is used almost a thousand times in the Qur'an; the word *muslim*, meaning "one who submits," is used less than a hundred.

Of course, members of this community eventually did embrace the name "Muslim" as part of their identity. But the process by which that happened – the *history* of how the early "Believers" movement grew into a community of "Muslims" – is precisely what we're studying. For that reason alone, it is crucial not to rush our story by starting to talk about the religion of "Islam" or seventh-century "Muslims." As with the followers of Jesus, who came to embrace their identity as "Christians" only about three generations after his death, so, too, would followers of Muhammad come to embrace their identity as "Muslims" only about a century after their prophet's death.

How, when, and why that happened are historical questions. They cannot be passed over because we think we know how the story of Islam may have started. One text from the seventh century CE confirms the workings of this complicated process.

The Constitution of Medina

For the members of the earliest community, Muhammad's companions, it was their identity as "Believers" which brought them together (*Key Debates* 14.1: Muhammad's "House" and the Development of Early Mosque Architecture). The importance of this term of self-identity is substantiated in a document, written in Arabic, that is not contained in the Qur'an. It was written around 622 CE, the year in which Muhammad left his home in Mecca to move north to the city of Yathrib. This text is known as the "Constitution of Medina," also called the *umma* document.

Unfortunately, no seventh-century copy of this artifact has yet been discovered, but scholars are virtually certain it existed. The text is known from the reports of two later writers – one living in the mid-eighth century CE, another in the ninth century CE. Although historians are naturally trained to be skeptical of documents attested in later authorities, scholars who have studied the text of the "Constitution of Medina" are virtually unanimous that it dates to the seventh century CE. For one, its language is filled with many archaic Arabic expressions dated to that time period. Secondly – and perhaps more significantly – it presents a view of Muhammad's movement that departs in radical ways from the stories which later developed about early Islam.

Key Debates 14.1 *Muhammad's House and the Development of Early Mosque Architecture*

After the emigration, in 622 CE, Muhammad acquired land in Yathrib where he built a house and a worship space, or *masjid*, for his community. (*Masjid* is the Arabic word for "mosque.") This famous story is recounted in many Arabic sources. It plays an important role in modern conversations about the development of Islamic architecture.

According to one of the prophet's first biographers, Ibn Sa'd of Baghdad (d. 844 CE), Muhammad let his camel take the lead in choosing the site where the Believers would worship. This trusted animal wandered upon a local animal pen and threshing floor which belonged to two orphans. The prophet offered to pay the orphans so that he could build a *masjid* on their land, but the boys graciously declined, insisting that they give it to Muhammad as a gift. Muhammad paid them anyway (Ibn Sa'd, *The Great Book of Generations*, volume 1.2.65). This space became Muhammad's house and the Believers' first mosque.

A robust tradition developed about what it looked like. Ibn Sa'd himself gives detailed measurements for its size and the materials from which it was constructed. The building was 100 cubits long by 100 cubits wide and was enclosed by a wall made of palm trunks and branches. Muhammad lived in rooms constructed of mud brick, covered with palm branches; and three gates allowed access into and out of the courtyard. The *qibla*, or direction of prayer, was marked to the north, facing Jerusalem (Ibn Sa'd, *The Great Book of Generations*, volume 1.2.65–66).

This ground plan is remarkably similar to later mosques. The eighth-century mosque in Damascus and the tenth-century mosque in Cordoba, on the Iberian peninsula,

share the same traits. This similarity has led some architectural historians to deduce that Muhammad's property was "a house only incidentally" and that, from the beginning, it "was intended … to serve as a focal point for the new Islamic community" (Robert Hillenbrand, *Islamic Architecture* [New York: Columbia University Press, 1994], p. 39). This claim – that Muhammad, in 622 CE, established the prototype for all later mosques – is provocative but not easy to evaluate. Arabic sources state that Muhammad's "house" was destroyed during an extensive renovation in 638 CE, and no archaeological evidence exists which can confirm or refute Ibn Sa'd's account.

Ibn Sa'd's story has also now come under scrutiny. For the measurements he gives happen to be the same as the courtyard of Solomon's First Temple in Jerusalem, as described in Jewish Scripture (Ezekiel 40.47). The broad outline of Ibn Sa'd's narrative – Muhammad finds a threshing floor, offers money to transform it, is graciously refused, then pays for it anyway – also mirrors an episode in Jewish Scripture (2 Samuel 24.18–25) which describes how King David laid the foundations for the Jerusalem Temple. For these reasons, one scholar has characterized the Arabic history of Muhammad's house as "an elaborate literary confection" (Jeremy Johns, "The 'House of the Prophet' and the Concept of the Mosque," in *Bayt al-Maqdis, Jerusalem and Early Islam*, ed. by Jeremy Johns [Oxford: Oxford University Press, 1999], pp. 59–112, at p. 107).

What Muhammad's property looked like in the seventh century CE will probably not be answered soon. Archaeological fieldwork is not currently permitted in Medina.

The events that led to the birth of this document are important. Muhammad's "emigration" to Yathrib in 622 CE, or *hijra,* would come to mark a crucial turning point for the Believers, largely because it was not a journey that happened under auspicious circumstances. Twelve years earlier in Mecca, in 610 CE – perhaps around the time he was forty, if his birth tradition can be accepted – Muhammad had begun to receive his revelations. Over the course of the next decade, he had brought this new, monotheistic message to the residents of his hometown. To the family in charge of the Ka'ba, people who had built a name for themselves and their city by successfully administering and growing their sanctuary, Muhammad's teachings aroused suspicion and maybe even fear about whether he intended to upset the status quo. In 622 CE, as a result of disagreements with the Quraysh, the family in charge of the sanctuary, Muhammad and his companions sought refuge in Yathrib.

Muhammad's "emigration" to Yathrib would prove foundational to his movement's development. Shortly after Muhammad's death, his followers would start to record time around their memory of that journey; the year of the emigration would now mark "year one" in their new community calendar. (Following the precedent for recording Christian time with "A.D." [*anno Domini,* "year of our Lord"], this new method of telling Islamic time is now abbreviated "A.H.," or *anno Hegirae* ["year of the *hijra*"].) The city of Yathrib itself would eventually come to be known by a different name, *al-medinat al-nabi,* "the city of the prophet," or Medina, in Saudi Arabia.

The "Constitution of Medina" was written shortly after Muhammad and his companions arrived in Yathrib. It outlines a settlement that was negotiated between Muhammad, his companions, and the leading families of Yathrib who were supporters of his movement. Throughout the text, the people who belong to Muhammad's movement are called the "Believers." The document as a whole articulates a plan for cooperation and mutual respect between participating parties, many of whom included local Jewish tribes living in this area of the Arabian peninsula:

> Whoever follows us among the Jews shall have assistance and equitable treatment; they shall not be oppressed, nor shall [any of us] gang up against them. The peace of the Believers is indivisible. No Believer shall make a [separate] peace to the exclusion of … [another] Believer in fighting in the path of God, except on the basis of equity and justice among them. … The Jews of [the local tribe] Banu 'Awf are a community [*umma*] with the Believers. (The "Constitution of Medina," sections 16–17, 25, trans. by F. Donner, *Muhammad and the Believers at the Origins of Islam* [Cambridge, MA: Belknap Press, 2010], pp. 227–232, based on the text from Ibn Ishaq [d. 767 CE])

The "Constitution of Medina" is an extraordinary source because it shows that Muhammad's vision for his early seventh-century community, or *umma,* was large enough to include other monotheists, like Yathrib's local Jewish families.

The constitution itself carried with it the authority that came from Muhammad's stature as an "apostle of God," the one to whom Allah had made his revelations. As the document states, "God [Allah] supports whatever is most righteous and upright in this treaty." This political allegiance – between Muhammad's emigrant group and his supporters in Yathrib – established a coalition that would eventually wrestle control of the Ka'ba from Mecca's leaders. It was also rooted in a shared commitment to the power and meaning of the prophet's "Recitations."

An apocalyptic component

In order to gain a fuller perspective of the social profile of the "Believers," we should examine some of the characteristics we can glean about them from the Qur'an. According to Islamic commentators, Muhammad's first revelations had come between 610 and 622 CE while he was living in Mecca. After the emigration to Yathrib, more followed. Taken together, these texts comprise the 114 chapters, or *suras*, of the Qur'an.

Among the many historical details that can emerge from a close reading of the text are two that deserve comment here. The first relates to the urgent nature of Muhammad's message. In many *suras*, listeners and readers are urged to change their ethical behavior because of the looming nature of the end times. This cosmic catastrophe lurks in the following verses, thought to have been revealed at Mecca:

> How many a sign is there in the heavens and the earth, which they pass by with face averted! And most of them believe not in God [Allah] except that they attribute partners (to Him). Deem they themselves secure from the coming on them of a pall of God's punishment, or the coming of the Hour suddenly while they are unaware? (*Qur'ān* 12 [Mecca]: 105–107, trans. by M. Pickthall [1938])

Here, those who have not joined the community of Believers are castigated for not recognizing the divine signs "in the heavens and the earth," cosmic signs which forecast the coming wrath of Allah. By contrast, those who *have* joined the movement, people who now follow the revelations to Muhammad, know that God's "punishment" demands they reset their moral and spiritual compass, especially when one considers the "coming of the Hour" (*Political Issues* 14.1: What Effect Did the Rise of Islam Have on Daily Life in the Christian Roman Empire?).

Political Issues 14.1   *What Effect Did the Rise of Islam Have on Daily Life in the Christian Roman Empire?*

After Muhammad's death (632 CE), the Believers' movement and its leaders expanded their territorial possessions via military means. By 633, the entire Arabian peninsula, not just isolated cities like Medina and Mecca, would be brought under their authority. During these battles, the Believers thought of themselves as striving, or fighting, for God. The Arabic word that expressed that idea is *jihad*.

The campaigns to acquire political authority across the peninsula, combined with an ideological belief that the Believers were doing God's work, pushed the community to wage even bolder campaigns. Soon, Muhammad's followers would arrive at the border of the Roman and Sasanian Empires. By 636 CE, the Roman army would be forced to engage this new military threat. At the battle of Yarmuk, in Roman Syria, fortune favored the Believers' army. Within two years, the territory of Roman Syria, as well as the land to its south – including Jerusalem – would fall from Roman hands.

The images of a fierce, relentless Islamic conquest, especially associated with the word *jihad*, can cloud our picture of daily life in the seventh century. Two documents, both written in Greek, offer a substantial rebuttal to those who think that the eastern Mediterranean was thrown into chaos with the spread of the Believers' movement. Both texts were laid in the ground as mosaics.

In Gadara (Hammat Gader, in Israel), we learn about an important repair to the city's baths that dates to the period of the Believers' expansion. According to the mosaic:

> In the days of the servant of God, Mu'awiya, the commander of the faithful, the hot baths of the people there [in Gadara] were saved and rebuilt by 'Abd Allah son of Abu Hashim, the governor, for the healing of the sick. [It was done] under the care of Ioannes, the official of Gadara on the 5th of December, on the second day of the week, in the 6th year of the indiction, in the 726th year since the colony's foundation, in the 42nd year according to the Arabs. (Translation adapted from R. Hoyland, *Seeing Islam as Others Saw It* [Princeton: Darwin Press, 1997], p. 690, no. 7)

The year A.H. 42 corresponds to 662–663 CE, which means this text dates about a generation after the Believers had conquered Roman Syria and the land around Jerusalem. Instead of speaking to an irreconcilable age of conflict, however, the announcement emphasizes the opposite. In Gadara, the new governor worked with residents to preserve and repair their hot springs. They did so likely because they shared a common goal in bringing the facilities back to life: boosting tourism.

Since Roman times, Gadara had been a destination for pleasure-seekers. One fourth-century CE writer dared to claim: "Gadara, a place which has warm baths in Syria, [is] inferior only to those at Baiae in Italy" (Eunapius, *Lives of the Philosophers*, section 458, LCL trans. by W. Wright [1921]). No doubt the town council approved of this publicity. Intense local pride, combined with steady revenue from visitors, likely explains why the Believers joined with locals to repair the springs in the seventh century CE. Even "the commander of the faithful" could recognize their benefits.

When did the early Believers expect this "Hour" to arrive exactly? It is an important question. As we have repeatedly learned from our studies of Hellenistic Judaism and early Christianity, apocalyptic thinking – even when it dwells on a Last Judgment and the end of the world – does not need to specify an imminent, or immediate, event for the speaker's message to have a certain energetic quality. What, then, can we deduce about the Believers' movement?

Evidence from the Qur'an suggests that they not only understood "the Hour" was approaching, soon, but that some of the first signs of this divine reckoning had already come: "The Hour drew near and the moon was rent in two," reads one sura (*Qur'ān* 54 [Mecca]: 1–5, trans. by M. Pickthall (1938)). "And if they behold a sign they turn away and say: 'Prolonged illusion.'" The text implies that people in Muhammad's lifetime have already been exposed to the warning signs that the "Hour" was near. It chastises anyone who interprets these signs as an "illusion."

An initial focus on Jerusalem

A second aspect of the Believers' movement is apparent when examining the chapters of the Qur'an. We can see that the Believers' understanding of which direction to pray was not the one handed down through Islamic tradition. Today, Muslims pray towards Mecca. The earliest Believers – driven from that desert sanctuary city, in effect, locked out of Muhammad's hometown – prayed the opposite direction: to Jerusalem.

From their earliest formation, a shared "direction of prayer" (qibla, in Arabic) had contributed to the Believers' strong sense of communal identity. When, in 630 CE, Muhammad marshaled the forces in Yathrib to march on Mecca, that community was given a new directional focus: the Ka'ba. Cleansing the shrine of its "pagan" character and taking forceful control of the city from the tribe who had managed it, Muhammad thus established Mecca as the center of the Believers' movement.

One important hint that the community's first qibla, or prayer direction, was changed after the emigration to Yathrib appears at sura 2.

> And when we made the House [at Mecca] a resort for people and a sanctuary [saying]: Take as your place of worship the place where Abraham stood.... The foolish of the people will say: What has turned them from the prayer direction (qibla) which they formerly observed? Say: To God belong the east and the west. He guides whom He wills to a straight path.... And we appointed the prayer direction which you formerly observed only that we might know him who follows the Messenger from him who turns on his heels. (Qur'ān 2 [Medina]: 124–126, 142–143, trans. by M. Pickthall, slightly modified [1938])

Although the text of the Qur'an does not name the city from which the Believers have turned their prayer, biographies of the prophet, like the one written by Ibn Sa'd, make clear that "the prayer direction which [the Believers] formerly observed" was Jerusalem.

There is also good circumstantial reason to think Jerusalem was the focus of their initial prayer. Many of the Believers' contemporaries, both Christians and Jews, thought that Jerusalem would be the setting for the explosive end-time events described in their own traditions. For a community steeped in apocalyptic imagery, as Muhammad's early community was, Jerusalem would have been a natural focus for their prayers. The Believers' awareness of this wider Mediterranean conversation – about the importance of Jerusalem in God's plans – would also explain why, in their military expansion, they soon made plans to seize it (Working With Sources 14.1: The Hunting Lodge at Qusayr 'Amra, Jordan; Figures 14.3 and 14.4).

Working With Sources 14.1

The Hunting Lodge at Qusayr ʿAmra, Jordan

Maintaining good diplomatic relations with Roman government was a high priority for leaders of the early Islamic Empire. Naturally, such meetings led to the potential for other kinds of dialogue between the Christian state and the Islamic state. The architecture and wall paintings from the site of Qusayr ʿAmra in modern Jordan, east of the capital Amman, offers a specific setting where these kinds of subtler exchanges took place.

Qusayr ʿAmra functioned as a hunting lodge, thought to have been built c.723–744 CE by Walid II, although a slightly earlier date in the eighth century has also been proposed (Garth Fowden, *Qusayr ʿAmra: Art and the Umayyad Elite in Late Antique Syria* [Berkeley: University of California Press, 2004]). Constructed of local limestone, it dazzled guests with a reception hall, a dining room, and a bathing establishment, where the Muslim governor of the region, who was known as an *amir*, or "military commander," hosted embassies and friends. The desert site helped the *amir* cultivate a working friendship with ambassadors sent south from the Roman Empire.

Qusayr ʿAmra's fine bathing amenities and sophisticated use of water showcased the wealth and technological resources of its owner and host.

Wall paintings inside the lodge also left an impression on guests. In the main entry hall, to the right of where the *amir* would have received visitors, was a scene of six intimidating figures. From their position high on the side wall, they would have looked like a parade of eminent dignitaries who had come to pay their respects to the *amir*, seated below. The paintings are in poor condition today, but four were labeled. They were known rulers of the Late Antique world. The four who are labeled are "Caesar" (ruler of the Roman Empire), "Khusrow" (or Shah, the King of the Sasanian Empire), "Roderick," King of the Visigoths in Spain, and "Negus," the honorary title of the ruler of Ethiopia. The identity of the remaining two is not certain. However, based on the fact that their four companions are heads of state, historians have plausibly deduced that one might be the ruler of a Central Asian kingdom along the Silk Road – perhaps Sogdiana, in Uzbekistan. The other might have depicted the emperor of China.

As prominent faces in the *amir*'s reception hall, these leaders would have caught any visitor's eye, even if the scene bringing them all together was a pictorial invention. The Sasanian Empire had ceased to exist in 651 CE when its last shah was assassinated. King Roderick of Spain died in 711 CE when the Visigothic kingdom was conquered by a Muslim army. The paintings in the reception hall do not commemorate an actual gathering, then; it affirms the political authority of the *amir* by arguing that he is the rightful successor of empires that have come and gone. It also does so by placing him in the context of still-powerful rulers, like the Roman emperor in Constantinople.

These paintings, like the hunting lodge as a whole, addressed Muslim and non-Muslim visitors alike. Each figure is labeled in two languages: Arabic and Greek. Since the sixth century CE, Greek had been made the official language of the Roman Empire, spoken by all its diplomats and ambassadors.

Figure 14.3 From the outside, the hunting lodge at Qusayr 'Amra appears to be a modest structure whose domes and vaults, nevertheless, give it a dramatic profile against the desert landscape. Built of local limestone, the lodge sits in an area east of the Jordan River valley (modern Jordan, about 50 miles outside Amman) at the base of a wadi, or canyon, that fills with rain. In the foreground, at left, is a cistern for storing water. The lodge's entrance, with its dramatic triple-vaulted room, lit by high windows, is at right. This photograph of the property faces south. Early to mid-eighth century CE. Photo credit: © Walter Ward, 2007.

Figure 14.4 In contrast to its unadorned exterior, Qusayr 'Amra's interior walls, including its entry vaults, are awash in frescoes. Some painted scenes show women nude, alluding to the luxuries of the bath. Others, such as these two panels, promoted values that were important to the Umayyad elite. Located on the east vault of the reception hall, they are part of thirty-two scenes which show ordinary men at work: transporting materials, pounding anvils, carving stone. Although their message is perhaps not immediately apparent today, the lodge's owner may have commissioned these scenes of daily life because he saw building, like patronage, as a metaphor for good governance – a value shared by the Umayyads' neighbors. Early to mid-eighth century CE. Photo credit: © B. O'Kane/Alamy Stock Photo.

Summary

By the beginning of the eighth century CE, individuals within the "Believers" community will have embraced the name "Muslim" to refer to their distinctive beliefs; and they will have taken political control of Egypt, Syria, and Sasanian Persia, as well as Jerusalem. There, the dynasty of rulers known as the Umayyads would make a powerful statement about their possession of the city. They would build a shrine, the Dome of the Rock, directly on the Temple Mount, a site which had lain barren since 70 CE under all Christian Roman emperors. The world of the Arabian peninsula, out of which the army of Muhammad's believers had emerged, was not cut off or isolated from the broader social and cultural currents of the Mediterranean, however.

Apocalyptic thinking, which was prevalent in both the kingdoms of western Europe – in the territories that had once been under Roman control – and the Roman Empire in the east was one such shared characteristic. The political maneuvering of the Roman and Sasanian states in and around the southern Arabian peninsula during the late sixth century CE also may have shaped the society and culture of cities like Mecca and Yathrib. And while, over the next two hundred years and beyond, Muhammad's followers would expand their territorial holdings through military victory, their conquests also came with significant degrees of diplomacy and cultural negotiation.

Even their vision of a divinely inspired government was little different than the ideology which had underpinned the Sasanian Empire before its collapse and which was currently upholding the Roman Empire in Constantinople.

Study Questions

1. Name some reasons why Jerusalem was an important city for Christians at the start of the seventh century CE.
2. What is the "Constitution of Medina," and how does it shed light on the community founded by Muhammad and followers?
3. What beliefs, ideas, and values did Muslims and Christians share in the seventh and eighth centuries CE? Be sure to cite specific evidence to support your analysis.
4. From a historical perspective, would you say that individuals and communities who hold monotheistic beliefs ("belief in one God") are fundamentally unable to live in a pluralistic society?

Suggested Readings

Patricia Crone, *Meccan Trade and the Rise of Islam* (Piscataway: Gorgias Press, 2004).

Fred Donner, *Muhammad and the Believers: At the Origins of Islam* (Cambridge, MA: Belknap Press, 2012).

Jodi Magness, *The Archaeology of The Holy Land: From the Destruction of Solomon's Temple to the Muslim Conquest* (New York: Cambridge University Press, 2012).

Marcus Milwright, *An Introduction to Islamic Archaeology* (Edinburgh: Edinburgh University Press, 2010).

Glossary

A.D. ("Anno Domini") Latin for "In the Year of our Lord," a dating system that was first proposed in the sixth century CE.

A.H. ("Anno Hegirae") Latin for "In the Year of the Emigration (*hijra*)," this system of reckoning time is modeled after the Latin A.D. to express the Islamic custom of dating time from the year of Muhammad's journey from Mecca to Yathrib (Medina) in 622 CE.

amir A "military commander" within the early Islamic empire.

basileos **(plural:** *basileoi***)** The Greek word which captured the idea of the Latin "*imperator*," or emperor; it could also, however, be understood as "king." East Romans referred to their ruler as *basileos*.

Christ From the Greek word "Anointed," a word which Jesus' followers used to articulate their belief that Jesus was the "Messiah." It is not Jesus' last name, and its use in historical writing is highly questionable since not everyone, then or now, believes Jesus was the "Messiah."

Christianismos A Greek word, coined in the early second century CE. Often translated as "Christianity," so that it appears as something distinct from Judaism, this word was likely invented to capture a sense of "identifying openly as a 'Christian.'" As a term, then, it says very little about whether Christians saw themselves as having separated from their Jewish heritage or whether Christianity as a religion had parted ways from Judaism.

comes A special advisor to the emperor, or "count."

communitas As proposed by the anthropologist Victor Turner (1920–1983), this Latin word captures the social bonds that tie people together after a rite of passage, or initiation. To emphasize that this social connection endures even after individuals depart, Turner used the Latin word "*communitas*" to distinguish it from the common word for a gathering.

consul A government executive who served beneath the emperor although largely a ceremonial position. It had existed during the Republican period when the two consuls of Rome acted largely as the government's chief executives. By the later Empire, it was a political honor to hold the title.

A Social and Cultural History of Late Antiquity, First Edition. Douglas Boin.
© 2018 John Wiley & Sons, Inc. Published 2018 by John Wiley & Sons, Inc.

cosmocrator A Greek word usually used to refer to the Roman emperor's status as "ruler of the known world."

diocese One of twelve super-provinces created as part of Diocletian's restructuring of the Roman state in the late third century CE.

domus (**plural:** *domus*) The Latin word for "house."

dux The military governor of a province, as opposed to its civilian commander, the *praeses*.

episcopalis audientia The Latin phrase for "bishop's audience," a legal option for Romans who wished to have their grievances tried by a Christian church official, not by judges in the traditional Roman legal system.

episcopos (**plural:** *episcopoi*) Greek for "overseer," it later became one of the terms used to designate a "bishop" in the early Christian community. There is no historical evidence for the establishment of any such office prior to the first century CE, however.

epistula (**plural:** *epistulae*) The Latin word meaning "letter," or piece of correspondence; in a legal context, an emperor's letter had the force of law.

flamen (**plural:** *flamines*) Provincial priests of Rome's imperial cult, they oversaw sacrifices and temples for the deified rulers in the capital cities of the provinces where they lived.

gnōsis Greek for "knowledge," it became associated with teachers and holy men who professed to have hidden ideas which only their disciples could understand.

haram An Arabic word for a "sanctuary," in general.

hijra Arabic for "emigration," this word is commonly used to refer to the occasion in 622 CE when Muhammad left his home in Mecca and journeyed to a new home in Yathrib (Medina).

Ioudaïsmos A Greek word coined during the late Second Temple period, it is used for the first time in the anonymously written text known as 2 Maccabees and for a second time two hundred years later in Paul's letter to the Galatians. Often misleadingly translated "Judaism," it began its life as a contentious term and referred to one specific cultural way of "being Jewish." It was not an idea with which all Jews in antiquity necessarily identified.

jihad An Arabic word which expresses the idea of striving, or struggling, for God.

magister officiorum Master of the Imperial Offices, a chief-of-staff figure in the late Roman Empire who oversaw couriers, communications, interpreters, and the emperor's schedule.

menorah (**plural:** *menarot*) A seven-branched candlestick which was one of the objects used in Jewish Temple rituals. In the third century CE, it became a popular symbol for Jewish communities looking to reassert their lost connection to the Temple in Jerusalem.

mu'min (**plural:** *mu'minum*) A "Believer," in Arabic; in the first generations of Muhammad's movement, the word was overwhelmingly preferred by members inside the group to refer to themselves.

Notitia Dignitatum This "List of Offices" describes Rome's governmental structure in both the eastern and western Mediterranean around 400 CE.

oratio The emperor's "speech" before the Senate, in which he could articulate new law.

paganus (**plural:** *pagani*) A Latin word which had multiple meanings. It could refer to a "civilian," the antonym of an "enlisted soldier," or it could designate "country folk," an antonym for "city dweller." In the fourth century, militant followers of Jesus used *paganus* in the former way: to question the beliefs of other Christians whose cultural compromises they scorned. Only in the fifth century did Christians begin to use the word in the second sense, to refer to their non-Christian neighbors as "rustics" or "hicks."

paludamentum A military cloak sported by Roman emperors in battle.

pietas Latin noun which encapsulated the idea of devotion to the gods, to one's family, and to the Roman state. Its Greek equivalent was *eusebeia*.

pontifex maximus Latin title held by the emperors to designate their authority as "Chief Priest" of the state.

praefectus urbi Prefect of the City of Rome, an office akin to mayor.

praeses The civilian governor of a province, as opposed to its military commander, the *dux*.

praetorian prefecture Four administrative regions which were created in the early fourth century CE; their chiefs, called praetorian prefects, functioned as the government oversight for the twelve dioceses.

***proseuche* (plural: *proseuchai*)** Greek word for "prayer hall," it is a common term for Jewish meeting spaces in the Hellenistic and early Roman period.

proskynesis A Greek word loosely meaning "to kneel down in an act of worship"; it became part of Roman political ritual in the second and third centuries CE and remained a feature of political and diplomatic ritual throughout Late Antiquity.

pseudepigraphic Adjective used to designate writings which were forged, including texts in the Christian Scripture like the letters of Timothy and Titus, attributed to Paul but which were written later.

qibla For Muslims, the word that designates the "direction of prayer."

quaestor sacri palatini Chief Legal Officer in the Sacred Palace; he heard cases on the emperor's behalf and met with citizens who petitioned the imperial house.

refrigerium A funerary banquet at which family and friends gathered at the deceased's tomb to pour offerings for the dead and commemorate their passing.

***religio* (plural: *religiones*)** The set of worship practices that were deemed socially and culturally acceptable to the Roman people and state; its Greek equivalent was *threskeia*.

***saeculum* (plural: *saecula*)** The Latin word for "sacred time" or "age"; Romans used it to refer to an Etruscan religious idea that the lifespan of the world was structured into discrete segments. The end of one unit and the beginning of the next was celebrated as an important event. The deceptively similar English word "secular" is a misleading translation of it since, in antiquity, it denoted a sacred concept.

Sasanians Rulers who founded a new Persian empire which existed from 224–651 CE.

Second Temple Judaism The period in Jewish history from 539 BCE–70 CE. It began after the liberation from captivity in Babylon when Jews returned to Jerusalem and began building a Second Temple. (The first had been destroyed by the Babylonians.) It ended in 70 CE when Romans destroyed the Temple.

solidus A gold coin, also known in Greek as a *nomisma*. This form of currency was introduced into the Roman economy at the end of the third century CE.

***superstitio* (plural: *superstitiones*)** The Latin word which designated those worship practices, rituals, or beliefs which were stigmatized as questionably Roman and were therefore judged to be socially unacceptable.

sura A "chapter" in the Qur'an.

Tetrarchy The "Rule of Four" instituted by Diocletian in 293 CE, it was headed by two senior Augustuses (Latin plural: Augusti) and two junior Caesars (Latin plural: Caesares). It became obsolete with the rise of Constantine as sole emperor in 324 CE.

threskeia The Greek word for "worship," it held similar connotations as the Latin word *religio*.

***titulus* (plural: *tituli*)** A Latin legal term meaning "title," or "inscription." It was used to designate properties that had been gifted, or donated, to another person.

umma Arabic for "community."

vicarius The administrative head of a super-province, or diocese.

vir clarissimus Gold social status, the lowest tier, among Roman senators.

vir illustris Platinum social status, the highest achievable, among Roman senators.

vir spectabilis Silver social status among Roman senators.

Index

A Social and Cultural History of Late Antiquity, First Edition. Douglas Boin.
© 2018 John Wiley & Sons, Inc. Published 2018 by John Wiley & Sons, Inc.